Yale French Studies

SPECIAL ISSUE

After the Age of Suspicion: The French Novel Today

Yale French Studies

Charles A. Porter, *Special editor for this issue*
Liliane Greene, Managing editor
Editorial board: Peter Brooks (Chairman), Ora Avni,
   Shoshana Felman, Richard Goodkin, Christopher
   Miller, Charles Porter, Christopher Rivers, Allan
   Stoekl, Brigitte Szymanek, Helen Williams
Staff: Lauren Doyle-McCombs
Editorial office: 315 William L. Harkness Hall
Mailing address: 2504A Yale Station, New Haven,
   Connecticut 06520
Sales and subscription office:
   Yale University Press, 92A Yale Station
   New Haven, Connecticut 06520
This issue is published with the support of the French
   Embassy.

Designed by James J. Johnson and set in Trump
Medieval Roman by The Composing Room of
Michigan, Inc. Printed in the United States of America
by The Vail-Ballou Press, Binghamton, N.Y.
ISSN 0044-0078
ISBN for this issue 0-300-04386-4

CHARLES A. PORTER

Foreword

The novel came under siege in France around the time of the Second World War. A certain number of thoughtful and influential writers claimed to find the legacy of Balzac and Flaubert, as it had been developed by such earlier twentieth-century masters as Proust, Mauriac, and Malraux, both pretentious and fraudulent. In *La Nausée* (1938) Sartre scathingly attacked the novel's claim to be a reflection of reality. The theorists of the "Nouveau Roman," starting with Nathalie Sarraute (*L'Ere du soupçon*, 1950, 1956), and Alain Robbe-Grillet (*Pour un Nouveau Roman*, 1963), questioned authors' "omniscience" and the positivistic bases and middle-class bias of the novel as it had been generally practiced up through the '30s. Interest developed in the work of experimental writers, both French and foreign, who, instead of centering their novels around plot and character development, highlighted language, style, and texture, or tried out unusual typographical arrangements. The influence of Faulkner and James Joyce (in some cases via Samuel Beckett), Kafka and Borges, began to displace Balzac and Dostoevsky; the movies and the comic strip suggested other new narrative possibilities. Freud lurked in the background.

The "new" novels of writers like Robbe-Grillet, Sarraute, Michel Butor, Marguerite Duras, Claude Simon, and Claude Ollier, fascinated some readers in the 1950s and 1960s with their intellectual games, intricate formal schemes, discontinuities, turning inward upon themselves—and irritated others, many of whom simply refused to read them. Before long, some said, the new novelists had become "classics": that is, read mostly by critics and literary theorists—and in *classes* (most often, according to mischievous commentators, university classes in the United States).

Still viable, more traditional forms of fiction had not, of course, disappeared. Publishers continued to provide an abundance of traditional novels, and they found an avid readership. Detective fiction, where the plot was what mattered most, remained popular. There seemed to be no

1

end to autobiographical (or seemingly autobiographical) novels, rich in "character" and—often—psychopathology. Historical and adventure novels continued to emphasize both plot and character.

Since the 1970s, however, plot and character seem to be once again everywhere in the ascendency. Several of the recondite "new novelists" have recently published autobiographical pieces that appear in their structure and form almost old-fashioned, compared to their earlier works. Newly popular novelists are frequently making use of "normal" sentence and chapter structure, credible characters, and one-directional plots in stories that directly reflect recent, or less recent, historical and social reality.

The writers presented in this volume fall into at least three, *non-mutually* exclusive categories: established novelists formerly renowned for their experiments with form who seem recently to have turned to less experimental techniques; seemingly more traditional writers who have begun to emerge since the high period of the Nouveau Roman; and, finally, various uncategorizable writers, some who have been around throughout the period of the new novel and some who have emerged since, who are and remain simply themselves. Our selection cannot claim, except in its diversity, to be "representative" of the talented host of writers who are publishing fiction in the France of the 1970s and 1980s, but we have tried to provide our reader with examples of some of the best narrative prose available. These pieces indicate not only that the novel is not "dead," but also that it is enjoying a rather vigorous life in today's France.

Our presentations focus on the texts we have selected and translated for English-language readers. Our introductions stress what in these texts characterizes their author at this point in his or her work. Readers who wish to pursue their study of individual novelists in other texts or through critical evaluations of them will find suggestions here or in the accompanying notes or selected bibliography. Most of the texts we feature come from novels or variously disguised autobiographical writings. There is also an important original interview with Philippe Sollers.

Students of literature should be impressed with the quality of the prose in these pieces: these authors take their craft to heart. Literary historians will note how the writers' voices, however idiosyncratic, are tending to express themselves in canonical forms: the subject matter is often not "classical," certainly, but the style is schooled. With surprising frequency these texts are writings in the tradition of Proust, Camus, or the detective story: Proust for the omnipresent autobiographical "I" and the emphasis on the writing of a book resembling the book one has in hand; Camus for the limpidity of the prose and seeming objectivity of the style; the detective story for its suspense and emphasis on plot.

On the other hand something clearly has changed since mid-century.

Passion and commitment have been replaced by a cool ironic detachment. Literary language has been liberated to talk, and talk freely, about once taboo subjects (sex, especially, but not only); one notes, for example, Tournier's use of "potentially palatable form" to present "offensive and bizarre content." Women writing fiction appear much more aggressive in asserting their right to be heard in all their specificity, and in their struggle they are even taking on the sacrosanct French language. Moreover, writers of fiction are now assuming an audience that has mastered the "new novel" and remains willing to work hard in order to understand— or simply follow—difficult textual sequences. Though the prose of these writers is usually now more "ordinary" than, for instance, the mammoth sentences in some of Beckett's or Claude Simon's novels, their texts still often teem with unmarked changes of person or scene, half-hidden transitions, ambiguous references. Similarly their narrative techniques often seem to have been devised so as to conceal the origin (or "authority") of the words expressed. Knowing what comes "before" and what "after," or which of two versions of a story is the "right" one, is not now considered to be necessarily a reader's right, and Sarrautian "tropisms" frequently replace old-fashioned, "straightforward" "analysis" of "character."

May it be claimed that we now find ourselves "After the Age of Suspicion," as the title of this volume implies? Perhaps. Certain of the standard features of the 1920s and 1930s that had tended to disappear in the Nouveau Roman do not seem to be present in the works of the novelists here presented either, or, if they are present, they lie semihidden in the background: there is little of the moral or philosophical high seriousness of Mauriac and Malraux, Céline and Bernanos, little of the political "engagement" of Malraux and others, little of the earnestness of Saint-Exupéry or the intellectual and good-humored comedy of writers like Queneau. But in their apolitical, *psychological* seriousness the authors here presented still manifest a continuity with major concerns of the New Novel. Other kinds of continuity can be noted in the form (a linguistico/psychoanalytic form, with frequent elements of detective fiction thrown in) of their omnipresent, intense soul-searching, or in the way in which they show their words striving against the temptation (or the inability) to remain silent, or the way they favor scenes of violence, or privilege an uncanonical—such as an illiterate's, or a madwoman's— point of view.

Their prose, on the other hand, *looks* somehow more traditional. We must assume that neither the apolitical appearance nor the traditional look of the prose is simple or innocent. As several of our introductions point out, a seemingly objective description (in Le Clézio, Modiano, or Perec, for instance), may be a false front only partly hiding real terror and revulsion against the horrors of modern history and the anguish of modern life. Similarly a return to "ordinary" prose and structure can signify self-satire, or an aggressive or defiant stance against what had become a new tradition. There is humor in some of these pieces, but it is usually a bitter humor; in all of them, not far below the surface, lurks a great deal of tension.

In conclusion the editors of this volume wish to express their gratitude to all those who have collectively made it possible. This book results from a collaborative effort of the Yale French Department: more than two dozen of us, including some of our friends who are not at Yale, have worked at finding, introducing, translating these pieces. Few, and certainly none of us, can claim to have read all the fiction currently being published even in Paris. We have chosen according to our (and our friends') particular tastes and the chance encounters of the bookstore. Together we have tried to identify meaningful trends in today's French fiction, and we have attempted to combine exemplarity with representativeness, without, on the other hand, having too many illusions about our success at it. Peter Brooks, Chairman of the Yale French Department, has from the beginning provided us with institutional support and encouragement, and so have the editors of the Yale University Press. With patience and good humor the Managing Editor, Liliane Greene, ably assisted by Lauren Doyle-McCombs, has facilitated the Special Editor's work and kept us both on schedule; she has also exercised her acute literary eye and skillful pencil in double-checking the translations of texts that seemed at times to have been written in order to be untranslatable. Our special thanks, finally, go to the man who prodded us into thinking about this venture and arranged for its publication to be supported by a generous grant from the French Government: to Frédéric Berthet, accomplished man of letters, this book is gratefully dedicated.

I.

ERIC EIGENMANN

Nathalie Sarraute: The Use of Speech

"The Age of Suspicion": the legacy of this expression might suggest that its author, Nathalie Sarraute, would be among the contemporary French novelists best known in the United States. She has lectured a number of times in this country. All her books except for some plays and short essays have been translated into English and published in New York by George Braziller. A great deal has also been written in English, including articles in *Yale French Studies*, about her work and life.[1]

Nathalie Tcherniak was born in 1902 in Russia a short time before her parents separated. She moved back and forth between Russia and France until remaining definitively with her father in Paris in 1908. She studied English, history, and sociology in Paris, Oxford, and Berlin, then decided to enter law school in Paris, where she completed her studies in 1925. She married Raymond Sarraute, a fellow student, the same year.

Tropismes appeared in 1939 (Denoël): these eighteen sketches, written between 1932 and 1937, already contained the essential features of her future work. After her first novel, *Portrait d'un inconnu* (Marin, 1948), Gallimard became her regular publisher: *Martereau* (1953), *Le Planétarium* (1959), *Les Fruits d'or* (1963), and *Entre la vie et la mort* (1968) are all novels. She also wrote essays: four of them, in *L'Ere du soupçon* (1956), set out writing principles she has not abandoned since; "Paul Valéry et l'enfant d'éléphant" and "Flaubert le précurseur" were recently added in a new edition (1986). Two plays, *Le Silence* and *Le Mensonge*, were published in 1967.

Sarraute is also one of the contemporary French novelists who have been publishing over the longest period of time. Few studies address her production in the '70s and '80s, during which the so-called New Novel movement, with which she was associated, lost its vigor. This raises the possibility that her later texts differ substantially from the earlier ones. Her turning towards new genres (theater, autobiography) points to new directions. But a closer reading tempers such a conclusion.

---

1. I would like to express my thanks to David Pelizzari for his friendly help with the English version of this introduction.

One should remember that Sarraute always intended and managed to a large extent to break with plot and characterization such as they appear in the "traditional" novel. Instead she focuses on what she calls "tropisms": "the tenuous inner movements which slip by very rapidly on the threshold of our consciousness."[2] Tropisms can hardly be expressed or recreated except in a metaphorical "subconversation" or through the conversation they give rise to.

Her last two novels provide examples. In *Vous les entendez?* (1972) a father and a visiting friend are admiring an objet d'art the father is very proud to own, but he feels that his children, who are whispering and laughing upstairs, mock his old-fashioned world of values. From the given of this situation and from several points of view the characters' thoughts and speeches build up into scenes with ambiguous status: they may be actual, they may be imaginary.

Similar components create the scenes of *"Disent les imbéciles"* (1976). But here Sarraute dispenses even more with traditional narrative forms. The plot is not just minimal anymore, it actually bursts into fragments. What action occurs does so as tension between free-moving thought and the totalitarian power of formulae. Labels such as "fools say" alter, dismiss, or impose by virtue of the mere identity of the maker of a pronouncement, the ideas they are attached to. One cannot appeal the verdict; one cannot escape oversimplified categorization. The "characters," more numerous here though unidentifiable, are reduced to objects in someone else's discourse and to mere voices challenging each other.

Sarraute renounces the novel structure altogether in *L'Usage de la parole* (1980). It collects ten discrete sketches as *Tropismes* did, but under a more obvious unifying theme. One or two banal locutions pronounced in various small circles of people inspire every text (half-narrative and half-essay) in the mind of an authorial first-person who addresses a fictional reader about those locutions. Interlocutors and settings have no importance here other than letting speech be heard.

This book has more in common than one would expect with Sarraute's most recent work, *Enfance* (1983), an autobiography—though not really. The authorial first-person splits here into two narrative voices; there are almost no dates and no chronological order; historic truth (we are told) is not the point since memory matters more than what is remembered. Besides, this latter consists of details, preferably words again. Most of it is in the present tense, following the child's or narrator's stream of consciousness. Digressions frequently occur, even in the middle of the narration of never-realized hypothetical events. Significantly enough the title does not specify whose childhood the work is about, as though it were just *a* childhood. The fictionality of the text is thus preserved. *Enfance* indeed swerves slightly from the main line as a unique experiment for Sarraute at the end of her *oeuvre*. It does present more traditional—more childlike (?)—forms. But it remains too elusive a picture to achieve any physical or psychological cohesion. The primary concern is still tropisms. But the autobiographical background of Sarraute's inspiration for some recurrent tropisms in her writing is

2. Nathalie Sarraute, "The Inside of the Glove: Nathalie Sarraute Talks about her Plays," trans. Valerie Minogue, *Romance Studies* 4 (Summer 1984): 1.

now revealed, and perhaps dogmatism in the matter, insofar as New Novelists had any, is now over. . . .

Sarraute's growing inclination for the theater is worth noticing. *Théâtre* (1978) gathers four plays already published (*Le Silence* and *Le Mensonge* in 1967, *Isma* in 1970, *C'est beau* in 1973) with the previously unpublished *Elle est là*. Like *Pour un oui ou pour un non* two years later they all stage relatives who converse informally in an apartment or office. Their dialogue, however, developed as variations in recitation, runs a complex struggle for power through language. "Subconversation" is now completely subsumed into conversation.

A further analysis of Sarraute's recent work would confirm that it continues along earlier lines. It may even develop some of them more completely than ever before, since the novel structure, which had already been radically unsettled, is now abandoned for more open and polyphonic structures.

Both plot and character dissolve into dialogue, which is increasingly prevalent either as such or as the central object of the narration. Attention to tropisms, on the other hand, takes advantage of the fact that the dialogue fosters the inward action. Titles like *Vous les entendez?*, *"Disent les imbéciles,"* and *L'Usage de la parole*, as well as those of the six plays—all of them related to spoken words or speech, whereas none was before—together with Sarraute's dramaturgy are eloquent signs of her transforming focus on speech, which includes the intonation or articulation between the speaker and the words he or she speaks. There is a gap, a certain loose-jointedness, and Sarraute's writing is more and more about this. Her text reveals unsuspected dramas beneath apparently innocuous words, words that mask the dramas and at the same time bring them in part to the surface. What is pronounced in the texts resembles the commonplace and superficial conversations of everyday life, but Sarraute does not want to denounce conversation for its banality; on the contrary she regards such discourse as a privileged catalyst for tropisms.

The prevailing mode of dialogue matches the dominant temporal and spatial environments of her plots, that is to say, the here and now, as for a scene performed in a stage set. It also coheres with the withdrawal of the novelistic narrator behind the discourse of characters or of voices, again as in the theater. In this way the discourse itself acquires autonomy and thingness. A comparison with radio-theater—Sarraute's first plays were written for the radio—may be more useful. In her work words are focused on as physical objects entering and leaving human bodies, flying through the air, belonging to no one but forming a flow shared and conveyed by everyone who participates.

The connection of speech with sight, of gossiping with spying, of recitation with exhibition, and so on, should also be mentioned as one of the most interesting Sarrautean thematic knots. Whoever is being looked at has trouble expressing himself or herself except by means of a reassuring utterance borrowed in some way from other people. The speaker undergoes a feeling of dual subjective and objective personality; any struggle for unity and authenticity will always prove to be hopeless.

Not only did Nathalie Sarraute continue the evolution she had propounded in *L'Ere du soupçon* ("[the] dialogue . . . tends more and more, in the modern novel, to take the place left by action"),[3] she also succeeded in developing what she admired so much in the dialogues of the British writer Ivy Compton-Burnett:

... the inner movements, of which the dialogue is merely the outcome and, as it were, the furthermost point—usually prudently tipped to allow it to come up to the surface—try to extend their action into the dialogue itself.[4]

BIBLIOGRAPHY

I. Selected Works

Tropismes. Paris: Denoël, 1939.
Portrait d'un inconnu. Paris: Robert Marin, 1948.
Martereau. Paris: Gallimard, 1953.
L'Ere du soupçon. Paris: Gallimard, 1956.
Le Planétarium. Paris: Gallimard, 1959.
Les Fruits d'or. Paris: Gallimard, 1963.
Entre la vie et la mort. Paris: Gallimard, 1968.
Isma, Le Silence, La Mort. Paris: Gallimard, 1970.
Vous les entendez?. Paris: Gallimard, 1972.
"Disent les imbéciles." Paris: Gallimard, 1976.
Théâtre: Elle est là, C'est beau, Isma, Le Mensonge, Le Silence. Paris: Gallimard, 1978.
Enfance. Paris: Gallimard, 1983.

II. Selected Criticism

Allemand, André. *L'Oeuvre romanesque de Nathalie Sarraute.* Neuchâtel: La Baconnière, 1980.
Bell, Sheila M. *Nathalie Sarraute: A Bibliography.* London: Grant and Cutler, 1982. (A checklist)
Besser, Gretchen Rous. *Nathalie Sarraute.* Boston: Twayne Publishers, 1979.
Minogue, Valerie. *Nathalie Sarraute and the War of Words.* Edinburgh: Edinburgh University Press, 1981.
Watson-Williams, Helen. *The Novels of Nathalie Sarraute: Towards an Aesthetic.* Amsterdam: Rodopi, 1981.

3. Nathalie Sarraute, "Conversation and Subconversation," in *The Age of Suspicion,* trans. Maria Jolas (New York: Braziller, 1963), 98.
4. Ibid., 114.

NATHALIE SARRAUTE

*Disent les imbéciles**

Son nom. Il l'a perçu distinctement. Son nom, comme un déclic derrière son dos, suivi d'une décharge de petits plombs: « Pas intelligent? Vraiment? Tu crois? . . . —J'en suis sûr. Doué, c'est certain, mais pas intelligent. —Oui, peut-être, au fond . . . Il s'arrête, il flageole, la tête lui tourne, il va perdre connaissance, s'affaler . . . et eux le rattrapent . . . — Ah, enfin il nous attend . . . Lâcheur, va, grand rêveur. C'est qu'on a du mal à te suivre, tu cours devant nous comme un lièvre . . .

Sur le moment aucune douleur, juste cette faiblesse et une sensation inconnue, étrange, c'est elle que doivent éprouver ceux qui gisent, la moelle épinière blessée, quand ils veulent se relever et s'aperçoivent que leurs réflexes habituels ne jouent plus, que leurs jambes sont paralysées . . . un point vital en eux a dû être atteint.

Le centre. Le lieu secret où se trouvait l'état-major et d'où lui, chef suprême, les cartes étalées sous ses yeux, examinant la configuration du terrain, écoutant les rapports, prenant des décisions, dirigeait les opérations, une bombe l'a soufflé . . . il est projeté à terre, ses insignes arrachés, il est secoué, contraint à se relever et à marcher, poussé à coups de crosse, à coups de pied dans le troupeau grisâtre des captifs, tous portant la même tenue, classés dans la même catégorie: les imbéciles.

Impossible de se défendre, de contre-attaquer: il n'a plus d'arme. Impossible de s'évader, il n'y a pas où se réfugier, où qu'il aille il sera repris.

Et ça a commencé . . . c'est comme un dédoublement . . . Une part de lui-même par un effort pour survivre se détachant, se séparant, se traînant vers eux . . . essayant de se hisser à leur hauteur, de regarder à travers leurs jumelles, d'accommoder . . . Oui, je vois, je vois très bien . . . ce sont des dons. Je suis assez doué . . . Mais pour ce qui

Disent les imbéciles (Paris: Gallimard, 1976), 41–44. This passage is reprinted with the kind permission of Gallimard.

11

est . . . oui, vous avez raison. Ce n'est pas ce qu'on peut appeler de l'intelligence . . . Non . . . mais pourtant on ne peut pas me confondre avec les
autres, ceux dont on dit . . . —Mais écoutez-le, c'est vraiment un cas
curieux . . . Il reconnaît lui-même . . . C'est intéressant, ça mérite d'être
examiné de plus près . . . —Ah, vous voyez, mon cas n'est pas désespéré . . . Je pourrais peut-être obtenir une révision . . . peut-être une
réhabilitation? —Mais voyons, comment voulez-vous? Le malheureux
essaie de nous tromper. Il répète comme un perroquet ce que nous disons.
—Non, ce n'est pas juste, j'ai pris du recul depuis ce moment où j'ai
appris . . . C'était un choc. Une révélation. Mais depuis . . . —Quoi depuis? —Depuis, dès que je pense, quand je me permets de juger . . . je me
dis: ce ne doit pas être ça. Je me dis: ça ne tient pas . . . courte vue,
faiblesse du jugement . . . Forcément, puisque je ne suis pas intelligent. Il
y a donc là, reconnaissez-le, une parcelle de moi sauvée, un peu de tissu
vivant préservé, qu'il sera peut-être possible de cultiver, de développer, et
avec quoi j'arriverai à expulser le reste . . . —C'est vraiment touchant . . .
C'est rare, cette modestie, cette lucidité . . . Cette lucidité? Tu com-
mences, toi aussi, à m'inquiéter . . . Comment veux-tu que ce soit possible? Bien sûr, aidé, poussé, soutenu par nous, soumis à nous, terrorisé, il
parvient peut-être, sans savoir pourquoi, à force de répéter sans comprendre « je ne suis pas intelligent », à se persuader, à se méfier . . .

*Fools Say**

His name. He heard it distinctly . . . His name, like the click of a
trigger behind his back, followed by a volley of bird shot: "Not intelligent? Really? You think so? . . . —I'm sure. Gifted, that's certain, but
not intelligent. —Yes, perhaps, at bottom . . . He stops, he's shaking, his
head is swimming, he's about to lose consciousness, fall down . . . and
they catch him . . . —Ah, at last, he's waiting for us . . . Quitter, there,
always in the clouds. It's all we can do to follow you, you run from us like
a rabbit . . .

At the time, no pain, just that little weakness and a new, strange
sensation, it must be this sensation that people lying helpless, with an
injured spinal column, when they try to get up and realize that their usual

Fools Say (New York: Braziller, 1977), 34–36. Translated by Maria Jolas. This passage is reprinted with the kind permission of George Braziller.

reflexes have ceased functioning, that their legs are paralyzed . . . one of their vital points must have been affected . . .

The center. The secret spot where the General Staff is located and from where he, the Commander-in-Chief, all the maps spread out for him to see, examining the lay of the land, listening to reports, taking decisions, directing operations, a bomb hit it . . . he is thrown to the ground, his insignia torn off, he is shaken, obliged to get up and walk, pushed forward by blows from rifle butts, kicks, into the gray flock of the prisoners, all dressed alike, classified in the same category: fools.

Impossible to defend oneself, to counterattack: he has been disarmed. Impossible to escape, there's no place to hide, wherever he goes he'll be caught.

And it started . . . a sort of dual personality . . . One part of himself, in an effort to survive, coming unattached, separating, crawling towards them . . . trying to pull himself up to their height, to see through their spectacles, to adapt . . . Yes, I see, I see very clearly . . . they are gifts. I am rather gifted . . . But as regards . . . yes, you're right. It's not what you might call intelligence . . . No . . . and yet I can't be mistaken for the others, the ones about whom they say . . . —Do listen to him, it's really a curious case . . . He himself acknowledges . . . It's interesting, it would be worth examining more closely . . . —So you see, my case is not a desperate one . . . I could perhaps get a re-examination . . . perhaps a rehabilitation? —Now see here, how could you? The poor creature is trying to outwit us. He repeats what we say like a parrot . . . —No, that's not true, I have kept my distance ever since I found out . . . That was a shock. A revelation . . . But since . . . —How do you mean since? —Since then, whenever I think, when I allow myself to judge . . . I tell myself, I tell myself: that doesn't hold water . . . shortsighted, weak judgement . . . Necessarily, since I'm not intelligent. So we have there, admit it, a bit of myself that has been saved, a bit of live tissue that has been preserved, that it will be perhaps possible to cultivate, to develop, and with which I'll succeed in getting rid of the rest . . . —That's really touching . . . It's rare, such modesty, such perspicacity . . . Such perspicacity? You too are beginning to make me anxious . . . How do you expect it to be possible? Of course, if he's helped, prodded, propped up by us, ruled by us, terrorized, without knowing why, by dint of repeating without understanding it, "I am not intelligent," he may succeed in persuading himself, in being on his guard . . .

NATHALIE SARRAUTE

L'Usage de la parole*

LE MOT AMOUR

C'était au fond d'un petit café enfumé, mal éclairé, probablement d'une buvette de gare . . . il me semble qu'on entendait des bruits de trains, des coups de sifflet . . . mais peu importe . . . ce qui d'une brume jaunâtre ressort, c'est de chaque côté de la table deux visages presque effacés et surtout deux voix . . . je ne les perçois pas non plus avec netteté, je ne saurais pas les reconnaître . . . ce qui me parvient maintenant ce sont les paroles que ces voix portent . . . et même pas les paroles exactement, je ne les ai pas retenues . . . mais cela ne fait rien non plus, je peux facilement inventer des paroles du même ordre, les plus banales qui soient . . . de celles que deux personnes étrangères l'une à l'autre peuvent échanger au cours d'une rencontre quelconque, à une table de café . . . est-ce sur le goût de ce qu'elles boivent . . . une orangeade ou bien du thé? ou sur les avantages et les inconvénients des voyages en train, en avion . . . ou sur n'importe quoi, je vous laisse, si vous le voulez, en imaginer d'autres . . . mais ce que je ne peux pas vous laisser, ce qui dans ces paroles pour quelques instants m'appartient, ce qui m'attire, me taquine . . . c'est . . . je ne sais pas . . . c'est peut-être cette impression qu'elles donnent . . . de légèreté . . . elles semblent voleter, aériennes . . . on dirait que ce qu'elles portent . . . le goût de la grenadine, la fatigue des voyages en train . . . ce qu'on peut trouver de plus banal, de plus modeste, de plus discret, ne les emplit pas complètement, laisse en elles des espaces vides où quelque chose qui ne peut trouver sa place nulle part, dans aucune parole, aucune n'a été prévue pour le recevoir . . . quelque chose d'invisible, d'impondérable, d'impalpable est venu s'abriter . . .

*L'Usage de la parole (Paris: Gallimard, 1980), 67–71. This passage is reprinted with the kind permission of Gallimard.

Ces paroles peu lestées, dilatées, s'élèvent, flottent, légèrement ballottées, se posent doucement, effleurent à peine . . .

On pourrait, en observant ces paroles porteuses de platitudes et la légèreté avec laquelle elles se posent, effleurent, rebondissent, les voir pareilles à des cailloux minces et plats voletant, faisant des ricochets.

Mais cette image exacte à première vue et séduisante est de celles qu'il faut se contraindre à effacer, auxquelles il vaut mieux renoncer avant qu'elles ne vous égarent. Elle aurait immanquablement fait apparatre celui par qui ces cailloux sont lancés et son geste montrant du savoir-faire, de l'habileté . . . elle aurait fait oublier ce qui dans ces paroles m'attire, ce qui revient me hanter . . . ces espaces vides en elles où, à l'abri de choses modestes et effacées, vacille, tremble . . . venu d'où?

Ceux de qui aussi naturellement, aussi irrésistiblement que l'air qu'ils expirent cela s'exhale ne sauraient pas nous renseigner. Le lieu en eux d'où cela émane n'a jamais été décrit, il est dans une région que personne, si bien muni qu'il soit des mots les plus effilés et pénétrants, ne peut atteindre . . . aucun mot n'a pu venir ici prospecter, fouiller, saisir, extraire, montrer . . .

D'un côté à l'autre de la table les paroles circulent . . . elles sont comme des rayons que des miroirs identiques placés l'un en face de l'autre réfléchiraient sous un même angle, comme des ondes . . . « C'est agréable, ces lumières . . . On ne voit plus partout que des éclairages au néon . . . Les trains sur des petites distances . . . »

Les paroles à peine lestées, parcourues de vibrations, de radiations, jaillissent . . . venues d'un lieu intact où pour la première fois, une première et unique fois . . . sourd, frémit . . . à la source même . . . à la naissance . . .

Mais oui, bien sûr, ça ne pouvait pas manquer, je vous entends, vous l'avez dit, nous l'avons dit ensemble . . . voilà ce que c'est que d'avoir l'outrecuidance de s'introduire dans ces lieux préservés, de briser leur silence ne serait-ce qu'avec des murmures, des balbutiements, avec les mots les plus timides, prudents . . . Qu'on les laisse pénétrer et il est sûr qu'ils en amèneront d'autres . . . Celui-ci: « naissance » . . . à sa suite a amené . . . trop tard pour l'empêcher d'entrer, le voici, il est là . . . de ce mot: « naissance » le mot « de » est sorti aussitôt, s'est tendu comme un bras, tirant à soi, énorme, faisant un grand vacarme, le mot « amour » . . . « La naissance de l'amour . . . »

The Use of Speech*

THE WORD LOVE

It was at the back of a smoky, ill-lit little café, probably a station buffet . . . I rather think you could hear the sounds of trains, whistles blowing . . . but that's of no importance . . . what stands out from a yellowish haze is, on either side of the table, two blurred faces, and above all two voices . . . I can't make them out very clearly either, I wouldn't be able to recognize them . . . what reaches me now is the words these voices conveyed . . . and not exactly the words even, I don't remember them . . . but that doesn't matter either, I can easily invent other words of the same order, the most banal imaginable . . . the kind that two strangers are likely to exchange in the course of any ordinary meeting, at a café table . . . whether they are about the taste of what they are drinking . . . orangeade, or maybe tea? or about the advantages or disadvantages of travelling by train, by plane . . . or about anything you like, I'll leave it to you, if you like, to imagine others . . . but what I cannot leave to you, what for a few moments belongs to me in these words, what attracts me, what tantalizes me . . . is . . . I don't know . . . perhaps it's the impression . . . of lightness . . . they make . . . they seem fluttering, ethereal . . . it's as if what they convey . . . the taste of the grenadine, the fatigue of train journeys . . . the most banal, the most modest, the most unobtrusive things imaginable, doesn't completely fill them, leaves voids in them in which something that can find its place nowhere, in no word, none has been provided to receive it . . . something invisible, imponderable, impalpable, has come to take refuge . . .

These scarcely ballasted, dilated words rise, float, bob about gently, then softly alight, barely skim . . .

When we observe these platitude-carrying words, and the lightness with which they touch down, skim, rebound, we could compare them to thin, flat stones flying through the air, ricocheting.

But this fascinating image, which at first sight seems accurate, is one of those you have to force yourself to efface, which it would be better to abandon before they lead you astray. It would inevitably result in the appearance of the person by whom the stones are thrown, and the savoir-faire and skill of his movement . . . it would have made you forget what it is in these words that attracts me, what it is that returns to haunt me . . . those voids in which, sheltered by modest, unpretentious things, there vacillates . . . trembles . . . where has it come from?

The Use of Speech (New York: Braziller, 1986), 65–69. Translated by Barbara Wright in consultation with the author. This passage is reprinted with the kind permission of Braziller.

Those people from whom this is exhaled just as naturally, just as irresistibly, as the air they breathe out, wouldn't be able to enlighten us. The place within them from which it emanates has never been described, it's a region that no one, no matter how well equipped he may be with the most perfectly sharpened, the most penetrating words, can ever reach . . . no word has managed to come here to prospect, to search, to seize, to extract, to show . . .

From one side of the table to the other, words circulate . . . they are like rays which identical mirrors placed opposite one another would reflect at the same angle, like waves . . . "Isn't this lighting nice . . . These days you see nothing but neon . . . Trains, for short journeys . . ."

Words, barely ballasted, permeated by vibrations, by radiations, spurt out . . . coming from an intact place where for the first time, for the first and unique time . . . there wells up, quivers . . . at the very source, at the birth . . .

But yes, of course, it had to happen, I can hear you, you said that, we said it together . . . that's what it is to have the presumption to insinuate oneself into these forbidden places, to shatter their silence if only by murmurs, by babblings . . . with the most timid, prudent words . . . Let them once penetrate and they are certain to introduce others . . . This one: "birth" . . . brought in its wake . . . too late to stop in entering, it's coming, it's here . . . from the word: "birth" the word "of" immediately emerged, stretched itself out like an arm and pulled towards it, enormous, making a terrific din, the word "love" . . . "The birth of love . . ."

NATHALIE SARRAUTE

*Elle est là**

H 2: Vous savez, je ne sais pas ce qui m'arrive . . . c'est étrange . . . (*L'air surpris:*) J'accepte. Oui. (*Ton furieux:*) J'accepte. (*Ton accablé:*) J'accepte. (*Ton calmé:*) J'accepte. (*Ton ferme, décidé:*) J'accepte. Qu'elle garde en elle son idée. Qu'elle la couve. Qu'elle la soigne. Qu'elle l'engraisse . . . ça m'est égal . . .

H 3: Ce n'est pas possible? . . . Ne me dites pas que vous êtes devenu un de ces indifférents . . . un de ces tièdes pour qui les idées . . .

H 2: Mais voyons! comment pouvez-vous penser ça . . . Non, pas du tout.

H 3: Alors, peut-être que pour ne plus souffrir, vous avez trouvé un clou qui a chassé? Un bon gros clou?

H 2: Oh non, pas de clou. Rien n'a pu chasser . . . mon idée à moi est là, comme on dit « elle m'habite » . . . Et pourtant j'accepte que l'autre, la sienne là-bas, qu'elle vive . . .

H 3: Ah, donc vous en prenez votre parti. A l'impossible nul n'est tenu, n'est-ce pas?

H 2: Non, pas du tout, vous vous trompez.

H 3: Vous prenez votre mal en patience.

H 2: Non non, ce n'est pas ça.

H 3: Vous faites contre mauvaise fortune bon cœur.

H 2: Non, vous n'y êtes pas du tout. Vous feriez mieux de donner votre langue au chat.

H 3: Bon, je la donne.

H 2: Alors, sachez que je suis content. Très satisfait. C'est tout ce que je demande: la sienne chez elle, la mienne chez moi. Chacun pour soi et Dieu pour tous. Ne plus rien extirper chez personne. Plus d'incursions.

H 3: Mais dites-moi, c'est ce qui s'appelle la « tolérance ». Ah j'en

Elle est là (Paris: Gallimard, 1978), 35–37. This passage is reprinted with the kind permission of Gallimard.

connais, là (*montre la salle*), qui seront contents. Plus besoin de nous lancer des boulettes de papier pour nous rappeler aux bons sentiments. Et c'est vous maintenant qui donnez l'exemple . . .

H 2: Quoi? Ça de nouveau, la tolérance? Toujours ces mots qui enserrent, qui déforment . . . parce que j'ai dit que son idée à elle peut bien vivre, s'engraisser, aussitôt ça y est, on croit que tout est rentré dans l'ordre. C'est de la tolérance . . . Eh bien non, il ne s'agit pas de ça. C'est à mon idée à moi, à elle seule, que je pense . . . Je ne veux plus qu'elle s'avilisse . . . plus de contacts, de corps à corps répugnants . . . Qu'on nous laisse seuls, elle et moi. Tout seuls . . .

Un silence.

Pardonnez-moi, je ne voudrais pas vous vexer, c'est gênant de vous dire ça, à vous . . . vous avez été si bon, si patient . . . et j'ai tant abusé . . . Mais maintenant, voyez-vous, je n'ai plus besoin d'aide . . . Plus besoin du soutien de personne. Nous n'avons besoin que de ça: être seuls, tout seuls, mon idée et moi. Et même . . . c'est drôle . . . vous voyez comme on change . . . et même ça nous aiderait si vous étiez contre nous . . . Oui, c'est ainsi. Que tous soient contre nous. Vous. L'ami qui était là tout à l'heure . . . d'ailleurs comment savoir si lorsqu'il approuvait . . . si ce n'était pas par politesse . . . par paresse . . . et vous-même, peut-être . . . par gentillesse . . . sait-on jamais . . . Mais c'est fini. Plus besoin de sonder les reins et les cœurs. Oui, tous contre. Eux aussi, là . . . Rien que de l'imaginer . . . c'est étrange . . . ça me fait du bien . . . Mais je ne l'imagine pas . . . je sens qu'eux, ils m'ont exaucé . . . Mon souhait, d'ailleurs, est un de ceux qui d'ordinaire ont le plus de chances d'être comblés. Regardez-les. Voyez où ils sont, où ils se tiennent, à quelle distance . . . une distance que ne peut pas franchir la sympathie, aucune connivence. Ces regards fixes, braqués . . .

Silence.

C'est drôle, maintenant je crois que je commence pour la première fois à comprendre . . . Une petite chose, une toute petite chose sans importance vous conduit parfois ainsi là où l'on n'aurait jamais cru qu'on pourrait arriver . . . tout au fond de la solitude . . . dans les caves, les casemates, les cachots, les tortures, quand les fusils sont épaulés, quand le canon du revolver appuie sur la nuque, quand la corde s'enroule, quand la hache va tomber . . . à ce moment qu'on nomme suprême . . . avec quelle violence elle se redresse . . . elle se dégage hors de son enveloppe éclatée, elle s'épand, elle, la vérité même . . . la vérité . . . elle seule . . . par sa seule existence elle ordonne . . . tout autour d'elle, docilement, rien ne lui résiste . . . tout autour d'elle s'ordonne . . . elle il-

lumine . . . (*la lumière baisse*) . . . quelle clarté . . . quel ordre . . . Ah
voilà . . . c'est le moment . . . c'est la fin . . . Mais juste pour moi, mais
moi je ne suis rien, moi je n'existe pas . . . et elle, avec quelle force . . .
hors de son enveloppe éclatée, elle se dresse, elle se libère, elle se ré-
pand . . . elle éclaire (*la lumière baisse*) . . . personne ne peut . . . c'est
ainsi . . . contre elle on ne peut rien . . . on le sait bien, (*la lumière baisse*)
n'est-ce pas, on le dit bien: toujours la vérité triomphe . . . pour elle il n'y
a rien à craindre . . . ah elle sait se défendre . . . (*la lumière s'éteint*) par sa
seule existence . . . par sa seule présence . . . seule . . . toute seule . . . si
seule . . .

Elle est là

M 2: You know, I don't know what is happening to me . . . it's
strange . . . (*Air of surprise:*) I accept it. Yes. (*Furious:*) I accept it. (*Overwhelmed:*) I accept it. (*Calm:*) I accept it. (*Firm, decided:*) I accept it. Let
her keep her idea inside herself. Let her hatch it. Let her take care of it.
Let her fatten it up. . . . It's all the same to me . . .
M 3: Is it possible? Don't tell me that you have become one of those
indifferent people . . . one of those lukewarm people for whom ideas . . .
M 2: Come, come! how can you think that . . . No, not at all.
M 3: Well, maybe in order not to suffer anymore, you've replaced the old
with the new? A good fat new one?
M 2: Oh no, not a new one. Nothing could drive it out . . . it's mine, so to
speak, "it's taken root". . . . And nevertheless, I accept that the other
one, hers over there, has the right to live also . . .
M 3: Ah, then you are coming to terms with it. One can't expect miracles,
right?
M 2: No, that's not it at all, you're wrong.
M 3: You're bearing up under it.
M 2: No, no, that's not it.
M 3: You're making the best of it.
M 2: No, you don't understand at all. You would do better to give up and
stop trying.
M 3: All right, I give up.
M 2: Well, then, know that I am glad. Very satisfied. That's all I ask: her
idea for her, and mine for me. Every man for himself and devil take the
hindmost. Nothing more extracted from anyone. No more inroads.
M 3: But say, this is what is called "tolerance." Ah, I know some of them,

there (*points to the hall*) who will be happy. No further need to throw spit balls at us to bring us back to order. And now it's you who are giving the example . . .

M 2: What? That again, tolerance? Always these words that grab, that deform . . . because I said that her idea can live, can get fat, right away that's it, everyone believes that everything is back to normal. It's tolerance. . . . Well, no, it's not a question of that. It's my idea, and that alone, that I'm thinking about. . . . I no longer wanted it to be dragged into the mud . . . no more touching, no more repulsive embraces. . . . Leave us alone, it and me. All alone . . .

A silence.

Excuse me, I didn't want to annoy you, it's hard to say that to you . . . you've been so good, so patient . . . and I've taken such advantage. . . . But now, you see, I don't need any more help. . . . No further need of support from anyone. We only need this: to be alone, all alone, my idea and me. And even . . . it's funny . . . you see how one changes . . . and it would even help us if you were against us. . . . Yes, that's how it is. Let them all be against us. You. The friend who was there just a while ago . . . besides, when he was approving, how would one know whether . . . whether it wasn't out of politeness . . . or laziness . . . and you yourself, maybe . . . in kindness . . . does one ever know. . . . But it's over. No more need to sound out hearts and minds. Yes, all are against it. They are too, out there. . . . Just to imagine it . . . it's strange . . . it does me good. . . . But I don't imagine it. . . . I sense that *they*'ve granted my wish. . . . My wish, besides, is one of those that normally have a better chance of being fulfilled. Look at them. See where they are, where they hold themselves, at what a distance . . . a distance that sympathy cannot cross, no complicity. These fixed gazes, trained on . . .

Silence.

It's funny, now I believe that for the first time I'm beginning to understand. . . . A little thing, a tiny little thing without importance sometimes brings you there where you would never have believed that you could arrive . . . right to the depths of solitude . . . in the cellars, the blockhouses, the dungeons, the torture chambers, when the shotguns are shouldered, when the barrel of the revolver is pressed against the neck, when the cord winds up, when the blade is about to fall . . . at that moment this so-called supreme moment . . . how violently it rights itself . . . it separates itself from its shattered covering, it spreads, truth itself . . . truth . . . alone . . . by its very existence it makes order . . . of everything around it, obediently, nothing resists it . . . everything around it becomes organized . . . it illuminates . . . (*the light dims*) . . . what light . . . what order. . . . Ah, there it is . . . it's time . . . it's the end. . . . But only for me, but I am nothing, I don't exist . . . and truth, with what strength . . . outside of its burst shell, it rights itself, it liberates itself, it spreads out . . . it lights the way . . . (*the light dims*) . . . no one can . . . it's that way . . . against it one can do nothing . . . it's well known (*the light dims*), isn't it, it's often said: truth always triumphs . . . for truth, there is nothing to fear . . . ah, it knows how to defend itself . . . (*the light is extinguished*) by its very existence . . . by its very presence . . . alone . . . all alone . . . so alone . . .

TRANSLATED BY MARIE-ANNE FLEMING

NATHALIE SARRAUTE

*Enfance**

« Cher petit oreiller, doux et chaud sous ma tête, plein de plume choisie, et blanc et fait pour moi . . . » tout en récitant, j'entends ma petite voix que je rends plus aiguë qu'elle ne l'est pour qu'elle soit la voix d'une toute petite fille, et aussi la niaiserie affectée de mes intonations . . . je perçois parfaitement combien est fausse, ridicule, cette imitation de l'innocence, de la naïveté d'un petit enfant, mais il est trop tard, je me suis laissé faire, je n'ai pas osé résister quand on m'a soulevée sous les bras et placée debout sur cette chaise pour qu'on me voie mieux . . . si on me laissait par terre, on ne me verrait pas bien, ma tête dépasserait à peine la longue table à laquelle sont assis, de chaque côté d'une mariée tout en blanc, des gens qui me regardent, qui attendent . . . j'ai été poussée, j'ai basculé dans cette voix, dans ce ton, je ne peux plus reculer, je dois avancer affublée de ce déguisement de bébé, de bêta, me voici arrivée à l'endroit où il me faut singer l'effroi, j'arrondis mes lèvres, j'ouvre mes yeux tout grands, ma voix monte, vibre . . . « Quand on a peur du loup, du vent, de la tempête . . . » et puis la tendre, candide émotion . . . « Cher petit oreiller, comme je dors bien sur toi . . . », je parcours jusqu'au bout ce chemin de la soumission, de l'abject renoncement à ce qu'on se sent être, à ce qu'on est pour de bon, mes joues brûlent, tandis qu'on me descend de ma chaise, que je fais de mon propre gré une petite révérence de fillette sage et bien élevé et cours me cacher . . . auprès de qui? . . . qu'est-ce que je faisais là? . . . qui m'avait amenée? . . . sous les rires approbateurs, les exclamations amusées, attendries, les forts claquements des mains . . .

Enfance (Paris: Gallimard, 1983), 60–61. This passage is reprinted with the kind permission of Gallimard.

*Childhood**

"Dearest little pillow, with choicest feathers sewn, so soft and warm beneath my head, and made for me alone . . ." as I recite, I can hear my little voice, which I am making shriller than it really is because I want it to be the voice of a very little girl, and I can also hear the affected silliness of my intonation . . . I am perfectly well aware of how false, how ridiculous is this imitation of the innocence, the naiveté of a little child, but it's too late, I've let myself in for it, I didn't dare resist when they picked me up under my arms and stood me on that chair so that they could see me better . . . if they left me on the floor, they wouldn't be able to see me properly, my head would hardly reach above the long table where, on either side of a bride dressed all in white, people are sitting, looking at me, waiting . . . I have been pushed, I have fallen, into this voice, this tone, I can't retreat, I have to advance, masquerading under this disguise of a baby, a silly goose, and now I've come to the place where I have to feign terror, I part my lips, I open my eyes wide, my voice rises, vibrates . . . "When you're afraid of the wolf, of the wind, of the storm . . ." and then, the tender, naive emotion . . . "Dearest little pillow, how well I sleep on you . . ." I follow it through to the bitter end, this path of submission, of abject renunciation of everything I feel myself to be, of everything I really am, my cheeks are burning, while they lift me down from my chair, while of my own accord I make the little curtsey of the well-brought up, good little girl and run off to hide . . . in whose lap? . . . what was I doing there? . . . who had taken me there? . . . to the approving laughs, the amused, sympathetic exclamations, the loud clapping . . .

Childhood (New York: Braziller, 1984), 52–53. Translated by Barbara Wright in consultation with the author. This passage is reprinted with the kind permission of Braziller.

MICHAEL SYROTINSKI

Henri Thomas: Relics of the Past

For someone whose first novel was published in 1940, and who is now probably the most regular contributor to the *Nouvelle Revue Française* with his monthly "Amorces," it is somewhat surprising that Henri Thomas is not better known. These laconic, very personal observations on life and literature were recently collected together and published as a kind of fragmented autobiography, *Le Migrateur* (1983), and this title well defines the drifting movement of Thomas's novels, novels which are themselves autobiographical in nature. This interplay between autobiography and the writing of fiction is itself characteristic of his novels, so much so that it would be difficult to determine with any certainty whether his personal experiences provide the material for his novels, or whether Thomas, who now spends most of his time alone on the tiny island of Houat off the coast of Brittany, is living out the life of one of his own characters.

Henri Thomas has published twelve novels in all, the most recent being *Une saison volée* in 1986. The corpus of his published works, however, is much larger, since he has written seven collections of poetry, several volumes of short stories, and translations into French of Shakespeare, Mosley, Melville, Junger, Stifte, Kleist, Goethe, and Pushkin. His work has earned him three major literary awards in France. He worked for a while in London at the BBC, and was Visiting Professor at Brandeis University in the late 1950s. It was while in the United States, during a stay at Harvard University, that he became a friend of Paul de Man, who was still at the beginning of his academic career, and who fascinated Thomas. He subsequently became the "hero" of Thomas's novel *Le Parjure*, which has attained a degree of notoriety among students of de Man. His experiences abroad explain the English and American settings of several of his stories (*La Nuit de Londres, John Perkins* among others). In France he was close to the group of writers affiliated with the NRF—Gide, Artaud, Paulhan, Pierre Leyris, Brice Parain, Raymond Queneau—although he has never openly associated himself with any literary movement or school.

The uncertain negotiation between autobiography and fiction confers upon the novels of Thomas a deceptive homogeneity. There is an almost obsessional return to certain decisive moments in childhood that reminds one of the writing of Louis-René des Forêts, and one character, Paul Souvrault, reappears at different stages of his life, giving the novels the appearance of a *Bildungsroman*. This

25

unfolding of an autobiographical self is at the same time an attempt to recover the self via the mediation of a succession of fictional analogues. As Jean Roudaut points out, however, in his article "Les Petits hasards inquiétants" [Disquieting little accidents], the "realism" of Henri Thomas is not what it seems: "La formation qu'ils narrent est sans fin, tout comme le livre, dans l'oeuvre, est en écho de lui-même." [The education they recount is endless, just as the book echoes itself throughout Thomas's works.] The autobiographical enterprise is continually stymied as each novel gets caught up in a process of self-interrogation, and it seems that this feature of the book "en écho de lui-même" is in some way connected to, even motivates, this failure.

The novels often present self-doubting authors (such as the narrators of *Le Précepteur* and *Le Promontoire*, and Louis Vince in *Le Croc des chiffonniers*) who write in order to understand why they are writing, and who are overshadowed by authors who have "made it" (Gilbert Delorme in *Le Promontoire*, Marcelin Bauge in *Le Croc des chiffonniers*). The process of writing invades the existence of the writers, and seems to carry them away, irresistibly. The narrator of *Le Précepteur* says of writing: "La venue dans mon existence de ce travail imprévu a modifié tout le reste" [The coming into my life of this unforeseen work has changed everything else], and the novels could be said to constitute an interminable response to the question posed by the *je* of *Le Promontoire*: "Qu'est-ce qui m'a pris de commencer, quand je ne suis pas écrivain, et je n'ai pas envie de le devenir?" [Why on earth did I start, when I'm not a writer, and have no desire to become one?].

Jean Roudaut has also pointed out how the events of the novels are triggered off by strange little incidents or accidents. *La Relique*, for example, begins with the theft of the bone of the little finger of an obscure saint from its reliquary, and in *Le Promontoire* the narrator's entrapment on a distant, barely inhabited headland is occasioned when he finds himself one day carrying the coffee urn at the funeral of one of the villagers, and is slowly pulled into the life of the community. The novels proceed to exhaust the narrative interest generated by these chance beginnings only to continue in an aimless migratory movement which is variously referred to by Thomas as a *dérive* [drifting], an *égarement* [straying], or an *errance* [wandering].

It might seem, then, at these moments of specular self-representation, or of *mise en abyme*, that Thomas is just one more introspective *nouveau romancier*, cleverly disguised as a writer of realistic fiction, who has turned away from the political or social or historical dimension of his time. But this would be wrong, since his novels, if they resist the appeal of "modernity" of much contemporary fiction, are also indifferent to the technical innovation and experimentation that is the hallmark of the *nouveau roman*. Indeed, Thomas has recently criticized the *nouveau roman* for its inertia, and its lack of "soul." (*La Quinzaine littéraire*, June 1985.) Whilst eschewing more formal considerations of novel-writing, Henri Thomas pursues a sustained and deep-seated meditation on what it is to write (novels), a meditation which also profoundly engages questions of history, time, memory, and chance. It may or may not be an accident that this convergence of concerns places Thomas close to the Walter Benjamin of "Theses on the philosophy of history." If Thomas appears to "turn his back" on history, this aptly calls to mind Benjamin's famous description of Klee's "Angelus Novus" as the "angel of history" flying backwards into the future. Thomas's prose, like that of Benjamin, is uncompromising in its perpetual critical lucidity.

The novel from which the following excerpts are taken, *Le Croc des chiffonniers*, brings us even closer to another study by Benjamin: his essay on Baudelaire, "A lyric poet in the era of High Capitalism." Benjamin was the first critic to read Baudelaire in the context of the shifting experiences of life in a big city in the middle of the nineteenth century, and of the various phenomena produced by "high capitalism." The ragpickers of this novel's title were very much a product of this era, and Louis Vince's great-great-grandfather, who lived around the time of Napoleon III, was probably one of the first generation of ragpickers. They became the focus of a great deal of curiosity, and Baudelaire the city poet and the "flâneur" was quick to see the poetic potential of such a figure. It is his poem "Le Vin des chiffonniers" which provides Thomas with one of his two epigraphs to the novel: "Butant et se cognant aux murs comme un poète" [Bumping and banging oneself against the walls like a poet].

Louis Vince, an old man as the novel opens, was born into generations of ragpickers, who had made a fortune in the trade. The mock-heroic tone of the story is evident in the reference at one point to the "Ragpickers' Empire," which was in fact the original title of the novel. Louis, however, had become a fairly successful novelist in the prime of his life, having won recognition (and a rosette of the Legion of Honor) with his novel—later made into a film—entitled *Le Croc des chiffonniers*, the story of his father's life. While Louis Vince's novel recounts the rising fortunes of his father, the one we read tells of Louis's inexorable decline. The central chain of events is presented as a memory of the decisive moments in Louis's fall from grace: his flight from Marcelin Bauge's house in the forest, after he had been lured there by Dorine and Bauge's wife, Francine; the chance meeting with an old friend, Martine, in Chartres; and his return on the train to Paris, accompanied by a young girl, Julie, who tags along behind him. The flight through the forest merges with a previous flight when Louis, as a fourteen-year-old boy, ran away from school.

This superimposing of different layers of memories is not chronologically consistent, but the deliberate blurring of temporal frames of reference is more in the nature of a blending together that holds out the promise of a satisfying plenitude. The burden of the novel—which also invites us to make the intertextual connections with the other novels—is this attempt to join up the past with the present, to close off the temporal circle of his life, to recover his self. Hence the other epigraph, from Hegel: "—la venue à soi-même de l'esprit absolu" [the becoming-self of Absolute Spirit]. With this in mind, we can now turn to a consideration of the significance of the *croc*, the ragpicker's hook. The ragpicker collecting objects that have been discarded as valueless by others can clearly be read as a figure for the activity of re-collection, the gathering up of the worn-out debris of the past in the ragbag of one's memory. The completion of an "esprit absolu" would depend upon the complete recovery of the past through the activity of remembrance. The book that Louis wrote starts out: "Tout a commencé par les peaux de lapin" [It all started with the rabbit skins.] The rabbit skins were, as Louis remarks, in fact added to the rags and scrap metal his father had already begun to collect. This expansion of the trade marked the decline of the family business, since there was nothing left for Louis to collect: "Le père ramassait tout, sauf ça: les mots. Au petit Louis, il n'est resté que cela: les mots" [The father gathered up everything, except that: words. All that was left for little Louis was that: words].

The narrative recollection of the past, even if it is a fabrication of the actual events, is valorized as something resistant to the erosive passage of time, as a means of recuperating the value with which his forefathers had reinvested the "worthless" objects they had collected, a value which was fast disappearing. The superiority of the writer-ragpicker lies in his ability to synthesize the past and the present by the use of symbols which would unite past collection with present recollection. The *croc* is, however, more than just a symbol of recollection; the very possibility of a successful putting together of the fragmented pieces of the past is dependent upon the synthesizing power of the symbol, just as the *symbolon* requires its broken pieces to be matched up again. Thus the *croc* is a symbol of writing, a symbol of symbol, or a figure of figuration. Thomas's novels abound in such figures, which seem to hold the key to their salvation. This is not to overstate the case, since Louis's flight and painful journey back to Paris is referred to at several points as a sort of calvary. The relic in the novel of the same title is a further, very suggestive, case in point.

Why, then, are these symbols literally rejected at the end of the novels? The answer may have to do precisely with keys and locks. In *Le Croc des chiffonniers* the entire sequence of events in the middle section of the novel is determined by a crucial moment when Louis has returned to his apartment after a party at which a friend, Serrurier, collapsed and was taken off to the hospital. Louis goes to bed, and is awakened by Dorine, who was able to enter his apartment because he had left the key in the lock ("serrure") of his door: "N'avait-il pas glissé sur les mots, dans un instant d'absence, devant sa porte: serrure, Serrurier, c'est Serrurier qui l'a détourné d'*agir*—" [Did he not slip on his words, in a moment of absence, in front of his door: serrure, Serrurier, it was Serrurier who distracted him from *acting*—]. Such unpredictable slippages of language, which are beyond the reach and control of the writer-ragpicker, are worrying little leftovers. All the more so since these irretrievable linguistic accidents are able to generate a story, and a story of the retrieval of one's life at that. It would not be quite so disruptive were they not, as is often the case, entrusted with so much metaphorical responsibility. How are we to read the scene towards the end of the novel when Louis discovers the "message" Dorine had slipped ["glissé"] into his keyhole?: "Cette fois, le papier enroulé contient une petite feuille morte. Ça doit venir du bois-taillis autour de la maison Bauge" [This time, the rolled up piece of paper contains a little dead leaf. It must have come from the trees in the copse around Bauge's house]. Is it an accident that this "feuille morte" takes us to the "feuille blanche"—the blank sheet of paper on which the child Louis was unable to write to his mother—and, in the plural, to the "feuilles" of Marcelin Bauge's book which Louis crushes into the ground? It also takes us, more pertinently, to the pages of Louis's own book, which he also wishes would go back to where it came from, to the "débris des choses." It is perhaps the unsettling prospect of writing under the constant risk of such uncertainty that explains, in the novel, an opposing tension of suspicion towards narrative recovery. Yet, as we read early on, where his book goes, Louis goes too: ". . . auteur de quelques livres, dont un seul le suit, le porte encore . . ." [". . . author of a few books, only one of which follows him, and is still carrying him along. . ."].

A similar sense of being "carried along" by the writing, fully aware of its attendant risks and unpredictability, characterizes the novels of Henri Thomas, and makes our reading of them an activity which is equally vagrant and unpredictable. The refusal of Thomas to seek a way out of this *errance*—like Louis refusing to return to Bauge's house in the forest—marks the significance of his contribution to the contemporary French novel. Thomas's novels never claim to be anything *other* than novels, but rather provide the space that allows for the emergence of the irretrievable "otherness" that inhabits the novelistic enterprise itself.

BIBLIOGRAPHY

I. SELECTED WORKS

Le Seau à charbon. Paris: Gallimard, 1940, novel.
Le Précepteur. Paris: Gallimard, 1942, novel.
La Vie ensemble. Paris: Gallimard, 1943, novel.
Les Déserteurs. Paris: Gallimard, 1951, novel.
La Nuit de Londres. Paris: Gallimard, 1956, novel.
Histoires de Pierrot et quelques autres. Paris: Gallimard, 1960, short stories.
La Dernière année. Paris: Gallimard, 1960, novel.
John Perkins. Paris: Gallimard, Prix Médicis, 1960, novel.
Le Promontoire. Paris: Gallimard, Prix Femina, 1961, novel.
Le Parjure. Paris: Gallimard, 1964, novel.
La Relique. Paris: Gallimard, 1969, novel.
Tristan le dépossédé. Paris: Gallimard, 1978, short stories.
Le Migrateur. Paris: Gallimard, 1983, autobiographical essay.
Le Croc des chiffonniers. Paris: Gallimard, 1985, novel.
Une Saison volée. Paris: Gallimard, 1986, novel.

II. SELECTED CRITICISM

Interview with Marcel Bisiaux in *La Quinzaine littéraire*, 441 (1–15 June 1985): 10–11.
Roudaut, Jean. "Les Petits hasards inquiétants," *NRF* 326 (March 1980).

HENRI THOMAS

*Le Croc des chiffonniers**

Après Chartres, quand on va vers l'ouest, l'horizon sur la droite, peu éloigné, est fermé un certain temps par une ligne irrégulière de forêts qui cachent l'arrière-pays, puis s'abaissent et sont oubliées, si même elles ont été remarquées des voyageurs. Il y en eut un, cependant, qui n'a jamais fait ce trajet sans lever les yeux vers ce proche horizon—, y retrouvant une chose qui retenait son regard jusqu'à ce qu'une ondulation de la plaine la dérobe.

Les années passaient; les trains étaient devenus plus rapides; au printemps, les champs de colza en fleur—il y en a toujours eu là-bas—, filaient « comme un rêve », disait la dame voyageant avec Louis Vince. « Que dites-vous! . . . » disait-il, et il se demandait s'il n'allait pas lui raconter ce qui s'était passé là-bas, ce qui lui était arrivé, il y avait plusieurs années. Il avait pensé, une fois: « Je veux tout lui dire »,—il avait même cherché des mots pour commencer, et puis il avait renoncé. C'était fini depuis trop longtemps, tout cela. Les mots existaient, dans cette vieille boîte à outils, sa tête, autant que pour raconter n'importe quoi,— mais pour *cela*, ils devenaient affreux, et même, tout au fond, dans le creux où cela s'était achevé, là-bas, les mots griffaient salement, à moins de les mouiller, parfaitement, de les tremper dans une rosée noire qui colle à l'esprit.

Choses gardées et perdues, si longtemps que le monde a eu le temps de changer; on le voit différent, au moins, ne serait-ce que parce que la vue s'est affaiblie. Aujourd'hui, il y a les tours des nouveaux silos à blé dressés près de la voie ferrée, et l'autoroute derrière, un camion-citerne jaune, un autre, des voitures plus rapides que le train, d'autres qui se maintiennent à sa hauteur . . . L'horizon . . . Où sont les forêts? Dépassées, quand le léger trouble lui détourne l'esprit,—les forêts sont déjà loin en arrière. Ou

Le Croc des chiffonniers (Paris: Gallimard, 1985), 13–16, 51–63, 141–46. This passage is reprinted with the kind permission of Gallimard.

30

bien c'est plus loin encore—il n'a pas levé les yeux, c'est comme s'il avait oublié—, le train glisse sur les rails continus, sans chocs—quelqu'un a attiré son attention sur cette nouveauté, pas si récente d'ailleurs—, il a la conviction soudaine, encore une fois, que tout doit se raconter, sortir de lui, quoi, comme . . . comme . . . ce qui n'existe que si on le dit. Et si personne n'est là, cela se dit tout de même, pas besoin d'articuler comme un vieux comédien remâchant son rôle. Tout sera dit, *quidquid latet adparebit*—nous avons chanté cela pour rigoler, aux fenêtres des mansardes, dans le grand lycée, *nil inultum remanebit*, le jour où l'on introduisait Poincaré au Panthéon. C'est loin, et moralement c'est tout près, toutes les voix de ces jours-là sont mêlées dans le bruit du train, pas moyen de les distinguer mais elles sont toutes là: on est sorti du rail continu, le train frappe des coups pressés qui sont comme *mort mort mort*.

Les bois sont presque noirs sur l'horizon; le printemps pluvieux fonce toutes les couleurs; une trouée de soleil, et les champs de colza éblouissent, les étendues de blé sont des lacs profonds. Il happe tout ce qui vient, et le jette au diable, avec tout le reste, ce qu'il a vu, qui lui colle à l'âme, et tout le caché, le disparu; l'oublié, *quidquid latet*, derrière ce qui est là, tout le temps passé qui fait le poids de maintenant, la nuque blonde à côté de lui dans ce train, un jour, le fil d'or échappé dans le cou,—le vrai fil d'or autour de la taille de la jeune fille, un jour, toujours un autre jour, nuit, jour, nuit, vite enfui et tellement précis au passage.

Louis Vince, vieil homme, auteur de quelques livres dont un seul le suit, le porte encore, cette année, jusqu'à l'hôtel Forban de Roscoff

. . . .

Louis s'éloigne, d'abord à grandes enjambées, qui font craquer les herbes sèches, puis à pas silencieux. Il distingue, un instant, sur les troncs de quelques arbres, le reflet des fenêtres éclairées, mais les voix sont déjà loin, les lueurs s'effacent. Il va maintenant d'un pas de promeneur inquiet, un peu trop rapide, sans regarder à droite ni à gauche. Le passage entre les arbres n'est peut-être pas un sentier mais la marche y est facile; c'est comme les premiers pas d'une promenade dans un parc, l'après-midi, quand on sort des maisons étouffantes. Dans les parcs, il y a d'autres promeneurs, comme il y a des sentiers à suivre. Personne ne se promène ici, et il n'y a pas de chemin. Quelqu'un se tient appuyé contre un arbre, Louis ne l'aurait pas aperçu sans le point rouge de la cigarette. Un de ces impossibles guetteurs qu'il faut fuir, Louis est certain que ce n'est pas le type aux canards. Il y a un va-et-vient dans ces bois, Marcelin Bauge a dû errer comme cela, il a connu l'empire des chiffonniers, c'est pourquoi il a compris Louis qui s'enfuyait. Louis, sans s'arrêter, fait un geste de la main vers le ciel laiteux, au-dessus du sentier, un signe pour personne, pour tout ce qui vole dans la nuit. Il y a un peu de brouillard à l'endroit où se trouve l'étang; la voiture de Dorine sera bien cachée, cette nuit.

Il s'éloigne vers la lisière des bois; le sol s'élève en approchant du talus qui longe la forêt de ce côté. Le chemin qu'ils avaient pris pour arriver passe par là. Avant la descente, Louis se retourne: les bois derrière lui ne sont pas noirs, ils flottent dans une pâleur qui est même plus claire que le ciel. C'est sans doute la brume sur les étangs. Quelques lumières filent dans la plaine, là où Dorine a tourné pour monter vers les bois—, ces mauvaises forêts sans villages où l'on est guetté, où Marcelin Bauge se débat en s'en allant chez les morts.

Il ira de ce côté, il marchera sous le couvert des premiers arbres, à la lisière. Derrière le talus, bornage d'autrefois qui s'efface, il y a un sentier, presque un chemin par endroits, et c'est là que s'en va Louis Vince, l'enfant, le vieil homme, l'ami des chiffonniers, l'homme éternel, et allez! Il marche plus vite, il respire plus largement. Le sentier s'écarte de la lisière, les arbres se resserrent, on ne voit plus le trou noir de la plaine avec ses lumières en mouvement, l'air que Louis respire a cette odeur des bois nocturnes, ce goût d'automne qui fait que l'esprit sursaute comme un animal qui se réveille et flaire le monde de la nuit. La trouée du sentier devant lui s'éclaire assez nettement pour ressembler à une porte ouverte. Ici les feuilles mortes ont glissé dans le creux et le pied s'y enfonce; Francine disait que ces sous-bois sont humides, une couche d'argile y retient l'eau, il n'y fait bon qu'au fort de l'été, quand la terre est craquelée.

S'ils cherchent à y comprendre quelque chose, ils diront qu'il a repris sa liberté. Ils se demanderont dans quelle direction . . . Dorine va se fâcher . . . Bauge est capable de les avoir rassurées, avant qu'elles ne l'aident à regagner sa chambre et avaler ses tranquillisants. Si Louis a disparu, c'est pour aller lire *Le glaviot* ailleurs, les endroits ne manquent pas. Et Bauge s'est rendormi, et les femmes ont senti le froid qui gagnait la maison, l'oubli leur viendra avec la chaleur, quand elles seront ensemble.

Le sentier monte, descend, suit une longue pente. Louis Vince garde le même pas, son pas, celui qui l'a mené le long de la vie jusqu'ici, depuis le jour où il s'est sauvé du collège, à quinze ans,—ils l'ont su tout de suite, le concierge l'avait vu filer, le répétiteur Simonin l'avait rattrapé à bicyclette. Rien compris, Simonin,—rien compris le professeur Beaumont, avec son « Rien ne tient à moi, je ne tiens à rien »—et lui, Louis-Loulou, est-ce qu'il comprenait? Il ne s'agissait pas de comprendre. Quelque chose l'a tiré très fort en arrière, il a perdu son pas dès qu'il s'est assis dans le pré au bord de la route, contre un arbre. La plaine bruissante, le ciel, les vols de papillons jaunes autour de lui, c'était si nouveau, terrible,—et c'était lui, tout venait à lui pour être lui; il l'a senti comme un choc dans son cœur. *Il ne pouvait pas le dire.*

Le sentier est sorti des taillis, Louis sent le vent d'Ouest qui lui baigne le visage et il écoute en marchant le bruit que fait l'automne, une plainte intermittente qui vient de si loin qu'elle n'est presque plus rien ici, dans le maigre taillis. Le professeur l'avait regardé, pas méchant du tout. Il pardonnait, il comprenait: « Votre désespoir d'adolescent: je ne tiens à rien, rien ne tient à moi. » Et Louis chialait, pas moyen de se retenir. « Oui, oui, oui! » Et c'est faux, il y avait autre chose. Comme le mensonge est lourd! Il chialait par impuissance à s'expliquer. Et maintenant? Maintenant, peut-il expliquer? Tout venait à lui, les vagues d'herbe haute, les courants du ciel, et, lui presque étalé dans l'herbe au ras de l'horizon, le bleu foncé du jour qui bougeait entre les hautes herbes et les toits des maisons. Il fallait passer là-bas, d'abord dans un bureau de tabac pour acheter un timbre. Il n'est pas allé là-bas, Louis Vince, l'enfant, le petit Loulou. Il avait tiré la feuille blanche de son cartable, puis le crayon, il s'était redressé, le dos contre l'arbre, et sur la feuille blanche, il n'avait rien écrit. Il ne pouvait pas écrire: chère maman. Il voyait sa mère, qui ne sait pas, et qui va savoir. Ce n'est pas la frousse qui l'a rendu docile quand le pion Simonin est arrivé sur sa bicyclette. Loulou suffoquait, chialait, Simonin n'a pas dit un mot. Mais qu'est-ce qu'il a Louis Vince? Mais qu'est-ce que c'est? Il a suffi qu'il pense à sa mère, seule dans l'école du village, et le cœur lui a manqué; il n'est plus revenu en marchant, mais en courant. Simonin, devant lui, s'arrêtait de temps en temps, et le regardait venir.

Louis Vince s'assied sur le talus. Dorine? Quoi, Dorine? Il la voit comme elle était chez Germaine, et chez lui le matin. « Il n'y a personne en face pour me voir? » Dire qu'il n'a pas envie de la revoir, ce n'est pas assez; il ne veut pas penser à elle, un noir dégoût lui racle l'esprit. Est-ce bien, est-ce mal? Personne ne répond à Louis Vince. Rien ne le tire vers Dorine, rien ne le ramène à cette maison. Rien. Ce serait peut-être bien, de se retourner et de refaire tranquillement le chemin. Un vieil homme qui revient lentement d'une petite virée dans la forêt la nuit—ce serait rassurant. Seulement, c'est impossible.

Louis Vince a repris sa marche. Il n'y a plus d'arbres, pas même de buissons autour de lui, mais le sentier est descendu dans un creux des collines, car du côté de la plaine les lumières n'apparaissent plus, elles sont cachées par une grande vague noire qui continue, plus ou moins haute, comme une vraie vague qui bougerait: il ne faut pas trop chercher ce que c'est. Le sentier tourne, insensiblement; il vacille à droite et à gauche, la pente est incertaine, comme est la teinte du sol pâle. Louis penche avec le sentier, docilement. Il n'entend plus ses pas, depuis qu'il ne foule plus les brindilles et les herbes sèches mais un sous-sol muet comme un tapis. Cette pâleur sous ses pas, depuis qu'il est sorti du sous-bois, ce n'est pas du sable, mais de la poussière; un peu plus, et ce serait . . . quelque chose qui n'existe pas. Il s'est arrêté, et il s'agenouille; il applique ses deux paumes sur cette poussière qui est fraîche et reçoit bien l'empreinte invisible. Il a touché la terre déserte, qui ne pense rien, sans voix ni lumière, la terre qui se cache sous le ciel. Il est bien là, longtemps, couché en chien de fusil, en position fœtale dirait Serrurier s'il était vivant,—la joue contre la poussière qui tiédit. Sol abandonné, sol de rien du tout. Ce n'est pas la première fois que Louis se couche en travers d'un sentier, les yeux fermés, mais c'est la bonne, rien à regretter. Il aime cette poussière comme un mort aime la terre, en attendant la résurrection. Une fois, une fois pour toutes, et c'est lui, aujourd'hui, cette nuit, il faut qu'un homme soit complètement ce qu'il a été et ce qu'il sera. Le fugueur de quatorze ans, ce qu'il cherchait sans le savoir, c'était cela. Puisque Louis le vieux a retrouvé Louis le petit fugueur, ils sont ensemble, ils ont retrouvé le chemin dans la nuit. Il faut aller plus loin pour en savoir davantage, mais ils ont tout le temps . . . « jusqu'à la fin du monde », dit le gosse. Il s'était dit cela en s'enfuyant, Louis l'avait oublié, c'est de nouveau là: jusqu'à la fin du monde. Et pas d'*auprès de ma blonde*, pense Louis. Elle est restée là-bas, près de la mare aux canards. On a le temps. Plus de cinquante années ont été nécessaires, mais le résultat est là, tout à coup, tout ensemble, qui le fait toucher terre, tomber dans la poussière fraîche, et il se relèvera pour l'emporter, le moment venu, loin dans la nuit noire . . . Pas la nuit noire, la terre est un brouillard clair, c'est seulement le livre qui a glissé de sa poche, *Le glaviot* de Marcelin Bauge. Louis, sans ouvrir les yeux, le retrouve, ouvert dans la poussière, les pages qui ont touché le sol sont déjà humides. Il n'y a pas de rosée sur l'herbe, c'est l'humeur de la terre qui se prend au papier, elle l'attire, pour qu'il disparaisse. Le froissement des feuilles est comme une agitation de bête dans l'obscurité. Louis arrête ce bruit en étranglant l'animal, en l'écrasant contre terre. Ça deviendra ce que ça a toujours été, un ramassis de pages froissées, terreuses,—non: mieux que ça! Louis s'est relevé, ses genoux tremblent, il ne voit autour de lui que de grandes taches informes qui changent de place, reviennent, chavirent . . . c'est le vent qui les souffle. Qu'il emporte *Le glaviot!* Louis jette le livre aussi fort qu'il peut, du côté de la forêt. Il jetterait bien un autre livre, le sien, *Le croc des chiffonniers,* la vie du père par le fils, la fortune faite à partir des débris des choses. Qu'elle y retourne!

La marche est un peu moins facile, le sentier s'est enfoncé entre deux bords rapprochés contre lesquels Louis bute du genou, pour peu qu'il vacille d'un côté. Le fond blanchâtre n'est guère visible, et surtout, Louis marche avec une légèreté mécanique, une confiance, un abandon, qui l'ont envoyé sur le talus deux fois avant la sortie de cette espèce de sentier creux. Ce n'est rien!

Il va d'un bon pas, maintenant que le sol est sans embûche, loin devant lui, car une vague clarté règne à présent, le proche horizon tranche nettement la nuit. Qu'est-ce qui te prend? Qu'est-ce qui te prend? Il répète encore: qu'est-ce qui te prend? Ce n'est pas pour s'interroger: il y a longtemps que la réponse a été donnée, et oubliée, parce que la marche a tout pris. Ce qui l'a pris, c'est de marcher comme cela, la tête baissée pour distinguer le sentier devant lui, rien d'autre. *Où le père a passé passera bien l'enfant* . . . Il faut changer ça. *Où l'enfant a passé* . . . Ce n'est pas ça. *Où l'enfant a eu peur*, le vieil homme passe, et l'enfant avec lui . . . L'enfant Louis Vince a eu peur; les premières fois, il était rappelé en arrière vers la mère qu'il fallait retrouver avant qu'elle ait peur, elle. Ce que le môme Louis voulait en sortant de la ville, ce matin-là, c'est ce que Louis accomplit maintenant dans la nuit qui lui saute au visage. Il ne l'aime pas tellement, ce môme, il en a plutôt pitié, il en a peur aussi. Quand lui est-il revenu à l'idée, le petit Louis des rues de Mulhouse? Quand il hésitait, trébuchait dans le sentier, dans l'étourdissement avant de tomber, et il était là: c'était moi, c'était nous! Et Louis s'est lancé à grands pas, vers où l'enfant voulait aller, mais il s'était couché au premier choc. C'est cette nuit qu'il s'est relevé, après toutes ces années, furieux, terrible! Oh, ces idées-là passent comme ce qui lui frôle le visage par instants, les esprits de la nuit qui vont, qui viennent. Il y a la fatigue aussi, celle que l'enfant ne connaissait pas et qu'il ne veut toujours pas connaître, rien ne le rappelle plus en arrière, il veut foncer, il a trouvé le chemin! Une minute de repos tout de même, dit Louis, là, dans le talus, tiens, je serre mon manteau, on n'a pas froid? Non. Le sommeil les prend aussitôt.

. . . .

Il y a quelque chose dans la serrure. Connu: Dorine a souvent glissé de ces messages dans le trou—*À bientôt?* Cette fois, le papier enroulé contient une petite feuille morte. Ça doit venir du bois-taillis autour de la maison Bauge.

« Oui, c'est plutôt grand chez toi, dit Julie. Il y a de la poussière. Des collants sur le séchoir. C'est qui?

—Je n'en sais plus rien. »

Il y a aussi du linge jeté dans la baignoire; on y trouverait bien un slip rose, un slip noir.

« Mon grand-père était chiffonnier, dit Louis. C'est pour ça que tout traîne. Un jour, je ramasse, et allez . . .

—Et des livres, et des livres! dit Julie. Pourquoi que tu dis chiffonnier?

—Parce que c'est vrai. Viens voir. »

Là, dans la pièce aux livres, il lève la lampe au bout de son fil, elle éclaire l'objet, suspendu au mur, le long crochet en métal poli dont la pointe recourbée brille comme une griffe.

« On était chiffonnier de père en fils. Sauf moi, et mon père, ferrailleur, papa, quelqu'un! C'est le croc de l'arrière-grand-père, une relique dans la famille, l'arrière-arrière-grand-père du temps de Napoléon trois. »

Julie détourne les yeux; elle n'aime pas cette chose au mur, ni les livres dans les casiers, ni ces affaires dans les coins, des trucs de femme encore? Il y a un parfum ici, les fenêtres n'ont pas été ouvertes. Elle étend le bras, et presse le commutateur. Les voitures qui tournent au carrefour font courir des bandes de clarté au plafond, plus rapides, plus lentes, immobiles un instant, c'est cela qu'elle voulait voir. Elle dit: « C'est du cinéma . . . Chiffonnier qu'on est, faut se laver tout de même . . . Aussi, t'as pas faim? »

Elle s'est endormie aussitôt fourrée dans le lit, tournée vers le mur. Elle était sortie nue de la salle de bains, et a traversé la pièce aux livres pour gagner la chambre. Il l'a regardée, elle n'est pas venue vers lui, mais elle a dit, en cambrant le maigre buste: « Ils sont petits, c'est pas de ma faute. » Par la porte qu'elle a laissée ouverte, il voit le haut du lit, dans l'ombre. Ses cheveux qu'elle a lavés s'étalent noirs sur l'oreiller, et c'est sa main qui dépasse un peu du drap, les doigts ouverts; elle dort. Comme elle dort!

Commence, Louis Vince, tu as fait ta tournée, la grande. Ce que tu as ramené, tiens-le bien, ne perds pas l'idée, quelle idée? Elle a roulé toute la nuit, et dans l'hôtel Voisin elle est passée, par les mains de Martine, sur les pieds nus, les ongles vernis,—et tout cela n'était rien encore, petite limaille pour l'idée, qui lui collait à l'esprit, quand il a peiné dans les rues. Trop lourd alors, il a été renversé, l'idée s'est retournée avec lui. Le serveur blond a vu la glissade, il a relevé ce client qui croule, lui seul, et pourquoi pas?

Le premier venu est dans le secret, la plus pauvre fille, la gringalette aux cuisses maigres qui s'endort tout de suite est dans le secret, jusqu'au fond. Va voir le secret, Louis, ne tombe pas, appuie-toi au mur. On s'est bien tiré d'affaire, pour venir ici,—elle sans billet, et lui qui a vomi, et elle . . . Quand elle barbotait dans la baignoire, tout à l'heure, elle a crié: « Louis! Le crochet de ton grand-père, j'aime pas ça, c'est dégueu. T'es pas chiffonnier, Louis, t'es pas chiffonnier! » Elle chantait cela.

Pas chiffonnier, Julie, c'est vrai, c'est fini. C'est à mon tour maintenant de passer de l'autre côté, dans le tas, avec l'idée, on se défile, on est tranquille, on va au fond.

Il avait mangé trop vite, et trop, de ces boîtes ouvertes par Julie, et bu cette bouteille qui restait de Dorine. Le dégoût. Il va vomir encore, dans la cuisine, sans personne, comme c'est arrivé plusieurs fois, ces derniers temps. Le dégoût? Le mal qui se précise? Cette robe jetée dans un coin, bon Dieu! c'est Dorine, qui s'est changée en partant, il y a . . . deux jours . . . des années . . . Ça va mieux, comme chaque fois. Mais dormir, dormir? . . . Sur le canapé, où il a passé des nuits de l'hiver, quand il travaillait. Travaillera-t-il jamais de nouveau? C'est bien comme c'est. La porte sur la chambre est ouverte. Julie se retourne, soupire, dort. Il entend la pluie sur la verrière du photographe, dans la cour.

Julie Trottat aura disparu le lendemain. Il sera malade, très malade. Il guérira, encore une fois. Il sera le vieil homme, encore, dans ce train, qui lève les yeux vers l'horizon rapproché. La poussière d'une cimenterie blanchit l'herbe des collines, où le vent dominant la chasse. Le vieil homme porte machinalement la main au revers de sa veste. Il sourit, est-ce à cette voyageuse assise non loin de lui, qu'il ne connaît pas? Il n'a pas retrouvé au revers de sa veste la rosette de la Légion d'honneur; cela vaut tout au plus un haussement d'épaule, à peine.

Marcelin Bauge est mort, mais *Le glaviot* vient de passer en livre de poche. Louis Vince l'a repêché.

Houat, 2 octobre 1984.

The Ragpicker's Hook

After Chartres, as you travel further west, the horizon, not far off to the right, is obscured for a bit by an irregular line of forest which hides the land beyond before it starts to thin out, and is forgotten, if indeed it was ever noticed at all by the travellers. There was one traveller, however, who never made this journey without looking up to watch this nearby horizon—finding something there which held his attention until an undulation in the plain took it away.

The years passed; the trains had become faster; in the springtime the fields off lowering rapeseed—it has always grown over there—flew by "like a dream," the lady travelling with Louis Vince said. "What are you saying! . . ." he said, and he wondered if he was not going to tell her everything that had happened there, that had happened to him, several years ago. He had once thought on one occasion, "I want to tell her everything,"—he had even searched for the words with which to begin, and then he had given up. All that had been over for a long time now. The words were there, in that old tool box of a head of his, enough words to talk about anything—but for *that,* they became awful, and down in the depths, in the hollow space where it had ended, the words clawed in a nasty way, unless he made them wet, perfectly, by dipping them in a black dew that clung to his mind.

Things kept and lost for so long that the world had had time to change; you see it differently now, at least, if only because your sight has gotten weaker. Today there are the new grain elevators standing next to the railroad tracks, and the highway behind them, a yellow tank-truck, and another, cars faster than the train, others which keep up with it. . . . The horizon . . . . Where is the forest? Already gone by, by the time his mind had been vaguely troubled by this distraction—the forest is already far behind. Or perhaps it's further on—he hasn't looked up, it's as if he had forgotten—the train glides along over the straight tracks, without any jolts—someone drew his attention to this novelty, which isn't really that recent,—he has a sudden conviction, once again, that everything must be told, you know, come out of him, like . . . like . . . something that only exists if it is told. And if no one is there, it should still be told, no need to enunciate like an old actor practicing his lines. All will be told, *quidquid latet adparebit*—we sang that for a laugh from the attic windows in high school, *nil inultum remanebit*, the day they put Poincaré in the Pantheon. It's far away, and yet morally speaking it's nearby, all the voices of those days are blended in with the noise of the train, no way to make them out but they're all there: we've gone off the straight track, the train jolts in hurried bumps that sound like *dead, dead, dead.*

The woods are almost dark on the horizon; the rainy spring darkens all the colors; the sun breaks through, and the fields of rapeseed dazzle, the expanses of wheat are deep lakes. He snatches up everything that comes, and throws it to the devil, with everything else, everything he's seen, which clings to his soul, and everything that's hidden, that has disappeared or been forgotten, *quidquid latet*, behind what is there, all of the past that makes up the weight of the present, the nape of the neck with its blond hairs next to him in this train, one day, the golden thread come loose onto the neck—the real golden thread around the young girl's waist, one day, always another day, night, day, night, quickly flown by and so precise in its passage.

Louis Vince, an old man and the author of a few books, only one of which follows him, and is still carrying him along, this year to the Forban Hotel in Roscoff . . .

. . . .

Louis runs away, at first with giant strides which make the dry grass crackle, then with silent steps. For a second he makes out the reflection of lit windows on the trunks of a few trees, but the voices are already distant, the light fading. Now he goes along like someone walking nervously, slightly too fast, without looking left or right. The way between the trees might not be a path, but it's easy to walk through them; it's like the first steps of a walk in the park in the afternoon, when you leave your stuffy house. In the parks, there are other people out for a walk, just as there are paths to follow. No one goes for a walk here, and there is no path. Someone is leaning against a tree, Louis wouldn't have noticed him except for the red glow of the cigarette. One of these impossible peeping-toms you have to steer clear of, Louis is sure that it's not the guy who was with the ducks. People come and go in these woods, Marcelin Bauge must have just wandered about like that, he knew the ragpicker's empire. Which is why he understood Louis's running away. Without stopping, Louis gestures towards the milky sky above the path, a sign for no one, for everything that flies in the night. There's a little bit of fog where the pond is; Dorine's car will be well hidden tonight.

He goes off towards the edge of the woods; the ground rises up as he gets nearer to the bank that follows the edge of the forest on this side. The path they had taken to get there goes through that way. Before heading down, Louis turns around: the woods behind him are not black, they are floating in a pale light which is even brighter than the sky. It's probably the mist over the pond. A few lights flicker on the plain, over by where Dorine turned to go up towards the woods—these horrible forests without villages where people watch you, where Marcelin Bauge is struggling as he goes off to join the dead.

He'll go over that way, he'll walk under the cover of the first trees, at the edge of the forest. Behind the bank, a former boundary marking which has begun to disappear, there is a track, which almost turns into a path in places, and that's where Louis Vince goes, the child, the old man, the friend of the ragpickers, the eternal man, and off with you! He walks faster, he breathes more deeply. The path leaves the edge of the forest, the trees get thicker, the black hole of the plain with its moving lights is no longer visible, the air Louis breathes has that smell of night woods, that taste of fall which makes the mind jump like an animal that wakes up and sniffs the night world. The break in the path ahead of him becomes so clear that it looks like an open door. Here the dead leaves have collected in the hollow and your feet sink into them; Francine was saying that this undergrowth was wet, there's a layer of clay that holds the water, it's only good at the height of the summer, when the earth is cracked.

If they try to understand why he did it, they'll say he got his freedom back. They'll wonder what direction. . . . Dorine will get angry. . . . Bauge could well have reassured them, before they help him back to his room to swallow his tranquilizers. If Louis has disappeared, it's in order to go and read *The Glob of Spit* somewhere else, there's no shortage of places. And Bauge has gone back to sleep, and the women have felt the cold that was creeping into the house, they'll forget once it starts to get warm, when they're together.

The path goes up and down, following a long slope. Louis Vince walks along at the same pace, his pace, the one he has kept throughout his life until now, from the day he ran away from boarding school, when he was fifteen—they knew right away, the superintendant had seen him run off, Simonin the monitor had caught up with him on his bicycle. Simonin didn't understand anything—Mr. Beaumont didn't understand anything, with his "I have no meaning for anyone and nothing has any meaning for me"—and Louis-Loulou, did *he* understand? It wasn't a question of understanding. Something jerked him back violently, he lost his pace once he sat down against a tree in a meadow at the edge of the road. The rustle of the plain, the sky, the yellow butterflies fluttering around him, all this was so new, and terrible—and it was him, everything came to him in order to be him; he felt it like a shock to his heart. *He could not say it.*

The path left the woods, Louis feels the west wind caress his face and while walking, listens to the noise that autumn makes, an intermittent moaning that comes from so far away that it's barely audible here, in the sparse woods. The teacher had looked at him, not mean at all. He forgave him, he understood: "It's just your adolescent despair: I have no meaning for anyone and nothing has any meaning for me." And Louis was blubbering away, no way to stop. "Yes, yes, yes!" And it wasn't true, there was something else. Lies are so heavy! He was blubbering because he wasn't able to explain himself. And now? Can he explain now? Everything came to him, the waves of tall grass, the currents of the sky, himself almost spread out in the grass on the horizon, the dark blue of the twilight shifting between the tall grasses and the roofs of the houses. He had to go that way, first of all to a tobacconists' to buy a stamp. He didn't go that way, Louis Vince, the child, little Loulou. He had pulled the blank sheet of paper out of his satchel, then the pencil, he'd sat up, with his back against the tree, and on the blank sheet of paper he had written nothing. He couldn't write: Dear Mama. He saw his mother, who doesn't know and is going to know. It wasn't being scared stiff that made him docile when Simonin the monitor arrived on his bicycle. Loulou was suffocating, blubbering, Simonin didn't say a word. What on earth is the matter with Louis Vince? What's wrong? All he had to do was think of his mother, alone in the village school, and he lost heart; he didn't walk, but ran back. Ahead of him, Simonin stopped from time to time to watch him coming along.

Louis Vince sits down on the bank. Dorine? What about Dorine? He sees her as she was at Germaine's, at his house in the morning. "Is there anyone across the way who could see me?" It's not enough just to say he just doesn't want to see her again; he doesn't want to think of her, a black kind of disgust grates on his mind. Is it good, is it bad? No one answers Louis Vince. Nothing is pulling him towards Dorine, nothing is bringing him back to that house. Nothing. It might be good to turn around and quietly retrace his steps. An old man coming back slowly from a little walk in the forest at night—that would be reassuring. Except, it's impossible.

Louis Vince has set off again. There are no more trees, or even bushes around him, but the path has gone down into a hollow in the hills, because on the side where the plain is the lights are no longer visible, they are hidden by a large black wave that goes on and on, more or less high, like a real wave which would move: it's not too good an idea to try to find out what it is. The path turns imperceptibly; it veers right and left, the slope is uncertain, as is the color of the pale ground. Louis lists docilely with the path. He doesn't hear his steps any more, since he's no longer walking on twigs and dry leaves, but on earth that is as silent as a carpet. This paleness under his steps, ever since he's left the woods, is not sand, but dust; if it were any finer, it would be . . . something which doesn't exist. He has stopped, and is kneeling down; he places the palms of his hands on the dust which is cool and easily forms an invisible imprint. He has touched this deserted ground, which doesn't have any thoughts, or voice or light, the earth that hides under the sky. He stays there for a long time, lying like a hunting dog, in a fetal position, as Serrurier would say if he were still alive—his cheek against the warming dust. Abandoned ground, worthless ground. It's not the first time Louis Vince has lain across a path with his eyes closed, but this time it's right, no regrets. He loves this dust as a dead man loves the earth while he waits for the resurrection. Once, once and for all, and it's him, today, tonight, a man has to be completely what he has been and what he will be. This was what the fourteen-year-old runaway was looking for without knowing it. Since Louis the old man has caught up with Louis the little runaway, they're together, they've found the path in the night again. They have to go further to know more but they have all the time, "until the end of the world," the kid says. He'd said that to himself when he ran away, Louis had forgotten it, but there it is again: until the end of the world. And none of this *With a Blonde at My Side*, Louis thinks. She stayed over there, by the duck pond. There's plenty of time. It took over fifty years, but the end result is there, suddenly, all together, making him touch the ground, fall into the cool dust, and he'll get up again to take it away when it's time, far away into the dark night. . . . Not the dark night, the earth is a bright fog, it's only the book that slipped out of his pocket, *The Glob of Spit* by Marcelin Bauge. Louis finds it again without opening his eyes, lying open in the dust, the pages that touched the ground are already wet. There's no dew on the grass, it's the wetness of the earth that's seeping into the paper, pulling it down so that it disappears. The rustling of the pages is like an animal stirring in the darkness. Louis stops this noise by strangling the animal, crushing it against the ground. It will become what it has always been, a bunch of crumpled, soiled pages—no: better yet! Louis has picked himself up, his knees are trembling, he sees nothing around him but large shapeless spots that shift about, come back, spin over . . . it's the wind blowing them. Let it carry *The Glob of Spit* away! Louis throws the book as hard as he can, towards the forest. He would like to throw away another book, his own book, *The Ragpicker's Hook*, the father's life written by the son, a fortune made from debris. Let it go back where it came from!

It's getting less easy to walk, the path has disappeared between two banks that are close together, against which Louis knocks his knee whenever he sways even slightly to one side. The whitish ground is barely visible, and what's more, Louis is walking with a mechanical lightness, a confidence and abandon that have made him fall twice onto the bank before getting out of this sunken path. Never mind!

He's walking at a good pace now that the ground is free of pitfalls, far ahead of him, for now there's a vague brightness all around, the horizon nearby clearly stands out against the night. What's gotten into you? What's gotten into you? He repeats it again: What's gotten into you? He's not really asking himself this question: the answer was given, and forgotten, a long time ago, because the walking has taken everything. What's gotten into him is that he's walking like this, his head down to make out the path in front of him, and nothing else. *Where the father has gone the child will go too.* That needs changing. *Where the child has gone. . . .* That's not it. *Where the child was afraid,* the old man is going, and the child with him. . . . Louis Vince the child was afraid; the first times, he was called back to his mother whom he had to find before she became afraid. What Louis the kid wanted when he left the town that morning was what Louis is now accomplishing in the night which leaps at his face. He doesn't really like that kid, it's more that he is sorry for him, he's afraid of him too. When did the little Louis of the streets of Mulhouse come back to mind? When he was hesitating, stumbling on the path, in his bewilderment before falling, and there he was: it was me, it was us! And Louis strode off, towards where the child wanted to go, but he had lain down at the first shock. It is tonight that he has picked himself up again, after all these years, furious, terrible! Ah, these ideas go by like the thing that brushes against his face now and again, the spirits of the night that come and go. There's also his tiredness, the tiredness the child didn't know and that he still doesn't want to know, nothing is calling him back anymore, he wants to forge ahead, he's found the path! Let's just rest a minute, says Louis, over there, on the bank, look, I'll pull my coat on tight, we're not cold, are we? No. They fall asleep straight away.

. . . .

There's something in the lock. He knows: Dorine often slipped messages into the keyhold, like "See you soon?" This time, the rolled up piece of paper contains a little dead leaf. It must have come from the trees in the copse around the Bauge house.

"Yeah, your place is pretty big," says Julie. "It's dusty. Pantyhose on the drying rack. Whose are they?"

"I don't know anymore."

There are also some dirty clothes thrown into the bathtub; you might well find a pair of pink panties, a pair of black panties.

"My grandfather was a ragpicker," says Louis. "That's why there's all this stuff lying around. One day I'll pick it all up, and that'll be that. . . ."

"And books and books!" says Julie. "Why did you say ragpicker?"

"Because it's true. Come and see."

There, in the room with the books, he lifts the lamp up as far as its cord will stretch, it lights up the object hanging on the wall, the long hook of polished metal whose curved point shines like a claw.

"We were ragpickers from one generation to the next. Except me, and my father, a scrap metal dealer, he was really somebody, my Dad. This is my great-grandfather's hook, a family relic, it was originally my great-great-grandfather's from the time of Napoleon the Third."

Julie turns her eyes away, she doesn't like this thing on the wall, nor the books in their cases, nor all this stuff in the corners, maybe more women's things? There's a certain smell in here, the windows haven't been opened. She stretches out her arm and turns off the light switch. The cars that turn at the intersection send bands of light running across the ceiling, faster, slower, still for a second, that's what she wanted to see. She says, "It's all for show. . . . You may be a ragpicker, but you still have to wash. . . . And anyway, aren't you hungry?"

She fell asleep straight away, nestled in the bed, turned to the wall. She had come out of the bathroom naked, and crossed the room with the books to get to the bedroom. He looked at her, she didn't come towards him, but she said, pushing out her skinny chest: "They're small, it's not my fault." Through the door that she's left open he sees the head of the bed in the shadows. Her hair, which she's washed, is a mass of black strewn across the pillow, and her hand, open, sticks out from under the sheet; she's sleeping. She's sleeping so soundly!

Begin, Louis Vince, you've done your rounds, this is the big one. Hold on tight to what you've brought back, don't lose the idea, what idea? It rolled around all night long, and in the Voisin hotel, it passed through Martine's hands, over her bare feet, her polished nails—and all that was still nothing, little bits of filings for the idea that clung to his mind when he struggled through the streets. Then it got too heavy, he was knocked over, and the idea went over with him. The blond bartender saw him slip, he picked up this customer who's falling, on his own, and why not?

The first person to come along knows the secret, the poorest girl, the puny little thing with the skinny thighs, who falls asleep straight away knows the secret, down to its core. Go look at the secret, Louis, don't fall over, lean against the wall. We've managed to get out of a tight spot, to come here—she without a ticket, and he who's thrown up, and she. . . . When she was splashing about in the bathtub just now, she shouted: "Louis! I don't like your grandfather's hook, it's gross. You're not a rag-picker, Louis, you're not a ragpicker!" She sang it.

Not a ragpicker, Julie, it's true, it's over. It's my turn now to go over to the other side, into the crowd, with the idea, you just sneak off, you get some peace, you get to the bottom.

He had eaten too much, and too quickly, from the cans that Julie had opened, and had drunk the bottle that Dorine had left behind. Disgust. He's going to throw up again in the kitchen, with no one around, as he has several times recently. Disgust? Is it the sickness getting clearer? That dress thrown into the corner, for Christ's sake! it's Dorine, who changed before she left . . . two days ago . . . years ago. . . . He's feeling better, as always. But what about sleeping, what about sleeping? . . . On the couch, where he spent the winter nights, when he was working. Will he ever work again? Things are good just as they are. The door to the bedroom is open. Julie turns over, sighs, sleeps. He hears the rain on the photographer's glass roof in the courtyard.

Julie Trottat will have disappeared the next day. He'll be sick, very sick. He'll get better, once again. Once again he'll be the old man in that train who looks up at the nearby horizon. The dust from a cement works whitens the grass on the hills, where the prevailing wind blows it. The old man brings his hand up mechanically to his lapel. He smiles, is it at the woman sitting not far from him, whom he doesn't know? He hasn't found the rosette of the Legion of Honor on his lapel; that's worth at the most a shrug of the shoulders, if that.

Marcelin Bauge is dead, but *The Glob of Spit* has just come out in paperback. Louis Vince fished it out again.

Houat, 2 October 1984.

Translated by Michael Syrotinski

BARBARA VINKEN

Claude Simon: The Stained Paper

Claude Simon, born in 1913 in Tananarive, Madagascar, grew up on a vineyard near Perpignan in Southern France. He began to write at the age of twenty-seven after trying "painting and revolution." Though he came to writing/literature/text rather late in life, it was with all the more intensity. *Les Géorgiques*, published in 1981, is his fourteenth novel.

Simon is a member of the last great "school" of French fiction which is called "the new novel." Claude Simon received the Nobel Prize for Literature in 1985: He no longer needs an introduction, for he has done so extensively himself in his *Discours de Stockholm*, which has appeared in many, slightly different, versions. As for the autobiographical material here cited, it is useless, even impossible to ask if it is "fictive" or "authentic." As a literary text, it is necessarily a mask, stylization, the supreme camouflage of the writer Simon behind "the man."

I am now an old man, and, like many inhabitants of this old Europe, the first part of my life was rather eventful: I witnessed a revolution, I fought a war under particularly murderous conditions (I belonged to one of those regiments cold-bloodedly sacrificed by officers from the beginning, and of which there remained very little by the end of the first week), I was taken prisoner, I experienced hunger, physical labor to the point of exhaustion, I escaped, I was gravely ill, many times close to death, violent or natural, I encountered the most diverse types of people—priests as well as church burners, peaceful bourgeois as well as anarchists, philosophers as well as the illiterate; I shared my bread with crooks and ended up travelling here and there in the world . . . and still, I have not yet, at the age of 72, discovered any sense in all of it, unless, as Barthes said after Shakespeare, "if the world signifies something, it is that it signifies nothing"—except that it is.

Simon thus sketches out with considerable pathos the life of a man who has experienced everything. His religious, political, and intellectual antitheses encompass the possible extremes of life in the world. The experience of marginality, suffering, and brushes with death have all left their trace. This eventful life can be summed up in a laconic phrase, a key to antimetaphysical thought, formulated by Barthes, who refers in his turn to Shakespeare. "If the world signifies something, it is that it signifies nothing."

45

Simon's position in literary history can be summed up in three "posts": post-realist, post-visionary, and post-Sartrian. These three "posts" are obviously not reactions to literary texts; they are rather positions taken against a certain discourse on literature and thus of an essentially polemic nature. If Balzac has become a kind of *tête de turc* [whipping boy], it is not as the author of *La Comédie humaine*, but as the object and paradigm of academic discourse. Since Barthes's reading of Balzac we all know—and Simon probably always knew it—that Balzac's texts are no more "realist" and no more represent a reality that might exist outside of them than any text labeled "New Novel." Perhaps they provoke more easily the "effect of the real" because they produce or reproduce a structure with which we are accustomed to constitute reality, which must, perhaps definitively, be that of yesterday: namely a plausible psychologism, a certain causality, stories with a beginning and an end, and a temporal, linear development.

By showing us that it is merely a question of effect, Simon's texts have the potential to disillusion. For Simon, as for Lévi-Strauss, writing is essentially a matter of what he liked to call "tinkering." He turns to Valéry to characterize his relation to the text: "If I am questioned, if people worry (which happens sometimes, and rather intensely) about what I meant, . . . I would respond that I didn't want to mean, but to do, and that it is this intention to do that required what I said." In his literary texts, Simon thus has "nothing to say," no message to deliver. In his polemic against "engaged" literature, he does not, however, resort to an estheticism for which literature would be gratuitous and all literary texts a mere play of forms. Simon is committed to literature: "Because to live is to read and because man is shaped by language, whatever work finally transforms language cannot by the same token avoid transforming man." It is precisely by featuring esthetics that he is far more radical than any "engaged" literature.

Simon's texts became from the beginning the paradigm for structuralist criticism. While the greater part of his work is centered on the signifier, one can, however summarily, distinguish two different approaches. A truly structuralist analysis proves to be strictly rhetorical. It is based on Jakobson's fundamental distinction between metaphor and metonymy and strives to explain, with these two categories, how the Simonian text functions, with its innumerable ruptures that break up the unity of the text (generators, transits). In spite of this fragmentation, this incoherence, and though there is no unity either on the level of the anecdote, a unity is established through a subtle network of metonymy and metaphor, which works on the level of the signified as well as on that of the signifier. The text tells only the story of its own literarity; it is the allegory of its own functioning: "fiction develops as the allegory of the writing that erects it" (Ricardou). This nonmonolithic writing assumes the resources of a palimpsest.

Its palimpsestic character has electrified more recent interpretations. By analyzing intertextual relationships in *La Bataille de Pharsale*, Georges Raillard has concretized and refined the topos of a reference to Proust. The relationship between texts—Proust's text cited in Simon's—is anamorphic. They read each other, they are models for reciprocal readings, one for the other; this process is thematized in the anamorphic tool par excellence, the cylinder. In his subtle interpretation of *Géorgiques*, Roger Dragonetti reads generation in the text as an allegory of the generation of the text—both of which are, in certain ways, failed or "*claudicant*" [limping].

These "stories" are not, however, part of the anecdote. It is the work of the signifier that secretes them. As cryptic stories, they resist any effort at deciphering. This unreadable texture, this story of unreadability can be traced, as I have demonstrated, through an allegorization of the body-text relation. Roger Dragonetti has proposed the Immaculate Conception as the allegorization of such a relation in the *Géorgiques*. These allegorizations are not represented; the impossible representation, which provokes desire for the figure, does not cease to figure its own unreadability.

In *Leçon de choses* (1975), of which I have chosen a passage for demonstration, "la leçon de choses" is what the *Petit Robert* refers to as "méthode d'enseignement qui consiste à familiariser les enfants avec les objets usuels, des productions naturelles" [a method of teaching designed to familiarize children with common things, natural phenomena]. A schoolbook of this title is read in *Leçon de choses* by a young soldier with some difficulty (narrational context of this part of the story: the German invasion of Alsace at the beginning of World War II). Our reading of the *Leçon* doubles the difficult learning of this ficticious reader; it is the reading of his reading. A troubled reading, to be sure, troubled by darkness, threatened by unreadability: "Les illustrations," read by the young man in his book, "représentant des montagnes rocheuses, des carrières, des scieurs de long . . . ne sont plus sur les pages que des rectangles noirs." [The illustrations, representing rocky mountains, quarries, sawyers of construction wood . . . are no more than black rectangles on the page.] A reading of figures that is troubled in that it "illustrates" the difficult relation between writings and illustration. The illustrations become animated, they develop into "real" stories. By a strange inversion, or irony, the reality that should be represented through the illustration is, on the contrary, engendered by illustration. *Leçon de choses* is thus a treatise *on* figures as well as a reading *of* figures; it is grounded in figures of reading. Its title reflects and rereads contemporary treatises like Foucault's *Les Mots et les choses* (1966) and Althusser's "Leçon de lecture" in *Lire le capital* (1968).

But the title *Leçon de choses* evokes yet another reading, *lectio*, according to the first entry of the *Petit Robert* under the heading "leçon": "lecture des textes de l'Ecriture ou des Pères de l'Eglise, qu'on lit ou qu'on chante aux offices nocturnes" [reading of Scripture or of the church fathers read or sung during the evening masses]. In addition to the manifold meaning of the term "leçon", we learn about the rhetorical "coloring," the nocturnal "milieu," of Simon's text. We find traces of a *lectio* in this older sense of the word in the calendar, quoted in the text, which contains a litany of saints and, therefore, has to be read as a *contrafactura* (analogous to the musical transposition of a religious theme into a worldly lyric) that evokes, in reverse, profane texts, notably Proust's *Recherche*: "Sainte Gilberte, Odette, Albertine."

The passage here presented gives a good example of the highly complicated structure of the later novels, the segmentation of overlapping stories, or, better, storylike fragments of narration, which prove all "reality" in these texts to be side effects of an intricate network of signifiers. The "principle of structure" involved can be identified as two types, or, rather, models, of what has come to be called in recent years "allegories of reading." In the course of *Leçon de choses*, problematic readability is varied along the *leitmotif* of black and white. It crystallizes in the two conflicting allegories of Medusa's hair and the Immaculate Conception of the Virgin Mary. Reverberations of both motifs are to be found throughout the book. There is a mason by the name of Jesus living in the "Camino del la Virgen," and the spiritual vehicle of conception familiar from medieval iconography is travestied in a gull with a "plumage immaculé". In the scene at hand, a young woman, without any known relation to the mason, is called Estelle, that is the star symbolizing Mary's immaculate condition. The same woman is associated with the cyclamen, flower of Mary, as we read in another of Simon's works, where he combines this flower with the appropriate line from the *Ave Maria*: "cyclamen ou plutôt lilas fané *fructus ventris tui*" (*La chevelure de Bérénice*). The signifier "maculé," however, does not itself appear in the scene that finally allows for the deciphering of the allegory. But it occurs earlier in the book and there it stands for the qualifications of the newspaper that covers the news on "papier maculé." The later scene fulfills the earlier appearance of the word in that it deals with a "maculé," instead of the Immaculate Conception.

The intercourse reported occurs between the woman Estelle and a man, whom she meets at night in the fields near her house. She is afraid of becoming pregnant and insists that he should withdraw before ejaculation. But he "ne fait pas attention," and she tries to wipe her cunt with her panties. Almost desperate, she throws her arms around his neck, while he now tells her to be careful not to stain his clothes. Outraged, she stammers "espèce de espèce de espèce de." Her words are marked by mutilation and omission: the moment before, she hadn't finished the word "tacher" properly; now she doesn't finish "espèce de con." Her stumbling, however, reveals exactly what she means: The man "a taché son con." But his sperm, "black" as ink, leaves no traces in her "dark flesh."

Ironically, the chapter is entitled "La charge de Reichshoffen," apparently to take advantage of the double entendre of the sexual and the military ("to shoot one's load"). But there is a pun involved that is more complicated and more substantial. The Alsatian spelling "Reichshoffen" for Reichshofen permits the reading of the name of this place not far from the German border as "hope for the Reich," i.e., the kingdom of heaven as in the German *Pater noster* ("Dein Reich komme"), as well as the Third Reich that seeks the territory of an older Reich in this region. The theological definition of the Immaculate Conception, which has, as a matter of fact, nothing to do with the more popular opinions on the Annunciation, frees the Virgin of the collective hope for a "kingdom to come," while ejaculation, metaphorized in terms of exploding warheads, points to an altogether different ending of history.

The thematic contrafactura of the Immaculate Conception has a hermeneutical "point." The Immaculate Conception is the very model of cognitive efficacy; the word becomes flesh that in its turn illuminates the darkness of the world and thereby makes it intelligible. In Simon's text, though, the model of transparence is perverted into the true allegory of a complete failure, the failure to read. Nothing remains but "les langues pendantes de papier décollé" who "laissent apparaître le plâtre humide," first sentence of the first as well as the last chapter of the "lesson" that is to be taken, learned and read, from Simon. Against the grain of the first allegory we perceive another, second allegory of reading, Medusa. Her principal attribute, the hair "mouillé," "strié," runs through the whole of Simon's text, surfacing here and there, revealing finally the "character" of all writing "comme celle d'une chevelure reptilienne et visqueuse." This allegory also goes back to medieval sources and surfaces in this text "via" Dante, "1, rue Dante, 1" (thus the fictive editor's address of the "Leçon de choses" quoted within the text of *Leçon de choses*). Blinding through Eros (les langues pendantes, pendantes de désir), the Medusa petrifies and brings death. Within the spiritual death that is the inability to read and the incapacity to understand, everything becomes dark. Last sentence: "Tout est complètement noir."

BIBLIOGRAPHY

I. Selected Works

Le Tricheur. Paris: Sagittaire, 1945.
La Corde raide. Paris: Sagittaire, 1947.
Gulliver. Paris: Calmann-Lévy, 1952.
Le Sacre du printemps. Paris: Calmann-Lévy, 1954.
Le Vent. Paris: Minuit, 1957.
L'Herbe. Paris: Minuit, 1958.
La Route des Flandres. Paris: Minuit, 1960. With an essay by J. Ricardou, Paris: UGE, 1963; with an essay by L. Dällenbach. Paris: Minuit, 1982.
Le Palace. Paris: Minuit, 1962.
Histoire. Paris: Minuit, 1967.
La Bataille de Pharsale. Paris: Minuit, 1969.
Orion aveugle. Paris: Skira, 1970; illustrations of photographs, drawings, and paintings by Rauschenberg, Poussin, Dubuffet, Picasso and others.
Les Corps conducteurs. Paris: Minuit, 1971.
Triptyque. Paris: Minuit, 1973.
Leçon de choses. Paris: Minuit, 1975.
Les Géorgiques. Paris: Minuit, 1981.

II. Selected Criticism

Dällenbach, Lucien, Roger Dragonetti, Georges Raillard, Jean Starobinski. *Sur Claude Simon.* Paris: Minuit, 1987.
Duncan, Alastair B., ed. *Claude Simon—New Directions.* Edinburgh: Scottish Academic Press, 1985. (Bibliography 156–64).
Ricardou, Jean, ed. *Claude Simon: Colloque de Cerisy.* Paris: UGE, 1975 (Bibliography 432–43).
Sarkonak, Ralph. *Claude Simon, Les Carrefours du texte.* Trinity College, Toronto: Paratexte, 1986.

III. Special Issues

"Claude Simon," *Entretiens* 31 (1972).
"Claude Simon," *Sub-stance* 8 (1974).

"Claude Simon," *Etudes littéraires* 1 (1976).

"La Terre et la guerre dans l'oeuvre de Claude Simon," *Critique* 38, no. 414 (1981) (Bibliography 1244–52).

"Claude Simon," *The Review of Contemporary Fiction* (1985).

CLAUDE SIMON

Leçon de choses*

LA CHARGE DE REICHSHOFFEN

Le hibou hulule de nouveau. Le pourvoyeur répète encore dans un souffle là vous avez entendu vous avez entendu? Les yeux du tireur scrutent la nuit. Les silhouettes confuses du groupe formé par les trois soldats aux visages tendus vers la fenêtre se dessinent vaguement dans l'ombre de la pièce. La masse noire du bois semble flotter comme une île au-dessus des écharpes de brume. Les saccades précipitées qui secouent le bassin de l'homme prennent fin sur une dernière poussée après laquelle il se tient étroitement collé aux fesses de la jeune femme, cramponné à ses hanches, tandis qu'à l'intérieur de la chair obscure le long membre raidi se tend encore, lâchant de longues giclées de sperme noir. Au bout d'un moment les muscles de l'homme se relâchent et il caresse doucement les hanches nues cependant que le dos et les épaules de la femme continuent à être secoués de tressaillements nerveux. Peu à peu, tandis que le soir tombe, la mer se teinte d'une couleur plombée et verdâtre. En avant de la falaise, les roches qu'elle recouvre et découvre tour à tour apparaissent et disparaissent, luisantes et d'un violet sombre, entourées d'une bave d'écume que chaque nouvelle vague étire paresseusement derrière elle comme une traîne. Les yeux accoutumés à l'obscurité distinguent les larges plaques blanches et noires aux contours sinueux et imbriqués qui épousent les reliefs du corps puissant au ventre renflé, aux os saillants sous le cuir épais. L'œil gauche de la vache est noyé dans une tache obscure à peu près de la grandeur d'une assiette. La conjonctive rose et les longs cils pâles de l'œil droit se confondent avec le pelage clair qui l'entoure. La rumeur violente du sang dans les oreilles s'apaise par degrés. Le menton levé, la pomme d'Adam saillante sous la peau grise et mal rasée, le vieil ouvrier boutonne soigneusement le col de sa chemise. Le petit bouton nacré aux

*Leçon de choses (Paris: Minuit, 1976), 163–73. This passage is reprinted with the kind permission of Editions de Minuit.

reflets bleu-vert et mauves échappe plusieurs fois à ses doigts maladroits. Tâtonnant à sa recherche et le menton toujours levé, il bouge légèrement celui-ci, le pointant à droite et à gauche en même temps que, les paupières à demi baissées, son regard dirigé vers le sol, il dit quelque chose au jeune maçon. Déjà prêt, celui-ci repose son sac, va chercher un balai presque dépourvu de poils appuyé contre l'un des murs et dégage le centre de la pièce de quelques gravats qu'il pousse sous l'un des échafaudages. Des nuages de poussière s'élèvent à chacun de ses mouvements. Le vieil ouvrier a fini de boutonner son col et dit ça va bien comme ça pourvu qu'il y ait un passage. L'une des pointes du col est restée relevée. Maintenu par le seul bouton du bas qui tiraille le tissu à hauteur de la taille, le revers lustré du veston bâille en formant une poche. A l'emplacement du bouton manquant une petite mèche de fils noirs et torsadés sort du tissu. Le pourvoyeur est maintenant étendu à plat ventre à même le carrelage parmi les gravats. Ses épaules sont agitées de soubresauts et de tremblements convulsifs. La tête cachée dans ses bras croisés il sanglote nerveusement. Les ronflements de l'ivrogne qui s'est recouché sur le lit privé maintenant de son matelas s'élèvent régulièrement. Le servant du fusil-mitrailleur est allé s'asseoir contre le mur et tire à de lents intervalles sur un nouveau cigare. De temps à autre, pour atténuer le feu qui brûle sa langue et son palais, il tâtonne de le main gauche dans le noir à la recherche du bocal de fruits qu'il a transporté près de lui et le porte à ses lèvres. Il lampe une gorgée de sirop qu'il garde un moment dans sa bouche avant de l'avaler. Parfois il recrache un menu fragment de plâtre resté accroché au bord poisseux du bocal ou en suspension dans le sirop. Le chargeur est assis de biais sur la table et regarde par la fenêtre le paysage nocturne et simplifié où se distinguent seulement des masses plus ou moins sombres sous le ciel piqué de rares étoiles. Une fois encore la chouette hulule dans l'épaisseur du bois. Il dit allons voyons en caressant les cheveux dénoués et en tapotant affectueusement l'épaule de la jeune femme. Elle est adossée à la barrière. Elle pleure. Elle dit au milieu de ses sanglots vous m'aviez promis. Il dit voyons il n'y aura r. Elle se baisse et tâtonne dans l'herbe noire à la recherche de sa culotte déchirée. Elle se redresse. Elle répète vous m'aviez promis vous m'aviez promis. Sans cesser de parler et de renifler, elle soulève sa jupe et se baisse en écartant les jambes. Les pieds rapprochés, les genoux ouverts, les jambes pâles dessinent dans la nuit un losange approximatif. Elle essuie son con avec un pan du tissu déchiré. Elle l'enfonce dans sa vulve. Elle sent ses doigts gluants de sperme. Elle dit oh mon dieu vous m'aviez promis. Elle fouille aussi profond qu'elle peut dans son vagin en fléchissant encore plus les genoux pour écarter les cuisses. Elle a l'air d'une grenouille. Après avoir rangé le balai, le jeune ouvrier époussette de quelques tapes son pantalon propre d'où s'échappe un léger nuage de poussière et reprend son sac de sportif, en tissu écossais, qu'il rejette par-dessus son épaule, retenant d'une main, deux doigts en crochet, le cordon qui en serre l'ouverture. Un moment encore les deux ouvriers restent là, debout et prêts à partir, s'attardant à discuter sans doute du travail du lendemain car le plus âgé agite à plusieurs reprises son doigt tendu en direction de l'un ou l'autre des échafaudages et de la saignée horizontale pratiquée dans le mur. Tout en discutant, il roule encore une cigarette. Le goulot de la bouteille de vin enveloppée de papier-journal soulève l'un des côtés du rabat de la musette repoussée sur ses reins. Sur la feuille déchirée et grise on peut lire en caractères gras des fragments de mots composant un titre: . . . IERS (vacanciers?) . . . IVRE (suivre?) ÉCRAS . . . (écrasés?) . . . EUX (affreux?) AC . . . (accident?) . . . EMENT (effondrement?) EN . . . (ensevelis?) . . . UT . . . (chute?) ROCH . . . (rochers?) COR . . . (corniche?). Dans le verger le merle chante de nouveau. La tête inclinée sur le côté, le vieux maçon bat à plusieurs reprises la pierre de son briquet, qui illumine chaque fois sa figure d'une brève lueur. A la fin la flamme fait sortir de l'ombre les reliefs du visage raviné et des mains aux larges doigts. Il remet le briquet dans sa poche et l'un suivant l'autre les deux hommes se dirigent vers la porte. On achève de charger sur le plateau d'un camion les caissettes pleines de soles, de seiches, de maquereaux rayés, de daurades, et les curieux se dispersent. Les pêcheurs ont mis à sécher sur un filin tendu obliquement à partir de la poupe leurs cirés jaunes ou brique. La brise de terre qui se lève balance faiblement les pantalons et les suroîts raides comme des planches, aux jambes et aux bras écartés. Il ne reste bientôt plus sur la plage déserte que les quatre ou cinq grosses barques noires, quelques canots et un groupe de jeunes filles assises en rond comme pour quelque cérémonial secret et d'où fusent parfois de frais éclats de rire. Non loin d'elles deux gamins ramassent des galets plats qu'ils lancent d'un geste vif au ras de l'eau sur laquelle ils ricochent plusieurs fois en soulevant des aigrettes étincelantes de plus en plus rapprochées avant de disparaître. La haute falaise, la plage, s'enténèbrent peu à peu. Maintenant on ne distingue plus que la tache claire formée par le groupe de jeunes filles et les mouettes posées sur l'eau, à quelques mètres du rivage, comme des canards, s'élevant et descendant aux passages paresseux des vagues. Elle répète oh mon dieu oh mon dieu et Charles s'il arrive quelque chose. Il bredouille une phrase confuse comme pas de risques mais vous n'avez pas voulu je. Elle dit rageusement Non je n'ai pas voulu! pour qui me pre. Les sanglots l'étouffent. Il lui tapote gauchement l'épaule, porte à sa bouche le mince cigare qu'il tient entre deux doigts, se ravise et l'éloigne de ses lèvres sans l'allumer. Il lui tapote de nouveau l'épaule en répétant allons voyons allons. Elle continue à s'essuyer, d'un geste maintenant machinal. Elle dit vous m'aviez promis vous m'aviez promis que vous feriez attention. Il dit allons. Elle laisse retomber sa jupe. Elle tient le morceau de tissu trempé et gluant roulé en boule dans sa main. Elle a un geste comme pour le jeter puis se ravise. Elle dit s'il arrive quelque chose s'il arrive quelque chose je suis sûre que ça arrivera je n'ai pas vous avez tout lâché vous. Il dit allons voyons. Les petites grenouilles coassent toujours, assourdissantes. On n'entend que les faibles bruits de sanglots qui s'échappent de la gorge du pourvoyeur, comme des cris de souris ou un rat qui couine. Le tireur continue à aspirer de lentes bouffées de son cigare dont chaque fois la faible lueur croissant et décroissant extrait de l'ombre son visage qui se fond de nouveau dans l'obscurité. Brusquement, sans qu'aucun bruit ni aucun mouvement visible l'ait annoncé, le chuintement rapide d'une fusée tirée de derrière ou de l'intérieur du petit bois déchire le silence. Le bruit soyeux de l'air froissé s'intensifie et décroît rapidement tandis que le sillage d'étincelles s'élève en ondulant dans le ciel noir. Arrivée très haut, en bout de course, la tête de la fusée éclate, éparpillant autour d'elle une pluie de brandons. Le tireur et le chargeur ont sursauté et sont maintenant debout près de l'arme devant la fenêtre. Troublé quelques instants, le calme opaque de la nuit s'installe de nouveau. Au bout d'un moment les grenouilles qui s'étaient arrêtées de chanter relancent l'une après l'autre leur cri, d'abord timidement, puis s'enhardissant, puis, comme avant, toutes ensemble. Le pourvoyeur couché sur le carrelage s'est vivement redressé. Appuyé sur un coude il regarde par la fenêtre le ciel de soie grise où les dernières étincelles dispersées en gerbe retombent et s'éteignent l'une après l'autre. Sa voix geignarde s'élève encore une fois et dit les salauds tu parles s'ils ne savent pas qu'on est là attendez voir demain matin qu'est-ce que j'avais dit? Personne ne répond. Parvenu presque à la porte, le jeune maçon avise l'image tombée sur le sol et se baisse pour la ramasser. Il l'époussette et la tourne vers la lumière. Sur la marge de papier vert olive et pelucheux où elle est collée on peut lire en lettres autrefois dorées: L'ILLUSTRATION. Il tient l'image à bout de bras, clignant des yeux, comme un myope, en penchant légèrement la tête sur le côté. Il lit la légende en caractères bâtons noirs sous les rochers battus par les vagues: Les Tas de Pois (Finistère). Il dit mince ça doit être chouette. Il contemple encore l'image quelques instants d'un air pensif. Sur le seuil le vieil ouvrier se retourne et dit alors tu viens? Le jeune maçon desserre ses doigts et, glissant en oblique, l'image retombe parmi les gravats. Il rejoint son compagnon et la pièce reste vide. Les deux gamins qui faisaient des ricochets sont partis. Le cercle clair des jeunes filles poursuivant leurs rites secrets ponctués de brusques éclats de rires est à peu près indistinct. Soudain, au fond de l'horizon où le ciel ne se sépare plus maintenant de la mer, scintille sur la gauche la brève lueur d'un phare qui disparaît aussitôt, reparaît, s'éteint pendant quelques secondes, reparaît deux fois coup sur coup, démasquée et occultée tour à tour selon un rythme codé avec une régularité de métronome comme si l'œil—pas l'oreille: l'œil—pouvait percevoir quelque part à travers le bruit paisible et régulier du ressac l'implacable grignotement des roues dentées, des engrenages, de l'échappement fractionnant le temps en menus intervalles comptabilisés, comme si quelque signal venu d'étoiles, d'astres lointains gravitant à des millions d'années-lumière les avait tout à coup mis en mouvement pour marquer l'instant, la seconde précise de la séparation du jour et de la nuit, déclenchant en même temps l'apparition soudaine d'un fugitif chemin de reflets sur l'étendue ténébreuse qui ne se distingue plus de la plage que par une incessante mouvance, confusément perçue, de noires et statiques ondulations, comme celles d'une chevelure liquide reptilienne et visqueuse. Elle jette soudain ses bras autour des épaules de l'homme et se serre convulsivement contre lui. Il dit voyons allons et lui caresse les cheveux. Elle dit mon chéri mon chéri vous m'aimez dites-moi que vous m'aimez s'il arrive quelque chose vous ne m'. Il dit mais voyons je. Elle dit jurez-le-moi vous ne me. Il dit mais voyons bien sûr Attention ma chérie vous allez me tacher. Elle dit vous t . . . Il se dégage doucement du bras qui enserre ses épaules et dont la main tient la boule de tissu gluant. Il dit mais bien sûr ma chérie bien sûr. Elle regarde sa main serrée sur l'étoffe froissée et mouillée. Elle répète vous tach. Il dit voyons ma chérie. Elle crie vous tacher espèce de. Il dit voyons ne criez pas on pourrait vous ent. Elle crie espèce de espèce de espèce de. Elle tourne brusquement le dos et part en courant. Il crie Voyons. Il crie Estelle. Il crie Estelle écoutez-moi! Estelle, Élodie, Émilie, Élisabeth, Hélène, Sylvie, Gilberte, Édith, Odette. Il fait quelques pas dans la direction où elle s'est enfuie. La tache de la robe sombre s'éloigne ou plutôt semble rester sur place, agitée de faibles secousses, en diminuant de grandeur. Il s'arrête et reste là, le mince cigare entre deux de ses doigts. Il dit à mi-voix quelque chose d'indistinct. La tache de la robe s'est fondue dans la masse noire du bois. Il revient s'accoter à la barrière. Il tire de sa poche une boîte d'allumettes et en frotte une. Il prend soudain conscience de la présence de la vache presque au-dessus de lui, toujours immobile, gigantesque. A la lueur de la flamme il voit ses doigts, le pouce, l'index et le majeur réunis sur l'allumette. Il tire deux ou trois bouffées du cigare. Il se tient ainsi quelques instants, laissant se consumer l'allumette maintenant éloignée de l'extrémité du cigare. Il peut voir le museau humide et baveux de la vache. Il peut voir son œil fardé de noir, l'autre bordé de rose pâle et sa frange de cils soyeux et décolorés comme ceux d'un albinos. L'allumette lui brûle les doigts. Il la laisse tomber et elle s'éteint dans l'herbe. Tout est complètement noir.

The World About Us*

The owl hoots again. The ammunition-server repeats again in a single breath there did you hear did you hear? The gunner's eyes search the night. The blurred shapes of the group consisting of the three soldiers with their faces turned towards the window is dimly outlined in the darkness of the room. The dark mass of the woods seems to float like an island above the wraiths of mist. The abrupt jolting which shakes the man's pelvis culminates in a final thrust after which he holds himself clamped hard to the young woman's buttocks, gripping her hips, while within her dark flesh the long, stiff penis stiffens still further, releasing long spurts of black sperm. After a while the man's muscles relax and he gently strokes the naked hips while the woman's back and shoulders continue to shake and quiver. Gradually, as evening draws on, the sea is tinged with a leaden, greenish color. In front of the cliffs, the rocks which the sea successively covers and uncovers appear and disappear, gleaming and darkly violet, surrounded by foaming froth which each new wave draws lazily out behind it like a train. Eyes accustomed to the darkness make out the broad, black and white patches with sinuous, overlapping contours which take the shape of the powerful body with its swelling belly, its bones jutting under the thick hide. The cow's left eye is lost in a dark patch about the size of a plate. The pink conjunctiva and the long, pale lashes of the right eye merge into the light-colored coat surrounding it. The violent din of the blood in the ears gradually calms down. With his chin lifted up, his Adam's apple jutting under the gray, unshaven skin, the old workman carefully buttons his shirt collar. The little pearly button with its blue-green and mauve reflections several times evades his clumsy fingers. Fumbling, he moves his chin, still lifted, a little to the right and to the left, while with his eyelids half-lowered, his gaze directed downwards, he says something to the young builder. Ready to go, the latter puts down his bag, fetches a practically bristleless broom leaning against one of the walls and clears the center of the room, sweeping the rubbish under one of the scaffoldings. Clouds of dust rise up at each of his movements. The old workman has finished buttoning up his collar and says that's fine so long as there's a pathway. One corner of his collar is still sticking up. The jacket's shiny lapels, secured only by the lower button which tugs on the cloth at the level of the waist, gape like a pouch.

The World About Us (Princeton, N.J.: Ontario Review Press, 1983), 109–16. Translated by Daniel Weissbort. This passage is reprinted with the kind permission of Ontario Review Press.

A twisted fringe of black threads sticks out from the cloth in the place of the missing button. The ammunition-server is now stretched out flat on his stomach on the tiled floor amid the rubble. His shoulders quiver, shuddering, convulsively. With his head buried in his crossed arms, he sobs tremulously. An even snoring comes from the drunken man who is once again recumbent on the bed now stripped of its mattress. The Bren gunner has sat down with his back to the wall and is puffing at a new cigar with long pauses in between. From time to time, to mitigate the burning sensation on his tongue and palate, he gropes left-handed in the darkness for the fruit jar which he then raises to his lips. He takes in a mouthful of juice which he holds in his mouth for a while before gulping it down. Occasionally he spits out a morsel of plaster which has remained clinging to the sticky edge of the bowl or floating in the juice. The loader is seated sideways on the table and is gazing out of the window at a nocturnal landscape of simple, more or less dark shapes under a sky sparsely studded with stars. Once again the owl hoots in the depth of the woods. He says don't worry stroking the young woman's loose hair and patting her shoulder affectionately. She is leaning back against the gate. She is weeping. In the midst of her sobbing she says you promised me. He says don't worry nothing'll. She bends down and gropes about in the dark grass for her torn panties. She stands up straight again. She repeats you promised me you promised me. Still talking and sniffing, she lifts her skirt and bends, spreading her legs. With her feet together, her knees parted, the pale legs make a rough diamond-shape in the night. She wipes her cunt with a flap of the torn material. She pushes it up into her vulva. She feels her fingers sticky with sperm. She says oh dear you promised me. She burrows as deeply as she can in her vagina, flexing her knees even more to separate her thighs. She looks like a frog. After he has put the broom away, the young workman brushes down his clean trousers, a light cloud of dust rising from them, and picks up his tartan sports bag again, throwing it over his shoulder while keeping the cord which closes it hooked round two fingers of one hand. For a little while longer the two workmen remain standing there, ready to go, no doubt discussing tomorrow's work, since the older one wags his finger several times at one or another of the scaffoldings and the horizontal groove that has been made in the wall. As he talks, he rolls another cigarette. The neck of the wine bottle wrapped in newspaper lifts up one side of the flap of his haversack which he has pushed back onto his loins. On the torn, gray sheet, fragments of words in bold letters making up a headline can be read: . . . ERS (holidaymakers?) . . . OL . . . (follow?) CRU . . . (crushed?) WO . . . (worn?) AC . . . (accident?) SUB . . . (subsidence?) EN . . . (engulfed?) . . . AND . . . (landslide?) . . . VER . . . (overhang?). The blackbird is again singing in the orchard. His head to one side, the old builder flicks his lighter, fleetingly illuminating his face each time. Finally the flame picks out the features of his lined face and his hands with their broad fingers. He puts the lighter back into his pocket and one following the other the two men walk towards the door. The boxes full of sole, cuttlefish, striped mackerel, sea bream are finally all loaded onto the flat truck and the onlookers disperse. The fishermen have laid out their yellow or brick-red oilskins to dry on a rope stretched obliquely from the stern. The land breeze which has sprung up makes the trousers and souwesters sway slightly, stiff as planks, with spread arms and legs. Soon nothing remains on the deserted beach except the four or five large, black boats, a few dinghies and a group of girls, from whom come occasional bursts of clear laughter, seated in a circle as though for some secret rite. Not far from them two children are picking up flat pebbles and skimming them briskly at the water which they glance off several times raising plumes of spray closer and closer together before vanishing. The tall cliff, the beach, are gradually plunged in darkness. Now all that can be discerned is the bright patch formed by the group of girls and the gulls floating on the water, several yards from the shore, like ducks, rising and falling with the lazy passage of the waves. She repeats oh dear oh dear and Charles what if something happens. He mumbles something indistinct like there's no danger but you didn't want me to. She says furiously No I didn't! What do you ta. She is overcome by sobbing. He pats her shoulder awkwardly, lifts the thin cigar he is holding between two fingers to his mouth, thinks better of it and removes it from his lips without lighting it. Again he pats her shoulder repeating don't worry don't worry. She continues to wipe herself mechanically. She says you promised me you promised you'd be careful. He says don't worry. She lets her skirt fall back into place. She holds the sodden, sticky piece of material rolled up in a ball in her hand. She makes as though to throw it away and then changes her mind. She says what if something happens what if something happens I'm sure something is going to happen I didn't you let it all go. He says don't worry. The little frogs are still croaking, deafeningly. All that can be heard are faint, sobbing sounds coming from the ammunition-loader's throat, like the squeaking of mice or a rat squealing. The gunner continues to puff slowly on his cigar, its faint glow brightening and fading each time, picking his face out of the darkness into which it then melts again. Suddenly, without any audible or visible warning, the swift sizzle of a flare fired from beyond or within the little woods shatters the silence. The silky sound of the ruffled air swells and decreases rapidly while the wake of sparks undulates in the black sky. When it is very high, at the apex of its flight, the rocket head explodes, showering firebrands about it. The gunner and loader, shocked into action, are now standing near the weapon in front of the window. Disturbed for a few moments, the deep calm of the night is again restored. After a while the frogs which had stopped croaking start up again one after another, cautiously at first, then growing bolder, then, as before, all together. The ammunition-server lying on the tiles has lifted himself up abruptly. Leaning on an elbow he gazes through the window at the gray silk of the sky where the last scattered sparks are fanning out and dying one after the other. His whining voice is heard once again saying the bastards if you think they don't know we're here you wait till tomorrow morning what did I tell you? No one answers. When he has almost reached the door, the young builder notices the picture which has fallen onto the floor and bends to pick it up. He dusts it off and turns it towards the light. On the margin of fluffy, olive-green paper to which it is stuck can be read in what used to be gilt lettering: ILLUSTRATION. He holds the picture at arms' length, screwing up his eyes myopically, leaning his head slightly to one side. He reads the caption in block letters under the rocks pounded by the waves: *Les Tas de Pois* (Finisterre). He says gosh that must be great. He gazes thoughtfully at the picture for a few more moments. The old workman turns round on the threshold and says well are you coming? The young builder releases the picture which slides sideways back into the rubbish. He rejoins his mate and the room is now empty. The two children who were skipping stones have left. The bright ring of girls pursuing their secret rite punctuated by sudden bursts of laughter is blurry now. Suddenly, on the distant horizon where sky and sea are no longer separate, to the left, there is the brief flash of a light-house light, vanishing and then reappearing, going out for a few seconds, then reappearing twice in rapid succession, covered then uncovered in turns according to some secret rhythm with metronomic regularity as though the eye—not the ear: the eye—through the calm, even sound of the surf could somewhere catch the remorseless grinding of cogwheels, of gears, an escapement dividing time up into tiny accountable segments, as though some signal emanating from the stars, from distant luminaries revolving millions of light years away had suddenly set them in motion to mark that particular moment, the precise second when day separates itself from night, casting at the same time a sudden, ephemeral pathway of reflections across the dark expanse, distinguishable from the beach only by its endless, dimly perceivable mobility of blacks and static undulations, like the fluid, reptilian viscosity of hair. Suddenly she throws her arms around the man's shoulders and presses convulsively against him. He says don't worry and strokes her hair. She says darling darling tell me you love me tell me you love me if something happens you wo. He says of course I. She says swear to me you won't. He says of course not Careful darling you'll dirty my. She says I'll d . . . He cautiously disengages himself from the arm encircling his shoulders and the hand holding the ball of sticky material. He says of course darling of course. She looks at her hand grasping the crumpled, damp material. She repeats I'll dir. He says oh darling. She cries I'll dirty you you. He says don't shout dear someone might hea. She cries you you you. She turns abruptly and departs at a run.

He shouts Oh come on. He shouts Estelle. He shouts Estelle listen to me! Estelle, Élodie, Emily, Elizabeth, Helen, Sylvia, Gilberte, Edith, Odette. He takes a few steps in the direction she has fled. The patch made by her dark dress moves further away or rather seems to remain in one place, jerking a little as it diminishes in size. He stops and stands there, holding the thin cigar between two fingers. He says something indistinct under his breath. The patch has melted now into the dark mass of the woods. He goes back to the gate and props himself up against it. He takes a box of matches from his pocket and strikes one. He suddenly becomes aware of the cow which is standing almost above him, still motionless, immense. In the light of the flame he can see his fingers, the thumb, index and second fingers joined around the match. He puffs two or three times on the cigar. He stands like this for a few moments, letting the match now removed from the end of the cigar burn out. He can see the cow's moist, slobbering muzzle. He can see its eye with the black border, the other one encircled in pale pink and the silky fringe of its eyelashes, colorless as an albino's. The match burns his fingers. He drops it and it goes out in the grass. All is completely black.

CATHERINE CUSSET

Marguerite Duras

Marguerite Duras was born April 4, 1914 near Saigon, in Indochina. After the death of her father Henri Donnadieu, a professor of mathematics, Marguerite Donnadieu spent her childhood in Indochina with her mother and her brothers, in places that later provided the settings for several of her novels. In 1924 an event that strongly marked Marguerite Duras's adolescence took place: with ten years' worth of savings, her mother bought a plot of land in Cambodia that turned out to be unfarmable, resulting in the family's financial ruin.

Marguerite Duras left Cambodia for France at the age of seventeen; from 1935 to 1941, she worked as a secretary for the Colonial Ministry. She began to publish around 1941, fulfilling a desire to write that she had asserted since childhood against the wishes of her mother, who had wanted her to pursue a scientific career. In 1939 Duras married Robert Antelme, whose return from the concentration camps she recounted in a book published in 1985 under the title *La Douleur*. Immediately following the war she divorced Robert Antelme and joined the Communist party. Duras published *Les Impudents* in 1941 and *La Vie tranquille* in 1944; in 1950 *Un barrage contre le Pacifique*, published by Gallimard, made her famous.

And so began Marguerite Duras's intense career as novelist, playwright, screen writer, and film director. Her books and films, considered difficult, are addressed to a restricted intellectual public. Marguerite Duras does not try to reach a large audience, but rather the "ten thousand spectators who make the films and who, against all odds, create a place for them in cinema or reject them" (*Les Cahiers du cinéma* 313 [June 1980]). But if Duras's cinema has met with "quantitative failure" as she calls it, her written works have had a different fate: her play *L'Amante anglaise* won the Prix Ibsen in 1970; in 1985 *L'Amant* was awarded the Prix Goncourt, making Duras a best-selling author.

A large number of autobiographical writings published by or about Marguerite Duras in the last ten years illustrate her popularity. In *Les Lieux de Marguerite Duras*, an interview with Michelle Porte, Duras speaks of the three places where she lives, and emphasizes the importance of the habitats of women, who are themselves "the dwelling place of the child." *M.D.* is a narrative written in 1985 by the life companion of Marguerite Duras, Yann Andréa, in which he tells of the struggle against death and madness that the writer had to endure during a treatment for alcoholism in the American Hospital in Paris. In *La Vie matérielle*, a text that appeared in 1987, Duras speaks to us in her own way about a few components of her daily material life, and explains how her life has been organized around three main poles: love, alcohol, and writing.

The literary career of Marguerite Duras unfolded with *Un barrage contre le Pacifique*, which is in a sense the matrix of her other books. The destruction by the waters of the Pacific of the dam built by Duras's mother to protect her land is a real event in the life of Marguerite Duras, but is also the metaphor of the only event that takes place in her novels: the passionate event. "My nightmares, my dreams of horror are always related to the tide, to invasions by water," says Duras during her interview with Michelle Porte. The surging waters of the Pacific break down the dam, that is, the attempt to channel life, to make it normal and possible through profit and thrift. But the strength of the Pacific is incommensurable with human defenses: confronted with the cruelty of the Pacific, the mother slowly sinks into madness. What force is this that surges so violently, like the Pacific, in the writings of Duras?

One is tempted to respond: Love. Love seems to be the incandescent center of Duras's fiction. All of her books, *Le Marin de Gibraltar, Le Ravissement de Lol V. Stein, Hiroshima mon amour, L'Amant*, to name just a few, are stories of love encounters. Marguerite Duras wrote in 1987, in *La Vie matérielle*: "A book is the story of two people who love. That's it: who love without being forewarned."

But the element that surges in the novels of Duras is not love, even if every text is the story of a love encounter that opens a dialogue between a man and a woman. The structure of her writing is complex: the discovery of love that occurs between a man and a woman takes place in the eyes of memory of another who observes it and tells of it; this "other" is always a woman. The simple dialogical relation is transformed into a complex triangular relation: the event that is as powerful as the Pacific is not love, but love as it is lived through the eyes, the silence of a woman. Marguerite Duras's writing is a woman's writing, in this sense: "For thousands of years, silence has been synonymous with women. Therefore, literature *is* women. It's women whether it speaks of women or is created by women" (*La Vie matérielle*). Women, in Marguerite Duras's work, are witnesses of a love that happens to others, or even to themselves as others: witnesses, martyrs in the etymological sense, women are subjected to the passion of seeing, a passion in which they lose their identity. The woman's gaze is an absence of self in which her own image is not reflected, but the love of two other people. "All the women in my books, regardless of their age, spring from the character of Lol V. Stein, that is, from a certain self-effacement." The "V" signifies the tearing apart of the subject, the loss of her identity, as she stands before the window where she loses herself in the contemplation of the couple: ". . . the window, this mirror that reflected nothing and before which she could only feel with delight the eviction of her being that she so desired" (*Le Ravissement de Lol V. Stein*).

Marguerite Duras places silence, literature, and women together as components of the same equation. The writing of Marguerite Duras is a writing of silence: things are not said explicitly but suggested in short sentences where abstract nouns replace adjectives, producing a theatrical effect which dramatizes her writing. This sober and silent writing is the event (ex-venire) of a woman: a woman leaves the social, masculine world where she is condemned to silence and enters into "la folie," madness, the fascination with the spectacle of the Other. Nevertheless, men are not absent from the narratives of Duras: on the contrary, they play important roles as narrators, as in *Le Ravissement de Lol. V. Stein*, or at least as partners of a dialogue, as in *Moderato cantabile*. They are themselves fascinated by the mystery of feminine madness and attempt to approach and read it, to make it speak: the masculine voice is necessary to give shape to this silence, to this specifically feminine emptiness. Madness is a feminine illness par excellence, an illness of pain, as Julia Kristeva calls it, or of the absence of pain, which is essentially the same thing. In the mesmerizing contemplation of what happens to another or to oneself as "other," an enormous vacuum is created in which the loss of subjectivity occurs; this loss is at the same time absolute subjectivity, and the beginning of literature.

TRANSLATED BY DEIDRE DAWSON

BIBLIOGRAPHY

I. SELECTED WORKS

Les Impudents. Paris: Plon, 1941.
La Vie tranquille. Paris: Gallimard, 1945.
Un Barrage contre le Pacifique. Paris: Gallimard, 1950.
Le Marin de Gibraltar. Paris: Gallimard, 1952.
Les Petits chevaux de Tarquinia. Paris: Gallimard, 1953.
Des journées entières dans les arbres. Paris: Gallimard, 1954.
Le Square. Paris: Gallimard, 1955.
Moderato cantabile. Paris: Minuit, 1958.
Les Viaducs de Seine et Oise. Paris: Gallimard, 1959.
Dix heures et demie du soir en été. Paris: Gallimard, 1960.
Hiroshima, mon amour. Paris: Gallimard, 1960.
Une aussi longue absence. Paris: Gallimard, 1961.
L'Après-midi de Monsieur Andesmas. Paris: Gallimard, 1962.
Le Ravissement de Lol V. Stein. Paris: Gallimard, 1964.
Théâtre I: Les Eaux et forêts, Le Square, La Musica. Paris: Gallimard, 1965.
Le Vice-consul. Paris: Gallimard, 1965.
L'Amante anglaise. Paris: Gallimard, 1967.
Théâtre II: Suzanna Andler, Des Journées entières dans les arbres, Yes peut-être, Le Shaga, Un Homme est venu me voir. Paris: Gallimard, 1968.
Détruire, dit-elle. Paris: Minuit, 1969.
Abahn, Sabana, David. Paris: Gallimard, 1970.
L'Amour. Paris: Gallimard, 1971.
Nathalie Granger, suivie de La Femme du Gange. Paris: Gallimard, 1973.
Le Camion, suivi de Entretien avec Michelle Porte. Paris: Minuit, 1977.
L'Eden cinéma. Paris: Mercure de France, 1977.
Véra Baxter ou les plages de l'Atlantique. Paris: Albatros, 1980.
L'Homme assis dans le couloir. Paris: Minuit, 1980.
L'Eté 80. Paris: Minuit, 1980.

Les Yeux verts, in *Cahiers du Cinéma* (1980).
Agatha. Paris: Minuit, 1980.
Outside. Paris: Albin Michel, 1980.
L'Homme atlantique. Paris: Minuit, 1982.
Savannah Bay. Paris: Minuit, 1982.
La Maladie de la mort. Paris: Minuit, 1982.
Théâtre III. Paris: Gallimard, 1984.
L'Amant. Paris: Minuit, 1984.
La Douleur. Paris: P.O.L., 1985.
Les Yeux bleus cheveux noirs. Paris: Minuit, 1986.
La Pute de la côte normande. Paris: Minuit, 1987.
La Vie matérielle. Paris: P.O.L., 1987.
Emily L. Paris: Minuit, 1987.

II. Selected Criticism

Etude sur l'oeuvre littéraire, théâtrale et cinématographique de Marguerite Duras. Paris: Editions Albatros, 1976. With articles by Jacques Lacan and Maurice Blanchot.

Alleins, Madeleine. *Marguerite Duras, médium du réel.* Lausanne: L'Age d'homme, 1984.

Borgomano, Madeleine. *Duras: Une Lecture des fantasmes.* Belgium: Cistre, 1985.

Kristeva, Julia. "La Maladie de la douleur: Duras," in *Le Soleil noir de la mélancolie.* Paris: Gallimard, 1987.

Lamy, Suzanne, André Roy. *Marguerite Duras à Montréal.* Montreal: Editions Spirales, 1981.

Marini, Marcelle. *Territoires du féminin avec Marguerite Duras.* Paris: Minuit, 1977.

Murphy, Carole. *Alienation and Absence in the Novels of Marguerite Duras.* French Forum, Lexington: Kentucky, 1982.

Willis, Sharon. *Marguerite Duras: Writing on the Body.* Urbana, Ill.: University of Illinois Press, 1987.

MARGUERITE DURAS

*Un Barrage contre le Pacifique**

Le moment propice à la construction des barrages arriva.

Les hommes avaient charrié les rondins depuis la piste jusqu'à la mer et ils s'étaient mis au travail. La mère descendait avec eux à l'aube et revenait le soir en même temps qu'eux. Suzanne et Joseph avaient beaucoup chassé pendant ce temps-là. Ç'avait été pour eux aussi une période d'espoir. Ils croyaient à ce qu'entreprenait leur mère: dès que la récolte serait terminée, ils pourraient faire un long voyage à la ville et d'ici trois ans quitter définitivement la plaine.

Le soir, parfois, la mère faisait distribuer de la quinine et du tabac aux paysans et à cette occasion elle leur parlait des changements prochains de leur existence. Ils riaient avec elle, à l'avance, de la tête que feraient les agents cadastraux devant les récoltes fabuleuses qu'ils auraient bientôt. Point par point elle leur racontait son histoire et leur parlait longuement de l'organisation du marché des concessions. Pour mieux encore soutenir leur élan, elle leur expliquait aussi comment les expropriations, dont beaucoup avaient été victimes au profit des poivriers chinois, étaient elles aussi explicables par l'ignominie des agents de Kam. Elle leur parlait dans l'enthousiasme, ne pouvant résister à la tentation de leur faire partager sa récente initiation et sa compréhension maintenant parfaite de la technique concessionnaire des agents de Kam. Elle se libérait enfin de tout un passé d'illusions et d'ignorance et c'était comme si elle avait découvert un nouveau langage, une nouvelle culture, elle ne pouvait se rassasier d'en parler.

. . . .

La saison des pluies était arrivée. La mère avait fait de très grands semis près du bungalow. Les mêmes hommes qui avaient construit les

Un Barrage contre le Pacifique (Paris: Gallimard, 1950), 47–48. This passage is reprinted with the kind permission of Gallimard.

barrages étaient venus faire le repiquage du paddy dans le grand quadri-
latère fermé par les branches des barrages.

Deux mois avaient passé. La mère descendait souvent pour voir ver-
dir les jeunes plants. Ça commençait toujours par pousser jusqu'à la
grande marée de juillet.

Puis, en juillet, la mer était montée comme d'habitude à l'assaut de la
plaine. Les barrages n'étaient pas assez puissants. Ils avaient été rongés
par les crabes nains des rizières. En une nuit, ils s'effondrèrent.

The Sea Wall*

The auspicious moment for the building of the sea walls came at last.
First, the men transported the logs from the road to the sea, then they set
to work digging. Ma went down with them at dawn every day and returned with them at night. Suzanne and Joseph had hunted constantly
during the period and they, too, had had hope. They believed in Ma's
undertaking. They were sure that, as soon as the first harvest should have
been made, they would make a long journey to the city and within three
years they would definitely be able to leave the plain.

Sometimes in the evenings Ma distributed quinine and tobacco to
the peasants, and on these occasions she spoke to them of the imminent
changes in their existence. They laughed with her, in advance, at the
faces the cadastral agents would pull when they would see the fabulous
harvests soon to be made on the salvaged land. Point by point she recounted her story to them, at long length she described the organization
of the trading activities that would be arranged for the concessions of the
plain. The better to maintain their hopes, she explained to them how the
expropriations, of which many had been victims to the profit of the
Chinese pepper-planters, could also be attributed to the agents of Kam
and their dastardly dealings. She spoke with enthusiasm, not being able
to resist sharing with them her recent initiation into their peculation, the
techniques by which the Kam agents crushed them. She freed herself at
last from a whole past of illusions and ignorance, and it was as though she
had discovered a new language, a new culture. She could not finish talking about it.

· ·

*The Sea Wall (New York: Pellegrini & Cudahy, 1952), 43–45. Translated by Herma
Briffault.

The rainy season came. Ma had sowed a vast seed bank near the bungalow. The same men who had constructed the sea walls came to take the seedlings and replant them in the big rice field which was surrounded by the sections of the dikes.

Two months passed. Ma often went to see the greening young plants. They always began to grow just before the great tides of July.

Then, in July, the sea had risen as usual, in an assault on the plain. The sea walls had not been strong enough. The logs had been eaten through by the dwarf crabs of the paddies. In one single night the sea walls had collapsed.

Le Ravissement de Lol V. Stein*

Lorsque Michael Richardson se tourna vers Lol et qu'il l'invita à danser pour la dernière fois de leur vie, Tatiana Karl l'avait trouvé pâli et sous le coup d'une préoccupation subite si envahissante qu'elle sut qu'il avait bien regardé, lui aussi, la femme qui venait d'entrer.
. . . .

Il était devenu différent. Tout le monde pouvait le voir. Voir qu'il n'était plus celui qu'on croyait. Lol le regardait, le regardait changer.

Les yeux de Michael Richardson s'étaient éclaircis. Son visage s'était resserré dans la plénitude de la maturité. De la douleur s'y lisait, mais vieille, du premier âge.

Aussitôt qu'on le revoyait ainsi, on comprenait que rien, aucun mot, aucune violence au monde n'aurait eu raison du changement de Michael Richardson. Qu'il lui faudrait maintenant être vécu jusqu'au bout. Elle commençait déjà, la nouvelle histoire de Michael Richardson, à se faire.

Cette vision et cette certitude ne parurent pas s'accompagner chez Lol de souffrance.

Tatiana la trouva elle-même changée. Elle guettait l'événement, couvait son immensité, sa précision d'horlogerie. Si elle avait été l'agent même non seulement de sa venue mais de son succès, Lol n'aurait pas été plus fascinée.

Elle dansa encore une fois avec Michael Richardson. Ce fut la dernière fois.

La femme était seule, un peu à l'écart du buffet, sa fille avait rejoint

*Le Ravissement de Lol V. Stein (Paris: Gallimard, 1964), 17–18. This passage is reprinted with the kind permission of Gallimard.

un groupe de connaissances vers la porte du bal. Michael Richardson se dirigea vers elle dans une émotion si intense qu'on prenait peur à l'idée qu'il aurait pu être éconduit. Lol, suspendue, attendit, elle aussi. La femme ne refusa pas.

Ils étaient partis sur la piste de danse. Lol les avait regardés, une femme dont le cœur est libre de tout engagement, très âgée, regarde ainsi ses enfants s'éloigner, elle parut les aimer.

The Ravishing of Lol V. Stein*

When Michael Richardson turned around to Lol and asked her to dance for the last time in their lives, Tatiana noticed that he had grown suddenly pale, and was so suddenly lost in his own thoughts that she knew that he too had looked at the woman who had just come in.

. . . .

He had become different. It was obvious to everyone. Obvious that he was no longer the same person they had thought he was. Lol was watching him, watching him change.

Michael Richardson's eyes had grown brighter. His face had shrunk into the fullness of maturity. Pain was etched upon it, ancient, primordial pain.

The moment they saw him again this way, they knew that nothing— no word, no earthly act of violence—could have the least effect upon the change in Michael Richardson. That he now had to be played out to the bitter end. Michael Richardson's new tale had already begun to take shape.

In Lol, this vision and this conviction did not appear to be accompanied by any sign of suffering.

Tatiana found Lol herself changed. She watched and waited for what would come next, brooded over the enormity of it, its clocklike precision. If she herself had been the agent not only of its advent but of what would come of it, Lol could not have been more fascinated by it.

She danced once again with Michael Richardson. It was the last time.

The woman was alone, standing slightly off to one side of the buffet, her daughter had gone over to join a group of acquaintances near the door to the ballroom. Michael Richardson made his way over to her, prey to an

*The Ravishing of Lol V. Stein. Translated by Richard Seaver. (New York: Grove Press, 1967). Reprinted with the kind permission of Grove Press.

emotion so intense that they were frightened at the very thought that he might be refused. Lol, left hanging there, waited, waited like the others. The woman did not refuse.

They had walked out onto the dance floor. Lol had watched them, the way a woman whose heart is wholly unattached, a very old woman, watches her children leave her: she seemed to love them.

MARGUERITE DURAS

L'Amant*

Elle lui dit: je préférerais que vous ne m'aimiez pas. Même si vous m'aimez je voudrais que vous fassiez comme d'habitude avec les femmes. Il la regarde comme épouvanté, il demande: c'est ce que vous voulez? Elle dit que oui. Il a commencé à souffrir là, dans la chambre, pour la première fois, il ne ment plus sur ce point. Il lui dit que déjà il sait qu'elle ne l'aimera jamais. Elle le laisse dire. D'abord elle dit qu'elle ne sait pas. Puis elle le laisse dire.

Il dit qu'il est seul, atrocement seul avec cet amour qu'il a pour elle. Elle lui dit qu'elle aussi elle est seule. Elle ne dit pas avec quoi. Il dit: vous m'avez suivi jusqu'ici comme vous auriez suivi n'importe qui. Elle répond qu'elle ne peut pas savoir, qu'elle n'a encore jamais suivi personne dans une chambre. Elle lui dit qu'elle ne veut pas qu'il lui parle, que ce qu'elle veut c'est qu'il fasse comme d'habitude il fait avec les femmes qu'il emmène dans sa garçonnière. Elle le supplie de faire de cette façon-là.

Il a arraché la robe, il la jette, il a arraché le petit slip de coton blanc et il la porte ainsi nue jusqu'au lit. Et alors il se tourne de l'autre côté du lit et il pleure. Et elle, lente, patiente, elle le ramène vers elle et elle commence à le déshabiller. Les yeux fermés, elle le fait. Lentement. Il veut faire des gestes pour l'aider. Elle lui demande de ne pas bouger. Laisse-moi. Elle dit qu'elle veut le faire elle. Elle le fait. Elle le déshabille. Quand elle le lui demande il déplace son corps dans le lit, mais à peine, avec légèreté, comme pour ne pas la réveiller.

La peau est d'une somptueuse douceur. Le corps. Le corps est maigre, sans force, sans muscles, il pourrait avoir été malade, être en convales-

*L'Amant (Paris: Minuit, 1984), 48–50. This passage is reprinted with the kind permission of Editions de Minuit.

cence, il est imberbe, sans virilité autre que celle du sexe, il est très faible, il paraît être à la merci d'une insulte, souffrant. Elle ne le regarde pas au visage. Elle ne le regarde pas. Elle le touche. Elle touche la douceur du sexe, de la peau, elle caresse la couleur dorée, l'inconnue nouveauté. Il gémit, il pleure. Il est dans un amour abominable.

Et pleurant il le fait. D'abord il y a la douleur. Et puis après cette douleur est prise à son tour, elle est changée, lentement arrachée, emportée vers la jouissance, embrassée à elle.

La mer, sans forme, simplement incomparable.

The Lover*

She says, I'd rather you didn't love me. But if you do, I'd like you to do as you usually do with women. He looks at her in horror, asks, Is that what you want? She says it is. He's started to suffer here in this room, for the first time, he's no longer lying about it. He says he knows already she'll never love him. She lets him say it. At first she says she doesn't know. Then she lets him say it.

He says he's lonely, horribly lonely because of this love he feels for her. She says she's lonely too. She doesn't say why. He says, You've come here with me as you might have gone anywhere with anyone. She says she can't say, so far she's never gone into a bedroom with anyone. She tells him she doesn't want him to talk, what she wants is for him to do as he usually does with the women he brings to his flat. She begs him to do that.

He's torn off the dress, he throws it down. He's torn off her little white cotton panties and carries her over like that, naked, to the bed. And there he turns away and weeps. And she, slow, patient, draws him to her and starts to undress him. With her eyes shut. Slowly. He makes as if to help her. She tells him to keep still. Let me do it. She says she wants to do it. And she does. Undresses him. When she tells him to, he moves his body in the bed, but carefully, gently, as if not to wake her.

The skin is sumptuously soft. The body. The body is thin, lacking in strength, in muscle, he may have been ill, may be convalescent, he's

*The Lover (New York: Pantheon, 1985), 37–38. Translated by Barbara Bray. This passage is reprinted with the kind permission of Pantheon Books, a division of Random House, Inc.

hairless, nothing masculine about him but his sex, he's weak, probably a helpless prey to insult, vulnerable. She doesn't look him in the face. Doesn't look at him at all. She touches him. Touches the softness of his sex, his skin, caresses his goldenness, the strange novelty. He moans, weeps. In dreadful love.

And, weeping, he makes love. At first, pain. And then the pain is possessed in its turn, changed, slowly drawn away, borne toward pleasure, clasped to it.

The sea, formless, simply beyond compare.

MARGUERITE DURAS

*La Vie matérielle**

On manque d'un dieu. Ce vide qu'on découvre un jour d'adolescence rien ne peut faire qu'il n'ait jamais eu lieu. L'alcool a été fait pour supporter le vide de l'univers, le balancement des planètes, leur rotation imperturbable dans l'espace, leur silencieuse indifférence à l'endroit de votre douleur. L'homme qui boit est un homme interplanétaire. C'est dans un espace interplanétaire qu'il se meut. C'est là qu'il guette. L'alcool ne console en rien, il ne meuble pas les espaces psychologiques de l'individu, il ne remplace que le manque de Dieu. Il ne console pas l'homme. C'est le contraire, l'alcool conforte l'homme dans sa folie, il le transporte dans les régions souveraines où il est le maître de sa destinée. Aucun être humain, aucune femme, aucun poème, aucune musique, aucune littérature, aucune peinture ne peut remplacer l'alcool dans cette fonction qu'il a auprès de l'homme, l'illusion de la création capitale. Il est là pour la remplacer. Et il le fait auprès de toute une partie du monde qui aurait dû croire en Dieu et qui n'y croit plus. L'alcool est stérile. Les paroles de l'homme qui sont dites dans la nuit de l'ivresse s'évanouissent avec elle une fois le jour venu. L'ivresse ne crée rien, elle ne va pas dans les paroles, elle obscurcit l'intelligence, elle la repose. J'ai parlé dans l'alcool. L'illusion est totale: ce que vous dites, personne ne l'a encore dit. Mais l'alcool ne crée rien qui demeure. C'est le vent. Comme les paroles. J'ai écrit dans l'alcool, j'avais une faculté à tenir l'ivresse en respect qui me venait sans doute de l'horreur de la soûlographie. Je ne buvais jamais pour être saoule. Je ne buvais jamais vite. Je buvais tout le temps et je n'étais jamais saoule. J'étais retirée du monde, inatteignable, mais pas saoule.

. . . .

Ça fonctionne comme une centrale, un corps alcoolique, comme un ensemble de compartiments différents tous reliés entre eux par la person-

La Vie matérielle (Paris: P.O.L., 1987), 22–25. This passage is reprinted with the kind permission of P.O.L.

73

ne tout entière. C'est le cerveau qui est pris en premier. C'est la pensée. Le bonheur par la pensée d'abord et puis le corps. Il est gagné, imbibé peu à peu, et porté—c'est le mot: porté. C'est à partir d'un certain temps qu'on a le choix: boire jusqu'à l'insensibilité, la perte de l'identité, ou en rester aux prémices du bonheur. Mourir en quelque sorte, chaque jour, ou bien encore vivre.

Material Life

A god is missing. This emptiness that you discover on an adolescent day, nothing can keep it from having taken place. Alcohol was made to put up with the emptiness of the universe, the swinging of the planets, their imperturbable rotation in space, their silent indifference to the place of your pain. The man who drinks is an interplanetary man. He moves in an interplanetary space. It is there that he watches. Alcohol in no way consoles, it does not fill in the psychological spaces of the individual, it only replaces the absence of God. It doesn't console man. It's just the opposite, alcohol comforts man in his madness, it transports him into sovereign regions where he is the master of his destiny. No human being, no woman, no poem, no music, no literature, no painting can replace alcohol in the function it has for man, the illusion of capital creation. It is there to replace that. And it does this for a large number of people who should have believed in God and who no longer believe in him. Alcohol is sterile. The words that a man says in a night of drunkenness fade away with it at dawn. Drunkenness creates nothing, it doesn't enter into words, it obscures the intelligence and restores it. I have spoken in alcohol. The illusion is total: what you say, no one has ever said before. But alcohol creates nothing that remains. It is wind. Like words. I have written in alcohol; I was skillful at holding drunkenness at bay, which I doubtless got from fear of "drunkography." I never drank to get drunk. I never drank fast. I drank all the time and I was never drunk. I was withdrawn from the world, beyond reach, but not drunk.

. . . .

The alcoholic body functions like a switchboard, like a set of different compartments all linked together by the whole person. It's the brain that gets taken first. It's thought. Happiness first for the mind then for the body. It's won, imbibed little by little and carried—that's the word: carried. It's after a certain point in time that one has the choice: drink to the point of insensibility, of loss of identity, or stay with the first fruits of happiness. You sort of die, every day, or you continue living.

TRANSLATED BY LAUREN DOYLE-McCOMBS

RINDALA EL-KHOURY

Louis-René des Forêts
Speaking Our Silence

Reading a book by Louis-René des Forêts is an event: an experience so stunning and staggering that it, itself, is unspeakable and can only be read through its effects. It is precisely this unspeakability that seems to be the most specific impact of des Forêts's work. Indeed, it is astonishing for someone interested in this author's work to find out that, except for a few articles scattered throughout the last twenty years, nothing substantial has been written on him. However, des Forêts is recognized by Georges Bataille and Maurice Blanchot, among others, as one of the few authors one should not just read but upon whom one should pause and reflect; an author that engages his reader in every way. Marguerite Duras, whose work has been read extensively, declared that des Forêts is one of the few authors that deeply influenced her writing. And yet, when one mentions des Forêts's name, an interrogative silence sets in. "Who is he? What has he written?" seems to be the only response even in the most well-read circles.

Des Forêts's work is indeed surrounded by this unspeakability, an unspeakability that has been translated into a pervasive silence. This silence has not only been fostered by those who do not read him but has even been corroborated by those who do. Louis-René des Forêts himself, by not publishing for over fifteen years, materializes this silence. We, readers or potential readers, are ineluctably confronted by this silence. At the moment that we perceive it as silence, it "becomes" silence in regard to us: when we are exposed to it, we become impregnated by it. This silence is now addressed to us and we have become implicated in it. The silence around Louis-René des Forêts assumes "meaning" because we can perceive it. Once intrigued by it, we must turn to des Forêts's texts, as the focus around which silence has settled. We feel compelled to interrogate these texts, to make them speak. This silence has then provoked in its recipient a desire to make it speak. It has led to an inquiring gesture: a gesture that asks this silence to speak its own silence, its own reason to be silent. Our gesture indicates our incapacity to live this silence as silence. To leave it unaddressed could render us silent—making us aware of our own terrifying capacity to remain silent. Our silence might, in turn, engender or perpetuate new silences. It becomes a menace by revealing that any silence carries a self-perpetuating capacity of creating yet another silence. Our gesture reveals that the menace which turns silence into a specter is the very menace which leads to this silence.

In turning to Louis-René des Forêts's two main texts, *Le Bavard* and *La Chambre des enfants*, published in 1946 and 1960 respectively, we find that silence is the central concern. In *Le Bavard*, the speaking "I" compares himself to a babbler and in his babbling adds that his friends say that he is "silence itself." He declares that he "feels like talking" and yet insists that he has "absolutely nothing to say." By presenting his own speech as empty words and while talking compulsively, the speaking "I" makes us suspicious of the nature of his speech. To read it as speech would be to ignore the speaking "I's" warning, while to heed that warning is to start interrogating the notion of "chattering." Because his chattering is compulsive and excessive, it empties words of any particular meaning, thereby rendering discourse meaningless. However, to hear meaninglessness in speech is to understand how speech and silence overlap while they are simultaneously interwoven. An excess of words stifles speech by annulling it in the very gesture through which it is presented; it does, however, discover silence in that annulment. Too many words reveal that silence can constrain speech and therefore that speech can reveal silence. In his talking gesture, the speaking "I" addresses the problematic of speech and silence and offers insight into their incessant struggle.

La Chambre des enfants, a book of short stories, presents three stories about a child who refuses to speak. The vehemence of this refusal of speech belies a total belief in speech's power and can be read as the symptom of an acute suspicion of its capacity to mean. The silence of each of these children identifies them as characters. These children use silence as a weapon while they become its victims. The fourth story presents a character who, through his singing, speaks to his audience, to what is most "elementary" in them. The text suggests that singing occupies a particular space where speech and silence are interwoven. Singing contains the possibility of meaning that speech carries or that which silence withholds.

Des Forêts's fiction revolves around a silence that both contaminates and is contaminated by speech. Constant interlocutors, speech and silence both obscure and define one another. Therefore, at the moment that we ask silence to speak itself we find, at the core of this silence, the questioning of a speaking gesture. By responding to the silence around and within des Forêts's texts, we make it speak to us. In asking silence to speak we speak back to it: our question reveals our desire to speak. Moreover by addressing our question to des Forêts's texts, texts which unveil the presence of silence in speech, this question is returned to us with the silence that it bears. Hearing this silence in and around this author's work reflects our desire to hear our own silence as well as acts out our desire to make our silence speak.

When one reads des Forêts's work as a gesture that addresses the inherent silence that is the source of speech as well as its paralyzing motor, the author's long silences become overwhelming. The threatening call for surrender that emanates from the power of this silence reverberates. The threat of silence that haunts any attempt to face it is rendered palpable: silence holds a real menace that propels anyone who questions it back into more silence. Louis-René des Forêts's silence echoes then, as both a menace and a protection. But when, in 1984, a short extract of *Ostinato* is published, this echo becomes a call. *Ostinato* cries out the anguish that this silence has quieted and yet exacerbated. The need to break the silence is now an unavoidable but yet devastating need:

Se taire, non, il n'en avait plus les moyens, même s'il connut un tremblement de haine et d'effroi à entendre sa voix remonter de l'abîme où il croyait l'avoir à tout jamais précipitée et perdue. Non, il n'était déjà plus de force à lui résister: évanouie seulement, voilée peut-être, mais encore là, insistante, inébranlable, comme pour le prendre en défaut de vigilance et le rejeter dans un nouveau tourment.

Louis-René des Forêts confronts the need to speak while he realizes that speech springs from the very menace that binds him to silence. Not surrendering to this enraged struggle which threatens to demolish him, *Ostinato* "puts into words" this devastation and offers it as the only justifiable speaking gesture.

BIBLIOGRAPHY

I. WORKS

Les Mendiants. Paris: Gallimard, 1943, definitive edition in 1986.
Le Bavard. Paris: Gallimard, collection l'Imaginaire, 1947; updated in 1973.
La Chambre des Enfants. Paris: Gallimard, collection l'Imaginaire, 1960.
Un Malade en Forêt. Excerpt from *La Chambre des Enfants.* Paris: Fata Morgana, 1985.
Les Mégères de la mer. Paris: Mercure de France, 1967.
Voies et détours de la fiction. Paris: Fata Morgana, 1985.
Le Malheur au Lido. Paris: Fata Morgana, 1987.
Ostinato. Excerpted in *NRF,* 372 (January 1984): 1–64.
Ostinato. Excerpted in *L'Ire des Vents,* 15–16 (1987): 203–39.

II. CRITICISM

Bonnefoy, Yves. "Une Ecriture de notre temps (L.-R. Des Forêts)" *Nouvelle Revue Française* 402–03 (July–August, 1986): 1–43; 404 (September 1986): 60–77; 405 (October 1986): 30–50; 406 (November 1986): 29–50; 407 (December 1986): 30–49; 408 (January 1987): 38–55.

LOUIS-RENÉ DES FORÊTS

*Ostinato**

Heureux renversement par lequel ce qui n'a pas eu lieu se reconnaît à distance comme un produit innocent de la mémoire. De même qu'un ciel sans soleil et sans nuage serait réduit à la fade inanité de sa surface bleue où le regard se noierait d'ennui et que le ciel nocturne privé d'étoiles n'offre à la contemplation que sa noirceur insignifiante, faisant de nous des aveugles, une telle opération pour qui s'y livre sans calcul et sans frein répond à la nécessité de restituer son dû à un monde endormi que seuls les temps forts illuminent.

Tout le reste est un champ de ruines perdu dans la nuit.

. . . .

CHUTES

Enfouir le visage dans ses mains et se désintéresser du monde tout en le surveillant du coin de l'œil pour se prémunir contre ses mauvais coups, d'ailleurs bien en vain, c'est toujours lui avec son poids dévorant qui aura le dernier mot.

Hors la loi fuyant le vacarme forain des grands maîtres de la vanité, tournicotant à la dérive sur son ombre, avec combien de compagnons délaissés derrière lui, flairant, démasquant les impostures sans venir à bout de la sienne, toujours occupé fébrilement à faire et à défaire, brouillant tout sur ce mauvais chemin d'où il ne s'écarte que pour se fourvoyer davantage.

Non pas cela fut. Cela est, qui ne demandait qu'un peu de temps et l'abandon au courant de la langue pour refaire surface.

*Ostinato, NRF 372(January 1984): 38–51. This passage is reprinted with the kind permission of Louis-René des Forêts.

D'une vision en défaut il tire sa vérité propre comme celle de sa relation avec le monde, et c'est elle qui le garantit contre le vain souci d'exactitude, les attestations, les mises au point, les travestissements de la mauvaise foi dont n'a que faire un homme affecté d'une incorrigible déficience de la vue.

Mémoire, infatigable mémoire qui multiple ses leurres avec un art retors, mémoire turbulente comme un enfant qui court de chambre en chambre et que la main ne peut retenir.

Ce n'est là qu'un monde qui meurt lentement devant l'autre qui renaît sous de fabuleuses couleurs pour s'assombrir et retourner comme il se doit à l'état de rien.

Il ne possède rien dont il n'aspire aussitôt à se défaire, sans toutefois y parvenir, moins possédant que possédé par une surabondance d'images fastueuses où il voit la preuve de son inaptitude à modérer le mouvement qui l'entraîne bien au-delà de cette part de lui-même que son peu d'éclat rend impropre à la magnification mystificatrice. Négliger les régions arides où se trahit l'insuffisance de l'être ne répond nullement à une volonté préméditée de se prendre ni de se donner pour qui n'aurait respiré que l'air des sommets, mais au besoin insatiable d'aller plus loin, encore et encore plus loin, toute illusion écartée d'infléchir le parcours en le subordonnant à une fin incompatible avec sa nature qui est de n'en viser aucune et de se poursuivre indéfiniment.

C'est aussi que la recherche scrupuleuse de la vérité, l'absurde prétention à tout dire sont des instances auxquelles se soumettre reviendrait à s'enfermer dans les limites d'un dessein et manquer du même coup par souci de probité ce que les seules forces du hasard sans cesse remises en jeu à la faveur du langage et conditionnées par lui désignent au point le plus reculé comme le centre actif, la substance souterraine dont l'être se nourrit, quelle que soit la perte d'intensité qu'entraîne une représentation approximative qui, liée à la durée changeante d'une vie, doit varier ses reprises et s'en remettre pour chacune d'elle aux occasions de la chance, hors de toute sujétion à un ordre préétabli ou de conformité respectueuse à la réalité des faits derrière laquelle se dissimule comme la braise sous la cendre ce que les mots ont pour mission de ranimer.

À se tracer un chemin ou à suivre un chemin déjà tracé il court également le risque de se fourvoyer et, qu'il le sache bien, dans les deux cas il n'y aura aucun signe pour l'en avertir, pas même la vilaine grimace du doute qui l'accompagne sans le guider, tout juste bon à ralentir sa marche qu'il poursuivra donc aussi obstinément qu'en vain, aveuglé par un reste de foi en son étoile depuis longtemps éteinte, continuant à chercher tantôt avec fébrilité, comme s'il y allait de sa vie, tantôt calmement comme pour vérifier qu'il ne trouvera rien.

Qui sait si l'emploi de la forme verbale du présent comme la désignation à la troisième personne ne relèvent pas tout bonnement de la lâcheté: rompre avec le temps présent, s'abriter derrière l'ambiguïté protectrice de la fiction? Et cependant une voix s'élève aussitôt qui, sans trouver d'arguments décisifs à lui opposer, s'insurge avec véhémence contre les grossières simplifications de la psychologie.

L'esprit appelle à lui les images où il croit se reconnaître et, pourvu que ce soit sans préméditation mais dans le sens et selon des voies qui correspondent à leur secrète nécessité, elles vivent alors de toute la force qu'il met à les rendre aussi présentes que les réalités les plus aiguës du moment, aidé en cela par le fait que pour une large part ce qui est advenu autrefois ne trouve à se produire que sous la pleine lumière d'aujourd'hui. Rien ici qui réponde à une attitude calculée, rien qui n'obéisse au mouvement naturel et impérieux du ainsi-en-est-il parce qu'il ne saurait en être autrement.

Encore faudrait-il pour s'en prévaloir que la nécessité porte en elle sa justification.

À tout ce qu'on s'efforce de lui remettre en mémoire et dont il n'a que faire, il souscrit les yeux fermés, qui est sa façon de l'exclure comme chose insignifiante justement sanctionnée par l'oubli.

Ce mutisme, à se prolonger indûment, bien loin d'approfondir, dérange le silence. L'heure est venue de congédier ceux auxquels il n'aura parlé que pour se taire.

Des mirages, rien que des mirages façonnés par les mots pour peupler le désert de l'oubli.

Il ne trouve aplomb que sur son propre vide, ignorant vers où va ce chemin qu'il reconnaît parfois curieusement à des traces qui ne sont pas les siennes, ne sachant pas davantage pourquoi il s'y est engagé avec tant de présomption, si même à le poursuivre obstinément il aura aucune chance de déboucher sur le lieu encore insoupçonné de sa destination.

Trajet aveugle qui l'exalte, qui l'exaspère comme la lecture d'un récit dont l'auteur eût été conduit à différer sans cesse le dénouement. S'il s'achemine vers un but inconnu auquel il ne devra jamais toucher, quelle force mystérieuse l'empêche d'y renoncer? Une sorte de courage ou une sorte de lâcheté? La vigueur séductrice d'une langue qu'il avait congédiée, mais peut-être aussi bien sa pauvreté, l'attrait de sa pauvreté. Le sombre plaisir de trahir son vœu, celui de remplir un office désespéré en donnant sans y croire valeur vivante à des figures dont l'apparition désordonnée ne se règle pas sur le travail de la raison? La fatigue de l'âge, et l'impuissance à se taire qui souvent s'y rattache? (Blessé à mort, le héros d'opéra n'en continue pas moins de chanter sans mesurer son souffle, avec une mâle énergie, et c'est comme si tout son sang jaillissait et se répandait à flots sous les espèces de sa voix jusqu'à la rémission dernière.) Par quel démon s'est-il laissé tirer d'une apathie si durement acquise? Pourquoi cette fièvre sur le tard dont la ténacité est l'un des traits les plus troublants, toutes ces brûlantes images comme surgies à l'état brut d'un foyer souterrain proliférant avec la force d'une épidémie qu'aucun moyen, même s'il en était encore temps, ne serait assez puissant pour juguler, et les pauses destinées à en ralentir le débit, loin de leur donner un coup d'arrêt, ne servant qu'à en prolonger les effets et à en libérer de nouvelles prises à leur tour dans un mouvement aussi irrésistible que celui de la vie, et qui n'aura de terme cette fois que par extinction naturelle, défection subite, le sommeil sans rêve et laconique de la mort.

Une incrédulité si radicale qu'elle en arrive à ébranler ses propres fondements. Mais laisser la défiance s'introduire au cœur du doute—mettre en doute la légitimité du doute—, est-ce encore douter?

En fait de remède contre l'incohérence, il n'a que sa main droite, bien qu'elle lui obéisse paresseusement et même le plus souvent pas du tout, courant à vide, butant contre les obstacles, lâchant prise au lieu de retenir, comme en proie à une agitation superflue qui, loin d'apporter la guérison, accroît le désordre auquel elle donne toutefois un semblant de cohésion. Qu'elle reste un seul jour inerte sur la table, et le tourment du manque se déchaîne.

Il suffirait d'un peu d'ardeur et d'abandon pour remettre en mouvement l'esprit abîmé dans la contemplation de son dénuement, la main engourdie par la froideur hostile du papier. Mais rien d'autre qu'attendre, seul comme un pauvre, le retour de la grâce, son premier signe dans le silence de ces murs, le mot éclair, la formule décisive qui ouvrirait la voie vers un domaine d'autant plus inaccessible que le désir d'y accéder paralyse les élans et, faute de s'approprier l'objet qui lui manque, retombe dans l'inertie.

Expectative qui d'ordinaire n'en est pas moins tout le contraire de la passivité, car ce désir douloureusement tendu, irréalisable sans le concours de forces occasionnelles, exige que, pour se préparer à les saisir, on lutte à chaque instant contre la tentation du repos.

Il attend, il ne peut qu'attendre, et c'est comme si tout autour de lui demeurait suspendu à cette attente de la chance. Que le désir qui s'exaspère et échoue à la capter finisse par s'éteindre, ce ne sera jamais que partie remise: la déconvenue n'a fait que relancer absurdement la volonté d'agir, le jeu ne valût-il pas d'être poursuivi—et il lui arrive d'en rire, sans pour autant y renoncer, à deux doigts de trouver il ne saura jamais quoi, peu de chose sans doute, une autre raison de rire, mais jaune cette fois, ce peu hypothétique comptant pour si peu qu'il ne répondrait pas au grand rêve présomptueux de l'esprit.

Ces images qui se dressent pour construire et qui retombent sans pouvoir donner forme cohérente à un temps aussi indistinct que les régions les plus reculées de l'enfance. Encore un petit effort. Mais à quoi bon? Et il s'endort sur sa tâche, tel le piètre écolier de jadis que l'énoncé d'un problème inscrit au tableau suffisait à plonger dans la torpeur, d'où le tirait en sursaut la honte d'avoir à remettre copie blanche, bien que son inaptitude à résoudre correctement ces devinettes rebutantes ne lui laissât aucune chance d'éviter les sarcasmes du maître qui en savourait l'effet tout comme à le voir bondir et se contorsionner sous la morsure du fouet.

Il ne se presse pas d'arriver comme s'il disposait d'un temps sans limite ou qu'il eût d'ores et déjà perdu tout espoir d'une issue, auquel cas cette nonchalance serait le signe d'un abandon imminent, mais pourquoi ici plutôt que là? De même qu'il ne s'est jamais proposé aucun but ni soucié de voir plus loin que le sol à ses pieds, il ne mettra pas le point final avant sa propre fin.

Combien de moments et de figures inoubliables dont on dirait que par méfiance du langage ils se refusent à reprendre vie, comme préférant au grand jour la discrète pénombre d'une mémoire individuelle vouée à disparaître avec eux: il n'est pas de lieux plus sûrs que la mort et l'oubli.

L'expression du désespoir a comme toute autre sa rhétorique propre à laquelle les plus désespérés s'abandonnent sans retenue et ne tentent de s'opposer que ceux qui trouvent à lui substituer quelque forme inhabituelle un apaisement au moins momentané, peut-être une manière de revanche sur le mal qui les ronge, dont on ne dira pas, pour autant qu'ils le font servir à des fins esthétiques et savent en tirer de beaux effets, qu'il ne correspond à aucune expérience vécue, qu'il n'est que le ressort d'une fiction destinée par la mise en œuvre de subtils procédés à donner comme au théâtre l'illusion d'une vie tourmentée. Peu importe par quels moyens cet effet de suggestion est atteint: ceux qui les emploient avec art, et ce terme serait-il pris dans un sens dépréciatif, n'en demeurent pas moins habités par le désespoir, tous également sans défense devant lui qu'aucune arme verbale, fût-elle inédite et de la qualité la plus fine, ne parviendra jamais à conjurer.

Les faux départs et les renoncements sans retour: sa gloire secrète, son unique gloire.

Que le chemin semble infini à celui dont le temps est compté, lequel néanmoins le poursuit sans précipitation, et il est vrai que rien ne le presse, car le terme serait-il en vue qu'il lui apparaîtrait toujours infiniment lointain, à jamais inaccessible, peut-être même indésirable pour autant qu'y parvenir signifie briser le mouvement aventureux de la recherche qui l'anime, entrer dans une passivité mortelle, faire en somme comme si, la question résolue, il ne lui restait désormais qu'à se laisser glisser sans effort vers sa propre fin, à vivre ses derniers jours dans la niaise satisfaction d'une existence accomplie, toute couronnée de souvenirs et de sagesse sénile, où il n'aurait plus à vaincre que les misères du corps, rien à attendre que ce froid qui viendra bientôt l'envelopper.

Il marche à présent d'un pas de somnambule sur une terre appauvrie où ne lui parvient que la sèche odeur de sa récolte abandonnée, ce monceau de feuilles froissées auxquelles il a mis froidement le feu.

Serait-il temps de réparer les dommages qu'il n'en ferait rien, faute de savoir aujourd'hui comment s'y prendre. Vieux compagnon sans emploi qui a perdu la main.

Las d'attendre sur la berge, il se jette à l'eau. Où est-il maintenant? Sur l'autre rive à refaire provision d'énergie. Et ainsi de suite jusqu'à ce que ses dernières forces l'abandonnent au milieu du courant.

Au fil du temps, mais que ce fil vienne à se perdre et le temps n'est que matière confuse, masse amorphe, rumeur aussi inconsistante qu'un discours dont rien du premier au dernier mot n'aurait retenu l'attention.

Laisser sa pensée tourner autour de la mort n'est en définitive qu'un exercice risible auquel viendra mettre fin tôt ou tard la vraie souffrance du corps à l'agonie.

Comment malgré tout ne pas y revenir et même s'y attarder, non pas dans un but d'ascèse á la manière du moine des images pieuses qu'on voit devant un crâne méditer sur sa condition mortelle, mais pour assouvir un désir angoissé, et en rire aussi sans doute, de ce rire qui écarte l'angoisse, par lequel cependant l'angoisse s'exprime sous l'apparence de la désinvolture—un rire à peine différent de celui que suscite une plaisanterie macabre d'autant plus irrésistible qu'elle tranche sur la gravité des circonstances, qu'elle est par les rieurs eux-mêmes jugée de mauvais goût.

Désir et peur mêlés dans la certitude de tout perdre, auxquels, fût-ce par un rire irrévérencieux, on ne parvient pas à donner le change, car bafouer la mort à partir de ses signes extérieurs ou des rites de deuil qui l'entourent, c'est montrer qu'elle garde son pouvoir obsédant. Mais si chacun doit reconnaître, à moins de s'abuser, que la prendre comme objet de dérision n'est qu'un subterfuge, une comédie qu'on se joue sans y croire pour déguiser en rire son horreur de l'anéantissement et qui de toutes façons ne règle rien, s'il admet qu'en libérer l'esprit excède les forces humaines soumises à la loi inexorable de l'espèce, pour autant que l'esprit n'accepte pas la possibilité d'une défaite, il se défend d'instinct soit dans le mouvement irraisonné de la jeunesse par un appétit de vivre qui sonne comme un joyeux défi soit à son déclin par le pauvre expédient de la raillerie, et souvent du cynisme le plus grossier qui ne trompe ni ne choque personne, pas plus que n'impressionnent les déclarations tapageuses d'un lâche pour sauver la face. (Il n'y faudrait qu'un peu plus de légèreté, autant dire ce qui nous manque à nous autres qui ne sommes pas de purs esprits, mais des êtres frappés d'une lourde malédiction, dont la vie précaire comme celle des bêtes est sans cesse et de toutes parts menacée.)

Plus il lutte, plus il cède du terrain. Que ce combat acharné l'entraîne à la longue vers sa perte ne fait aucun doute, et c'est justement pareille certitude qui l'empêche d'y renoncer. Même s'il pense avec non moins de certitude qu'il s'en faudrait d'un rien pour l'emporter, combattre signifie que ce rien lui fera toujours défaut.

Toute possibilité de souffler comme de revenir en arrière lui étant retirée, ce vagabondage forcé lui donne l'illusion de couvrir des distances et d'avancer du même pas que la passion qui le conduit là où il trouvera peut-être ce qu'à défaut de chercher il avait longtemps attendu, mais quoi au juste il n'en sait rien, et c'est de son ignorance de la fin poursuivie qu'il tire la force de persévérer sur une voie qui en vaut bien une autre, même si elle semble destinée à faire trébucher plus qu'à être parcourue. En est-il d'ailleurs aucune qui puisse s'emprunter sans risque et mener dans la bonne direction? L'explorateur d'une terre inconnue met autant d'énergie à en affronter les périls qu'à en reculer les limites: l'absence de repères, l'hostilité des éléments et d'une nature encore brute le stimulent plutôt qu'elles ne l'arrêtent.

De ce chaos désolé tout cependant l'engagerait à se détourner si ce n'était ruiner le mouvement qui l'y a conduit, signer son échec avant même d'avoir échoué. Il lui faut donc aller son chemin jusqu'aux bornes extrêmes de l'endurance, dût-il se déchirer cruellement aux épines, traverser en suffoquant tous les feux de l'enfer pour ne déclarer forfait qu'à la veille d'en toucher le terme qui sera le moment de mourir comme chacun sans avoir établi sa preuve.

Se croire capable de renverser tous les obstacles, sauf le dernier en vue duquel venir seulement à bout des autres ne compterait pour rien.

Il a oublié entre-temps où le mène son chemin sur lequel, passé le point de non-retour, il marque le pas, et c'est tout comme s'il avait atteint sa destination.

Son exaspération, ses défis, sa brûlure . . . Mais il ne se reconnaît à la fin qu'au plus près du silence.

De l'envol à la chute, tous ces grands espaces paisibles désertés par la mémoire.

Ne pouvant rien faire ici du peu qu'il a retenu, refusant d'obéir laborieusement aux règles de l'harmonie, ne voulant plus rien entendre ni voir, il franchit d'un bond brutal la faille qu'il retournera combler s'il en a demain le désir, la force et le temps.

Sans remettre en cause le principe d'une célébration de la vie, mais comme de haut on sonde le fond du désastre, côtoyer l'abîme toujours d'un peu plus près, au risque de perdre pied devant la vision béante qui se creuse vertigineusement pour en défendre les abords.

Deux décennies pèsent moins que le trait fulgurant venu en une seconde frapper, déraciner, trancher au plus vif, mettre en pièces . . .

Après la courte saison des fables, ses lueurs éblouissantes, la force rapide de son action, tout se brouille et s'éteint qui ne reprend figure que sous les traits de la gaieté perdue, les derniers élans refroidis par la sage, la trop clairvoyante raison, dissipées les chimères du cœur, la magie des fêtes, la dévotion au langage—et pire, bien pire, l'accord tant de fois recherché rompu par ce rapt sec comme la décharge d'une arme à feu, la grâce incarnée, la beauté si fière inacceptablement anéantie, la douleur sans mesure qu'attise au réveil sa douce apparition dans les rêves de chaque nuit, le vœu de retrait bientôt délié par le déferlement de la vie qui toujours l'emporte à la fin, mais ne découvre en se retirant qu'un champ de décombres.

Comment l'entendre, elle qui leur parle maintenant de si loin avec si peu de mots que la distance rend de jour en jour plus rares, la vie retrouvée plus difficiles à saisir?

Ostinato

Happy upheaval by which what never took place becomes aware of its being from afar as an offshoot of memory.

Just as a sunless and cloudless sky is reduced to the inanity of its blue surface, where the gaze drowns of boredom, and just as the night shorn of its stars, offers only meaningless darkness to the gaze, making blindmen of us—for the one who yields without afterthoughts or hesitation, such an operation answers to the necessity of restituting its right to a world asleep, illuminated only by accented time.

Everything else is a field of ruins lost in the night.

. . . .

Falls

Burying his face in his hands and distancing himself from the world, all the while watching it from the corner of his eye in order to avert its blows, moreover in vain, it's always the world with its devouring weight which will have the last word.

Outlaw fleeing the fair's din of the great masters of vanity, wandering up and down, adrift on his shadow, with how many companions left behind him, sniffing, unmasking shams without overcoming his own, always feverishly busy, doing and undoing, blurring everything on this wrong road from which he strays only to lose his way even more.

Not was. Is, only asked for a little time and abandon to the drift of language to reemerge.

From a defective vision he takes his own truth like that of his relation with the world, and that truth is what protects him from the vain worry of exactitude, attestations, conclusions, the travesties of bad faith that a man afflicted with weak sight wants nothing to do with.

Memory, indefatigable memory that multiplies its illusions with a wily art, memory as turbulent as a child who runs from room to room and can't be held back by any hand.

There it's only a world that dies slowly in front of the other which is reborn in fabulous color only to darken and return, as it must, to a state of nothingness.

He possesses nothing which he doesn't immediately hope to get rid of, without however succeeding; less possessing than possessed by an overabundance of sumptuous images in which he sees the proof of his inaptitude in moderating the motion that pulls him well past this part of himself that his dullness makes improper for mystifying magnification. Neglecting the arid regions where the being's insufficiency is betrayed does not correspond at all to a premeditated will to assume himself, or pretend to be someone who could breathe only rarified mountain air, but if need be to the insatiable need to go further, further and further still, rejecting any illusion of bending the trajectory while subordinating it to an end incompatible with his nature which is precisely not to aim at any, and to pursue himself indefinitely.

It is also that the scrupulous search for truth, the absurd pretension to say it all, are solicitations which, if heeded, would mean the imprisonment within the limits of a plan and thereby missing out, out of a scruple about integrity, what chance alone constantly put into question by language and conditioned by it, name at the most distant point as the active center, the subterranean substance which while it nourishes the being, whatever the loss of intensity may be which an approximate representation entails, which, tied to the changeable duration of a life, must vary its repetitions and trust itself to luck in every case, removed from any subjection to a preestablished order or any respectful conformity to reality: and yet what words are made to revive is hidden behind that reality like embers under ashes.

Whether he traces a path or follows a path already traced he runs equally the risk of losing his way in any case; let him be aware that in both cases no sign will warn him, not even the nasty grimace of doubt that accompanies him without guiding him, just good enough to slow down his progress that he will pursue therefore as obstinately as in vain, blinded by a glimmer of faith in his star long extinguished, continuing his search, now feverishly, as if his life depended on it, now calmly, as if to prove that he will find nothing.

Who knows if the use of the present tense, like the choice of the third person does not arise quite simply from cowardice: breaking with present time, shielding oneself behind the protective ambiguity of fiction? And yet a voice arises immediately which, without finding decisive arguments to oppose it, revolts vehemently against the gross simplifications of psychology.

The mind seeks out the self reflecting images wherein it believes it recognizes itself and, as long as it is without premeditation but in the direction of and along their innermost secrets, then they live with the strength that he invents to make them as present as the most acute realities of the moment, helped in this by the fact that what happened in the past can for the most part only be manifested in the present. Nothing here that implies calculation, nothing that doesn't obey the natural and imperious movement of absolute necessity that could not be otherwise.

Still, in order to take advantage of that state, necessity would have to carry its justification within itself.

To anything that anyone tries to restore to his memory and that he does not care about, he subscribes, blindly, which is his way of excluding it as an insignificant thing justly relegated to forgetfulness.

This mutism, prolonging itself unduly, far from deepening silence, disturbs it. The time has come to dismiss those with whom he spoke merely to remain silent.

Mirages, nothing but mirages fashioned by words to people the desert of forgetfulness.

He finds balance only in his own void, not heeding the direction this path follows, this path that he oddly recognizes at times by traces that are not his own, not knowing anymore about why he engaged himself in it so presumptuously, even if by following it obstinately he will ever have any chance of emerging at the still unsuspected site of his destination.

Blind journey that exalts him, that exasperates him like reading a tale whose author had been led to defer the denouement indefinitely. If he makes his way toward an unknown goal that he may never reach, what mysterious force prevents him from renouncing it? A kind of courage or a kind of cowardice? Is it the seductive vigor of a language that he had dismissed, but perhaps his poverty just as well, the appeal of his poverty. The somber pleasure of betraying his vow, the vow of fulfilling a hopeless task by investing—without belief—figures with a vitality whose disordered apparitions do not comply with reason. The fatigue of age, and the incapacity to be silent which often accompanies it? (Fatally wounded, the operatic hero continues nevertheless to sing without stinting his breath, with male energy, which he expends as if all his blood spurted forth and spread in waves in the sound of his voice until the end.) By what demon did he allow himself to be wrenched from an apathy so painstakingly acquired? Why this fever late in life whose tenacity is one of the most stirring traits, all of these burning images as if erupting in the rough from an underground hearth proliferating with the power of an epidemic that no means, even were there still time, would have the power to quell, and the pauses meant to slow the output, far from putting a brake on them, merely to prolong its effects and to free new ones in turn, in a movement as irresistible as life's, and whose end will finally be achieved by natural extinction, sudden defection, the laconic, dreamless sleep of death.

An incredulity so radical that it succeeds in shaking its own foundations. But to let distrust insinuate itself into the very heart of doubt—to question the legitimacy of doubt—is that still doubting?

As a remedy against incoherence, he has only his right hand, although it obeys him lazily and most often, not at all, running aimlessly, butting against obstacles, letting go instead of holding on, as if prey to a superfluous agitation which, far from healing, heightens the disorder to which it does however lend a semblance of cohesion. Let it lie but one day inert on the table, and the torment of emptiness is unleashed.

A little ardor and abandon would be enough to start up again the mind rapt in the contemplation of its penury, the hand numbed by the hostile coldness of the paper. But there is nothing to do but wait, as abandoned as a poor man, for the return of grace, its first sign in the silence of these walls, the flashword, the decisive formula that will open the path toward a domain all the more inaccessible because the desire to reach it paralyzes all attempts, and the failure to appropriate the needed object, falls back into inertia.

Expectation that ordinarily is nevertheless the complete opposite of passivity, for this desire, painfully taut, unrealizable without the complicity of casual forces, requires that, in order to be ready to seize them, one fight at every moment against the temptation of rest.

He waits, he can only wait, and it is as if everything around him remained in suspense during this waiting for chance. If the desire that tries desperately and fails to capture chance is finally spent, it will never merely be anything but postponed: the setback was merely an absurd spur to the will to act, the game worth playing or not—and he even laughs about it, without however renouncing it, on the verge of finding he will never know what, not much doubtless, another reason to laugh, but hollowly this time, this hypothetical little, counting for so little that it would not satisfy the great presumptuous dream of the spirit.

These images that rise up to build and fall back without being able to give a coherent form to a time as indistinct as the most hidden recesses of childhood. One more little effort. But what's the use? And he falls asleep on his task, like the wretched schoolboy of long ago who was plunged into a torpor by the presentation of a problem inscribed on the blackboard; he would be pulled out with a start by the shame of having to hand in a blank page, although his inability to solve those repellent guessing games did not allow him to escape the sarcasm of the teacher who savored its effect on him, just as he savored seeing the schoolboy jump and writhe under the bite of the whip.

He is in no hurry to arrive, as if he had unlimited time at his disposal or had already lost all hope of an outcome, in which case this nonchalance would be the sign of imminent giving up, but why now rather than later? Just as he never set himself any goal, nor cared to see further than the ground at his feet, he will not end it all before his own end.

How many unforgettable moments and faces, it seems as if they refuse to come back to life through distrust of language, as if preferring to the bright light of day the discreet penumbra of an individual memory destined to disappear with them: there are no places more secure than death and oblivion.

The expression of despair has, like any other expression, its own rhetoric to which the most desperate abandon themselves without restraint and only those who find a way of substituting some unusual form for it attempt to oppose a momentary appeasement, perhaps a kind of revenge on the pain which gnaws at them, about which one will not say, just so long as they make it serve esthetic ends and know how to glean fine effects from it, that it doesn't correspond to any lived experience, that it is only the resource of a fiction destined by the impulse of subtle procedures to give, as in the theater, the illusion of a tormented life. It matters little by what means this suggestive effect is achieved: those who employ them artfully, and this term may be taken in a derogatory sense, are none the less all inhabited by despair, equally defenseless before it which no verbal weapon, be it original and of the finest quality, will ever succeed in exorcizing.

False departures and definitive renunciations: his secret glory, his unique glory.

How infinite the way seems to him whose time is counted, who nevertheless pursues it without precipitation, and it is true that there is no hurry, for even if the end were in sight it would appear to him infinitely far away, forever inaccessible, and perhaps even undesirable inasmuch as arriving there means breaking the adventurous movement of the quest that propels him, entering into a mortal passivity, all in all, doing as if, the question resolved, he only had to let himself slide effortlessly toward his own end, living his last days in the inane satisfaction of an accomplished existence all wreathed in memories and senile wisdom, and where he would have only the woes of the body to overcome, nothing to wait for except the cold that will soon come to shroud him.

Now he walks like a sleepwalker on an impoverished earth where only the dry odor of its abandoned harvest reaches him, this heap of crushed leaves which he coolly sets aflame.

Even if there were time to repair the damages, he would do nothing for lack of knowing today how to go about it. Old journeyman without work who has lost his touch.

Weary of waiting on the bank, he throws himself into the water. Where is he now? On the other shore restoring his energy. And so on until his last forces abandon him in the middle of the current.

All along the stream of time, but let that stream get lost and time becomes mere confused matter, an amorphous mass, a rumor as empty as a speech unheard from the first to the last word.

Letting his thoughts dwell on death is ultimately nothing but a laughable exercise which the true suffering of a body in the throes of death will sooner or later put an end to.

How, in spite of everything, not to dwell on death and even to wallow in thoughts of it, not in an ascetic spirit as depicted in pious images of a monk whom one sees before a skull meditating on his mortality, but to appease an anguished desire, and probably also laugh at it, with the laugh that brushes anguish aside, through which anguish expresses itself nevertheless in a carefree way—a laugh hardly different from that elicited by a macabre joke, all the more irresistible because it contrasts with the gravity of the circumstances, and is judged by the jokers themselves to be in bad taste.

Desire and fear blended in the certainty of losing everything, which blend, though it be through an irreverential laugh, one does not succeed in fooling, for to scoff at death because of its exterior signs or the rites of mourning that surround it is to show that it retains its power to obsess. But if every one must recognize, lest one be self-deluded, that to take it as an object of derision is but a subterfuge, a part one performs without conviction in order to disguise one's horror of annihilation with a laugh, and which in any case solves nothing, if he concedes that liberating the spirit from it exceeds human resources subject to the inexorable laws of the species, inasmuch as the spirit does not accept the possibility of a defeat, he protects himself instinctively, whether in the unreasoned movement of youth by an appetite for life which rings like a joyous challenge, whether in his decline by the paltry expedient of mockery, and often of the crudest indecency which neither fools nor shocks anyone, no more impressive than a coward's uproarious declarations to save face. (One would only need a little more lightness, or one might as well say that that is what we lack, we who are not pure spirits, but beings struck down with a cursed heaviness, whose precarious lives, like those of animals, are constantly threatened on every front.)

The more he fights, the more ground he gives up. There is no doubt that this fierce combat finally leads him to his ruin and it's exactly this certainty that prevents him from renouncing it. Even if he thinks with no less certainty that the slightest thing would do him in, fighting means that he will always lack this slightest thing.

All possibility of catching his breath or retracing his steps having been denied him, this forced wandering gives him the illusion of covering ground and of advancing in step with the passion that drives him where he will perhaps find what, for lack of searching, he had long awaited, but what exactly it is he has no idea, and it is in his very ignorance of the pursued end that he finds the strength to persevere on a path which is as good as any other, even if it seems destined to make him stumble more than to be travelled. Besides, does one exist which can be followed without risk and lead in the right direction? The explorer of an uncharted region puts as much energy into confronting its perils as into extending its boundaries: the absence of landmarks, the hostility of the elements and of a still untamed nature stimulate rather than halt him.
Everything would however tempt him to turn away from this desolate chaos, if it didn't ruin the impulse that drove him there, seal his failure even before failing. He therefore has to follow his path to the extreme limits of endurance, even though he must be cruelly ripped by thorns, traverse, though suffocating, all the fires of hell to withdraw only on the eve of reaching the fulfillment which will be the moment to die like anyone else without having proven anything.

Believing himself capable of overcoming all obstacles, except the last, whose failure would negate the victory over all others.

He has forgotten in the meantime where his path leads him, on which, past the point of no return, he marks time, and it's as if he had reached his destination.

His exasperation, his challenges, his burning . . . but at the end he knows himself only as closest to silence.

From flight to the fall, all these great peaceful spaces deserted by memory.

Incapable of doing anything here with the little that he has retained, refusing to obey laboriously the rules of harmony, not wanting to hear or see anything more, he crosses in a single brutal leap the gap that he will return to fill if tomorrow he still has the desire, the strength, and the time to do it.

Without putting into question again the principle of a celebration of life, but as from high up one probes the depth of disaster, skirting the abyss always a little closer, at the risk of losing his footing before the gaping vision that is dizzily hollowed out to defend the surrounding area.

Two decades weigh less than the lightning flash come in one second to strike, uproot, slice to the core, rend asunder . . .

After the short season of fables, its dazzling lights, the rapid force of its action, everything becomes confused and is extinguished that doesn't take shape again under the traits of lost gaiety, the last attempts chilled by wise, too-clairvoyant reason, the chimeras of the heart, the magic of celebrations, devotion to language, all dissipated—and worse, much worse, the accord sought after so many times broken by this abduction as sharp as the discharge of a firearm, grace incarnate, beauty so proud unacceptably annihilated, pain without measure that fans, upon awakening, its soft apparition in the dreams of each night, the vow of retreat quickly undone by the surge of life which always wins out in the end, but discovers upon withdrawing only a field of rubble.

How to hear her, she who speaks to them now from so far away, with so few words that distance renders rarer day by day, that rediscovered life renders more difficult to grasp?

TRANSLATED BY JOANIKO KOHCHI

MARTINE REID

Robert Pinget

Robert Pinget was born in Geneva on July 19, 1919. After earning a law degree, he came to Paris and, as a painter, he took part in several exhibitions. In 1950, he taught drawing in England. A year later, he published his first work, *Entre Fantoine et Agapa*. He traveled in Europe, North Africa, and Israel (a journey related in *Le Renard et la boussole*). A close friend of Beckett, he translated *Tous ceux qui tombent*; in return, Beckett did a translation of Pinget's radio play *La Manivelle* (under the title *The Old Tune*). In 1963, Pinget received the Prix des Critiques for his novel *L'Inquisitoire*, and in 1965 he was awarded the Prix Femina for *Quelqu'un*. He has since published many novels and plays. *L'Ennemi*, his twenty-fifth work, was released in 1987.

The author whom a journalist once called "the man who writes with his ears"[1] has been *harnessed* to the "chose littéraire" for over thirty-five years. I use the word "harnessed" on purpose. If Pinget still chooses to refer to such images as "harness" and "plow," it is because rustic work constitutes for him the ideal metaphor. It emphasizes, in the context of perpetual motion, repeated each season, both the fundamental and the obtuse nature of the writer's task.

Since the publication of his first work in 1951, Pinget has kept dismantling the traditional narrative forms, creating a deliberately repetitive and indeed obsessive style. With a single-minded faithfulness he has untiringly listened and given a voice to the places and characters that have emerged from his fiction.[2] To speak in literature, whether it is theater or a novel, is first of all, for Pinget, to communicate a *tone*. "For me, the preliminary work consists in selecting among the many components of my [voice], the one I am interested in at the time," the author observed when urged to disclose his esthetic principles at the Colloque de Cerisy in 1971. "I then isolate and embody it until a character emerges, who becomes the narrator and with whom I identify."[3] The ear, Pinget added, "makes

1. The expression is by Didier Eribon commenting on *Monsieur Songe* in *Libération* (7 April 1982).

2. Tony Duvert sees in the novelist's "toponymic and patronymic apparatus" a "reserve," sort of a "fictional substance" from which the author derives new narrative resources. "La Parole et la fiction," *Critique* (May 1968): 443.

3. "Pseudo-principes d'esthétique," *Nouveau roman: hier, aujourd'hui*, vol. 2 (Paris: UGE, 10/18), 311.

97

tyrannical demands. . . . I am not interested in what is said or meant, but in the way it is said." . . .[4]

The reader of *Quelqu'un*, of *Libera* or of *Passacaille* soon realizes, however, that this "way to say things" which forms the subject of the novel is not as innocent as it first appears. In fact, it is the very heart of the fictional process which is at stake. As Tony Duvert has quite rightly pointed out,[5] Pinget first defines a narrative frame (with characters and events); he then organizes the variations of this fictional unit around the axis which supports the novel. From that moment on, the characters turn into more than "paper beings"; they are *performers* who, under a given name, play out the polymorphic characteristics of their "roles." There is not one plot, but several, and not one of them is more "true" or more plausible than another. Through the infinite multiplication of details, dialogue, and narrative accidents, fiction yields its full ludic potential. In Pinget, "the novel invents itself," as Robbe-Grillet put it.[6]

We now take for granted that the Nouveau Roman does not exist any more. The seven writers who belonged to it have gradually drifted away from the declamatory manifestos published, especially in the '60s, by such peremptory writers as Robbe-Grillet and Jean Ricardou. We have witnessed, for the past few years, the resurgence of a certain "humanism" once denigrated.[7] What appears to be a return to a more traditional literature, can be observed in many recent publications which are either autobiographical, or nearly so.[8] The political implications of such an itinerary still need to be assessed. They would show, among other things, that the "novelty" (or the "modernity" of the form) does not necessarily accompany a critical reevaluation of the ideological presuppositions behind every attempt to represent.[9]

In this respect, there is no doubt that Pinget's extremely inventive literary production, despite its relative conservatism, has never ceased serving as a vehicle for a fundamental idealism. This is clearly the case in his recent publications, particularly since *L'Apocryphe*,[10] where, without forsaking his characteristic tone, he keeps repeating the "essential" questions.

4. Ibid., 311–12.

5. Op. cit., especially 449 ff. See also, on *Passacaille*, F. Meyer's remarks in "Robert Pinget: le livre disséminé comme fiction, narration et objet," *Nouveau Roman: hier, aujourd'hui*, vol. 2, 299–310.

6. *Pour un nouveau roman* (Paris: Editions de Minuit, 1963), (on *Mahu ou le matériau*).

7. We borrow the term from B. Poirot-Delpech commenting on Robbe-Grillet's *Miroir qui revient*, *Le Monde* (19 January 1985).

8. Nathalie Sarraute published *Enfance* (Gallimard, 1983), Alain Robbe-Grillet *Le Miroir qui revient* (Editions de Minuit, 1985), Claude Ollier *Cahier d'écolier* (Flammarion, 1985). Claude Simon's latest novel (*Les Géorgiques*, Minuit, 1981) revives the themes of family and geneology.

9. The question has been debated. See, for instance, A. Robbe-Grillet, "Sur quelques notions périmées, l'engagement," in *Pour un nouveau roman*, 33 ff., which valorizes, against all forms of political thought, the novel "for nothing"; R. Jean, "Politique et nouveau roman," *Nouveau roman: hier, aujourd'hui*, vol. 1, 363–71; Jean Ricardou remains faithful to the definition of modernity as the abolition of "the ideological valorization of the reproduction of meaning," *Nouveaux problèmes du roman* (Paris: Seuil, 1978), 17 ff.

10. As far as I know, this text is Pinget's last novel translated into English.

"Not finished," the narrator declares in the opening scene of *Charrue*, "I'll come back to it."[11] It's a question of telling us, once again, a certain way of living literature, this fierce and inexplicable injunction to put things in writing only to be, later, often unhappy with it. To speak of "it," to show himself grappling with the old demons, is the only way Pinget can imagine writing his memoirs.[12] *Charrue* is in the form of notes, replies from his friend Mortin, bits of plots, mininovels imagined in a few lines, reflections and aphorisms. It is like a subtle "ars poetica" written with irony and feigned detachment. The author, who is the first to admit it, has, after all, never stopped being a "moraliste."[13] Pinget's latest books are sparer. They are mere props for a text composed of fragments. They reflect the effectively rarefying process the author has committed himself to—and which he discourages our commenting on: "to say that words or the practice of writing progressively lead the poet to silence," he says, "is to say that his breathing dwindles until his last breath. No need to paraphrase the obvious. As clever as all developments about this subject may be, they are futile."[14]

In *Testament bizarre* (1986), which directly follows *Charrue*,[15] Pinget attempts again to let "the broken machine or sign-trap"[16] formed by language speak inside him. A consenting prisoner of the drudgery of discourse and memory, he no longer resists a "circular, convoluted and regressive" narrative form (70). All narrative techniques fused, writing which has quite rightly been described as "perpetual reexamination" (71), is doomed to repeat: "The neverending . . . story . . . grabs memory and never lets go of it . . . in the paradise of endless repetitions . . . endless repetitions . . ." (64).

Here the question that underlies writing and the origin of all literary discourse does not extend beyond the narration of what is elsewhere simply called "fate." What word can adequately name the unnameable enterprise? "Whim or stuff and nonsense," the author replies (108). The "testament" ends with a few simple words in the form of questions ("You?," "To be alone?," "Literature?," "Fear?"). From the text's stammering syntax a final narrative emerges, the only conceivable one, when "nothing" and "end" become only one word: "Is he dying?" (103). Like Beckett, whom he here recalls in every way, Pinget keeps jogging down his literary path, pondering endlessly the unavoidable questions, which he calls ironically "the music of nothingness" (65).

"Holding the pen confers on the hand which has mastered it a 'semblance' of reality," (82) the author observes in *Charrue*. It is, again, around this "semblance" that the characters in Pinget's latest novel take their places: the master, his nephew, an old servant along with a few other familiar characters. As in his

11. *Charrue* (Paris: Minuit, 1985), 9.
12. *Charrue*, 27.
13. These are Pinget's own terms, at the very end of *Harnais*: "After reading a few pages of Monsieur Songe's diaries, his friend Mortin says to him after all you are a moralist. Monsieur Songe bursts out laughing and replies I wonder what could someone possibly be when he takes upon himself to write . . . at least in French" (58).
14. *Charrue*, 25.
15. According to Michèle Bernstein, the plays were written for a German radio station, prior to his latest novel ("Solitudes de l'innombrable Mortin," *Libération*, 23 January 1986).
16. *Un Testament bizarre* (Paris: Minuit, 1986), 63. Page numbers will henceforth be indicated in the text.

previous works, time, old age, a faulty memory are the *enemy* against which writing obstinately persists in designating, in an awkward and incomplete way, the major fable, a story impossible to tell, signalling from a distance to all Pinget's novels: part of an unsolvable crime, an impossible inquest, an unprovable guilt, an irrepressible urge to speak.

In the one hundred and forty-four sections, which most often never exceed one page, the narrative reiterates, with these characters, Pinget's favorite themes, yet with increasing detachment. The number of blank pages is multiplied, especially towards the end. Thus, Pinget emphasizes the ultimate stretching of the narrative matter which, henceforth, is merely the place to hallucinate the innumerable previous narratives of the past. The novel ends as it started, with the portrait of an ancestor, both a figure of death and of the obstinate presence of eternity. This portrait attests to the slow effacement of the narrative and the voice: at the end, it stands alone, his eyes fixed on the "now indiscernable workspace of his taciturn descendant."[17] Is that Pinget's last word?

Translated by Brigitte Szymanek

BIBLIOGRAPHY

I. Selected Works

Entre Fantoine et Agapa. Paris: Minuit, 1951, short stories.
Mahu ou le matériau. Paris: Minuit, 1952, novel.
Le Renard et la boussole. Paris: Minuit, 1953, novel.
Graal flibuste. Paris: Minuit, 1956, novel.
Baga. Paris: Minuit, 1958, novel.
Le Fiston. Paris: Minuit, 1959, novel.
Lettre morte. Paris: Minuit, 1959, two-act play.
La Manivelle. Paris: Minuit, 1960, radio play.
Clope au dossier. Paris: Minuit, 1961, novel.
Ici ou ailleurs, Architruc, L'Hypothèse. Paris: Minuit, 1961, theater.
L'Inquisitoire. Paris: Minuit, 1962, novel.
Autour de Mortin. Paris: Minuit, 1965, dialogues.
Quelqu'un. Paris: Minuit, 1965, novel.
Le Libera. Paris: Minuit, 1968, novel.
Passacaille. Paris: Minuit, 1969, novel.
Identité, followed by *Abel et Bela.* Paris: Minuit, 1971, theater.
Fable. Paris: Minuit, 1971, narrative.
Paralchimie, L'Hypothèse, Nuit. Paris: Minuit, 1973, theater.
Cette voix. Paris: Minuit, 1975, novel.
L'Apocryphe. Paris: Minuit, 1980, novel.
Monsieur Songe. Paris: Minuit, 1982, novel.
Le Harnais. Paris: Minuit, 1984, novel.
Charrue. Paris: Minuit, 1985, novel.

17. *L'Ennemi* (Paris: Minuit, 1987), 144.

Un Testament bizarre. Paris: Minuit, 1986, novel.
L'Ennemi. Paris: Minuit, 1987, novel.

II. Selected Criticism

La Revue des belles lettres. Geneva (1982).
The Review of Contemporary Fiction. 3, ed. Jack Kerouac, no. 2 (1983).
Critique (October 1987).

ROBERT PINGET

*Charrue**

○

A un jeune romancier qui s'évertue à camper, comme il dit, des personnages, monsieur Songe conseille en termes gracieux de décamper d'abord du sien. Apprendre à écrire c'est se mettre à l'école de l'humilité. Tout le temps après de jouer à l'auteur.

○

Le délayage journalistique le hérisse tellement qu'il ne peut plus lire que les manchettes des journaux et les gros titres. Son information s'en ressent et il le déplore. Il en est réduit par un dernier acquit de conscience à imaginer l'article ou le commentaire, quitte à se fourvoyer complètement et aboutir à des conclusions n'ayant rien à voir avec la réalité, ce qui fait pouffer son entourage. Mais il préfère ce ridicule-là à celui de s'efforcer d'emmagasiner des textes qui le rendent malade.

Mais il prévoit avec angoisse le moment où toute lecture aura cet effet. Qu'est-ce qu'il lui restera pour se meubler l'esprit? Son ami le rassure en lui disant le peu d'esprit qui te reste suffira à meubler ton silence.

Cette réponse abrupte sonne si bien à l'oreille du vieux . . . qu'il s'en méfie. Vaut-il pas mieux se détruire la santé à lire des délayages instructifs quoique nauséeux que de se réconforter à l'ouïe de formules élégantes mais captieuses?

Bref en attendant le silence il n'aura guère que la ressource de se rappeler ses lectures, seul mobilier de l'esprit. Jusqu'à ce qu'il n'ait plus qu'un tabouret à sa disposition.

*Charrue (Paris: Minuit, 1985), 20–39. This passage is reprinted with the kind permission of Editions de Minuit.

○

Attention de ne pas donner dans le genre précieux qui est le plus facile. Et si la facilité l'amuse? Qu'il se remette plutôt au jeu de l'oie.

Ou bien

A force de rechercher l'exercice offrant le plus de difficulté il perdrait le goût de noter quoi que ce soit. Ce ne serait préjudiciable à personne sauf au chat vaniteux qui dort dans sa cervelle.

○

Prendre la plume c'est déjà se guinder dans une attitude. Remède, le crayon. Ensuite la craie sur l'ardoise. Et finalement l'index dans la poussière. Un grand exemple de ce geste-là. Bien difficile à suivre.

○

Est-ce que l'ennui de devoir s'exprimer dépasse celui de devoir se taire? S'agirait d'être au pied du mur pour en juger, or ce ne peut être le même mur dans les deux cas.

Rien à voir avec le dilemme faut-il ou ne faut-il pas.

○

Il constate que l'emploi d'un certain style lui fait oublier son identité. Le ton familier a disparu au profit d'un discours désincarné qui se modèle sur un poncif. Rien de plus grave.

Qu'y faire? Recommencer.

Il se relit. Qui pouvait bien parler avec ce ton-là? Même si les propos lui paraissent justes il lui faudra les reprendre jusqu'à ce que sa personne en resurgisse. Elle lui échappe à chaque mot et cette refonte est une torture.

Ou bien.

Il se répète en poursuivant ses exercices que le personnage qu'il évoque doit être le même que celui qui écrit, ce qui implique un effort de synthèse où l'un des deux perdrait des plumes, mais lequel? A moins qu'un troisième ne les récupère, maigre profit, mais sous quelle identité?

Ou bien.

Il ne doit jamais perdre de vue qu'il lui faut avant de formuler quoi que ce soit imaginer ce que formulerait le personnage de son choix et s'en inspirer. Mais il ne se rappelle plus pourquoi.

Ou bien.

Dieu que mon personnage m'assomme, qu'il gémit. Dire qu'il me faut l'ausculter jusqu'à ce que mort s'ensuive . . . Qui me l'impose? Un autre qui se cache derrière le mien et se vengerait de ma défection en en suscitant trois ou quatre de plus à ausculter, dépecer, disséquer jusqu'à ma damnation.

Ou bien.

Il se demande si à force de se questionner il ne finit pas par entendre les réposes d'un étranger. Si oui, quelle aubaine.

○

Dire que les mots, la pratique de l'écriture conduisent peu à peu le poète au silence c'est dire que sa respiration décline jusqu'à son dernier souffle. L'évidence ne requiert aucune paraphrase. Aussi savants que soient les développements sur ce thème ils sont vains.

○

Bien qu'il se félicite de n'avoir plus rien à dire il a de petits moments de regret, oh très brefs, relatifs à sa faculté passée de raconter drôlement les choses. Mais comme il n'aurait plus aujourd'hui personne à qui les raconter il rend grâce à la nature d'avoir fait coïncider sa déficience avec sa solitude.

○

Si la fatigue ne résultait que du travail il renoncerait à travailler. Mais elle provient aussi de l'inaction, qui lui est beaucoup plus douce.

○

Il demande à son ami vaudrait-il pas mieux éliminer toute tristesse de mes notes et n'en prendre que de gaies? L'autre répond question naïve, pour un maniaque comme toi la tristesse ne peut s'éliminer qu'à condition d'être notée, sinon aucune gaieté possible.

○

Un auteur lui dit même si la clique des critiques considérait que je décline en écrivant mes mémoires au lieu de récits ambitieux je m'en foutrais. Le progrès pour moi n'exige plus de continuer à plaire mais de me plaire à continuer.

Monsieur Songe juge la formule un peu spécieuse et la corrige en disant continuer c'est progresser à votre manière, non à celle d'autrui.

Et il ajoute, mais in petto, chacun prend son progrès où il le trouve.

○

L'art de dire. Beau casse-tête. Il y en a autant que de bons auteurs. Qu'est-ce qu'un bon auteur? Pas de recette pour le devenir. Ça doit réconforter pas mal de médiocres prétentieux.

Ou bien.

Tous ces pauvres gens de nos jours qui se mettent à écrire, que de désillusions les attendent.

Ou bien.

Untel fut un grand écrivain paraît-il. Comme le temps passe.

○

Une enquiquineuse lui dit oh une petite description seulement puisque vous prétendez n'imaginer plus rien, une toute petite description à publier dans notre journal, cher ami. Ce serait une grande faveur, nous devons élargir notre public, ne pas négliger les choses de l'esprit, et vous aviez un si joli tour dans vos billets d'autrefois.

Il répond je ne vois pas ce que je pourrais bien décrire, je ne quitte ma chambre qui m'ennuie que pour mon jardin où il ne pousse rien. Vraiment non je ne vois pas.

Elle reprend mais si mais si, une toute petite chose, n'importe, une gravure, une tabatière, que sais-je, trente lignes pas davantage, ce serait si gentil, j'insiste, vous devez ça à notre cher quotidien.

Pour se venger de la fâcheuse monsieur Songe une fois chez lui prend une feuille et décrit minutieusement son pot de chambre. D'abord vide, puis plein. Deux paragraphes qu'il envoie à la chère collaboratrice.

Ni accusé de réception ni publication.

○

La seule façon d'être connu dit-il est de se faire connaître. Aux ambitieux incapables d'un éclat, d'une parade, reste le recours de continuer à faire peu de bruit, avec acharnement, jusqu'au dégoût. Ils seront entendus.

Et aussi.

Qu'il soit impossible de rien dire de neuf n'effraie que les imbéciles. Et aussi.

Si on demandait à monsieur Songe pourquoi écrivez-vous il répondrait de quoi je me mêle. Et s'il se le demandait? Même réponse.

○

Il décide, n'ayant plus rien à perdre, d'utiliser sur ses vieux jours des expressions anciennes ou régionales qui lui sont familières.

D'une personne qui manque d'appétit il dira elle n'a pas plus faim que le pain. D'une autre qui est difficile à vivre, elle nous fait endêver. D'une situation pénible dont on ne sait comment se sortir, c'est la charrue à chien. De quelqu'un qui ne tient pas ses promesses, c'est un donneur de bonjours. D'une chose mal définie, ça n'est ni chou ni rave. D'une femme bête, c'est une saume. D'un goulu, c'est un béni-bouffe-tout. D'un fastueux repas, c'est un balthazar. D'un mets sans saveur, il n'a ni goût ni moût. D'une froide journée, les mouches ne tirent pas la langue. D'une proposition agréable, d'un cadeau inespéré, on l'accepte avec les quatre doigts et le pouce. D'un ivrogne, il se pique la ruche. D'une bonne chose à ne pas gaspiller, n'en pas perdre une farfalle.

Et cætera.

○

Il tombe parfois sur tel passage de ce qu'il appelle ses mémoires et y trouve des fautes si grossières qu'il se désole.

Son ami tâche alors de le réconforter et lui cite quelques inattentions d'auteurs célèbres. Il pousse la délicatesse jusqu'à prétendre que l'amour de la langue, attribut des poètes, n'a que faire de l'orthographe, de la syntaxe ni de tout le reste, inspiré qu'il est par un démon qui porte bien son nom.

Mais ce raisonnement qui frise l'absurde ne convainc ni le mémorialiste ni même l'ami consolateur.

○

L'art se fout des idées. En littérature il joue avec les mots, avec leur ordonnance et s'appelle alors poésie. Le roman de nos jours ne peut y atteindre qu'en se coupant du romanesque. Mais que de discipline, de métier et d'endurance cela implique.

Et aussi.

Le souci de l'effet est une faiblesse en art. On n'y doit tendre qu'à une vérité . . . sans trop savoir où elle se cache car elle vous oblige à mentir. Epuisante recherche.

Et aussi.

Progrès scientifique, progrès technique, progrès hygiénique, génétique, et cætera. Or l'art lui ne progresse pas, n'a jamais progressé et ne progressera jamais et pourtant propose depuis que le monde est monde des œuvres aussi diverses que parfaites.

Et aussi.

Il faut beaucoup de technique pour savoir s'en débarrasser. Vieux poncif.

○

Note roman.

Bien sûr qu'à la vue d'une belle chose monsieur Songe aurait encore la tentation d'en faire le point d'envol d'une description imaginaire qui à son tour donnerait naissance à une fable laquelle peu à peu s'étoffant de comparaisons, de récurrences, de contradictions et de divagations multipliées deviendrait finalement ce que faute de mieux il appellerait un roman, mais se sachant d'avance vaincu par le foisonnement des possibles il préfère au coin du feu rêvasser d'un problématique ouvrage où ses aspirations d'antan triompheraient de sa nonchalance.

Belle phrase. Sauf son ridicule.

○

Entamé la dernière étape de son parcours. Accepté de n'être plus l'objet des séductions de la fable. Qu'est-ce qu'il lui reste à tenter? Ne lui dites pas que le réel séduise.

○

Qui se venge du désamour de la vie en la faisant durer? Question malséante. Etrange qu'un certain agencement des mots fasse surgir un sens auquel on ne s'attendait pas.

Ou bien.

Avec trois mots pris au hasard on peut, le métier aidant, trouver une idée sûre.

○

Il craint à juste titre de ne plus dire dans ses notes que des choses touchantes ou fadasses. Faut-il continuer? Il sait bien que oui, il le faut, sans goût, sans but, dans le dénuement de tout sauf du réconfort dérisoire, incompréhensible, qui consiste à se le demander.

Et aussi.

Crever d'ennui à cette analyse inutile pour ne pas crever de regret de l'avoir écartée, avoue que ce n'est pas une vie dit-il à son ami. Et puis il constate que l'ami est absent. Où est-il? Où es-tu mon soutien, ma sauvegarde?

Cette dernière question il la juge irrecevable. Le pathétique n'est pas de son ressort. Alors pourquoi ne pas la biffer?

○

Il note un soir avant de s'endormir voir amour du prochain. Et le lendemain voulant développer il ne sait plus ni pourquoi ni comment.

○

Juin ses fleurs ses grillons ses parfums. Refrain qui revient chaque année à son heure. Peu après, iris églantine et sureau. Et plus tard un autre refrain. Et plus tard un autre et un autre jusqu'au déclin de l'année.

Ce qui fait dire au vieux eh bien si la décrépitude ne m'épargne pas et qu'un jour je ne voie ni n'entende plus rien j'aurai mes refrains pour compagnie et me tenir lieu de réconfort et de saisons.

○

Note roman.

S'il devait s'imaginer personnage de roman comment monsieur Songe se verrait-il? Vieux mais sans âge défini. Parfois barbu, parfois glabre. Le cheveu rare et argenté mais propre. Il va régulièrement chez le coiffeur. Parler des séances de coiffeur, de l'atmosphère de la boutique. Deux clients tout au plus. Odeur d'eau de Cologne qui ne domine pas celle de graillon venant de la cuisine attenante. Le patron ou l'apprenti en referme continuellement la porte qui s'ouvre par les courants d'air. On entend la femme du coiffeur parler toute seule dans sa cuisine ou à l'étage. Le patron en plaisante avec ses clients ou s'irrite.

Et cætera.

Et est-ce que dans la rue il se tient droit ou légèrement voûté? Est-ce qu'il a une canne? Est-ce qu'il tousse et s'arrête pour cracher?

Et est-ce qu'il parle volontiers aux commerçants? Ça c'est selon. Il a des aversions. Et des mouvements de sympathie imprévisibles.

Et cætera.

Et est-ce que . . .

La barbe.

○

Un matin de juillet bleu et or, assis dans son jardin parmi les fleurettes le vieux qui perd un peu la fiole se croit au paradis.

Plus tard sa lucidité reconquise lui tient lieu, à regret, de miracle.

○

Il devrait se forcer à noter sur-le-champ ce qui lui vient encore à l'esprit pour ne pas éprouver le plaisir de l'avoir oublié quelques minutes après, tant il est convaincu qu'on ne fait rien de bon sans déplaisir.

Savoir seulement s'il lui reste quelque chose à faire.

○

Il lui semble que le dégoût de soi-même n'est pas l'indice d'une haute moralité mais d'une faiblesse de caractère.

○

Plow

To a young novelist who is struggling to, as he puts it, flesh out his characters, Mr. Dream amiably advises that he first flush out his own. Learning to write means schooling yourself in humility. Plenty of time later to play author.

He finds journalistic blather so irritating that he can't read anything except the headlines anymore. As a result, the general state of his knowledge is suffering, a fact he deplores. In order to ease his conscience, he has been reduced to imagining the article or commentary, though it sometimes means he goes completely off the track and arrives at conclusions that have nothing to do with reality. While this makes those around him snigger, he prefers this kind of ridicule to going to the effort of stockpiling texts that make him sick.

Still he foresees with anguish the moment when all reading will have this effect. What will he fill his mind with then? His friend reassures him saying the little mind you have left will be quite enough to fill your silence.

This abrupt answer sounds so good to the old man . . . that he distrusts it. Isn't it better to ruin your health reading instructive if nauseating blather than to fortify yourself on elegant but specious formulae?

In short, while he awaits the silence, virtually his only recourse will be to recall his readings, sole baggage of his mind. Until he has nothing left but a footstool at his disposal.

Be careful not to lapse into the affected style which is the most facile. And if facility amuses him? Then let him go back to playing snakes and ladders instead.

Or else.

By seeking the exercise that offers the most difficulty he may lose his taste for noting down anything at all. This would not be detrimental to anyone but the conceited cat that is sleeping in his brain.

To pick up a pen is already to adopt a stilted attitude. Solution, a pencil. Then chalk on a slate. And finally a finger in the dust. A great example of that gesture. Very hard to follow.

Is the tediousness of having to express yourself greater than that of having to keep quiet? You'd have to have your back to the wall in order to say for sure, though it can't be the same wall in both cases.

Nothing to do with the dilemma should one or shouldn't one.

He notes that the use of a certain style makes him forget his identity. The familiar tone has given way to a disembodied discourse modeled on a cliché. Nothing more serious.

What to do about it? Begin again.

He rereads himself. Who could possibly be speaking in that tone? Even if the words seem right to him he must repeat them over and over until his personality reemerges. It escapes him with every word and this constant overhaul is torture.

Or else.

He repeats to himself, continuing his practice, that the character he evokes should be the same as the one who is writing, which implies an effort of synthesis whereby one of the two must lose out, but which one? Unless a third party were to bring them into line, meager profit, but under what identity?

Or else.

He must never lose sight of the fact that before formulating *anything* he first has to imagine what the character of his choice would formulate and draw his inspiration from that. But he no longer remembers why.

Or else.

God how my character bores me, how he moans and groans. And to think that I must diagnose him to death. . . . Who is making me do it? Someone else who is hiding behind my own and who would pay me back for my defection by creating three or four more for me to diagnose, dismember, dissect, until I'm damned in Hell.

Or else.

He wonders if by questioning himself like this he won't end up hearing a stranger's answers. If so, what good fortune.

To say that words, the practice of writing, lead the poet little by little to silence is like saying that his breathing gets shallower and shallower until his last breath. Evidence requires no paraphrase. However clever the variations on this theme may be, they are pointless.

Although he congratulates himself on no longer having anything to say, he occasionally has moments of regret, oh so brief, relating to his past ability to recount things humorously. But since today he no longer has anybody to recount them to he gives thanks to nature for having made his failure coincide with his solitude.

If fatigue only resulted from work he would give up working. But it also comes from inaction, from which he derives far more pleasure.

He asks his friend wouldn't it be better to eliminate all sadness from my notes and only make cheerful ones? The other answers naive question, for a fanatic like you sadness can only be eliminated by being noted, otherwise no possibility of cheerfulness.

An author says to him even if the gang of critics deemed that by writing my memoirs instead of ambitious tales I am going downhill I wouldn't give a damn. For me, progress no longer requires me to continue to please, just to please myself by continuing.

Mr. Dream judges the phrase a little specious and corrects it saying to continue is to progress in your own way, not in another's.

And he adds, but in petto, everyone makes his progress where he can.

The art of saying. Nice brain-racking task. There are as many of these as there are good authors. What is a good author? No recipe for becoming one. That should comfort not a few pretentious second-raters.

Or else.

All these poor folk nowadays setting out to write, what disillusionments await them.

Or else.

So-and-so was a great writer it seems. How time passes!

A real pain in the neck of a woman pesters him saying oh just one little description since you say you can't imagine anything anymore, one teeny little description to publish in our paper, oh please. You'd be doing us such a huge favor, we need to expand our audience, not overlook matters of the mind, and you used to have such a nice way of putting things.

He answers I don't see what I could very well describe, I only leave my room which bores me in order to go into my garden where nothing grows. Really no I don't see.

She carries on but yes but yes, one teeny little thing, anything, an etching, a snuffbox, I don't know, thirty lines at the most, it would be *so* kind of you, *please* I insist, you owe our little paper that much.

In order to get even with the tiresome woman, Mr. Dream, back at home, takes a sheet of paper and meticulously describes his chamberpot. First empty, then full. Two paragraphs that he sends to the dear lady contributor.

Neither return receipt nor publication.

The only way to be known he says is to make oneself known. Those ambitious people who are incapable of making a splash or a spectacle have only one recourse—to continue relentlessly to be very quiet, ad nauseam. They will be heard.

And also.

That it's impossible to say anything new only scares off idiots.

And also.

If *you* were to ask Mr. Dream why do you write he would answer what business is it of *yours*. And if he asked *himself*? Same answer.

He decides, having nothing left to lose, to use in his twilight years some archaic or regional expressions that he knows.

Of a person who has no appetite he'll say he hasn't got room for another bite. Of another who is hard to live with, he gets our goat. Of a tough situation one doesn't know how to get out of, it's the pits. Of someone who doesn't keep his promises, he's a regard-sender. Of an ill-defined thing, it's neither here nor there. Of a stupid woman, what a dumb bunny. Of a glutton, he's Mr. Greedy-Guts. Of a sumptuous meal, it's a Lucullan feast. Of a flavorless dish, it's as bland as sand. Of a cold day, it's too cold to spit. Of a pleasing proposal or an unexpected gift, one welcomes it with open arms. Of a drunkard, he's stewed to the gills. Of a good thing not to be wasted, don't lose a drop of it.

Et cetera.

Once in a while he comes across a passage of what he calls his memoirs and he gets all upset over the glaring mistakes he finds there.

Then his friend tries to comfort him, citing several famous authors' oversights. He is even so thoughtful as to proclaim that the love of language, proper to poets, has no need of spelling, grammar, and all the rest, inspired as it is by that special and fitting genius.

But this reasoning which borders on the absurd convinces neither the memoir writer nor the consoling friend.

Art doesn't give a damn about ideas. In literature it plays with words, with their order and then calls itself poetry. The novel these days can only achieve this by abandoning the novelistic. But what discipline, what skill and endurance *that* entails.

And also.

Caring about the effect is a weakness in art. One should only strive for truth . . . without ever really knowing where it is hidden since it forces you to tell lies. Exhausting search.

And also.

Scientific progress, technical progress, hygienic progress, genetic, et cetera. Now, *art* does not progress, has never progressed, will never progress and yet has since time immemorial brought forth works as diverse as they are perfect.

And also.

You have to have plenty of technique in order to be able to get rid of it. Old cliché.

Note on the novel.

Of course at the sight of a beautiful thing Mr. Dream would still be tempted to launch into an imaginative description which in turn would give rise to a fable which gradually filled out with comparisons, recurrences, contradictions, and increasing ramblings would finally become what he would call, for lack of a better term, a novel, but knowing himself to be defeated in advance by the burgeoning possibilities he prefers to daydream by the fireside about a problematic work in which his earlier aspirations would triumph over his nonchalance.

Nice sentence. Except its ridiculousness.

Having started the final leg of his journey. Having accepted no longer to be the object of the fable's seductions. What is there left for him to try? Don't tell him that the real seduces.

Who takes revenge for the unlove of life by making it last? Improper question. Strange that a certain arrangement of words produces a meaning one didn't expect.

Or else.

Given three words chosen at random one can, with enough expertise, come up with a sound idea.

He understandably fears no longer saying anything in his notes that isn't touching or insipid. Must he continue? He knows that yes, he must, without desire, without purpose, in the deprivation of everything except the derisory, incomprehensible comfort, which consists in wondering about it.

And also.

To die of boredom engaged in this useless analysis in order not to die of regret at having avoided it, admit that that's no life he says to his friend. And then he realizes that the friend is gone. Where is he? Where are you my rock and my salvation?

This last question he judges unacceptable. Pathos is not in his repertoire. So why not cross it out?

One night before falling asleep he notes see love of fellow man. And the next day wanting to develop it he no longer knows why or how.

June its flowers its crickets its perfumes. Refrain that returns every year in its time. Shortly after, iris wild rose and elderberry. And later another refrain. And later another and another until the close of the year.

Which makes the old man say well then if decrepitude doesn't spare me and one day I can't see or hear anything anymore my refrains will keep me company and take the place of comfort and seasons.

Note on the novel.

If he had to imagine himself a character in a novel how would Mr. Dream see himself? Old but of no particular age. Sometimes bearded, sometimes clean-shaven. Hair thin and silvery but clean. He goes to the barber regularly. Tell about his visits to the barber, the atmosphere in the shop. Two customers at the most. Scent of eau de cologne that doesn't cover up the burnt fat smell coming from the adjoining kitchen. The owner or his helper keeps closing the door that the wind keeps opening. You can hear the barber's wife talking to herself in her kitchen or on the landing. The owner jokes about it with his customers or he gets annoyed.

Et cetera.

And in the street does he stand up straight or is he slightly hunched over? Does he have a cane? Does he cough and stop to spit?

And does he talk freely with shopkeepers? That depends. He has certain aversions. And surprising bursts of sympathy.

Et cetera.

And does he . . .

Nuts.

On a blue and gold July morning, sitting in his garden among daisies the old man who's getting a little batty thinks he's in heaven.

Later his regained lucidity regrettably assumes the character of a miracle.

He must force himself to note down right away anything that still comes into his head in order not to experience the pleasure of having forgotten it a few minutes later, so convinced is he that one doesn't do anything worthwhile without displeasure.

If only he could know whether there is still something for him to do.

It seems to him that disgust with himself is not a sign of high moral standards but only of weakness of character.

TRANSLATED BY KAREN MCPHERSON

CHRISTOPHER RIVERS

Michel Tournier

Michel Tournier was born in Paris in 1924. After studying philosophy at the Sorbonne during World War II, he spent four years at the University of Tübingen. In 1950, upon his return to France, he failed the *agrégation* in philosophy and abandoned hopes of an academic career. In the years that followed, Tournier worked as a translator for the publishing firm Plon and, later, as a radio announcer for Radiodiffusion nationale and Europe 1. In the meantime, he continued to attempt to write a *roman philosophique,* a form through which he could express philosophical preoccupations within the traditional form of the novel. His first novel, *Vendredi ou les limbes du Pacifique,* was published in 1967 by Gallimard and met with critical and popular acclaim. It was awarded the *Grand Prix du Roman* by the Académie Française the same year. In 1970, Tournier published *Le Roi des Aulnes,* which received the Prix Goncourt, paving the way for Tournier's own election to the Académie Goncourt in 1972. Since then, Tournier has continued to publish novels and other writings with unusual regularity: *Les Météores* in 1975, *Le Vent Paraclet* (an autobiography *cum* literary manifesto) in 1977, *Le Coq de bruyère* (short stories) in 1978, *Gaspard, Melchior et Balthazar* in 1980, *Le Vol du vampire* (literary essays) in 1981, *Gilles et Jeanne* in 1983, *Le Vagabond immobile* in 1984 and, most recently, *La Goutte d'or* in 1986. In addition to this prodigious *oeuvre.* Tournier has also published a number of books for children and volumes of commentary on photography. He is frequently interviewed in the French press and on television and has established a somewhat notorious persona through his provocative on-the-record personal statements as well as the equally provocative content of his novels. Despite (or perhaps as a result of) the controversy he has created, Tournier's work is widely read and has been translated into more than twenty languages. He currently lives in a renovated parsonage in the Chevreuse valley, near Paris.

Michel Tournier is among the best known and most controversial contemporary French novelists. Both his work and his public persona have aroused suspicion, hostility, envy, admiration, adoration, factionalism, curiosity, and debate. It would not be inaccurate to describe Michel Tournier as a writer with something to offend everyone, some of the offense being taken at his form, some at his content. And yet he is widely read and discussed. The case of Tournier is thus a particularly intriguing one from the standpoint of its reception. It is also a unique

115

case for literary history, representing at once a return to traditional form in the novel and a subversion of this traditionalism by the bizarre content of the novels.

As a means of introduction, however, it would be useful to give a brief summary of Tournier's major works. His first novel, *Vendredi, ou les limbes du Pacifique*, is a retelling of Defoe's *Robinson Crusoe* as an odd kind of *mise-en-scène* of some of the highlights of Western philosophy. Tournier uses Robinson's solitude and the inevitable interior monologues which result from it as a means for expounding some of his favorite philosophical systems. While it is certainly quite possible to read *Vendredi* without being aware of the specific allusions to philosophy, it is not possible to escape the philosophical (detractors might say pseudophilosophical) content of the novel. *Vendredi's* conceptual agenda is inseparable from its "plot."

Le Roi des Aulnes, Tournier's second novel, shares its title with the French translation of Goethe's poem "Der Erlkönig." It is, like *Vendredi*, a sort of retelling of a preexisting text or "myth," in Tournier's terms. In this case, the driving force on both thematic and narrative levels is that of a powerful, obsessive image: a man carrying a child on his shoulders. The principal character, Abel Tiffauges, is a grotesque, gigantic auto mechanic living in Paris just before World War II. His is, to say the least, an unusual mentality, comprised of two basic components: firstly, an obsessive desire for experiences of "phorie" (from the Greek "to carry"), a unique, nongenital erotic experience he derives from carrying children on his shoulders and, secondly, his insistence on interpreting his own existence as an essential, predetermined myth of sorts through an elaborate system of perceived "signs." It is only in Fascist Germany that Abel blossoms into a sort of perverse selfhood (a fact which is understandably objectionable to many readers), but his final act, the ultimate "phorie," is to carry a Jewish boy to safety away from the Nazis. This signifies a reversal, a movement from the malevolent pole of "phorie" as represented by Goethe's "Erlkönig" and the notorious infanticide Bluebeard to the benevolent pole as represented by the legend of Saint Christopher.

Tournier's third novel, *Les Météores*, is the story of twin brothers whose twinship is so "perfect" that they seem to constitute a single entity. The twins represent the ideal coupling of an incestuous homosexual bond which rejects all otherness. This "perfect" relationship does not maintain its requisite stasis, however, as one of the twins, Jean, eventually feels the need to explore life outside the womb. The rest of the novel recounts Paul's global pursuit of Jean, finally ending in an accident in a tunnel joining the two halves of Berlin which results in Paul's loss of an arm and a leg.

If these first and most commented of Tournier's novels can be said to form a sort of thematic and formal trilogy (as William Cloonan has remarked in the only book-length study of Tournier published to date), it is probably because of the odd contiguity of narrating and philosophizing in each of them. This is also perhaps their most striking characteristic. On the thematic level, this is effected through the juxtaposition of rambling introspection and picaresque, often grotesque adventures of the principal characters. These characters share another significant quality: a maniacal desire for order, for systems of interpretation, for explanation of their experience. They are obsessive theorizers. In direct contradiction to what he explicitly states as his philosophy of literature and the act of reading (in *Le*

Vent Paraclet and *Le Vol du vampire*), Tournier hemself enacts a constant process of interpretation of his text within his text. This phenomenon is frequently achieved with the help of the intertextual "myths" that form a basis for many of his novels. Many associations or references that, if left implicit, would normally provide at least a basis for a second-degree reading, a reader's own extratextual interpretation, are made explicit in Tournier's text itself, thus limiting the reader's ability to create his own system for interpreting the plot of the novel. The compulsion of Tournier's characters to perform literary self-analyses, in fact to interpret their own lives as if they were texts (and this at some length), can be both fascinating and frustrating for a would-be critic of his novels. This is not to say that it is impossible to comment or analyze them; it is rather to say that one of the most common tasks of literary analysis, that of reading textual signs as allusions either to other texts or to metaphysical concepts, has usually already been effected within the novel itself. Thus, the reader is forced to abandon his habitual practice of digging in and around the text and must instead rise above the text in order to be able to discern the play between narrative and its intratextual explication. To analyze Tournier's works, one is virtually obliged to perform a metainterpretation: one's own interpretation of the novel's interpretation of itself. It is perhaps this convolution of the act of reading that renders Tournier's work abhorent to some readers and fascinating to others; it is undeniably provocative.

An equally provocative quality of Tournier's novels lies in the seeming contradiction they embody. Seen in its most basic terms, this contradiction is simple; traditional form VS scandalous content. The narrative form of the novels incorporates various nineteenth-century paradigms, and is characterized by elaborate description, character development, and more or less linear narrative. From a purely formal standpoint, one could easily justify a classification of Tournier's work as a return to traditionalism, to the pre-Nouveau Roman. One might logically conclude from this that Tournier would thus be championed by the more "conservative" readers of French literature. This, however, is far from accurate, as many readers (and perhaps particularly the more traditionally minded ones) are repelled from potentially palatable form by offensive and bizarre content. Tournier's use of vivid, detailed, neonaturalist description technique to provide readers with memorable images of coprophilia, scatology, necrophilia, pedophila, vampirism, nazism, bestiality, incest, and garbage (to name but a few favorite themes) is a literary gesture not appreciated by all readers. Among those who might not be offended by such content are many who are instead equally offended by his use of "reactionary" literary devices such as plot and description. In the neo-*querelle des anciens et des modernes* that implicitly dominates many academic and literary circles, Tournier is often unacceptable to both sides. Tournier himself clearly defines his agenda in this statement from the autobiographical *Vent Paraclet:* "Mon propos n'est pas d'innover dans la forme, mais de faire passer au contraire dans une forme aussi traditionelle, préservée et rassurante que possible une matière ne possédant aucune de ces qualités." [My intention is not to innovate on the level of form, but on the contrary, to pass off, in as traditional, preserved, and reassuring a form as possible, a content which possesses none of those qualities.] To admit to admiring Tournier is to be suspected of being either a pervert, a literary reactionary, or both. The very controversy stirred up by his work, and the fundamental nature of the questions it provokes, is cause enough to assure Tournier a unique and significant place among contemporary French novelists.

If Tournier's first three novels can be seen as constituting a sort of trilogy in both form and content, his most recent, *La Goutte d'or* (1986), seems to be a return to analogous concerns. Although it is a shorter, less dense book told strictly from a third-person omniscient point of view, it shares with the others a tendency towards elaborate description, vivid and bizarre imagery, and a definite conceptual agenda. *La Goutte d'or* is the story of Idriss, a fifteen-year-old North African shepherd whose life is changed by a chance encounter with a camera-toting French couple in a Land Rover. They take his picture, and promise to send it to him. Although it never arrives, the very idea of its existence (to a boy raised with an Islamic mistrust of representations of the human form) suffices to lead him to Paris in search of the photograph. This quest for an image is of course not restricted to a sole photograph and, in typical Tournier fashion, becomes an exploration for, and of, the image. This theme of enslavement to images, already at play in the other novels, is both *mise-en-scène* through a series of picaresque adventures and explicitly presented in a passage near the end of the novel theorizing about the essential differences between the image as it exists in Western culture and the tradition of Arabic calligraphy. This passage opposes images and signs, thereby crystallizing one of the most persistent of Tournier's theoretical concerns. In *La Goutte d'or*, Tournier seems to have achieved a somewhat happier balance between plot and metaphysics than in the earlier novels and the result is a novel which maintains his philosophical preoccupations within the confines of an engaging and readable narrative. The following excerpt comes from the beginning of the novel, before Idriss leaves the desert. It includes what might be called the primal scene of the novel, in which Idriss has his first, fateful encounter with the West and its culture of images. As it also includes some bizarre and bloody imagery of its own that is exemplary of Tournier, the excerpt is a brief but significant sample of Tournier's work.

BIBLIOGRAPHY

I. Selected Works

Vendredi, ou les limbes du Pacifique. Paris: Gallimard, 1967, novel.
Le Roi des Aulnes. Paris: Gallimard, 1970, novel.
Les Météores. Paris: Gallimard, 1974, novel.
Le Vent Paraclet. Paris: Gallimard, 1977, essays.
Le Coq de bruyère. Paris: Gallimard, 1978, novel.
Gaspard, Melchior et Balthazar. Paris: Gallimard, 1980, novel.
Le Vol du vampire. Paris: Mercure de France, 1981, essays.
Gilles et Jeanne. Paris: Gallimard, 1983, novel.
La Goutte d'or. Paris: Gallimard, 1986, novel.

II. Selected Criticism

Bevan, David G. "Tournier's Photographer: A Modern Bluebeard?," *Modern Language Studies* 15, no. 3 (1985): 66–71.

Bougnoux, Daniel. "Des Métaphores à la phorie," *Critique* 28 (1972): 527–43.

Cloonan, William. "The Artist, Conscious and Unconscious, in *Le Roi des Aulnes*," *Kentucky Romance Quarterly* 29, no. 2 (1982): 191–200.

———. *Michel Tournier*. Boston: Twayne Publishers, 1985.

———. "The Spiritual Order of Michel Tournier," *Renascence* 36, no. 1–2 (1983–84): 77–86.

Deleuze, Gilles. "Michel Tournier et le monde sans autrui," In *Logique du sens*. Paris: Minuit, 1969.

Hayman, Ronald. "A Grand Scale: Ronald Hayman talks to Michel Tournier," *Literary Review* 67 (1984): 40–41.

Hueston, Penny. "An Interview with Michel Tournier," *Meanjin Quarterly* 38, no. 3 (1979): 400–05.

Magazine littéraire 138 (1978): 10–24. "Dossier sur Michel Tournier," 226 (1986): 12–37.

Shattuck, Roger. "Locating Michel Tournier," in *The Innocent Eye: On Modern Literature and the Arts*. New York: Farrar, Strauss, Giroux, 1984, 205–18.

Sud. Special Issue (1980). "Michel Tournier."

White, J. J. "Signs of disturbance: the semiological import of some recent fiction by Michel Tournier and Peter Handke," *Journal of European Fiction* 4, no. 3 (1974): 233–54.

Worton, Michael J. "Myth-Reference in *Le Roi des Aulnes*," *Stanford French Review* 6, no. 2–3 (1982): 299–310.

York, R. A. "Thematic Construction in *Le Roi des Aulnes*," *Orbis Litterarum* 36, no. 1 (1981): 76–81.

MICHEL TOURNIER

La Goutte d'or*

Où était Ibrahim? Sans doute avait-il accompagné ses chameaux vers une pâture éloignée, surgie en quelques heures à la faveur d'un orage? Idriss chercha sa trace autour de l'arbre, mais la terre était criblée d'empreintes qui mêlaient les larges soles des chameaux aux petits trous des sabots des chèvres et des moutons. Il décrivit alors un arc de cercle en s'éloignant du puits pour tenter de découvrir un indice sur la direction prise par le Chaamba. Il releva au passage la traînée irrégulière laissée par un varan, les minuscules étoiles trahissant le sautillement d'une gerboise, la trace triangulaire assez ancienne d'un fennec au galop. Il contourna un bloc de basalte dont la noirceur tranchait sur le reg de plus en plus éblouissant à mesure que le soleil montait à l'horizon. Et c'est alors qu'il découvrit une empreinte d'un intérêt si puissant qu'à l'instant le vide se fit dans son esprit. Il ne pensa plus ni à Ibrahim, ni à ses chameaux, ni à son propre troupeau. Seuls existaient ces deux rubans finement crénelés qui creusaient de faibles ornières dans la terre blanche, visibles jusqu'à l'infini. Une voiture, une automobile, dont personne n'avait parlé dans l'oasis, surgissait de la nuit avec sa charge de richesses matérielles et de mystère humain! Idriss, suffoquant d'excitation, se lança sur la trace du véhicule qui fuyait vers l'ouest.

Le soleil flambait en plein ciel quand il aperçut dans le tremblement de la terre surchauffée, glissant sur un boqueteau de tamaris, la silhouette pataude d'une Land Rover. Elle ne roulait pas très vite, mais Idriss n'avait aucune chance de la rattraper. D'ailleurs il n'y songeait pas. Cloué par l'étonnement et la timidité, il s'arrêta, bientôt entouré par ses moutons et ses chèvres. La Land Rover, braquant vers le nord, s'engageait maintenant sur la piste de Béni Abbès. Dans cinq minutes, elle serait hors de vue. Non. Elle ralentissait. Elle amorçait un demi-tour. Elle reprenait de la

---

*La Goutte d'or (Paris: Gallimard, 1986), 14–24. This passage is reprinted with the kind permission of Gallimard.

vitesse et fonçait droit sur lui. Il y avait deux personnes à bord, un homme au volant et à côté de lui une femme dont Idriss ne distingua d'abord que les cheveux blonds et les grosses lunettes noires. La voiture stoppa. La femme retira ses lunettes et sauta à terre. Ses cheveux flottaient en nappe décolorée sur ses épaules. Elle portait une chemisette kaki très échancrée et un short outrageusement court. Idriss remarqua aussi ses ballerines dorées et pensa qu'elle n'irait pas loin avec ça dans la pierraille environnante. Elle brandissait un appareil de photo.

—Hé petit! Ne bouge pas trop, je vais te photographier.

—Tu pourrais au moins lui demander son avis, grommela l'homme. Il y en a qui n'aiment pas ça.

—C'est bien à vous de le dire! remarqua la femme.

Idriss prêtait l'oreille et rassemblait les bribes de français qu'il possédait pour comprendre ce qui se disait. Visiblement il faisait l'objet d'une discussion entre l'homme et la femme, mais c'était la femme qui s'intéressait à lui, cela surtout le troublait.

—Ne te fais pas d'illusions, ironisa l'homme, il regarde beaucoup plus la voiture que toi!

C'est vrai qu'elle était imposante, cette voiture, trapue et blanche de poussière, hérissée de réservoirs, roues de secours, crics, extincteurs, câbles de remorquage, pelles, tôles de désensablement. Idriss admirait en connaisseur du désert ce véhicule de grande croisière, non sans affinité lointaine avec le chameau bâté. Les hommes qui possédaient un outil aussi prestigieux ne pouvaient être que des seigneurs.

—Je ne me fais pas d'illusions, dit la femme, mais je pense que pour lui il n'y a pas de différence. La voiture et nous, c'est le même monde étranger. Vous autant que moi, nous sommes des émanations de la Land Rover.

Elle avait plusieurs fois réarmé, et visait à nouveau Idriss et ses moutons. Elle le regardait maintenant en souriant, et, débarrassée de l'appareil de photo, elle paraissait enfin le voir normalement.

—Donne-moi la photo.

C'était les premiers mots que prononçait Idriss.

—Il veut sa photo, c'est normal, non? intervint l'homme. Tu vois, on devrait toujours emporter un appareil à développement instantané. Le pauvre gosse va être déçu.

La femme avait replacé l'appareil dans la voiture. Elle en sortit une carte enfermée dans un cadre de cellophane. Elle s'approcha d'Idriss.

—Impossible, mon gars. Il faut faire développer le film et demander des tirages. Ta photo, on te l'enverra. Regarde. On est là, tu vois: Tabelbala. La tache verte, c'est ton oasis. Demain Béni Abbès. Ensuite Béchar. Puis Oran. Là, le car-ferry. Vingt-cinq heures de mer. Marseille. Huit cents kilomètres d'autoroute. Paris. Et là, on t'envoie ta photo. Tu t'appelles comment?

Quand la Land Rover disparut en soulevant un nuage de poussière, Idriss n'était plus tout à fait le même homme. Il n'y avait à Tabelbala qu'une seule photographie. D'abord parce que les oasiens sont trop pauvres pour se soucier de photographie. Ensuite parce que l'image est redoutée par ces berbères musulmans. Ils lui prêtent un pouvoir maléfique; ils pensent qu'elle matérialise en quelque sorte le mauvais œil. Pourtant cette unique photo contribuait au prestige du caporal-chef Mogadem ben Abderrahman, l'oncle d'Idriss, qui avait rapporté de la campagne d'Italie une citation et la croix de guerre. Citation, croix de guerre et photo étaient visibles sur le mur de son gourbi, et sur l'image craquelée et un peu floue, on le reconnaissait tout flambant de jeunesse et d'ardeur avec deux camarades à l'air goguenard. Il n'y avait eu jusque-là qu'une photo à Tabelbala, pensait Idriss, désormais, il y en aura une autre, la mienne.

Il trottinait sur le reg blanc en direction du grand acacia d'Hassi Ourit. Il débordait de l'aventure qu'il venait de vivre et se réjouissait à l'avance de s'en prévaloir auprès d'Ibrahim. S'en prévaloir vraiment? Avec quelle preuve à l'appui? Si seulement on la lui avait donnée, sa photo! Mais non, son image roulait à cette heure vers Béni Abbès enfermée dans le boîtier de l'appareil, lui-même à l'abri de la Land Rover. La voiture devenait elle aussi irréelle à mesure qu'il progressait. Il allait quitter les traces des pneus. Plus rien bientôt ne démontrerait la réalité de la rencontre qu'il venait de faire.

Lorsqu'il arriva à Ourit, Ibrahim l'accueillit comme à l'accoutumée par une grêle de pierres. Cela non plus, on ne l'aurait pas fait entre oasiens. Ramasser une pierre, c'est déjà un geste d'hostilité, une menace qu'on est encore bien loin heureusement de mettre à exécution. Ibrahim s'amusait de l'adresse diabolique qu'il avait acquise en lançant des cailloux depuis sa plus petite enfance. Il atteignait infailliblement un corbeau en plein vol, un fennec en pleine course. Pour l'heure, voyant approcher son ami, il jouait en guise de bienvenue à faire gicler le sable à droite, à gauche, en face et jusque entre ses pieds, moins dans l'espoir de lui faire peur—Idriss savait depuis longtemps qu'il ne risquait rien— mais simplement pour manifester sa joie de le revoir sous une forme qui mêlait son agressivité et ses dons naturels. Il cessa lorsque la distance entre Idriss et lui fût devenue trop faible pour que le jeu présentât encore de l'intérêt.

—Viens ici! lui cria-t-il. Il y a du nouveau!

Voilà! C'était bien d'Ibrahim! Idriss faisait une rencontre inouïe. Il subissait l'épreuve de la photographie, par une femme blonde de surcroît, et devenait inopinément quelqu'un de comparable au caporal-chef Mogadem, et deux heures plus tard, c'était Ibrahim qui avait du nouveau à lui apprendre!

—J'ai une chamelle qui va mettre bas au puits Hassi el Hora. C'est à une heure d'ici. Le puits est pourri, mais il faut qu'elle boive. Nous allons y aller avec du lait.

Il prononçait le berbère en phrases hachées qui ressemblaient à autant d'aboiements impératifs. En même temps, son œil unique pétillait de lueurs ironiques, parce qu'Idriss n'était qu'un niais d'oasien, une « queue ronde », docile, doux, mais de peu de poids en face d'un chamelier chaamba. Un vieux mâle s'arcbouta et fit fuser un jet d'urine sur le sable. Ibrahim en profita pour s'y rincer les mains, parce qu'un Chaamba ne trait pas avec des mains sales. Puis il fit pivoter une femelle pour la placer en bonne position de traite et entreprit de dénouer le filet qui emprisonnait ses mamelles et les mettait à l'abri des chamelons du troupeau. Enfin il commença à tirer, debout sur une jambe, le pied gauche appuyé sur le genou droit, une jatte d'argile posée en équilibre sur sa cuisse gauche.

Idriss regardait les deux jets qui giclaient alternativement dans la jatte. En état de sous-alimentation permanente, il souffrait du désir que lui inspirait ce liquide blanc, chaud et vivant, capable de calmer à la fois sa soif et sa faim. La chamelle agita ses petites oreilles d'ours, et, ouvrant son anus, elle fit couler une diarrhée verte sur la face interne de ses cuisses, manifestations de confiance et d'abandon qui favorisaient la descente du lait.

Ibrahim s'arrêta de tirer quand il jugea avoir assez de lait pour en remplir une de ces gourdes séchées, munies d'un couvercle, qu'on suspend au flanc du chameau dans une résille de fibre de palmier. Il s'approcha du vieux mâle, et, sans avoir à le toucher, d'un simple cri guttural, il le fit baraquer. Puis il se jucha sur son garrot, le dos contre la bosse, et fit asseoir Idriss devant lui. Le chameau se releva en blatérant avec mauvaise humeur, et s'élança aussitôt vers le nord. Après avoir traversé une zone de terre rougeâtre semée d'une maigre brousse arborescente, ils s'engagèrent dans le lit d'un oued qu'ils remontèrent sur plusieurs kilomètres. Sculpté par l'eau—une eau qui n'avait plus coulé visiblement depuis des années—le sol présentait de vastes plaques lisses et durcies qui craquaient brutalement sous les larges pieds du chameau. Plusieurs fois les deux cavaliers faillirent être jetés à terre. La bête grondait de colère. Il fallut ralentir l'allure. Elle s'arrêta tout à fait au pied d'un rocher de basalte sous lequel elle avait flairé la présence d'une guelta. Ibrahim la laissa boire l'eau grise où zigzaguaient des insectes. Elle releva la tête, triste et hautaine, retroussa son mufle ruisselant d'eau, et poussa un brâme dans une odeur saline et sulfureuse. Puis la course reprit. A mesure qu'on approchait d'Hassi el Hora, Idriss percevait l'angoisse et l'impatience qui gagnaient son compagnon. Il y avait du malheur dans l'air, un instinct infaillible en avertissait le Chaamba.

Seule une levée de terre—les déblais très anciens et durcis du creusement—signalait la présence d'un puits. Ni bassin, ni murette, ni margelle, ce n'était qu'un trou rond dangereusement ouvert au ras du sol. Une fragile hutte de perches entrelacées de palmes attestait pourtant que les bergers connaissaient ce point d'eau, et s'y reposaient parfois à l'abri du soleil après y avoir abreuvé leurs bêtes. Pour l'heure il était désert. Mais de très loin l'œil unique d'Ibrahim distingua la silhouette grêle et fauve d'un chamelon nouveau-né, abandonné entre le puits et l'abri. Ses pires pressentiments se confirmaient.

Il sauta du chameau, et courut aussitôt au bord du puits. Idriss le vit s'engager sur la poutre la plus accessible de la charpente intérieure qui maintenait la terre des parois, et s'y coucher pour mieux scruter le fond du trou. Il n'y avait aucun doute possible. Altérée par la parturition, la chamelle s'était approchée du bord et avait basculé dans le vide. A ce moment le chamelon émit un beuglement plaintif et sa mère lui répondit: de la gueule du puits monta un râle amplifié comme par un gigantisque tuyau d'orgue. Idriss se pencha à son tour sur l'ouverture. Il ne vit d'abord que l'enchevêtrement des poutres fixant le coffrage des parois. Mais lorsque ses yeux furent accoutumés à l'ombre, il distingua des reflets lumineux et miroitants, une silhouette noire couchée sur le flanc et à demi immergée, et, comme un minuscule poinçon au bord de ce tableau sinistre, l'image de sa propre tête tendue et vive sur l'azur profond du ciel.

Ibrahim s'était relevé et courait vers la hutte. Il en revint avec une corde de cuir torsadée.

—Je vais descendre voir si la bête est blessée, expliqua-t-il. Sinon, on essaiera de la tirer de là avec l'aide des autres bergers. Si elle a une patte cassée, il faudra la tuer.

Puis ayant fixé le bout de la corde à une tête rocheuse, il se laissa glisser à l'intérieur. Il y eut un silence. Et bientôt sa voix monta en échos caverneux.

—Elle a une patte cassée. Je vais l'égorger et la dépecer. Tu remonteras les morceaux. Commence par mes vêtements.

Idriss remonta un léger ballot de hardes loqueteuses. Puis il attendit sans chercher à voir l'horrible travail auquel se livrait le Chaamba dans une eau boueuse à vingt mètres sous terre.

Le grand chameau s'était rapproché du chamelon, et, l'ayant longuement flairé, il s'était mis à le lécher tendrement. Idriss observait la scène avec amusement. Il était peu probable que le vieux mâle cédât à une soudaine vocation paternelle. Il devait plutôt apprécier sur le corps tremblant et humide du petit l'odeur violente de la mère. Quant au chamelon, éperdu d'esseulement, il se serrait contre ce protecteur inespéré, puis emporté par l'instinct, il fouillait du museau ses génitoires à la recherche d'hypothétiques mamelles.

Un appel impérieux arracha Idriss à sa contemplation. Il commença à haler la corde de cuir lourdement lestée. Bientôt il put attirer à lui une cuisse et une jambe encore tièdes de vie. Il porta cette pièce de boucherie dans l'ombre de la hutte. Aussitôt la voix du chamelier retentit à nouveau.

—Tire un seau d'eau, mélanges-y le lait que nous avons apporté, et fais boire le petit.

Ainsi Ibrahim, au plus fort du travail épuisant qu'il accomplissait, n'oubliait pas le chamelon, et il lui sacrifiait la seule nourriture dont il disposait. Idriss obéit à contrecœur, mais sans envisager la possibilité de désobéir, par exemple en buvant une partie du lait. Le courage surhumain de son compagnon le subjuguait. Le chamelon était incapable de boire. Idriss dut lui confectionner un biberon de fortune avec une bouteille dont il brisa le fond pour en faire une sorte d'entonnoir. Il avait à peine commencé ce nourrissage qu'un nouveau quartier de chamelle lui était expédié du fond du puits. Quand le soleil atteignit le sommet de sa course, il entendit Ibrahim se féliciter de la lumière directe dont il profitait. La cabane n'était plus qu'un amoncellement de quartiers de viande sur lesquels des essaims de mouches bleues vrombissaient furieusement dès qu'on les dérangeait. Mais ce qui inquiétait surtout Idriss, c'était que le ciel, encore vide une heure plus tôt, se peuplait de petites croix noires qui dérivaient lentement, paraissaient un moment immobiles, puis glissaient tout à coup en vol plané. Les vautours avaient tout vu, et ils s'apprêtaient à descendre. Pourtant ils étaient moins à craindre que les corbeaux dont l'audace et l'agressivité ne reculaient devant rien. Il imaginait ce que serait leur retour avec le chamelon à peine capable de marcher, le grand mâle balançant sur sa bosse une pyramide de viande fraîche, et la traînée noire et hurlante des corbeaux qui les suivraient.

Il fut surpris de voir tout à coup Ibrahim se hisser sur la poutre transversale du puits. Ce n'était qu'une vivante statue sculptée dans un limon sanglant. Ebloui par la lumière intense, il couvrit son visage de ses mains, et leva la tête vers le ciel. Puis ses mains glissèrent, et Idriss vit qu'un caillot de sang s'était logé dans son orbite creuse comme si son œil venait d'être arraché. Le Chaamba était ivre de tension, de fatigue et d'exaltation méridienne. Il leva les bras, et poussa un hurlement de triomphe et de défi. Puis il se mit à trépigner et à sauter en équilibre sur la poutre. Il avait pris son sexe dans sa main, et le tendait vers Idriss.

—Oh, queue ronde! Regarde! Moi, j'ai la queue pointue!

Il sauta encore sur le tronc vermoulu. Il y eut un craquement, et le Chaamba disparut comme un diable dans sa boîte. Un second craquement apprit à Idriss que le corps de son compagnon avait heurté la poutre maîtresse de la charpente, laquelle venait de céder à son tour. On eut dit alors qu'un tremblement de terre se produisait. Le sol remua. La cabane s'effondra sur les quartiers de la chamelle. Un nuage de poussière jaillit du puits vers le ciel, et Idriss y distingua le vol affolé d'innombrables chauves-souris qui passaient le jour dans la charpente du puits. La rupture des deux poutres avait entraîné l'effondrement de tout le coffrage qui retenait les parois du trou. Le puits s'était comblé d'un seul coup. Jusqu'à quel niveau? Où était Ibrahim?

Idriss s'approcha. A moins de deux mètres de profondeur, on voyait le sable mêlé de pièces de bois brisées. Il appela son compagnon. Sa voix frêle s'éleva dans un silence rendu plus sépulcral encore par la royauté du soleil en plein zénith. Alors la panique le prit. Il hurla de peur et courut droit devant lui. Il courut longtemps. Jusqu'à ce qu'il trébuche sur une souche et s'écroule sur le sable, secoué de sanglots. Mais il se relève aussitôt, les mains appliquées sur les oreilles. En collant sa joue sur le sol, il a cru entendre montant des profondeurs le rire de son ami enseveli vivant.

The Golden Droplet*

Where was Ibrahim? Had he perhaps taken his camels to a remote pasture created in just a few hours by a storm? Idris looked for traces of him around the tree, but the ground was riddled with prints in which the large soles of the camels were mixed up with the small holes made by the hooves of the goats and sheep. He then walked around in a cirle a short distance away from the well, trying to find some indication of the direction the Chaamba had taken. He spotted the irregular trail left by a monitor lizard, the tiny stars that betrayed the jumping action of a jerboa, the triangular and rather old trace of a fennec at the gallop. He walked around a lump of basalt whose blackness made a strong contrast with the reg, which was becoming more and more dazzling as the sun climbed up the horizon. And then he discovered some prints of such enormous interest that his mind immediately became a blank. He forgot all about Ibrahim and his camels, and even about his own herd. The only things that existed were the two finely serrated ribbons which had carved out shallow grooves in the white ground and were visible as far as the eye could see. A car, an automobile, a thing no one in the oasis had ever spoken about, had suddenly loomed up out of the darkness with its cargo of material riches and human mystery! Choking with excitement, Idris dashed off in pursuit of the vehicle, which was disappearing westward.

The sun was blazing high in the sky when he saw, in the quivering, overheated ground, gliding along by a tamarisk copse, the clumsy con-

*The Golden Droplet (New York: Doubleday, 1987), 4–12. Translated by Barbara Wright. This passage is reprinted with the kind permission of Doubleday.

tours of a Land-Rover. It wasn't traveling very fast, but Idris hadn't the slightest chance of catching up with it. Nor did he even dream of doing so. He stopped, immobilized by astonishment and timidity, and was soon surrounded by his sheep and goats. The Land-Rover, turning northward, was now starting along the track leading to Beni-Abbès. In five minutes it would be out of sight. No. It slowed down. It made a U-turn. It gathered speed and began to charge at him. There were two people in it, a man at the wheel and, sitting beside him, a woman; at first Idris could see nothing of her but her blonde hair and big sunglasses. The car stopped. The woman took off her glasses and jumped out. Her bleached hair hung down over her shoulders. She was wearing a very low-cut khaki top and a pair of outrageously abbreviated shorts. Idris also noticed her golden ballet slippers and thought that she wouldn't go far with them in the surrounding gravel. She was brandishing a camera.

"Hey, boy! Don't move too much, I'm going to photograph you."

"You might at least ask his opinion," the man muttered. "Some of these people don't like it."

"You're a fine one to say that!" the woman remarked.

Idris listened carefully and mustered up the oddments of French he possessed to try to understand what they were saying. It was obvious that he was the subject of an argument between the man and the woman, but that it was the woman who was interested in him, and this was what disturbed him the most.

"Don't delude yourself," said the man derisively, "he's much more interested in the car than he is in you!"

It was true that the car was impressive; squat, white with dust, bristling with cans, spare wheels, jacks, fire extinguishers, towropes, shovels, perforated metal sheets for freeing it from the sand. As a connoisseur of the desert, Idris admired this long-distance cruising vehicle which was not without some remote affinity with a sumpter camel. Men who possessed such prestigious implements could only be seigneurs.

"I'm not deluding myself," said the woman, "but I don't think he sees any difference. The car and us—it's the same foreign world. Both you and I are emanations of the Land-Rover."

She had wound her camera several times and was once again focusing it on Idris and his sheep. She was smiling now as she looked at him, and without her camera she finally seemed to be seeing him normally.

"Give me the photo."

These were the first words that Idris uttered.

"He wants his photo; only natural, isn't it?" the man put in. "We should always bring a Polaroid camera, you know. The poor kid will be disappointed."

The woman had put the camera back in the car. She brought out a map covered with cellophane. She went up to Idris.

"I can't possibly, young man. I have to get the film developed and printed. We'll send you your photo. Look. This is where we are, see? Tabelbala. The green patch is your oasis. Tomorrow Beni-Abbès. Then Béchar. Then Oran. There, the car ferry. Twenty-five hours on the sea. Marseille. Eight hundred kilometers on the autoroute. Paris. And from there, we'll send you your photo. What's your name?"

After the Land-Rover had disappeared, raising a cloud of dust, Idris was no longer quite the same man. There was only one photograph in Tabelbala. In the first place because the oasis dwellers are too poor to bother about photography. And next because the image is feared by these Muslim Berbers. They attribute a maleficent power to it; they believe that it in some way materializes the evil eye. And yet this unique photo contributed to the prestige of Lance Sergeant Mogadem ben Abderrahman, Idris's uncle, who had returned from the Italian campaign with a mention in dispatches and the Croix de Guerre. Mention, Croix de Guerre, and photo were all displayed on the wall of his gourbi, and in the cracked and rather fuzzy image he could be seen, bursting with youth and high spirits, in the company of two facetious-looking comrades. Up till then there had been only one photo in Tabelbala, thought Idris; from now on there will be another—mine.

He scurried along the white reg in the direction of the tall acacia tree at Hassi Ourit. He was bubbling over with the adventure he had just lived through and was already anticipating the pleasure of boasting about it to Ibrahim. Really boasting about it? What proof did he have? If only they had given him his photo! No, though, his image was now on its way to Beni-Abbès, shut inside the camera case, which itself was tucked away in the Land-Rover. The car too was fast becoming unreal, the farther away he got. He would soon be out of sight of its tire tracks. Any minute now there would be nothing to prove the reality of his recent encounter.

When he got to Ourit, Ibrahim greeted him as usual with a hail of stones. This too was something that oasis dwellers would never have done to each other. Picking up a stone is already a hostile gesture, although it is a threat that you are fortunately still a long way from carrying out. Ibrahim enjoyed the diabolical skill in stone throwing that he had acquired from his earliest childhood. He could unerringly hit a crow in full flight, a fennec at full gallop. For the moment, seeing his friend approach, as a welcoming gesture he was playing at making the sand spray up to his right, to his left, in front of him, and even between his feet, less in the hope of frightening him—Idris had long known that he was in no danger—than simply to manifest his pleasure at seeing him in a way that combined his aggressiveness with his natural gifts. He stopped when the distance between them had become too short for the game to present any further interest.

"Come here!" he cried. "I've got some news for you!"

There! That was Ibrahim all over! Idris had had an unheard-of experience. He had undergone the ordeal of photography, and by a blonde woman what was more, he had unexpectedly become someone comparable to Lance Sergeant Mogadem, and a couple of hours later it was Ibrahim who had news for him!

"One of my she-camels is going to drop her colt at the Hassi el Hora well. It's an hour from here. The well is rotten, but she has to drink. We must go there with some milk."

He pronounced the Berber language in staccato phrases which sounded like so many imperative barks. At the same time, his single eye was sparkling with irony, because Idris was only a foolish oasis dweller, a "round tail," docile, gentle, but no match for a Chaamba cameleer. An old male camel braced itself and spurted a stream of urine onto the sand. Ibrahim took advantage of this to rinse his hands, because a Chaamba doen't milk with dirty hands. Then he swung a she-camel around, to get her into the right position for milking, and started to untie the net imprisoning her teats to protect them from the colts in the herd. Finally he began to milk, standing on one leg, his left foot resting on his right knee, with a clay bowl balanced on his left thigh.

Idris watched the two jets squirting alternately into the bowl. In a permanent state of undernourishment, he suffered from the desire aroused him by this white, warm, living liquid that would have been capable of appeasing both his hunger and his thirst. The camel flapped her little bear's ears and, opening her anus, released a flood of green diarrhea onto the insides of her thighs, manifestation of the confidence and abandon induced by the flow of her milk.

Ibrahim stopped milking when he judged that he had enough milk to fill one of the dried gourds which are given a lid and hung from the camel's flank in a netting made of palm fibers. He went up to the old male and, without having to touch it, with a simple guttural cry made it kneel. Then he perched himself on its neck, his back leaning against its hump, and got Idris to sit in front of him. The camel stood up with an angry roar and immediately darted off toward the north. After crossing a zone of reddish earth strewn with the occasional treelike shrub, they entered the bed of a wadi and went up it for several kilometers. Carved out by the water—water which had obviously not flowed for several years—the ground consisted of vast, smooth, sunbaked patches which cracked violently under the broad feet of the camel. Several times the two riders were nearly thrown to the ground. The animal snarled with fury. They had to slow down. The camel came to a complete halt at the foot of a basalt rock under which it had scented the presence of a guelta. Ibrahim let it drink the gray water on which insects were zigzagging. It raised its sad, haughty head, dilated its dripping nostrils, and let out a roar that smelled of salt and sulfur. Then it began to run again. As they came closer to Hassi el

Hora, Idris could feel his companion's growing anxiety and impatience. There was misfortune in the air, as his unerring instinct warned the Chaamba.

The only sign of the presence of a well was a slight acclivity—the very old and hardened remains of the dug-out earth. Neither basin, nor curb, nor rim; it was merely a dangerously open round hole, flush with the ground. However, a flimsy hut of intertwined poles and palm branches showed that the shepherds knew this water hole and sometimes rested by it, protected from the sun, after watering their animals. For the time being it was deserted. But from a very long way away Ibrahim's one eye made out the spindly beige silhouette of a newborn camel colt, abandoned between the well and the shelter. His worst forebodings were confirmed.

He jumped down from the camel and ran straight to the edge of the well. Idris saw him climb down onto the most accessible beam of the inner framework supporting the earthen walls, and lie down on it to get a better look at the bottom of the hole. There was no possible doubt. Thirsty after her parturition, the she-camel had gone up to the edge of the well and toppled over into the void. At this moment the colt uttered a plaintive cry and its mother answered it: from the depths of the well came a groan amplified as if by a gigantic organ pipe. Idris too leaned over the opening. At first all he could see was the crisscross of the beams keeping the coffering of the walls in place. But when his eyes had grown accustomed to the darkness, he could make out luminous, glistening reflections, a black silhouette lying on its flank, half submerged, and, like a tiny pinprick at the edge of this sinister picture, the image of his own outstretched, living head against the deep azure of the sky.

Ibrahim had got out of the well and was running over to the hut. He came back with a twisted-leather rope.

"I'm going down to see whether the camel's injured," he said. "If not, we'll get the other shepherds to help us try and pull her out. If she's broken a leg, we shall have to kill her."

Then, having tied one end of the rope around the top of a projecting rock, he gently lowered himself into the well. There was a silence. But his voice soon came up in cavernous echoes.

"She's got a broken leg. I'm going to slit her throat and cut her up. You can bring up the pieces. Start with my clothes."

Idris pulled up a light bundle of rags. Then he waited, without trying to see the horrible job the Chaamba was doing in the muddy water twenty meters belowground.

The big camel had gone up to the colt. He sniffed at it for a long time and then began to lick it tenderly. Idris observed the scene with amusement. It was hardly likely that the old male would have succumbed to a sudden paternal vocation. More probably, he was appreciating the pungent smell of the mother on the trembling, humid body of the baby. As for the colt, desperate with solitude, it huddled up to this unexpected protector and then, driven by instinct, stuck its muzzle up into his genitals, searching for hypothetical teats.

An imperious call roused Idris from his contemplation. He began to haul the heavily weighted rope. Soon he was pulling up a thigh and a leg, still warm with life. He took this piece of meat over to the shade of the hut. The cameleer's voice immediately rang out again.

"Draw a bucket of water, mix it with the milk we brought, and give the baby a drink."

So even in the thick of the exhausting job he was doing, Ibrahim hadn't forgotten the colt, and was sacrificing to it the only nourishment he had at his disposal. Idris obeyed reluctantly, but without envisaging the possibility of disobeying, by drinking some of the milk, for instance. He was subjugated by the superhuman courage of his friend. The colt was incapable of drinking. Idris had to improvise a baby's bottle for it by breaking the bottom of an ordinary bottle and turning it into a kind of funnel. He had only just begun to feed the colt in this way when a new quarter from the she-camel was sent up from the bottom of the well. When the sun had reached its highest point, he heard Ibrahim congratulating himself on the direct light it was giving him. The cabin was now no more than an accumulation of quarters of meat over which swarms of bluebottles buzzed furiously the moment they were disturbed. But what particularly worried Idris was that the sky, which had been clear only an hour before, was now filled with slowly drifting little black crosses which for a moment seemed motionless but then suddenly began to hover. The vultures had seen everything and were getting ready to dive. Even so, they were less to be feared than the crows, whose audacity and aggressiveness stopped at nothing. He imagined what their return journey would be like, with the colt barely able to walk, the big male balancing a pyramid of fresh meat on its hump, and the black, screeching trail of crows that would follow them.

He was surprised to see Ibrahim suddenly hauling himself up onto the crossbeam of the well. He was nothing but a living statue sculptured in bloodstained clay. Dazzled by the strong light, he covered his face with his hands and raised his head up to the sky. Then his hands slipped, and Idris saw that a clot of blood had become lodged in his hollow orbit, as if his eye had just been put out. The Chaamba was intoxicated with tension, fatigue, and midday exaltation. He raised his arms and let out a howl of triumph and defiance. Then he began to jump up and down, balancing on the beam. He had taken his penis in his hand and was holding it out toward Idris.

"Oh, round tail! Look! *My* tail is pointed!"

Once again he jumped on the worm-eaten beam. There was a crack, and the Chaamba disappeared as if down a trapdoor. A second crack told Idris that his friend's body had hit the main beam and that too had given way. Then there was something like an earthquake. The ground moved. The cabin collapsed onto the quarters of the she-camel. A cloud of dust shot up into the sky from the well, and in its midst Idris could make out the panic-stricken flight of innumerable bats that spent the day in the framework of the well. The breaking of the two beams had led to the collapse of the whole coffering supporting the walls. The well had suddenly been filled in. Up to what level? Where was Ibrahim?

Idris went over to it. Less than two meters down, he could see sand mixed with broken bits of wood. He called his friend. His ineffectual voice sounded in a silence made still more sepulchral by the supremacy of the sun at its full zenith. Then he was seized with panic. He howled with fear and ran straight in front of him. He ran for a long time. Until he tripped over a tree stump and collapsed on the sand, shaken with sobs. But he got up at once, clasping his hands over his ears. Pressing his cheek to the ground, he thought he could hear, rising from the depths, the laughter of his friend . . . who had been buried alive.

MARINA KUNDU

Sébastien Japrisot

Sébastien Japrisot is an anagram which has concealed the identity of Jean-Baptiste Rossi from the crime fiction world for some twenty-five years. When he began writing at age seventeen, he signed his given name to a work which, rather intriguingly, bears the title *The False Start*. In 1962, he turned for the first time to the detective novel, and chose to adopt a pseudonym. His very latest offering was published in May of 1987. It is not a crime fiction piece, yet it manages still to reiterate the old enigma, lurking in so many of his writings: of what significance is his choice, a choice reduplicated in the texts by the displacement of the reference of each descriptive title—be it author, reader (ie., interpreter/detective), criminal, or victim?

Born in 1931, Jean-Baptiste was the grandson of southern Italian immigrants settled in Marseilles. His father abandons the family seven years later, allowing the protagonists of his son's formative experiences (and of his later fiction) to be women. Such is the case until Rossi's enrollment in a Jesuit secondary school. Here, he spends fifteen days of his baccalaureate preparation time writing his first novel, a story of adolescence and character discovery, completed in another fifteen days during his studies at the Sorbonne. He takes *Les Mal-Partis* to Robert Laffont, who publishes it in 1950. The book is awarded the prix de l'Unanimité in France that year by a distinguished jury, and is circulated in translation in England and the United States. At Laffont's request, Rossi himself at age twenty becomes the translator of another writer's story of adolescence, J. D. Salinger's first novel *The Catcher in the Rye (L'Attrape-Coeur)*, and eight years later Salinger's *Nine Stories*.[1] During this period, largely for financial reasons, Rossi pursues a career in advertising, working in Paris as a writer and later the manager in campaigns for such companies as Air France, Max Factor, and Formica. Meanwhile he satisfies his long-time interest in the cinema by doing the screenplay for and directing two film shorts: "La Machine à parler d'amour" in 1961 and "L'Idée fixe" in 1962.[2]

1. *Nouvelles* (Paris: Robert Laffont, 1963).
2. Producer Pierre Braumberger of Films de la Pléiade.

After leaving the advertising business and married with two children, Rossi turns to the detective novel. Robert Kanters at Denoël offers him a sizeable advance to write a story for their "Crime Club" collection. Just one month later, *Compartiments tueurs* and *Piège pour Cendrillon* are completed and signed—to protect his reputation from these first attempts at a new genre?—Sébastien Japrisot. Published respectively in May and November 1962, these two novels meet with unexpected success. Both are made into films, and *Piège pour Cendrillon*[3] wins the 1963 Grand Prix de Littérature policière. During a brief interval he (as Rossi) works with Trez on a satirical album called *L'Odyssexe*, which is made into a twelve-minute cartoon.[4] Japrisot's next suspense novel appears in September 1966: *La Dame dans l'auto avec des lunettes et un fusil*. Only three months later, it receives the prix d'Honneur in France, then the title Best Crime Novel in Britain.[5] Now not only critics of police fiction praise him but others as well. He is proud of his mention in Simone de Beauvoir's *All Said and Done*. [*Tout compte fait*].

His success now allows him to write directly for the screen: in 1968 Jean Herman directs *Adieu l'ami*; René Clément directs *Le Passenger de la pluie* and in 1972 *La Course du lièvre à travers les champs* (producer: Serge Silberman, publisher: Denoël), and he dabbles in directing, producing, and adaptation work as well, but with less success.[6] Japrisot returns to literature in September, 1978 with *L'Été meurtrier* which receives the Deux-Magots award that year. In 1984, his own screenplay adaptation receives the César du meilleur scénario (director, Jean Becker). There is an eight-year interval between *L'Été meurtrier* and *La Passion des femmes*, Japrisot's newest novel, published in August, 1986. Unhappily for those kept waiting, it does not approach the mastery of *Piège pour Cendrillon*, *La Dame dans l'auto*, or *L'Été meurtrier*, any one of which could be presented as his most fascinating and complex work. Denoël's latest Japrisot publication is a collection of early prose writings and poems, including *Les Mal-Partis*, *Visages de l'amour et de la haine*, *Le Bonheur du jour*, written between the ages of sixteen and nineteen. The title page alone requires a very careful reading:

Écrit par Jean-Baptiste Rossi
—Sébastien Japrisot

The text is written by one, signed by the other. Is the "author" clearly stating that the other is exterior to his *I*, thus irrevocably separating the two? Or is this an attempt to reconcile the existence of both in himself?

With the publication of *Écrit par Jean-Baptiste Rossi*, we are brought back full circle, to the writer of *Les Mal-Partis*—but we are brought there via the signature of Sébastien Japrisot. Japrisot states in the foreword that during the ten years separating the early pieces from his first detective novel, everything in his world accelerated.

3. Costa Gavras directs "Compartiments tueurs," André Cayatte "Piège pour Cendrillon."
4. Denoël publishes it, Twentieth Century Fox buys the cinema rights.
5. Anatol Litvak directs the film version.
6. "Toi," "Une Rose blanche peinte en rouge," "Histoire d'O."

J'avais beaucoup de peine à me reconnaître. C'est peut-être la vraie raison, sinon la seule, de mon pseudonyme. Pour ne point me quitter tout à fait, j'en voulais un qui fût l'anagramme de mon nom.

I was having a lot of trouble recognizing myself. This is maybe the real reason, if not the only one, for my pseudonym. In order not to forsake myself completely, I wanted one that was the anagram of my name. [Translation mine]

The questions this raises are absolutely fundamental: what does it mean to sign something? Does a name whose letters have been transposed still imply the same referent? How can we describe the space of identity in writing? Rossi, perceiving himself as other than he thought he was, changes his name, that is, his signature. He cannot claim his discourse as Rossi, yet he cannot abandon this name which signifies (in the linguistic sense) his identity, and therefore he chooses an exact anagram of it. The anagram, then, is the sought-after link; Japrisot is Rossi's link to Rossi. Of vital importance is the will to reach this state of being which was in existence before that threatening new awareness, that point where, for whatever reason, the person's sense of identity was altered.

These themes, obsessively present in the richest of Japrisot's texts, are perhaps most clearly seen through his heroine in *L'Été meurtrier*. Her whole story is in *her* name. If we were to rearrange the letters of her given name, *Éliane*, we would discover an anagram descriptive of a distinctive aspect of her personality as well as of the doubleness (which we shall explain) of her character: *aliené*. Within this anagram we would see also a *(a)lien(é)*, the link she seeks to her sense of identity. Her nickname, Elle, corroborates the fact of her search—as the third-person pronoun (a nuance lost in translation), it clearly indicates the enunciator's self-implied ambiguity of reference between herself and an other. We read the impulse that motivates her in these words: "Je serai Elle. Tout effacé." (See the penultimate paragraph of the passage). I will be she ("*elle*," the pronoun), but equally I will be *I* ("*Elle*," her name), once all that has come between the two is erased.

What incident was so traumatic as to shatter the notion Elle had of herself?— the sudden knowledge that her father was someone other than the man she had adored as her father in her childhood. This truth dissolved half her self, in that it took away the paternal link. The story of this book is the period of sickness she lives through (see the same paragraph), it is the devising and execution of her revenge for a crime committed twenty years previously by three men, one of whom was necessarily her father. The crime was the rape of her mother, its retribution would be the identification and destruction of the "bad" father, and the consequent restoration of the paternal relationship with the other man.

The reader follows the process of detection of the criminal's identity through the separate testimonies of four characters.[7] All are involved in Elle's plan of vengeance, all assume a wider reference than would be indicated by their individual designations as victim, witness, juror, or judge.[8] And yet no one of these

7. In *L'Été meurtrier*, he will have the satisfaction of discovering the rendering of one of these to be impossible!
8. Elle is the most complicated example of this. One glimpses the multiplicity of roles "L" takes on even in the chapter headings (in the French): "*Le* bourreau," "*La* victime," "*L*'acte d'accusation," and so on.

can arrest the fatal course of events. Like the analogous extratextual readers, they are trapped by the narrative situation—by the detective novel's peculiarity of being narrated backwards, inversely from the moment of the revelation of the criminal. For the investigator, the beginning is the state of no knowledge, whereas the author's beginning is the end, the knowledge of the key or "truth." In *L'Été meurtrier*, it is not until the last word of the novel that we reach the point from where the testimonies originated, too late to permit the sharing of information which might have prevented the catastrophe.

This feature of the suspense narrative is apt as a medium for Japrisot's own concerns.[9] Éliane's regressive course betrays her author's dilemma. In a sense, she is seeking to move away from a position of knowledge. The fulfillment of her quest would require the reestablishment of an earlier state, where the truth of the crime was a total mystery. It is not only the criminal's identity that is at stake in the process of detection, but also the investigator's. In avenging and solving the crime, Elle means to find her father, the link to the reunification of *I* and *she*, to the recovery of a self-identity. However, this is ultimately not permitted. The investigation has falsely promised one single interpretation. Both extra- and intratextual interpreters have been deceived by their belief that the work of reading a detective novel lies in moving towards the convergence of their perception and the author's information. Ending, access to the author's truth, perversely entails the permanent renunciation of a state of knowledge. Elle does find again the integrity of her childhood conciousness, but at the expense of abandoning her present sense of identity.

Is Japrisot's fate to be Éliane's? In *Piège pour Cendrillon*, he allowed two interpretations of the situation to coexist. In *La Dame dans l'auto*, the truth discovered at the end provided a reassuring explanation of the original misreading. The ultimate impossibility for the heroine of *L'Été meurtrier* to accommodate ambiguity implies that the author now considers the search to be more arduous. The all-consuming quest for identity, for what experience one can claim as one's own, are recurring themes in Japrisot. Those deceived by his double situations must contend with the intricacies of open readings, as he contends, with the problem of writing himself or inscribing his double name in writing.

BIBLIOGRAPHY

I. Novels

Les Mal-Partis. Paris: Robert Laffont, 1950.
Compartiments tueurs. Paris: Denoël, 1962.
Piège pour Cendrillon. Paris: Denoël, 1962.
La Dame dans l'auto avec des lunettes et un fusil. Paris: Denoël, 1966.
L'Eté meurtrier. Paris: Denoël, 1978.
La Passion des femmes. Paris: Denoël, 1986.
Ecrit par Jean-Baptiste Rossi. Paris: Denoël, 1987.

9. Of course, there are many ways in which his novels do not fit the various headings and subheadings of the detective story as defined by the often emphasized and over-rigid conventions of the genre.

II. Selected Criticism

Boisdeffre, Pierre de. "La Revue littéraire: Sébastien Japrisot: *L'Eté meurtrier*," *Nouvelle Revue des Deux Mondes* 12 (December 1977).

Boucher, Anthony. "Criminals at Large," *New York Times Book Review*. *The 10:30 from Marseilles* (17 November 1963); *A Trap for Cinderella* (31 July 1964); *The Lady in the Car with Glasses and a Gun* (10 December 1967).

F. D. "Japrisot ou Rossi," *Elle* (31 November 1977).

Felman, Shoshana. "De Sophocle à Japrisot (via Freud), ou pourquoi le policier," *Littérature* 49 (February 1983).

Gayot, Paul and Jacques Baudou. "Quand l'énigme fait peur: le suspense," *Français dans le Monde* 187 (August–September 1984).

Kanters, Robert. "Le Premier 'roman' de Sébastien Japrisot," *Figaro Littéraire* 1638 (15–16 October 1977).

Laski, Margharita. "New Novels," *The Observer* 8354 (15 July 1951).

Nourissier, François. "*Les Mal-Partis*, roman de Jean-Baptiste Rossi," *Les Nouvelles Littéraires* 2029 (21 July 1966).

Saletti, Robert. "L'Homme qui aimait les récits," *Spirale* 65 (November 1986).

Strouse, Jean. "Sébastien Japrisot: *One Deadly Summer*," *Newsweek* 95, no. 26 (30 June 1980).

SÉBASTIEN JAPRISOT

L'Eté meurtrier*

1.

Le lendemain soir, c'est Elle qui est venue au garage.

Quand elle est entrée avec son vélo à la main, juste après un orage qui avait inondé la rue, j'étais sous une voiture montée sur cric. Je ne voyais que ses jambes, mais j'ai su tout de suite que c'était elle. Ses jambes se sont approchées de la voiture jusqu'à la toucher, elle a levé la voix pour demander s'il n'y avait personne. J'étais allongé sur le dos, et quand j'ai déplacé le chariot que j'avais sous moi, j'ai vu que, contrairement à ce que tout le monde devait penser, elle portait une culotte. Blanche. Elle me regardait tranquillement d'en haut, elle m'a dit que son vélo était crevé, mais elle n'a pas bougé d'un centimètre. Je lui ai demandé de s'éloigner pour pouvoir sortir. Elle a pris plusieurs secondes pour le faire. J'essayais de mon mieux d'avoir la tête d'un dur de cinéma, de la regarder dans les yeux, pas autre chose. En fin de compte, elle a reculé d'un pas mais je me suis propulsé si fort qu'elle a trés bien compris qu'elle m'intimidait. (. . .)

(. . .) J'ai démonté la roue avant de son vélo, j'ai examiné la chambre à air. Je n'ai pas eu besoin de la passer à l'eau, elle n'était pas crevée mais déchirée. Sur plus de trois centimètres. Je lui ai demandé comment c'était arrivé, mais elle a soulevé son épaule gauche, elle n'a pas répondu.

Je lui ai dit que je n'avais pas de chambre à air pour remplacer la sienne. J'en avais chez moi, des vieilles de Mickey qui étaient encore bonnes, mais quand je lui ai proposé d'aller voir notre mère et de s'en faire donner une, elle n'a pas voulu. « Pour me faire attraper, merci. » Elle m'a demandé à quelle heure je finissais mon travail. Je lui ai dit que j'avais encore un bon moment à passer sous la voiture. Elle m'a dit qu'elle

*L'Eté meurtrier (Paris: Denoël, 1978), 52–61, 91–95, 278–84. These passages are reprinted with the kind permission of Denoël.

attendrait dehors. J'étais torse nu, il avait fait très chaud jusqu'à l'orage, et elle m'a dit que j'étais drôlement costaud. Je me faisais moins de souci pour mes chances, depuis que j'avais vu la déchirure de son pneu, mais c'était le premier mot agréable qu'elle me disait, j'étais content. Je me trompais d'ailleurs. Elle n'aimait pas les costauds. Ceux qui lui plaisaient, c'était les garçons minces comme des soupirs, plus ils étaient minces, plus ils lui plaisaient.

J'ai fini mon travail, je me suis lavé au fond du garage, j'ai passé ma chemise et j'ai crié à Juliette que je m'en allais. (. . .)

Elle m'attendait près de son vélo, assise sur le talus, les deux mains posées bien à plat sur l'herbe, parfaitement immobile. Je n'ai jamais vu personne qui sache rester immobile comme Elle. C'était stupéfiant. On pouvait croire que son cerveau même était bloqué, qu'il n'y avait plus rien au fond de ses grands yeux ouverts. Une fois, à la maison, elle ne m'a pas entendu venir, je suis resté immobile moi aussi, pour l'observer. Elle était véritablement une poupée. Elle était une poupée qui ne sert pas, qu'on a laissée assise entre deux murs dans un coin de la chambre. Dix siècles. A la fin, c'est moi qui ai bougé, j'allais devenir fou.

Nous avons traversé le village côte à côte, moi tenant son vélo d'une main et sa roue avant de l'autre. Plus exactement, nous avons descendu la rue—il n'y en a qu'une—et au fur et à mesure que nous avancions, tout le monde était sur le pas de sa porte pour nous regarder passer. Je dis bien tout le monde. Même un nouveau-né dans son landau. Je ne sais pas s'ils étaient là à cause de cet instinct animal qui pousse les gens à rester dehors après un orage ou s'ils avaient peur de manquer le spectacle de Pin-Pon avec la fille d'Eva Braun. En tout cas, nous ne pouvions pas parler. Brochard, devant son café, m'a fait un signe de la main et j'ai vaguement répondu. Les autres se sont contentés de nous suivre des yeux, avec des visages figés, sans se parler non plus. Même quand j'essayais la Delahaye, je n'avais jamais eu cette haie d'honneur. (. . .)

Il devait y avoir quelque chose dans l'air, cet après-midi-là—le ciel était comme lavé, d'un bleu intense—parce que notre mère, elle aussi, quand nous sommes entrés dans la cour, se tenait sur le pas de sa porte pour nous voir arriver. Je lui ai dit, de loin, que j'avais un vélo à réparer, je me suis dirigé tout droit vers l'appentis où je range le matériel de Mickey. Elles, elles ne se sont rien dit, même pas bonjour. Celle-là parce qu'on ne lui a jamais appris, et notre mère parce qu'elle se renferme devant tout ce qui porte jupe—y compris Georgette. Je crois que même un Écossais dans notre cour lui glacerait le sang.

Pendant que je remplaçais la chambre à air, Elle est allée s'asseoir sur le bac en bois de la source, à quelques pas de moi. Elle laissait sa main jouer dans l'eau mais elle ne me quittait pas des yeux. Je lui ai demandé si elle avait déchiré son pneu exprès, pour me voir. Elle m'a dit oui, « avec un taille-rosiers ». Je lui ai demandé si elle était venue exprès contre la voiture parce qu'elle savait que j'étais dessous. Elle m'a dit oui. Elle se rendait compte, depuis plusieurs jours, que je regardais ses jambes quand elle passait devant le garage. Avant d'entrer, elle avait même pensé à enlever sa culotte, rien que pour voir ma tête, mais Juliette la suivait des yeux par la fenêtre, elle n'avait pas pu.

(. . .)

Son vélo réparé, elle ne s'est pas pressée de se lever. Elle est d'abord restée assise comme elle était sur le bac de la source, un pied accroché au rebord et l'autre par terre pour que je voie bien ce qu'elle voulait me montrer, mais avec quelque chose dans les yeux qui était plus que de la déception, qui était triste, peut-être parce qu'elle sentait que son manège ne me faisait plus rien, qu'il m'écœurait même un peu. Je l'ai appris plus tard: quand elle sentait qu'elle perdait, à un jeu quelconque—elle jouait assez bien aux cartes—, elle avait le même air. Finalement, elle a rabaissé sa jambe pliée, puis sa jupe sur ses jambes, et ce n'est qu'après qu'elle s'est mise debout. Elle m'a demandé combien elle me devait. J'ai haussé les épaules. Elle m'a dit—et ce n'était plus sa voix habituelle, il m'a semblé qu'elle avait même perdu son accent: « Vous ne me raccompagnez pas? » Je l'ai raccompagnée. Elle voulait traîner le vélo, cette fois, mais j'ai dit non, que ce n'était pas gênant, je l'ai gardé.

Nous n'avons pas beaucoup parlé, en route. Elle m'a dit qu'elle aimait bien Marilyn Monroe et qu'elle avait gagné un concours de beauté, l'été d'avant, à Saint-Étienne-de-Tinée. Je lui ai dit que j'y étais avec mes frères, qu'elle était nettement la gagnante. Ensuite, tout le village se tenait à nouveau sur le pas de sa porte pour nous regarder passer, sauf le bébé dans son landau qui devait en avoir vu d'autres. Brochard m'a fait le même signe hésitant et j'ai répondu. J'avais l'impression que c'était le 1er avril et qu'on m'avait accroché un poisson dans le dos.

On s'est dit au revoir devant chez elle. Elle a repris sa bicyclette, elle m'a serré la main. Eva Braun était dehors, au fond de la cour, à redresser les fleurs que l'orage avait massacrées. Elle nous a regardés de loin, sans rien dire. Je lui ai crié bonsoir madame, mais je m'adressais à une statue. Je me suis écarté d'Elle, à reculons, quand tout à coup elle m'a demandé si je l'invitais toujours à dîner au restaurant. Je lui ai dit bien sûr, quand elle voudrait. Elle m'a dit: « Alors, ce soir, tout de suite? » La première chose qui m'est venue à l'esprit, c'est qu'il lui serait difficile de s'échapper. Elle m'a répondu: « Elle se débrouillera. » J'ai cru d'abord qu'elle parlait de sa mère, j'ai mis un instant à comprendre. Je ne savais pas encore qu'elle utilisait, quand ça lui chantait, la troisième personne pour parler d'elle-même ou de ceux à qui elle s'adressait. Avec elle, un simple « Passe-moi-le-sel » devenait un casse-tête.

Eva Braun nous observait, immobile de l'autre côté de la cour. Il était plus de sept heures. Il y avait encore de grandes taches de soleil en haut des montagnes, mais il faut une heure et demie, en allant le diable dans les virages, pour se rendre au restaurant où je voulais l'emmener. Je ne pouvais pas y aller en vêtements de travail et j'avais pensé à elle, dans la lumière des bougies, autrement qu'en jupe et en polo (. . .) Elle a compris cela sans que je lui dise. Il suffisait que je lui indique ce qu'elle devait mettre et elle en avait pour cinq minutes. J'allais faire le tour par-derrière—sa chambre donnait sur la pâture de Brochard—et elle me montrerait ses robes par la fenêtre. Voilà pourquoi je ne pouvais plus, à la fin, me passer d'elle. Elle donnait à la vie des coups d'accélérateur comme je n'en connaissais pas.

(. . .)

J'ai fait le tour de leur maison en longeant le mur du cimetière, comme un soir de la semaine précédente, mais je n'avais plus à me cacher. Il n'y avait rien ni personne dans la pâture, ils amènent les vaches plus tard dans l'été. Derrière la haie de ronces, à travers un bourdonnement d'abeilles, j'ai entendu Eva Braun qui parlait fort, en allemand, et Elle qui répondait. Je ne comprenais pas les mots mais je me doutais bien de ce qu'elles devaient se dire. Et puis, le silence.

Un moment après, Elle a ouvert sa fenêtre. Ils ont trois fenêtres, à l'étage, et c'était celle de droite. Elle m'a montré une robe rouge, une noire et une rose. Sur la robe noire, elle a plaqué une grosse fleur, pour me faire voir, puis une broche. Elle tendait chaque robe sur elle et, en me montrant la rouge, elle l'a lâchée d'une main pour relever la masse de ses cheveux noirs sur la tête. J'ai fait signe que non. Les deux autres me plaisaient bien, surtout la rose, qui était très courte, avec de fines bretelles. J'ai ouvert les mains comme un Napolitain pour dire que je ne savais pas laquelle choisir. Alors, elle a passé son polo par-dessus sa tête. Elle avait les seins nus et ils étaient comme je les avais devinés, fermes et gonflés, superbes pour sa minceur. Elle a enfilé d'abord la robe rose. Je n'en voyais que la moitié, à cause du rebord de la fenêtre. Puis, elle l'a enlevée, elle a voulu essayer la noire, mais il n'y avait pas à hésiter, j'ai agité désespérément l'index pour dire que c'était celle d'avant, la rose, que je préférais. Elle a compris, elle m'a fait un petit salut militaire. C'était un bon moment, l'un des meilleurs de ma vie. Quand j'y pense, j'aimerais tout recommencer.

2.

Bon. Je prends le taille-rosiers dans une main, la roue avant de mon vélo dans l'autre, et je me dis: « Fais attention. Après, tu ne pourras plus revenir en arrière. » Je frappe un bon coup et rien que pour sortir l'instrument, c'est un massacre.

Ensuite, Elle va voir Pin-Pon au garage pour qu'il répare le vélo. Ensuite il l'emmène dans sa cour. Elle a mis sa jupe beige évasée, son polo bleu marine avec un petit dauphin cousu sur la poitrine. Elle a mis une de ses culottes blanches en dentelle pour qu'il la voie jusqu'en haut. Elle a les jambes déjà bien bronzées, et l'intérieur des cuisses si doux, il se trompe de chambre à air, il ne sait plus où il en est. Ensuite, à la fenêtre de sa chambre, elle enlève son polo et elle lui montre ses beaux seins nus, il est droit comme un soldat de plomb derrière la haie de ronces, et elle se demande si c'est un fils de salaud ou simplement un pauvre crétin qu'elle devrait laisser tranquille. Quand je faiblis, je me déteste, je me tuerais. Ensuite, il y a la route, le restaurant. Pin-Pon bouge tout le temps. Dans la DS d'Henri IV, quand on monte une côte, il pousse sur son volant comme s'il voulait aider la saleté de voiture.

A table, il gamberge tant qu'il peut, mais toujours dans le même sens. Ce n'est pas comme je le croyais: « Est-ce qu'elle se laissera tringler ou non? » C'est autre chose. Je ne sais pas quoi. Ça me fait plaisir et ça me rend triste. (. . .)

(. . .)

Pin-Pon est brun, large d'épaules, avec des bras musclés. Il a une figure naïve, des yeux plus jeunes que son âge, j'aime bien sa manière de marcher. Ce qui me remue le plus, ce sont ses mains. Je les regarde pendant qu'il mange, je pense que dans une heure, ou même pas, elles vont me tenir, se crisper partout sur moi, je voudrais que ce soit répugnant et c'est le contraire. Je me déteste. Ou bien, alors, c'est l'effet du champagne. Je n'en ai pas bu beaucoup, mais je ne peux rien boire: ça me fait pleurer, ça me donne envie d'être une petite fille, je ne sais pas.

Dans la voiture, au retour, j'ai déjà pleuré toutes mes larmes. Je me dis qu'il va s'arrêter quelque part en route, abaisser le dossier des sièges et me le mettre soigné. Je me laisserai faire et puis, je prendrai une grosse pierre et je taperai sur sa tête et je taperai sur sa tête. Mais il ne fait rien de tout ça. C'est un brave Pin-Pon qui s'intéresse à Elle, qui essaie de comprendre ce qu'elle veut. Pauvre con. (. . .)

Et puis, on passe devant chez lui, mais il ne s'arrête pas, il faut que ce soit moi qui lui demande. Incroyable. Enfin, on traverse sa cour, en se tenant par la main, et je sens qu'il est embêté de m'emmener dans la maison, à cause de sa mère et de toute la sainte famille. On dit, lui et moi, en même temps: « Dans la grange. » A l'intérieur, c'est le noir. Il me dit: « Il y a une ampoule électrique, mais elle ne marche pas. » Un siècle. Et puis: « Ça vaut mieux d'ailleurs, qu'elle ne marche pas, parce que, quand elle marche, on ne peut plus l'arrêter. Il faut arracher les fils si on ne veut pas se ruiner. » Finalement, il me laisse là pour aller chercher une lampe à pétrole dans la maison.

Quand il revient, j'ai trouvé une échelle dans la clarté du dehors et un lit en haut, tout bancal et plein de poussière. Il me dit, en montant, que c'est le lit de mariage de sa tante. Dans le rond de sa lampe, pendant qu'il grimpe à l'échelle, je dois être comme un papillon au-dessus de lui, avec ma robe rose en corolle. (. . .)

Pin-Pon s'assoit sur le lit et m'attire devant lui. Il a les yeux levés vers moi, il y a beaucoup de gentillesse dans son regard. Il veut dire quelque chose et puis non, il ne le dit pas. Il passe ses mains sous ma robe. Je reste debout et je me laisse caresser. Il descend ma culotte et je soulève un pied, et puis l'autre, pour qu'il me l'enlève. Quand il met sa main entre mes jambes, il sait bien que j'ai envie. Alors il me fait basculer sur lui, sans que ses doigts me lâchent, il tire de l'autre main la fermeture de ma robe, il cherche mes seins. Celle-là est sur le ventre, par-dessus lui, le derrière nu comme pour la fessée, elle se voit comme ça, si excitante et sans défense, elle part une fois. Et tout le temps où elle est secouée, où elle a besoin de se plaindre et de gémir, je la regarde avec mon esprit immobile, ni dé-goûtée ni méprisante, rien, et je luis dis: « Oh! qu'est-ce qu'on te fait, ma petite Éliane, qu'est-ce qu'on te fait? » Sans même me marrer, seulement comme ça, mécaniquement, pour qu'elle aille au bout de son plaisir et qu'on n'en parle plus.

3.

Je me réveille au lever du jour, trempée de sueur. J'ai fait un rêve horrible. Je n'ai pas fermé les volets de la fenêtre et une clarté froide envahit peu à peu la chambre. J'entends Mickey qui prépare son café, en bas, juste au-dessous de moi. Pin-Pon n'est pas rentré. Je me lève et je vais jusqu'à l'armoire vérifier que le flacon est bien dans la poche de mon blazer rouge. Je le sors pour le regarder, pour vérifier que c'est le même. Dans mon rêve, c'est ma maman qu'on empoisonnait. Sous mes yeux, dans le bar de Digne. Je savais qu'elle allait mourir et je criais. Ensuite, ils lui arrachaient des poignées de cheveux, toute sa figure était couverte de sang. Mlle Dieu était là, et Pin-Pon et Touret. Mais pas Leballech. On disait qu'il allait venir et tout le monde riait et on m'obligeait à manger les cheveux de ma mère.

Je ne sais pas combien de temps je reste debout dans la chambre, toute nue. J'entends Mickey, dans la cour, qui essaie de faire partir son camion. Je vais à la fenêtre. Je me demande ce qu'il va faire, si tôt, un 14 juillet. Peut-être qu'il a ramené Georgette avec lui, cette nuit. Je ne peux pas voir si elle est dans la cabine. Je le regarde s'en aller, et puis j'enfile mon peignoir blanc marqué *Elle*, je descends à la cuisine. Il n'y a per-sonne. Je me fais du café, en me retournant plusieurs fois, parce que j'ai l'impression que quelqu'un est derrière moi. Finalement je sors avec mon bol et je m'assois sur le banc de pierre, près de la porte, et je bois mon café qui fume dans les premiers rayons du soleil rouge, entre les montagnes.

Ensuite, ça va mieux, comme toujours. Je marche pieds nus dans la cour et je vais jusque dans la prairie, derrière, où l'herbe est douce et mouillée. Je ne sais pas l'heure qu'il est. (. . .) Je trempe mes pieds dans l'eau de la rivière, mais elle est glacée, je ressors tout de suite. Je reste assise sur une grosse pierre, en essayant de ne penser à rien. Quand je ne pense à rien, je pense toujours aux mêmes conneries. Cette fois, je me revois mourir sur le divan bleu du Brusquet, le tête de Calamité entre mes genoux relevés. Elle m'a dit que c'était tellement fort que j'ai tiré sur ses cheveux, sans me rendre compte. C'est une chose qui a dû revenir dans ma saleté de rêve, j'imagine.

(. . .)

Je suis contente que Mlle Dieu ait téléphoné. C'est une vraie preuve d'amour. Enfin, je trouve. C'est une plus grande preuve d'amour que n'importe quoi d'avoir peur que quelqu'un se fasse du souci pour vous. Tout le monde—sauf ma mère—pense que si quelqu'un se fait du souci pour moi, je m'en fiche. Ce n'est pas vrai. Seigneur, non. Il ne faut pas que je montre mes sentiments, voilà tout. Qu'elle ait téléphoné chez Brochard, c'est une plus grande preuve d'amour que celle qu'elle pensait me donner, hier soir, à Digne, quand je l'ai retrouvée dans sa voiture. Elle était depuis longtemps à m'attendre, garée en face du *Provençal*. Passé les jérémiades parce que j'étais en retard, la première chose qu'elle m'a dite, c'est: « Je suis allée voir tes parents, samedi après-midi. Ta mère m'a montré ta robe de mariage. J'avais apporté une demande de reconnaissance de paternité pour ton père. Je n'ai pas pu le convaincre de la signer, mais tu verras, un jour ce sera rajouté sur ton livret de famille. »

Voilà. Samedi après-midi, je traînais en ville, je ne savais plus où aller pour me supporter. Après avoir téléphoné à Leballech, je pleurais en dedans comme cette pauvre conne peut pleurer en dehors. Elle est allée chez nous. Elle a cru qu'elle allait me rendre heureuse et que tout serait merveilleux et que je comprendrais enfin qu'elle m'aime comme elle dit, depuis que j'ai quatorze ans, ou quinze ans, depuis toujours. Je comprends, d'ailleurs. Je ne suis pas *insensible*, sûrement pas. Je ne suis pas *insensible*, ni *asociale*, ni *caractère pervers*, comme une orientatrice de merde l'a tapé à la machine, après des tests de merde, à Nice. Et un docteur avec elle, qui voulait presque m'enfermer. Seulement. Seulement, ce qui m'a traversé la tête, quand Calamité m'a raconté sa bonne action, ce n'est pas qu'elle m'aimait, ou que je devais sauter de joie à me fendre le crâne contre le toit de sa mini. Ce qui m'a traversé la tête, c'est qu'elle l'avait vu, *lui,* qu'elle lui avait parlé, qu'elle était entrée dans sa chambre, et moi pas. Et moi pas, voilà.

Je suis devant la fenêtre, le front contre la vitre. J'ai le soleil en face. Je me dis que j'irai le voir dans ma belle robe blanche, le jour du mariage, quand ils seront tous en train de boire et de rire et de se raconter leurs conneries. Pour la première fois depuis quatre ans, neuf mois et cinq jours. Et ensuite, avant que juillet se termine, Pin-Pon verra sa famille partir en lambeaux, comme la mienne. Il perdra ses frères comme j'ai perdu mon père. Où est mon père? Où est-il? J'ai de la peine quand j'imagine mon andouille de mère avec les trois salauds, ce jour de neige, je les hais pour ce qu'ils lui ont fait. Mais je m'en fiche, en fin de compte, voilà la vérité. Je m'en fiche quand je pense à ce qu'ils nous ont fait, à lui et à moi. Où est-il? J'ai frappé à coups de pelle un sale bonhomme qui n'était pas mon papa, un bonhomme que je ne connaissais pas—il faut que tu arrêtes, maintenant, arrête—il me disait: « Je te donnerai de l'argent. Je t'emmènerai en voyage. A Paris. »

Le soleil me brûle les yeux.

Je mettrai Pin-Pon en lambeaux. Il prendra un des fusils de son ordure de père et je lui dirai: « C'est Leballech, c'est Touret », pour qu'il les tue. Je serai Elle. Tout effacé. Je viendrai à mon papa et je lui dirai: « Ils sont morts tous les trois, maintenant. Je suis guérie et toi aussi. »

Je me rends bien compte que je suis dans l'escalier, assise sur une marche, une main sur la rampe. Ma joue est contre le bois verni et je vois par moments la cuisine en bas, la clarté de la fenêtre. Il n'y a pas de bruit, rien, seulement ma respiration. J'ai dû arracher mes faux ongles un à un, comme ça m'arrive, je les sens dans mon autre main, que je tiens fermée contre ma bouche. Je pleure en pensant à son visage. Il vient sur le chemin, jusqu'à notre maison. Il s'arrête à quelques pas de moi pour que j'aie à courir, pour que je saute dans ses bras. Il rit. Il crie: « Qu'est-ce qu'il a rapporté le papa, à sa chérie mignonne? Qu'est-ce qu'il a rapporté? » Rien ni personne ne pourra me faire entendre que c'est *avant*. Je veux, je veux que ce soit encore *maintenant*. Et que ça ne finisse jamais. Jamais.

*One Deadly Summer**

1.

The following evening Elle stopped by the garage.

When she came in, pushing her bike, just after a storm had flooded the street, I was under a jacked-up car. I could only see her legs, but I knew right away it was her. Her legs moved right up to the car, almost touching it. She raised her voice to ask if anyone was there. I was lying on my back, and when I shifted the trolley under me I saw that, contrary to what

One Deadly Summer (New York: Harcourt, Brace, Jovanovich, 1980; Penguin Books, 1981), 40–46, 65–68, 190–95. Translated by Alan Sheridan. These passages are reprinted with the kind permission of Harcourt, Brace, Jovanovich.

everyone thought, she did wear panties. They were white. She looked down at me calmly and said one of her tires was flat, but she didn't budge. I asked her to move away to let me get out. Several seconds passed before she did. I tried my best to act tough like some guy in a film, look her straight in the eyes, nothing else. Finally she took a step backward, and I propelled myself out so forcefully she realized I found her intimidating.

. . . .

I removed the front wheel of her bike and examined the inner tube. I didn't have to put it under water—it wasn't blown out, but torn, a tear about three centimeters. I asked her how it had happened, but she just shrugged her left shoulder and didn't answer.

I said I didn't have a spare inner tube to replace the old one. I had some at home, some old ones of Mickey's that were still good, but when I suggested she go to our place and get my mother to give her one, she didn't want to. "No thanks!" she said. "I don't want to get yelled at!" She asked me what time I finished work. I said I still had quite a bit to do under the car. She said she'd wait outside. I was stripped to the waist—it was very hot, and a storm was about to break again. She said I was really well built. I'd been less worried about my chances since I saw the tear in her tire, but it was the first pleasant thing she'd said to me. It made me feel good. But I was wrong. She didn't like well-built men. What she liked was slim young boys, thin as a breath.

I finished my work, washed my hands at the end of the garage, put on my shirt, and yelled up to Juliette that I was going.

. . . .

Elle was waiting by her bike, sitting on the embankment, her hands flat on the grass, quite still. I've never known anyone who could be as still as her. It was amazing. It was as if even her brain had stopped functioning. There was nothing at the back of her big, wide-open eyes. Once, in the house, she didn't hear me come in, and I stood quite still, too, and watched her. She really was like a doll—a doll you never pick up but leave sitting in the corner of the room. We stayed like that for ages. Finally I had to move. It was driving me crazy.

We walked through the village side by side; I held her bike with one hand and her front wheel with the other. Or, rather, we went down the street—there is only one—and as we went, everybody was out on the doorstep to watch us go by. And I mean everybody, even an infant in a baby carriage. I don't know whether they were there because of that animal instinct that drives people to stay outside after a storm, or whether they were afraid of missing the spectacle of Ping-Pong walking down the street with Eva Braun's daughter. Anyway, we couldn't say anything to each other. Brochard stood outside his café and gave me a vague wave of the hand. The others were content to follow us with their

eyes, faces transfixed, without saying a word. Even when I was trying out the Delahaye, I never had this guard of honor.
. . . .

There must have been something in the air that afternoon—the sky looked washed, a dark blue—because when we came into the yard Mamma, too, was standing outside on the doorstep. I called over to her that I had a bike to repair and went straight to the shed, where Mickey's equipment was kept. They said nothing to each other, not even hello. Elle because she had never been taught to, and Mamma because she closed up in front of anything wearing a skirt—including Georgette. I think even a Scotsman in our yard would make her blood freeze.

While I changed the inner tube, Elle went and sat on the wooden tank by the spring, a few meters away. She let her hand trail in the water, but she didn't take her eyes off me. I asked her if she had torn her tire on purpose, so as to see me. She said yes, "with a pair of garden shears." I asked her if she'd come so close to the car because she knew I was underneath. She said yes. She'd known for several days now that I was looking at her legs as she went by the garage. Before coming in, she'd even thought of taking off her panties, just to see the look on my face, but Juliette was watching her from the window and she couldn't.
. . . .

When I'd finished repairing her bike, she didn't seem in any hurry to get up. She just sat there on the tank, one foot wedged against the rim and the other on the ground so that I could see what she wanted to show me. There was something in her eyes that was more than disappointment, something sad, perhaps because she felt her tricks weren't working any more, maybe I was even getting a bit sick of them. I learned about it later: when she felt she was losing at some game—she was quite good at cards—she got that same look. Finally she straightened her leg, pulled her skirt down over her knees, and got up. She asked me how much she owed me. I shrugged my shoulders. Then she said—not in her usual voice, she almost seemed to have lost her accent—"Aren't you taking me home?" I took her home. She wanted to push the bike back this time, but I said no, it was no trouble; I carried it.

We didn't talk much on the way. She said how much she liked Marilyn Monroe, and how she'd won a beauty contest the summer before at Saint-Etienne-de-Tinée. I said I'd been there with my brothers, and she had won by a long shot. The whole village was out on the doorsteps to watch us go by again, except the baby in its carriage, who must have seen it all before. Brochard made the same hesitant sign, and I waved back. I felt as if it was April Fools' Day, and some trick was being played on me.

I said good-bye to her in front of her house. She took back her bike and shook hands. Eva Braun was outside, at the end of the yard, tending the flowers the storm had blown over. She looked at us but said nothing. I called out, "Good evening," but she might have been a statue. I was about to go when suddenly Elle asked if the invitation to dinner in the restaurant still held. I said of course, whenever she wanted to go. She said, "O.K. What about tonight, right away?" The first thing that occurred to me was that it would be difficult for her to get out of it. She said, "She'll manage." I thought at first she was talking about her mother. It took me some time to understand. I didn't know then that she was in the habit of using the third person when speaking of herself or of those she was talking to. With her, a mere "pass me the salt" became some kind of riddle.

Eva Braun stood watching us, from the other end of the yard. It had struck seven. There were still great patches of sun on the mountaintops, but it takes an hour and a half, what with all the twists and bends in the road, to get to the restaurant I wanted to take her to. I couldn't go in work clothes, and I imagined her, in the candlelight, wearing something other than a skirt and jersey. . . . She understood all that without my saying anything. I only had to say what she should wear and she'd be ready in five minutes. I was to go around to the back—her bedroom looked out over Brochard's field—and she would show me her dresses through the window. That's why, in the end, I couldn't give her up. She had a way of putting her foot on the accelerator I'd never met before.

. . . .

I walked around their house by the cemetery wall, like that time the week before, but this time I didn't have to hide. There was nothing and no one in the field—they bring the cows in later in summer. From behind the thorn hedge, which was full of buzzing bees, I could hear Eva Braun talking loudly in German and Elle answering back. I didn't understand what they were saying, but I had a good idea. Then it got quiet.

A minute later Elle opened her window. There were three upstairs windows, and hers was the one on the right. She showed me a red dress, a black one, and a pink one. She held a big flower against the black dress to show me, and then a brooch. She held each dress against her body, and when she showed me the red one, she kept it up with one hand, and with the other pushed back her thick black hair from her face. I gestured no. I liked the other two a lot, especially the pink one, which was very short, with narrow straps. I opened my arms wide like a Neopolitan to say I didn't know which one to choose. Then she took off her turtleneck jersey. She wasn't wearing a bra, and her tits were just as I'd imagined them, firm and big, pretty good considering how slim she was. First she put on the pink dress. I could only see half of it, because of the windowsill. Then she took it off. She wanted to try on the black one, but there was no doubt. I waved my finger desperately to say that it had to be the pink one. She understood and gave a little military salute. It was a good moment, one of the best in my life. When I think about it, I'd like to start all over again.

2.

O.K. I picked up the garden shears in one hand and front wheel of my bike in the other and said, "Be careful. Once you've done it, you won't be able to turn back." I gave it a great tear and pulled the shears out. It was a massacre.

Then Elle went to see Ping-Pong at the garage to get him to repair the bike. Then he took it back to his yard. Elle had on her flared beige skirt, her navy-blue turtleneck jersey with the little dolphin stiched on the front. She'd put on a pair of her white lace panties so that he could see them right up her skirt. Her legs were already well tanned and her thighs ever so soft. He was so worked up he didn't know what he was doing. He put the wrong inner tube back on. Then, at her bedroom window, she took off her jersey and showed him her beautiful bare breasts. He stood as straight as a toy soldier behind the thorn hedge, and she wondered whether he was just a bastard like all the others or some poor idiot she ought to leave alone. When I weaken, I hate myself—I'd even kill myself. Then there was the drive and the restaurant. Ping-Pong kept moving all the time. When we were going up a hill in Henri IV's DS, he leaned forward over the steering wheel as if he was urging the filthy old car on.

During the meal he did his best to keep up a conversation, but it was always the same story. It wasn't what I thought it would be, "Will she let me poke her or not?" It was something else. I don't know exactly what. I liked it, and it made me sad.

. . . .

Ping-Pong is dark. He has broad shoulders and muscular arms. He has a simple face, and his eyes look younger than he really is. I like the way he walks. What gets me most are his hands. I looked at them as he ate. I was thinking that in an hour or so they would be holding me, moving all over me—I wanted it to be repugnant, but it was the reverse. I hated myself. Unless it was the effect of the champagne. I didn't drink much, I can't really drink anything—I start crying and I want to be a little girl again. I don't know.

In the car, on the way back, I got over my tears. I said to myself, he'll stop somewhere on the way, fold back the rear seat, and start. I'd let him do it, then I'd pick up a rock and beat his head in. But he didn't try anything. He was just good old Ping-Pong, who was interested in Elle and tried to understand what she wanted. Poor bastard

. . . .

Then we went past his house, but he didn't stop—I had to ask him to. Incredible! At last we crossed his yard, hand in hand, and I felt he didn't want to take me into the house, because of his mother and the whole damned family. Both of us said, at the same time, "The barn." It was dark inside. He said, "There's an electric lamp, but it doesn't work." Another century went by and he said, "It's just as well because when it does work you can't stop it. You have to pull out the wires if you don't want to be ruined." Finally he left me there while he went in to get a kerosene lamp from the house.

By the time he got back, I'd found a ladder in the light from outside and a rickety, dusty old bed under the barn roof. As we were going up to it, he said it was his aunt's marriage bed. In the pool of light cast by his lamp as he climbed the ladder, I must have looked like a butterfly above him, in my coral-pink dress.

. . . .

Ping-Pong sat on the bed and drew me to him. He raised his eyes toward me. There was so much gentleness in them. He started to say something, then broke off. He put his hands under my dress. I stayed standing and let him feel me. He pulled down my panties, and I raised first one foot, then the other, so that he could take them off. When he put his hands between my legs, he knew very well I wanted it. Then he pulled me down toward him, without letting go. With the other hand he undid the zipper of my dress. He felt for my breasts. Elle is lying on her belly on top of him, her backside bare, as if she's going to be beaten. She sees herself like that, exciting and defenseless. And all the time she's moving up and down, moaning and groaning, I look down at her, from the stillness of my mind, feeling neither disgust nor contempt, nothing. I said to her, "Oh! What are they doing to you, my little Eliane, what are they doing to you?" I wasn't even laughing at myself—it was just like that, mechanical, so that she'd get to her pleasure and have done with it.

3.

I woke at dawn, drenched in sweat. I'd had a horrible dream. I hadn't closed the shutters, and a cold light was gradually invading the room. I heard Mickey getting his coffee ready downstairs, just below. Ping-Pong hadn't come back. I got up and went to the wardrobe to make sure the bottle was still in my red blazer pocket. I took it out and looked at it to make sure it was the same one. In my dream, it was my mother who was poisoned as I looked on, at the bar in Digne. I knew she was going to die, and I cried out. Then they started pulling handfuls of her hair out, and her face was covered with blood. Mlle Dieu was there, and Ping-Pong, and Touret, but not Leballech. Someone said he was coming, and everyone laughed and forced me to eat my mother's hair.

I don't know how long I stood in the room, naked. I heard Mickey in the yard, trying to get his truck going. I went to the window. I asked him what he was going to do so early on the Fourteenth of July. Maybe he'd brought Georgette back with him last night. I couldn't see whether she was in the truck. I watched him go off, then put on my white bathrobe with *Elle* embroidered on it and went down into the kitchen. There was no one there. I made myself some coffee, turning around several times because I had the feeling someone was behind me. Finally I went out with my bowl and sat down on the stone seat near the door to drink my coffee, which steamed in the first rays of the red sun, between the mountains.

Things got better, as always. I walked barefoot in the yard, going as far as the fields behind, where the grass was soft and damp. I had no idea what time it was . . . I wet my feet in the stream, but the water was icy, and I took them out right away. I sat down on a big stone, trying to think of nothing. When I think of nothing, I always think of the same crap. This time, I saw myself coming on the blue sofa in Le Brusquet, Calamity's head between my raised knees. She said it was so strong I pulled on her hair without realizing.

. . . .

I was pleased Mlle Dieu had called. That was a real proof of love, or at least I thought so. It's the greatest proof of love when people are concerned about your worrying about them. Everybody—except my mother—thinks that if someone is concerned about me, I don't care. It's not true. I just don't want to show my feelings, that's all. Telephoning Brochard is a greater proof of love than the one she thought she was giving me the night before, in Digne, when I got into her car. She'd been there a long time, waiting for me, across from the Provençal. When she got through with all the complaints about how late I was, the first thing she said to me was, "I went to see your parents on Saturday afternoon. Your mother showed me your wedding dress. I took them a request for recognition of paternity for your father. I didn't manage to persuade him to sign it, but you'll see, one day it will be part of your family file."

So there you are. Saturday afternoon, when I was wandering around town, not knowing what to do to pass the time. After calling Leballech, I'd been weeping inside like that idiot could cry outside. She'd gone to our home. She thought she would make me happy and everything would be marvelous and I'd finally understand that she'd loved me, as she said, since I was fourteen or fifteen, from the first moment she set eyes on me. I did understand, in fact, I wasn't *insensitive*, certainly not. I'm not *insensitive*, or *asocial*, or of a *perverse character*, as some shit of a social worker typed out after some idiotic tests they made me take in Nice. And there was a doctor with her who almost wanted to lock me up. And yet, and yet, what went through my head when Calamity told me about her good deed was not that she loved me, or that I should jump for joy and split my head open on the roof of her mini. What went through my head was that she had seen him, *him,* talked to him, gone into his room, and I hadn't. I hadn't—that was it.

I was standing at the window, my forehead against the glass. I was in the sun. I told myself I'd go see him in my white wedding dress, on my wedding day, when they were all drinking and laughing and telling their idiotic stories. For the first time in four years, nine months, and five days. And then, before the end of July, Ping-Pong would see his family fall apart as mine had done. He would lose his brothers, as I had lost my father. Where was my father? Where was he? It hurts me when I think of my fool of a mother with those three bastards, that snowy winter's day, and I hate them for what they did to her. But the truth is, I don't really care. I don't care when I think of what they've done to us, to her and to me. Where is he? I hit some dirty guy over the head with a spade, but he wasn't my daddy, he was some guy I didn't know. You must stop, now, stop. He used to say to me, "I'll give you money. I'll take you on a trip—to Paris."

The sun was hurting my eyes.

I would tear Ping Pong to shreds. He would get one of his filthy father's rifles, and I would say to him, "It's Leballech, it's Touret," and he'd kill them. I will be Elle. Wiped out. I shall come to my daddy and I shall say to him, "All three are dead now. I'm cured, and so are you."

I realized I was on the stairs, sitting on a step, holding the banister. My cheek was resting against the polished wood, and at times I could see the kitchen below, the brightness of the window. There was no noise, nothing, just my breathing. I'd had to pull off my false fingernails, one by one. I felt them in my other hand, which I held tight against my mouth. I cried when I thought of his face. He came along the path to our house. He stopped a few paces away from me so that I could run and jump into his arms. He laughed. "And what has Daddy brought back for his darling little girl?" he shouted. "What has he brought back?" Nothing and nobody could make me understand that that was *before*, I wanted it to be *now*, and to go on forever. Forever.

II.

CATHERINE CUSSET

A Different Measure of Time:
Writing or the Consciousness of Pleasure

*Interview with Philippe Sollers**

Catherine Cusset: *Le Coeur Absolu* tells of the creation of a secret society that has pleasure as its reason and ennui as its obsessive fear. What is ennui for you, Philippe Sollers?
Philippe Sollers: I will answer by speaking to you of time. *Le Coeur Absolu* is a book about time. All novels are, I think, works about time. The problem that I formulated for myself is a novelistic investigation, by narrative and by a certain number of montages, among them that of the secret society, about that which could accelerate time, slow it down, make a year appear longer or shorter; I asked myself what was a month, a week, a day, even what was an hour, a moment. To my great surprise, after having published this book, I received, from a historian, a study published in *La Revue historique* of 1986 about the libertine secret societies during the reign of Louis XV. I had no idea that there could have existed a large number of libertine societies in the eighteenth century; that is, societies for pleasure and not for knowledge, such as the societies that are always spoken of, namely freemasonry. In parallel with these secret societies, in the eighteenth century there proliferated pleasure societies where people gathered together in accordance with a certain number of affinities, codes, and rituals. The historian who sent me this study was convinced that my novel had intended to take up this eighteenth century tradition which deserved to be studied very seriously. One of these societies was called "The Society of the Moment." I was stunned: if I had had to choose a title other than *Le Coeur Absolu*, it would have been *The Society of the Moment, Novel*. It is a novel on the absolute heart of time. It is obvious, if you study time, that you must ask

*Conducted by Catherine Cusset, 29 June 1987 in Paris.

yourself about your instrument for measuring time. In *Le Coeur Absolu*, it is, of course, the greater or lesser *jouissance* of which one is capable.

C.C.: You say something different in *Le Coeur Absolu;* you say: the clock, or the measure of time, "it isn't the fuck but the consciousness that one has of it."

Ph.S.: Of course. By jouissance, I imply the consciousness that one has of pleasure. That is how I would define jouissance: not pleasure, but the consciousness that one has of it.

This measure of time will necessarily color all sentiments, all the classic affects that one experiences in the course of existence, and notably ennui. Ennui, to answer your question, is what makes you experience time as very lengthy, very burdensome.

C.C.: What is it that makes you experience time as very lengthy? Everything that isn't erotic?

Ph.S.: Yes. I believe that eroticism bores most people. Besides, it can be explained by the great Freudian trinity: inhibition, symptom, anxiety. Men are either inhibited or anxious with respect to eroticism, or else they suffer from the symptoms of it. What bores the narrator of *Le Coeur Absolu* may be called useless psychology. Let us say: everything that belongs to the domain of psychic reaction that does not serve the goal of pleasure.

C.C.: In your novel, you illustrate this rejection of all "useless psychology," since you don't introduce any conflict between the narrator S. and the women he frequents. Couldn't one reproach you, to some extent, for simplification?

Ph.S.: Certainly! How many complicated books there are, which have for principle the fact of not going straight to their sexual objective! One can create very lengthy narrations, provided that one avoids mentioning the sexual act itself. But since for me the relationships are established according to this measuring of time, a simplification of measures follows inevitably. I think that we are in a time when we must not hesitate to use simplification, because there are false complexities, false sophistications. This is one of the characteristics of our era, an extreme apparent complexity for the purpose of hiding ignorance about the simplest things. If, for my part, I erase these false complexities, it is in order to arrive at a different complexity.

C.C.: Which one?

Ph.S.: From the moment when sexual notation defines the space and the time in which we move—that is to say, that space and time are not constructed in order to arrive eventually at a sexual instance, but when one starts off from this sexual instance—the complexity is no longer in the repressions of the characters, in the metaphorization of their reciprocal impasses, in order to mark a failure or a physical obstacle. The complexity is in the sexual things themselves; it emerges from a large number of historical reinterpretations: in a mode that seems transparent, light, rapid, a large number of complex reinterpreted historical questions fill up the novel; for example, Casanova, or Dante. It's not obvious how to arrive at the reinterpretation of *The Divine Comedy* in parallel with Nabokov's *Lolita!*

I can give you a schema—simple and simplifying—once again, to explain this complexity to you in another way. You have three types of narrative: you have the narrative that introduces the narrator searching for a truth he does not intuit; for example, *La Recherche.* The contract accepted between the narrator and the reader is that through a considerable number of events, meanderings, echos, reduplications, one day, at the end of the narrative, truth in its entirety will be revealed. You are not supposed to doubt for a second the wish for truth on the part of the narrator, which is the very principle of the narration. You have another possibility: this is the contract of the Nabokov type, where the narrator tells you that he set off in search of truth and where you, the reader, discover that this narrator who claims to have set off in search of truth as in *La Vie de Sebastian Knight*—a fascinating book—does everything he can not to know, to know nothing about it. Which creates an extremely interesting narrative situation, because the passion to know nothing is equally deserving of novelistic presentation. Finally you have a third technique, evinced in the eighteenth-century novel, torrentially in Sade: the author knows everything in advance, his world view is completely determined, down to the smallest detail, philosophically radical, entirely assertive. He is going to present you with fugues and variations through this certainty that he is not searching for truth, he has it at the beginning. It is clear that I adopt this third point of view, the one of the narrator who knows everything and who can interpret everything. He is able to do this precisely because his sexual life is ordered in such a fashion that he has a complete certainty about sex which allows him to interpret all phenomena.

C.C.: You place yourself then in a libertine literary tradition, with the accent on sex, which extends from Sade to Bataille?

Ph.S.: Sade, yes. Bataille, I like very much; *Madame Edwarda* is an entirely sublime novel, but what I am doing is, I believe, very different. . . .

Bataille's position, you know, is eroticism as the approbation of life even into death. This conception of eroticism which verges on ruin, and ecstasy in ruin, corresponds, I think, to a certain state of European nihilism. I am trying on the contrary to have almost no further relation with nihilism. I am making a gesture of lightness. I eliminate negativity, and I bring it back in another manner, in order to highlight the difference: these are the epileptoid crises of the narrator of *Le Coeur Absolu*. It's a wink at Dostoyevsky. That's how I deal with the problem of nihilism, that is to say, the negative charge that there can be in sexual guilt. The big problem is to know why guilt happened to come into this sphere, how can it be that sex would engender guilt. I'm well aware that the Bible explains it to us, but this explanation is not sufficient. Because during certain periods, sex was an object of narrative just like all the others. If you read the Memoirs of Saint-Simon, you can see the way in which he writes down everything that has to do with sex, as if that did not have any importance.

C.C.: In *Le Coeur Absolu,* you speak a lot about Dante, Casanova, Sade, Mozart. Do you contrast centuries with each other, for example, the eighteenth century with the twentieth, or do you compare and contrast countries?

Ph.S.: I have the impression that the eighteenth century is not within time but on the contrary a sort of medium/mean time state. To think that the eighteenth century got started in the seventeenth century and led to the nineteenth century doesn't interest me a lot. I very much like Philippe Muray's book called *Le XIXème Siècle à travers les âges:* by very precise details, he shows quite well that the nineteenth century has a strange status which might be like a sort of definitive psychic regimen for humanity. I am very struck by the fact that we might start today to think about time outside of linearity; the reinterpretation that we might make of it presupposes that we lift many taboos; for example, the eighteenth century does not necessarily open onto the French Revolution (or rather, that revolution called French) and thence into the nineteenth century. For countries, it is similar: it's the reinterpretation of cultural localizations in a space which is not necessarily definitive, where sectioning can be carried out, and distributions different from those learned in school can be presented.

C.C.: In this space, do you contrast lighter Italy and France with weighty Germany? And where do you locate yourself in the Anglo-Saxon tradition?

Ph.S.: Polemically speaking, I have a tendency to set up a division between north and south. East and west I don't understand, for me, it's north and south everywhere. Pushkin is a southern author, for example. Faulkner is a southern author, just as Hemingway seeks the south throughout his life. A line of demarcation can really be traced between north and south; one can then quite well imagine an Anglo-Saxon south, a German south. . . . Nietzsche himself says it about Mozart: Mozart had faith in the south. And this is said by someone who himself did not want to be German because he felt something very frightening coming from it. I contrast the north and the south in that way everywhere, even in the interior of each individual: each one has a north side, a south side. . . .

C.C: Values change from the north to the south?

Ph.S.: It's a metaphorical locating. What does it mean: to be tempted by the south? That means to give the preference to sensation, to perception, to sensual technique, to physiology as thought, over concept, abstraction, calculation, philosophy in general. My polemic is very antiphilosophical. It seems obvious to me that German philosophy comes straight from the Reformation.

C.C.: What do you think of such a writer of erotic literature as the American Henry Miller?

Ph.S.: Not much. It is not enough to want to play at being southern in order to succeed easily at it. *Tropic of Cancer* is good, it's energetic, full of force. But sexual experimentation, instead of being burned and transformed into something else, becomes more and more charged with subliminal and esoteric references: all of the fundamentally Protestant ideology came back in his writing with time. Miller's case poses an interesting question: that of Americans in relation to Europe, to European obsessions: France, Italy, Spain. In the United States, repression is at its height, whether by repressive desublimation or by repression pure and simple; by repressive desublimation, I mean pornography, trivial display of skin, of no interest. You can therefore imagine the fantasy there is to discover, for someone born in Chicago or somewhere else, when that person has been subjected to the beating from the Presbyterian, Episcopalian—or whatever you like—billy club, to discover suddenly that *jouissance*, release, sensuality, exist.

C.C.: You appear keenly polemic in your novels with regard to a movement which is very powerful in the United States: feminism. Why this polemic?

Ph.S.: I am polemic with everything that is collective. Immediately I become fiery and furious. I reject everything that says "we." We, women. . . . It would be the same for "we, men . . ." business, the army. . . . Men, women, this or that, I don't know them. I wonder on the other hand about the reason why a certain number of bodies *en situation* insist on a "we": that allows them to reassure themselves cheaply, and to avoid questioning of the familiar "you." All the variable episodes of we, from the proletariat to feminism—which has adopted collectivist discourse— are sometimes necessary in the movement of History, it's very understandable. But that's bringing time back, once again, to an ill-at-ease time that is waiting, while conditions get better, until blossoming and fulfillment become possible; it's entirely contradictory to the here, now, right away.

I reject everything that says "we," everything that tries to reduce to the generic, that is to say, to the species, or to gender. Everything that does not define the real as intrinsically individual seems false and manipulated to me, for very bad reasons most of the time. My metaphysics are the theology of the subtle Duns Scotus; to wit: only the ultimate endpoint of the individual is real. Because there are no two sexualities alike. I want to say that *I*—not we—am a writer; all my life, and time as I conceive of it, is subordinated to the fact that *I* am a writer. That's all.

C.C.: Why that polemic, in your latest novel, against women writers, authors of bestsellers? You don't like women writers?

Ph.S.: No. When a woman writes about Eros, it is rather negative.

To make yet another simplification. . . . I am compelled to return to Freud, who is a valued ally for me. To simplify, let us say: Eros and Thanatos, the two eternal twins who divide and share the use that can be made of the drives. It is obvious that my sword belongs to Eros against Thanatos.

C.C.: According to you, women's writing is more on the side of Thanatos?

Ph.S.: Most often. . . . It is interesting to ask oneself why eroticism enunciated by a woman goes more to the side of melancholy and depression.

C.C.: You said a moment ago that your life was subordinated to the fact that you were a writer. Do you write regularly or only when you feel the desire? In other words: do you consider writing a profession or a pleasure?

Ph.S.: It's more serious than a profession or a pleasure. Pleasure sometimes, not always. . . . No, it's a matter of salvation. A mystic response!

It is a constant physiological technique. In the periods of writing, properly speaking, it requires a lot of time: in order to succeed in writing for seven hours a day, there must be twelve hours available. Writing is a question of time. Writing is time. Writing is necessary in order to measure time. An hour of writing is a tremendous thing; three days without writing is also a tremendous thing, but in the other sense: lost time. To recover lost time. Proust really had a tremendous intuition, because that is what it's all about.

C.C.: Do you write everyday?

Ph.S.: I write everyday, but often in a very condensed form. It is here that the notion of Joycean epiphany intervenes. What you see in the red notebook of *Le Coeur Absolu* are little epiphanies which lead next to developments. What is an epiphany? It's a very condensed notation, full of meaningless words for whoever reads it, which is destined to note something that happened that was so true, so exact—an attitude, a gesture, an intonation of voice—that, to explain it, it would need a lengthy development. Since one hasn't the time to do it, one notes it. Joyce's notebooks are full of epiphanies. Proust too. When you go back to the note, you get the whole landscape with it, the weather. The weather is very important: it's sunny, it's snowing, it's raining. . . . That is part of the time, the weather. It is one of the functions of time. With the epiphany, you know that you have noted that thing which will restore all the rest and from that point, it can be recounted.

C.C.: Do you consider the novelist to be the witness to his times?

Ph.S.: If you allow it to be seen by your contemporaries that you are a witness to their times, yes, witness, martyr even, in the etymological sense, if you make them feel that everything that they are in the process of saying and doing may be simply fiction, it's savage: that places doubt on the reality of life as it is really lived. A living person never felt less alive than a dead person; if you introduce a doubt into the mind, that can go very far.

C.C.: Writing transforms the real into fiction?

Ph.S.: Writing, as that which makes tangible the extreme relativity of time. One's contemporaries do not appreciate that you set yourself to making nasty little calculations about their time—*their* time; they think that they own it poor fools! It is very difficult to implant a suspicion in someone that he is not in the process of living *his* own life, but rather a series of repetitions of which he is not conscious. This is to be related to the apology that I am not afraid to make on behalf of Pavlov, an entirely misunderstood thinker and a very interesting character. The strictest Pavlovism seems to me to rule life in society, the stimulus-response process, as I say in *Le Coeur Absolu.* If you sow doubt in people whom you know, that they themselves are montages susceptible of being described in a work of fiction, a somewhat cubist assemblage of things found here and there, that has to bother them a lot.

C.C.: It is this disquiet, according to you, that explains the polemic that has opened up around your name, Philippe Sollers?

Ph.S.: It's Pavlovian. I can explain why.

C.C.: The critics haven't called you into question?

Ph.S.: No! I cannot challenge a device that is myself, that indicates the north and the south with precision. . . . But I know why I will never satisfy the critics. I can tell you who is for me and who is against me. It's very simple. I have for me the people who know me well in a certain number of networks, I have for me the scholars who favor the fact that I introduce learned subjects in an agreeable manner in novels; I don't have against me any mass hostility, which is important.

On the other hand, I have against me the entire critical and scholarly establishment, with a few rare exceptions. This entire establishment, which constitutes the literary customhouse, is unleashed against me. I call them the customs officers; or the clergy, if you prefer; the middle clergy, neither the high clergy nor the people, but the middle or lower clergy. Yes, let's state this in terms of clergy, it will be clearer for everyone. O.K.?

TRANSLATED BY MARIE-ANNE FLEMING

PHILIP BARNARD
CHERYL LESTER

Philippe Sollers: *Femmes*

Philippe Sollers has been a key figure of the Parisian literary-intellectual milieu for the past thirty years. Today, at the age of fifty-one, Sollers takes his place as one of the major French authors of the second half of the twentieth century. Thus far the career of this protean and always controversial writer and left-bank personality ("the dervish of the sixth arrondissement," as one reviewer put it) has been complex and eventful; Sollers's gift for self-transformation makes summaries of his career rapidly obsolete. Nevertheless, at this point one can divide his career into a *Tel Quel* period, from 1959 to 1982, and a Gallimard period, from 1982 to the present.

Born in Talence in 1937, within a stone's throw of the Haut Brion vineyards, educated in Bordeaux and Versailles, Sollers's first prose fictions, "Le Défi" and a somewhat Proustian novel entitled *Une Curieuse solitude,* appeared in 1957 and 1958 while Sollers was briefly a student in economics. Immediately hailed by Aragon, and Mauriac, who announced "I will have been the first to write this name," these works established Sollers as a young writer of great promise. During the 1960s and 1970s Sollers developed from a founding member of the *Tel Quel* group (along with the writer and art critic Marcelin Pleynet, in particular) to the organizing personality of that group and thus of the review which became the leading publication of the structuralist "revolution," with its fragile equilibrium of Marxist, psychoanalytic, philosophical, anthropological, and literary-theoretical forces. Sollers's first four novels during this period—*Le Parc* (1961), *Drame* (1965), *Nombres* (1968), and *Lois* (1972)—work past the formulas of the new novel toward the creation of plotless narrative structures which elicited the praise and commentary of the period's most notable voices, including Foucault, Derrida, Barthes, Lacan, and Kristeva. Without yet returning to plot and character, the novels *H* (1973) and *Paradis* (1981) transform the discrete segments and pronounced architecture of the earlier works into a continuous, unpunctuated flow of rhythmic prose. With these two novels, Sollers achieved a *tour de force* of modernist poetics whose clear precedents are Joyce and Faulkner. The powerful narrative voice that emerges in these works foregrounds song, chant, psalmody, and oral rhythms that point toward their sources in sacred texts and Dantean *epos.*

In 1982, leaving the rue Jacob and his relationship of over twenty years with the Editions du Seuil, Sollers moved to the rue Sébastien-Bottin and the more prestigious offices of Gallimard. At this point in his career, *Tel Quel* was rebaptised *L'Infini* and a resurrected Sollers embarked on a trilogy of best-selling and relatively traditional novels—*Femmes* (1982), *Portrait du joueur* (1984), and *Le Coeur absolu* (1987)—whose autobiographical posturing and provocative analysis of the French intellectual world have made him into a well-known media figure in the Paris of the 1980s. Although Sollers's novels have always had a certain reputation for "experimental" or theoretical sophistication, the first three Gallimard novels and a second volume of *Paradis* (1986) reestablished Sollers as a novelist with the ability to reach and provoke a wide reading public without sacrificing the intellectual and analytic rigor characteristic of his work. More than a simple "return" to plot and character, the trilogy recasts all the earlier tendencies of Sollers's work in the context of social and self-satire, utilizing traditional narrative staging as a framework for the two hallmarks of Sollersian writing whatever its form: his virtuosity as a prose stylist, and his analytic insistence on the primacy of sexuality and religion.

But in addition to the eleven novels he has written to date, the prolific range of Sollers's writing must also be taken into consideration. Parallel to the novels as well as within them, as an intrinsic part of their logic, Sollers has elaborated an impressive critical corpus. This critical writing extends from the metacommentary appended to "Le Défi" in 1957 through several volumes of essays on literature, painting, and music, to the recent book-length studies of Fragonard and Watteau. In addition, Sollers has published four volumes in interviews and many occasional writings, besides the uncollected literary and critical texts published throughout *Tel Quel* and *L'Infini*.

The following excerpt is drawn from *Femmes*, the novel that marked Sollers's transition from the status of an acclaimed avant-garde writer to that of a Socratic gadfly operating on a wider, more public stage. With *Femmes*, a six hundred-page semiautobiographical narrative, Sollers offers a critical exploration of intellectual life in Paris in the early 1980s. The question of women, and of feminism, is central to this exploration, for it represents the blind spot of the theoretical currents of the postwar period. The narrator—an American journalist and diarist whose observations and descriptions contrast him with the experimental and more abstracted stance of his close friend, the writer S., who ultimately edits the manuscript—records his theoretical and sexual encounters as a framework for the novel's many variations on representation and sexuality. The novel's open-ended series of picaresque episodes provides an account of Sollers's career, and establishes the basis for an on-going narrative that is continued in *Portrait du joueur* and *Le Coeur absolu*.

Given its episodic structure, this novel is conceived as dramatic tableau-painting on a large scale, much like the grand frescoes of Tiepolo referred to in the narrative's final Venetian scenes. Just as the portraiture of court personalities figures in the overall plan of Tiepolo's allegorical-historical scenes, or in the *Memoirs* of Saint-Simon, one of Sollers's favored authors, so too *Femmes* includes *roman à clef* portraits of Lacan, Barthes, Althusser, and others with whom Sollers was closely associated during the *Tel Quel* years.

The passage translated here is part of the novel's portrayal of Louis Althusser in the character of the professor and Marxist theoretician Laurent Lutz, whose name suggests both the Germanic origins of his theory, and *lutte*, the French term for "struggle." As in its treatment of Lacan and Barthes, the novel casts the fate of this thinker and his ideas in a tragic and elegiac light, juxtaposing his self-destructive madness with the senseless deaths of the other two figures. Sollers's master-thinkers, like the priest in Céline who stopped believing long ago, struggle for power and the control of belief, and pass away in efforts to ignore or eliminate what their theories exclude.

SELECTED CRITICISM

Scholarly criticism has been slow to recognize Sollers, and the current critical commonplaces continue to either overlook or misconstrue the essential outlines of his corpus by attempting to categorize Sollers's work (as avant-garde, post structuralist, etc., or, more recently and even more unlikely, as misogynist or as "selling out" to the French media) and to encapsulate it in a "movement" or theoretical formula that it easily exceeds. Paradoxically, however, what commentary there is is generally of a high standard and by notable critics. The following list gives the English translation, when available, of works by French authors.

Barthes, Roland. *Writer Sollers*. Trans. Philip Thody. Minneapolis: University of Minnesota Press, 1987. Barthes's collected essays on Sollers.
Derrida, Jacques. "Dissemination," in *Dissemination*. Trans. Barbara Johnson. Chicago: University of Chicago Press, 1981. On Sollers's *Drame* and *Nombres*.
Foucault, Michel. "Distance, aspect, origine" (1963), in *Théorie d'ensemble*. Paris: Seuil, 1968. On Sollers, Robbe-Grillet, and the evolution of the *Nouveau Roman*.
Hayman, David. "Introduction," in Philippe Sollers, *Writing and the Experience of Limits*. Trans. Philip Barnard with David Hayman. New York: Columbia University Press, 1983. The fullest general introduction to Sollers (up to *Paradis*) in English.
———. *Re-Formations: Toward a Mechanics of Modernist Fiction*. Ithaca, N.Y.: Cornell University Press, 1987. Discussions of Sollers appear on pages 95–102 and 137–143.
Heath, Stephen. *The Nouveau Roman*. Philadelphia: Temple University Press, 1972, 179–242. The best treatment in English of Sollers as the major successor of the *Nouveau Roman*.
Holz, Karl. *Destruktion und Konstruktion*. Frankfort am Main: Vittorio Klosterman, 1980. A lengthy final chapter on Sollers as successor to the French modernist lineage of Mallarmé, Breton, and Blanchot.
Houdebine, Jean-Louis. "Le Chant (ou sens vivant) des langues," *Tel Quel* 57 (1974): 85–116. On *Lois*. This issue of *Tel Quel* is entirely devoted to essays on Sollers.
———. "Le Souffle hyperbolique de Philippe Sollers," in *Excès de langages*. Paris: Denoël, 1984. The most consequential discussion of *Paradis* to date.
Kristeva, Julia. "L'Engendrement de la formule," in *Recherches pour une sémanalyse*. Paris: Seuil, 1969. On Sollers's *Nombres*.
———. "Polylogue," in *Polylogue*. Paris: Seuil, 1977. On *Lois* and *Paradis*.

Pleynet, Marcelin, "Dès Tambours," in *Art et littérature*. Paris: Seuil, 1977. On *Lois* and *Sur le matérialisme*.

Scarpetta, Guy. "Sollers ou l'écriture du passage," in *Eloge du cosmopolitisme*. Paris: Grasset, 1981. Sollers as the successor to the modernisms of Pound, Artaud, Kafka, and Beckett.

PHILIPPE SOLLERS

*Femmes**

Flora a bien connu Lutz, une de ses passions de toujours . . . Je pense à lui, maintenant, aux jours ouatés, rétrécis, qu'il traverse dans le service psychiatrique où il est interné, à Sainte-Anne . . . Là, d'ailleurs, où Fals enseignait, présentait ses malades . . . Le monde paradémoniaque est petit, on dirait qu'il finit toujours par se rassembler sur une tête d'épingle . . . Aimantation et diminution . . . Il pleut sans arrêt ces jours-ci. Je regarde par la fenêtre le ciel obstinément bas de Paris, comme Lutz est peut-être en train de le faire . . . Destinée invraisemblable des acteurs d'une époque. Comme s'ils étaient liés par le fil d'un roman en train de s'écrire. Un roman auquel personne ne croirait si c'était un roman. Et moi là-dedans? Finalement, je me suis trouvé là par hasard . . . Ou par une nécessité qui veut précisément que j'écrive ce livre. Je n'aurais pas dû être là autrement, voilà qui est sûr. Pas les mêmes intérêts, pas le même milieu, spectateur immédiat et dissimulé . . . Ou alors, il y a un dieu, du moins pour les écrivains . . . Un dieu étrange, fantasque, qui révèle ses plans peu à peu . . . Un dieu du récit à l'intérieur du récit, de la moralité silencieuse mais tissant la fable . . . Un dieu qui choisit son témoin de façon imprévisible, son secrétaire particulier, pas forcément celui qu'on croit, jamais celui qu'on croit . . . Attention à ce petit, là, les yeux brillants, qui ne dit rien et observe . . . Mis là uniquement pour voir, entendre, enregistrer, déchiffrer . . . S. m'approuve. Il soutient qu'il y a une vie toute spéciale pour celui qui est appelé à écrire réellement le dessous des événements . . . Une vie qui n'a rien à voir avec la vie . . . Une vie de la mort qui écrit . . . Raison pour laquelle, d'après lui, une certaine aiguille aimantée vient toujours se replacer dans l'axe « femmes » . . . Cherchez la femme et la flamme . . . Le pôle incurvé, là où le mensonge est le plus compact. Donc la vérité aussi. Lutz a donc fini par étrangler Anne, son amie qu'il avait tardé longuement à épouser . . . Il venait juste-

Femmes (Paris: Gallimard, 1983), 99–111. This passage is reprinted with the kind permission of Gallimard.

ment d'être opéré d'une hernie . . . Il allait de plus en plus mal, d'après ce qu'on m'a dit. Désillusion complète, amertume, vin rouge . . . Toute son existence lui paraissait être un naufrage absolu. Ici, nous entrons encore un peu plus avant dans la grande affaire communiste . . . On croit tout savoir là-dessus, on ne sait rien. Le communisme est autre chose que le communisme. Le fascisme aussi est différent de lui-même, et personne n'ose trop interroger ses racines, le fond de ténèbres où il se recharge, prend corps . . . Ce n'est pas ailleurs que ça se prépare, mais ici, bien ici . . . Question physiologique, plus qu'on ne l'imagine. On a dit beaucoup de choses sur tout cela, on n'a peut-être rien dit . . . Laurent Lutz avait commencé par être catholique, et bon catholique. Puis la Résistance, les camps, l'illumination scientifique . . . La philosophie et la science éclairant la marche de l'humanité enfin adulte, etc. Non pas tant l' « homme nouveau » que l'explication du processus global à l'intérieur duquel il y a de l' « homme » . . . L'ensemble à démonter, articuler, maîtriser . . . Quand je l'ai connu, c'était une étoile . . . Première grandeur . . . Qui n'avait aucun mal à réfuter les pensées molles contemporaines . . . Et toutes les pensées étaient molles aux yeux de Lutz . . . Sa pensée à lui était catégorique, mais avec élégance, une belle écriture, comme on dit. Je l'ai pas mal fréquenté, donc, quand je dérivais un peu dans la politique . . . On a beaucoup parlé . . . C'était l'époque où mon goût de la littérature avait fini par m'apparaître comme superficiel, insuffisant, coupable . . . Quelle idée! . . . J'avais attrapé le virus . . . Le microbe nihiliste . . . Le doute de soi, systématiquement injecté par le parti philosophique . . . La honte de soi, du plaisir, de l'égotisme, du jeu, de la liberté, du libertinage . . . Mon dieu, mon dieu, quelle erreur . . . Comme je me repens d'avoir pu cesser une seconde d'affirmer ma « superficialité » . . . Mon inconséquence . . . Mon irresponsabilité . . . Ma « perversité polymorphe » comme dirait Deb qui a beaucoup fait, à l'époque, pour me culpabiliser, elle aussi . . . Mais Deb, c'est compréhensible, justifiable. Il fallait m'amener au mariage . . . Dans ce but, toutes les propagandes sont bonnes pour déstabiliser l'instabilité. Même chose avec Flora, mais en sens inverse . . . Propagandes croisées . . . Tout cela s'équilibre . . . Ce qu'il y a de meilleur avec les femmes, c'est de les choisir comme pour un orchestre, une rosace contradictoire . . . De façon à se faire tout reprocher, tout, et le contraire de tout. Le concert est fascinant à entendre, chacune enfonce son clou selon ses intérêts. Il faut écouter sans rien dire, s'amuser sans trop le faire voir . . . Les basses continues du ressentiment . . . Les violons du regret . . . Les trombones de la menace et de la prédiction négative . . . Les clarinettes de l'ironie appuyée . . . Les flûtes de la moquerie . . . Les trompettes de la malédiction . . . La grosse caisse, ou les cymbales, de la demande d'argent . . . Le piano de la mélancolie . . . Les pizzicati de la contradiction mécanique . . . Et les voix . . . La « grosse voix » hystérique, surtout, ma préférée, quand elles se mettent à incarner la Loi qui devrait être là et tarde à mettre au pas cet homme qui n'obéit pas . . . Le soprano de l'insinuation calomnieuse . . . Le contralto de la dévalorisation . . . Bref, l'opéra rampant, ravageant . . .

Oui, c'était le temps où j'avais décidé, piqué au vif, de leur montrer que j'étais aussi un penseur . . . Que je pouvais, si je le voulais, disserter moi aussi sur les sujets les plus compliqués . . . Les plus lourds de conséquences . . . J'ai lu tout Hegel, je le jure . . . La *Phénoménologie de l'esprit*, la *Grande logique*, la plume à la main . . . Et Aristote . . . Et Platon . . . Et Spinoza . . . Et Leibniz, pour qui je garde un faible . . . Et Marx . . . Et Engels . . . Et Lénine . . . Les trente-six volumes de Lénine, parfaitement! Ah mais! Et Freud . . . Et Saussure . . . Et tout, et tout . . . Elles m'agaçaient, les filles, avec leur culte des philosophes-professeurs . . . J'avais un tel retard à combler, une telle existence bourgeoise à expier . . . Je voulais savoir . . . Quoi . . . Pourquoi . . . L'époque allait droit dans ce sens, comme c'est loin quand on y pense. . . Plus loin que les années 20 . . . Jamais la vision du monde PC n'a été plus forte que dans les années 70 . . . Je dis « PC », mais il faut nuancer . . . Il vaudrait mieux parler d'une grande nébuleuse « de gauche » allant des États-Unis au Japon, une galaxie entière avec ses amas, ses constellations, ses météores . . . Marxisme, psychanalyse, linguistique . . . « Nouveau roman » . . . Structuralisme . . . Eruptions de savoirs locaux . . . Épidémies de décorticages . . . Virtuosité dans le démontage microscopique . . . Eczémas de radiographies . . . Des « retours » à n'en plus finir, retours d'âge . . . A la fin du XIXᵉ . . . Aux pères fondateurs . . . Aux grands refondeurs . . . La coupure ici . . . Non, là! D'interminables débats . . . Le plus clair, dans tout ça, c'était une formidable entreprise de destruction du « Sujet » . . . Le Sujet, tel était l'ennemi . . . Comme autrefois, le cléricalisme . . . Un vertige, une avidité d'anonymat sans précédent . . . Volonté de suicide dans la rigueur . . . Ou plutôt de négation de soi, ultime affirmation de soi portée à l'incandescence . . . Bien entendu, sous ces déclarations fracassantes, les mêmes passions subsistaient, intactes . . . C'était la lutte pour le pouvoir entre les quelques noms qui abolissaient les noms . . . Intrigues, jalousies, vanité de tous les instants . . . Y avait-il une opposition? Non. Même pas. La « droite » et ses valeurs moisies individualistes s'était effondrée massivement, évaporée, dissoute . . . Elle l'est encore . . . Elle l'est définitivement . . . Je suis de gauche, vous êtes de gauche, nous sommes tous de gauche . . . A jamais . . . Pour l'éternité . . . D'ailleurs, le problème n'est pas là . . . Il s'agit de savoir s'il y a encore un personnage en ce monde avec 1° une vie intéressante et multiple; 2° une culture approfondie; 3° une originalité irréductible; 4° un style . . . Hélas, hélas . . . Pour s'en tenir aux Français—car je veux bien qu'il y ait un Américain, un Allemand, un Latino-Américain et un Jamaïquain—, que voyons-nous? Une catastrophe . . . Rien . . . Prenons les auteurs de Gallimard, puisqu'il n'y a qu'eux, c'est connu, et qu'il est parfaitement vain, en France, de vouloir être reconnu comme écrivain en dehors de la Banque Centrale . . . Jean-Marie Le Creuzot? Eric Medrano? Louis-Michel Tournedos? Tiens, c'est vrai que leurs noms sonnent tous en O! Oh! Oh! Tous de dos! Histoire d'O! On devrait peut-être les unifier sous un même pseudonyme . . . Lequel? Cocto? Giono? Corydo? En hommage à Gide? A l'aimable et définitif idéal français du ni trop ni trop peu, allusif, naturaliste, aphoristique, moraliste, et en tout cas, *litoteux*? La vérite sur les femmes, c'est-à-dire sur le temps lui-même, là? Vous n'y pensez pas! Je viens de m'emporter un peu devant S. qui m'écoute en souriant . . . Je n'ose pas trop développer devant lui l'autre partie de ma démonstration contre les « experiments », les trucs d'avant-garde . . . Ah, et puis après tout, tant pis . . . D'ailleurs, ce type me déroute, il n'est pas là où on le situe, il poursuit autre chose, ce n'est pas possible . . . Sa grosse machine, là, *Comédie*, collante, continue, biscornue . . . Après tout, c'est peut-être important, on ne sait jamais . . . Classique! Classique! Uniquement classique! Il va encore me répéter ça . . . Le con, il ne veut même plus s'expliquer . . . « Je me suis trop justifié, dit-il, maintenant motus . . . L'énigme en action . . . Le passant fermé . . . Hamlet . . . La légende . . . La pure volonté qui va . . . » Il rit. Il m'énerve. Les avant-gardes? Les « modernes »? Ce que j'en pense? Bafouillis analphabète . . . Prétention énorme . . . Obsessions sexuelles estropiées . . . Gribouillis, régurgitations, gâtisme en tout genre . . . Et, avec ça, des poses! L'ésotérisme en mission! Des signes de reconnaissance, des airs entendus, une volonté de ne rien savoir qui touche au prodige, une paresse infinie, une auto-satisfaction sans limites . . . On se demande ce qui les intronise et les autorise, les maintient en vie, les chérit comme des parasites cafouilleux d'un monde lui-même hébété, prostré . . . Ils vont et viennent avec leurs plaquettes, leurs revues débiles, leurs combines à dix personnes, toujours les mêmes, leurs petites perversités, leurs poétesses minables, leurs peintresses superchieuses, leurs audaces de caca-vomi . . . Je trouve S. trop indulgent avec tout ça. Complaisant . . . Clientéliste . . . « Mais non, mais non, il répond, toujours avec son sourire agaçant, croyez-moi, c'est très utile—Utile à quoi?—A la confusion.—Pourquoi la confusion?—Il faut avancer masqué, voyons . . . *Larvatus prodeo.*—Mais pourquoi? » Geste vague . . .

Revenons à Lutz . . . Du charme . . . Mais enfin, il était très malade . . . Même quand il était le phare intellectuel de la révolution possible, le guide des étudiants, l'espoir d'une rénovation dans le Parti (et pas seulement en France, mais dans le monde entier), il passait la moitié de son temps en clinique psychiatrique . . . En analyse d'un côté (mais pas dans l'école de Fals, d'où tirage entre eux), en électrochocs ou sels de lithium de l'autre . . . La maniaco-dépressive, la grande psychose-reine

de notre temps . . . La seule, la vraie, l'originelle, peut-être . . . Celle qui
expose le manque en tout cas . . . « L'épaisseur du manque. » . . . Le
Manque initial et final qu'aucune came ne pourra combler . . . Flora admirait Lutz . . . Le jalousait . . . Le contestait . . . L'adorait . . . Le dé-
testait . . . Le surveillait . . . Lui téléphonait . . . Lui écrivait . . . L'en-
gueulait . . . L'invitait . . . Lui retéléphonait . . . L'attaquait . . . Le
défendait . . . Enfin, il comptait pour elle . . . Elle était évidemment
amoureuse de lui, peut-être pas de lui, d'ailleurs, mais de sa fonction . . .
Guide en théorie révolutionnaire . . . Secrétaire général des concepts . . .
Trésorier de l'argumentation . . . Un type très doux, Lutz, pourtant . . . Il
faut dire qu'avec la répartition du pouvoir sur la planète encore hier, le
poste de dirigeant théorique en révolution pouvait prendre, d'un moment
à l'autre, toute son ampleur. Lutz aimait bien Flora, je crois, tout en étant
terrorisé par elle . . . Elle ne lui passait rien . . . Elle observait ses
moindres déplacements, ses articles, ses initiatives . . . Quoique anar-
chiste, Flora espérait toujours, comme tous les socialistes d'ailleurs,
comme toute la gauche en général, une mutation des partis communistes . . . Une transformation purificatrice . . . Une conversion . . . Lutz
aurait pu en être l'auteur ou l'occasion, et de proche en proche devenir
empereur de Marxavie, et elle, pourquoi pas, impératrice rouge, émi-
nence grise . . . Tsarine de choc . . . Catherine II et Voltaire . . . Enfin,
tout ça . . . Le goût passionné, naïf, émerveillé de Flora pour le pouvoir
m'a toujours fasciné . . . Parce qu'elle voulait, elle veut toujours que le
Pouvoir soit vrai, soit ce qu'il devrait être . . . Comme ça, elle se retrouve
toujours plus ou moins dans l'opposition . . . Ce qui fait sa
qualité . . . Elle ne pourrait pas s'empêcher de faire une remarque ironi-
que ou critique au Monarque absolu des univers . . . Rien que pour lui
faire sentir qu'en réalité il usurpe plus ou moins sa place à elle . . . Une
place qu'elle ne veut pas prendre non plus . . . « Que veut l'hystérique? a
dit Fals un jour . . . Un maître sur lequel elle règne. » Parole profonde. Je
l'avais citée à Lutz, impressionné. Mais Flora, c'est l'hystérie sans l'hystérie, le naturel en plein jour, la chose même . . . Elle se trompe rarement
sur quelqu'un ou sur une situation . . . Je l'écoute toujours plus ou
moins, même quand elle m'horripile . . . Elle sent les ondes, les forces,
les commencements, les forces, les fins . . . Je fais le plus souvent le
contraire de ce qu'elle me dit, mais c'est parce qu'elle me dit sans s'en
rendre compte, en réalité, le contraire de ce qu'elle me dit . . . Il faut
savoir lire . . . Entendre l'autre côté . . .

On est devenus plutôt amis, Lutz et moi. Paradoxe: mes demandes
philosophiques et politiques l'ennuyaient . . . Ce qu'il aurait voulu, lui,
c'était sortir de tout ça, justement, la révolution, la théorie, le marxisme,
et se cultiver, en savoir davantage sur le dehors qui avait continué pendant qu'il s'enfermait dans l'abstraction « scientifique ». Le dehors: littérature, peinture, musique . . . Qu'est-ce qui s'est fait, dans la vie, pen-

dant tout ce temps? Finalement, il sera allé d'un enfermement à l'autre . . . Je notais qu'il n'avait même pas de poste de télévision chez lui . . . Pour un penseur d'aujourd'hui . . . Et puis sa maladie . . . Et la maladie de sa maladie: sa femme, Anne . . . Je ne l'ai vue qu'une fois ou deux . . . Petite forme sèche à béret, plus âgée que lui, style institutrice . . . Extraordinairement antipathique . . . Je crois qu'il en avait une peur bleue . . . Résumons-nous: je les ai toujours vus trembler devant leurs femmes, ces philosophes, ces révolutionnaires, comme s'ils avouaient par là que la vraie divinité se trouve là . . . Quand ils disent « les masses », ils veulent dire leur femme . . . Au fond, c'est partout pareil . . . Le chien à la niche . . . Empoigné chez lui . . . Surveillé au lit . . . Lutz parlait d'Anne en baissant la voix . . . Je suppose qu'elle devait être le plus souvent odieuse avec lui dans le style habituel . . . Sois un homme . . . Davantage . . . Encore . . . Un peu de tenue, je t'en prie . . . Tu n'en feras jamais d'autres . . . Tu oublies qui tu es . . . Ce que tu représentes . . . Ce à quoi tu crois . . . Je ne comprends pas comment tu peux fréquenter des gens pareils . . . Quand je pense qu'on te croit fort, etc., etc. Elle l'empoisonnait . . . Elle lui pompait l'air . . . Il l'a asphyxiée . . . Une nuit . . . Depuis le temps qu'il y pensait, sûrement . . . Oh la cohabitation de la honte et de la haine, de la répugnance et du mépris, envers de l'idéalisation d'autrefois, quand l'autre devient le bruit insupportable d'un ronflement, d'un robinet, d'une chasse d'eau, quand le corps de l'autre n'est plus qu'une croûte couverte de plaques d'irritation et qui voient, et jugent! . . . Quand l'espace même, et le moindre geste, la moindre réflexion, sont électrisés par le refus global, définitif et cadenassé de ce volume respiratoire étranger . . . Tout proche . . . Froid comme un glacier qui avance, millimètre par millimètre . . . Quand le soulèvement de la poitrine de l'autre est une souffrance pour celui qui la ressent comme volée à sa propre intégrité . . . De l'intérieur des poumons, de la gorge . . . Elle s'est endormie, il veille . . . Il relit cet article sans intérêt . . . Il regarde ses livres sur une étagère spéciale, là, toute son œuvre traduite dans toutes les langues . . . Ces livres qu'il voudrait maintenant brûler . . . A ce moment-là, oui, la folie monte, et la folie n'est rien d'autre que le spasme de conscience suraiguë qui permet d'éclairer sa vie comme une immense petite bulle en folie . . . Et qui gonfle . . . Qui va crever . . . Il prend un foulard, il s'approche sans bruit de cette femme endormie à laquelle, tout compte fait, il doit tant; cette femme qui l'a supporté, aidé, encouragé, soigné dans sa névrose . . . Mais qui est devenue aussi, peu à peu, le miroir grimaçant de sa défaite, de son échec, de sa culpabilité sans raison . . . Il n'aspire qu'à une innocence infinie . . . A un grand relâchement . . . A desserrer l'étreinte de la tenaille des obligations imaginaires . . . Le Parti . . . La Base . . . La Direction . . . Les Masses . . . La Lutte des Classes . . . Le Mouvement de l'Histoire . . . La Stratégie . . . Le bal des majuscules sur l'échiquier de la pensée appli-

quée . . .Tous ces gens qui attendent de lui l'analyse correcte de la situation . . . L'explication du millième recul qui doit être compris comme
une réussite relative, un moment du long processus dont il ne faut jamais
désespérer, on n'a pas le droit de désespérer . . . Dialectique . . . Formules . . . On peut démontrer ce qu'on veut, c'est facile . . . On peut
toujours trouver la formule qui convient . . . Bond en avant . . . Retraite
élastique . . . Manœuvre indirecte . . . Approfondissement des contradictions . . . Période transitoire . . . Tournant . . . Les lettres qu'il reçoit
chaque jour des quatre coins du monde, son audience . . . L'héroïsme de
millions d'inconnus . . .

Anne dort. Elle a l'air déposée au-dessus de son sommeil, fragile,
légère. Son visage est sérieux. Même endormie, elle reste entière, ferme,
comme sont les femmes quand elles ont réussi à s'accrocher à une foi.
C'est ainsi parce que ça doit être ainsi . . . Elle est plus croyante que lui.
Elle n'a pas été contaminée par la casuistique . . . Elle est plus pure, au
fond, impeccable . . . Et insupportable parce qu'exigeant sans cesse de
lui, précisément, le sursaut, la cambrure, l'intransigeance, la fidélité . . .
Lui et son corps usé, ce ventre . . . Il rêve de longues vacances, de soleil, de
conversations pour rien, de promenades, de piscines et de jolies filles . . .
Il n'y croit plus, à l'Histoire. Il ne croit plus à rien. Il est fatigué, la mort ne
lui paraît plus comme autrefois et comme elles sont obligées de le penser,
elles, un détail négligeable, une simple formalité naturelle de la pièce qui
doit être jouée . . . Pourquoi? Parce que. Il a tout vu, les censures, les
condamnations, les réhabilitations, les nouvelles versions aussi fausses
que les anciennes, les cadavres qu'il vaut mieux oublier, les cris enterrés
dans la comptabilité . . . Il sait que, de toute façon, le rouage de la perversion générale, inévitable, est huilé dans ses moindres petites dents con-
crètes . . . Sur le papier, pourtant, tout devrait fonctionner comme il l'a
toujours dit, il ne s'est jamais vraiment trompé, une nuance là, peut-
être . . . Mais sur l'essentiel, il a toujours eu raison . . . En un sens, c'est
plutôt la réalité qui déraille . . . Qui n'en finit pas de dérailler . . . Staline . . . Mais quand même, Staline . . . Car, maintenant, c'est l'Opium
qui revient, la religion elle-même, ça, c'est vraiment le bouquet . . . D'où
a pu venir une telle fissure? Une si ahurissante fuite de sens? La vigilance
s'est relâchée . . . Dieu? Non, tout de même pas . . . Tout, mais pas ça! La
croisade de ce Pape . . . Ce Polonais . . . L'Islam . . . L'Ayatollah . . . Ré-
surgences, archaïsmes, il faudra encore nettoyer toute cette marée noire,
calmement, patiemment, montrer pourquoi et comment l'irrationnel se
reproduit quand les conditions du rationnel ont fait défaut dans la Théorie . . . Déviations . . . Régressions . . . Et la Chine qui a foutu le camp
dans la mécanique habituelle . . . On momifie le grand homme, on le
désavoue prudemment, on critique ses crimes simplement pour les adap-
ter à la nouvelle période, les moderniser en somme . . . « Libéralisation »
on appelle ça . . . On connaît la chanson . . . Il s'agit bien entendu de faire

la police moins visible, moins gênante pour obtenir des contrats d'affaires, plus efficace, plus habile, d'ailleurs, plus secrète . . . Perversion,
perversion . . . Partout . . . Le procès de Qiang Jing . . . Tout le monde a
tort . . . Tout le monde est criminel . . . Un crime de plus ou de moins,
quelle importance . . . C'est peut-être Staline qui a eu entièrement et
définitivement raison en posant les fondations de la nouvelle religion
universelle: « A la fin, c'est toujours la mort qui gagne. » . . . Ou alors,
c'est la mort qui vous le dit en personne: « A la fin, c'est toujours Staline
qui gagne. » Staline, le seul qui ait réussi? Ces nouvelles brochures, en
arabe, avec son portrait . . . Increvable Staline . . . Son rire, à la dimension de cette boulette qu'on appelle la terre . . . La terre vue depuis le
cosmos comme un point où résonne l'éclat de rire de Staline . . . Ou alors,
c'est Arthur Baron qui aurait eu raison, cet économiste borné, réactionnaire, social-democrate, représentant des Américains? Ce soi-disant penseur de la droite modérée, la plus dangereuse, ce juif intelligent mais
incapable de grande pensée . . . Qui s'en tient aux faits . . . Un
« faitaliste » comme disait Lénine . . . Baron a eu tous les honneurs . . .
Et lui, Lutz, est là dans son minuscule bureau poussiéreux de vieux garçon obstiné avec, à ses côtés, une femme irréprochable et intolérable qui,
dès demain, au petit déjeuner, va organiser l'enfer quotidien . . . Tu n'as
pas assez travaillé . . . Tu devrais intervenir . . . Je ne comprends pas
comment tu peux déjeuner avec ce réactionnaire mondain . . . Cet oppor-
tuniste . . . Lié à la CIA, sûrement . . . Et tu vas ensuite recevoir cette
intrigante! Cette putain! . . .

Au même moment, dans la nuit, Fals est à peu près dans les mêmes
dispositions d'esprit . . . Il sait qu'il n'en a plus pour longtemps . . . Lui
aussi regarde d'un œil intérieur épuisé, désabusé, sa longue route difficile . . . Partout, les petits hommes ont vaincu . . . Les puces . . . Ce
ramassis d'ordures nourri à ses frais . . . Sur son sang . . . Ces teignes
mentales . . . Ils occupent les places . . . Les institutions . . . Les institutions gagnent toujours . . . A la fin, c'est toujours la mort, c'est-à-dire les
institutions, qui gagne . . . Ah, le martyre de l'hérésie assumée, quelle
blague . . . C'est le dogme qui compte, l'orthodoxie . . . Mais on ne peut
pas dire ça . . . Surtout aux jeunes . . . Les autres n'ont pas les jeunes avec
eux . . . Fausse profondeur, travail de seconde main . . . Une pensée pour
ce pauvre Lutz qui est venu l'interrompre un jour . . . Ce crétin de Lutz
n'a jamais rien compris . . . Ces communistes . . . La congrégation communiste . . . Et dire qu'il a fallu, parfois, s'appuyer sur eux . . . Pour
vaincre le mépris d'acier des institutions académiques . . . D'ailleurs personne ne comprend rien. Petits hommes, petits hommes . . . Il y a à peine
une demi-heure de marche entre l'appartement de Fals et celui de Lutz. Il
est trois heures du matin. Supposons qu'ils aillent l'un vers l'autre, ils en
auraient, pourtant, des choses à se raconter, là, sous la lune d'hiver, du
côté du Luxembourg . . . Près du vieux parc solitaire et glacé . . . Com-

ment ils se sont épiés, espionnés, sabotés . . . Comment ils se sont en-
voyés de faux informateurs, de faux traîtres . . . Top secret! Microconfi-
dences . . . Luttes pour l'hégémonie . . . L'étudiant, l'étudiante . . . La
jeunesse . . . L'influence de l'avenir . . . Comme c'était puéril! Comme
c'était bête! Et puis, ils se fâcheraient presque tout de suite . . .
L'orgueil . . .

Qu'ils restent donc chez eux . . . Regardant la nuit . . . Et la mort qui
approche . . . Voilà, il ne reste plus que la sagesse antique, maintenant,
pas le moindre progrès de ce côté-là . . . Les stoïciens . . . Sartre est mort
cette année, après avoir fait une drôle d'autocritique . . . Sartre est resté à
mi-chemin, il a eu tous les honneurs lui aussi . . . Leur projet à eux était
quand même d'une autre taille, d'une autre rigueur dans son ambition . . . Marxisme; Psychanalyse . . . Le dehors, le dedans . . . A toi le
dehors, à moi le dedans . . . Le savoir absolu . . . Enfin . . . Qui aurait
commandé, ça c'est une autre affaire . . . L'Affaire, précisément . . .
Qu'est-ce que tout cela va devenir . . . Chacun va ronronner comme a-
vant . . . Des gens vont revenir s'installer sans avoir la plus petite idée de
ce qui s'est passé . . . Les philosophes dans leur coin, les curés de l'autre . . . Et personne ne se souviendra plus qu'il était trouvé, le lien, le joint
décisif de la nouvelle ère . . .

Fals ne dort pas, il souffre. La plus grande souffrance est quand même
d'avoir été obligé de passer son temps sur terre avec des imbéciles toujours en retard.

Lutz serre son foulard dans ses mains.

Il va le faire. Et puis il le fera pour lui.

Peut-être.

Le cou d'Anne. Mince et ridé. Elle respire doucement.

Il faut le faire. Il faut en finir avec cette tache noire qui bouche, là,
devant les yeux et depuis toujours, l'accès à l'air libre.

Il l'étrangle lentement. Il y a un moment, ici, indicible, un point de
mercure, suprême, déchirant, où l'acte ne peut plus être rattrapé. Arc
liquide . . . Jusqu'au bout.

Et tout bascule.

Poussière.

Le lendemain, Lutz est hagard, prostré, la police l'emmène, est interné, c'est aussitôt le scandale.

La délivrance.

Fals meurt quelques mois après.

C'est à l'enterrement d'Anne que tout le monde apprend brusquement qu'elle était juive. Un rabbin est là qui récite le Kaddisch. La litanie
est pathétique . . . Juive. Déportée. Communiste. Assassinée . . . Absolument antireligieuse pourtant . . .

Lutz est déclaré fou.

Fou comme la vérité.

Femmes

Flora knew Lutz well, he was one of her long-standing passions . . . I think of him now, of the padded, contracted days he spends at Sainte-Anne, the psychiatric hospital where they committed him . . . Which is also where Fals taught, and presented his patients . . . The parademonic world is small, it always seems to come together on the head of a pin . . . Magnetism and shrinking . . . It hasn't stopped raining for days. I'm looking out my window at the relentlessly low Parisian sky, as Lutz may be this very minute . . . The improbable destiny of an era's actors. As if they were connected by the thread of a novel in progress. A novel no one would believe if it were a novel. And my own role in it? Actually, I wound up there by accident . . . Or by a necessity that insisted I write this book. I wouldn't have been there otherwise, that much is certain. Not with the same interests, not in the same place, not as an immediate, surreptitious spectator . . . Or else there is a god, at least for writers . . . A strange, capricious god who reveals his plans little by little . . . A god of narrative within the narrative, a god of morality who doesn't speak but weaves the story . . . A god who unforeseeably selects his witness, his personal secretary, not necessarily who you think, never who you think . . . Be careful of that one over there, with the gleam in his eye, the one who keeps quiet and watches . . . Put there solely to see, to listen, to register, to decipher . . . S. approves of this. He maintains that there's a special life for whoever is called upon to write the underside of events . . . A life that has nothing to do with life . . . A life of the death that writes . . . Which is why, according to him, a certain magnetized needle always swings back toward the "woman" axis . . . *Cherchez la femme* and the flame . . . The curved pole, where the lies are most compact. And therefore the truth as well. And therefore Lutz ended up strangling Anne, the friend he waited so long to marry . . . He'd just had a hernia operation . . . I heard he was getting worse and worse. Complete disillusionment, bitterness, red wine . . . His entire existence seemed to him an absolute disaster. Here we make a little headway into the great Communist question . . . We think we know all about it, we don't know a thing. Communism is something other than Communism. Fascism too is different from itself, and no one dares question its roots, the depths of the shadows where it recharges, where it takes shape . . . It doesn't come from anywhere else, no, it starts here, right here . . . A physiological question, much more than we suspect. A lot has been said about all this, perhaps nothing's been said . . . Laurent Lutz started out as a Catholic, a good Catholic. Then the Resistance, the camps, scientific enlightenment . . . Philosophy and science illuminating the development of a humanity that had finally reached maturity, etc. Not so much the "new man" as the explanation of the global process within which there is "man" . . . An ensemble to be taken apart, articulated, mastered . . . When I met him, he was a star . . . Of the first magnitude . . . Who had no trouble refuting the inanity of contemporary thought . . . And in Lutz's eyes, it was all inane . . . His thinking was categorical, but with elegance, with style, as they say. So I saw him a lot during my little detour through politics . . . We talked a lot . . . This was the period when my taste for literature began to strike me as superficial, insufficient, guilty . . . What a notion! . . . I'd caught the virus . . . The nihilist microbe . . . Self-doubt, systematically injected by the philosophical party . . . Shame of self, of pleasure, of egotism, of play, of liberty, of libertinism . . . My god, my god, what a mistake . . . How I repent having for one second stopped affirming my "superficiality." . . . My illogicality . . . My irresponsibility . . . My "polymorphous perversity," as Deb would say, who did plenty, at the time, to convince me of my guilt . . . But with Deb it's comprehensible, justifiable. She had to lead me to marriage . . . Toward this end, any form of propaganda is admissible, so long as it destabilizes instability. Same thing with Flora, but in the opposite sense . . . Crossed propaganda . . . It all balances out . . . It's best to choose women as if for an orchestra, a rose window of contradictions . . . So that you get blamed for everything, for everything and for the opposite of everything. The concert makes terrific listening, each one attacks you according to her interests. You have to listen without speaking, amuse yourself without making it too obvious . . . The basso continuo of resentment . . . The violins of regret . . . The trombones of threat and negative prediction . . . The clarinets of emphatic irony. . . . The flutes of mockery . . . The trumpets of malediction. . . . The bass drum, or cymbals, demanding money . . . The piano of melancholy . . . The pizzicati of mechanical contradiction . . . And the voices . . . Especially the hysterical, "booming voice," my favorite, when they take it upon themselves to incarnate the Law that ought to be there but that's slow in putting this disobedient man in his place . . . The soprano of slanderous insinuation. . . . The contralto of devalorization . . . In short, the whole rampaging, ravaging opera . . .

Yes indeed, this was the time when, touched to the quick, I decided to show them that I too was a thinker. . . . That I too, if I so desired, could dissertate on the most complicated subjects . . . With the most weighty consequences . . . I read all of Hegel, I swear . . . *The Phenomenology of Spirit*, the *Science of Logic*, pen in hand . . . And Aristotle . . . And Plato . . . And Spinoza . . . And Leibniz, for whom I still have a weakness . . . And Marx . . . And Engels . . . And Lenin . . . The thirty-six volumes of Lenin, every one! Ah yes! And Freud . . . And Saussure . . . Every last one of them . . . These girls, they irritated me with their cult of philosopher-professors . . . I had so much to make up for, such a bourgeois existence to expiate. . . . I wanted to know . . . What . . . Why . . . The period was headed straight in that direction, it seems so long ago when you think of it . . . Farther away than the twenties . . . Never was the PC's vision of the world stronger than in the seventies . . . I say the "PC," but I ought to be more specific . . . It would be more accurate to speak of an immense, nebulous "left" extending from the United States to Japan, an entire galaxy with its own clusters, constellations, meteors . . . Marxism, psychoanalysis, linguistics . . . The "Nouveau Roman" . . . Structuralism . . . Eruptions of regional sciences . . . Epidemics of dissections . . . Virtuosity in microscopic dismantlings . . . Eczemas of x-ray analyses . . . The age of "returns," the age of menopause . . . A "return" to the end of the nineteenth century . . . To the founding fathers . . . To the great re-founders . . . Let's make the *coupure* here . . . No, there! Interminable debates . . . Clearest of all was a formidable attempt to destroy the "Subject." . . . The Subject, that was the enemy . . . Just as clericalism used to be . . . A dizziness, an unprecedented desire for anonymity . . . A will to suicide through rigor . . . Or rather to self-negation, an ultimate self-affirmation pushed to incandescence . . . Beneath this fracas of declamation, of course, the same passions subsisted intact . . . It was a power struggle between the few names who would abolish names . . . Plots, jealousies, vanity at every step . . . Was there an opposition? No. Not in the slightest. The "right" and its mildewed individualistic values was collapsing massively, evaporating, dissolving . . . It still is . . . For good . . . I'm on the left, you're on the left, everybody's on the left . . . Forever . . . For eternity . . . But that's not the problem . . . What matters is to know whether there's still one character on the planet who possesses 1) an interesting and multiple life; 2) profound culture; 3) irreducible originality; 4) style . . . Alas, alas . . . Speaking only of the French—there may be an American, a German, a Latin American, and a Jamaican, I'm willing to admit—what do we see? A catastrophe . . . Nothing . . . Take the authors Gallimard publishes, since, as everyone knows, they're the only ones that count, and since it's perfectly futile, in France, to hope for any recognition as a writer outside the Central Bank . . . Jean-Marie Le Creuzot? Eric Medrano? Louis-Michel Tournedos? Why, their names all seem to end in O! Oh! Oh! Very so-so! The Story of O! Perhaps they could all be incorporated under a single pseudonym . . . Which one? Cocto? Giono? Corydo? In hommage to Gide? To the amiable and definitive French ideal of neither too much nor too little, allusive, naturalistic, aphoristic, moralistic, and in any case *litotistic*? Any insight into the truth about women, in other words about time itself? Surely you jest! I've just gotten a little carried away in front of S., who's grinning as he listens . . . In front of him I don't dare get into the rest of my argument, the part against "experiments," avant-gardisms . . .

Ah, after all, it doesn't make any difference . . . Still, S. is disconcerting, he's never where you think he is, he's after something else, it can't be for real . . . That big machine of his, his *Comedy*, insistent, continuous, crazy . . . You never know, it may turn out to be important, after all . . . Classic! Classic! Only the classic! Now he'll tell me that one again . . . The bastard won't even take the trouble to explain himself anymore . . . "I've justified myself too much," he says, "now it's *motus* . . . The enigma in action . . . The inscrutable stranger . . . Hamlet . . . The legend . . . Pure will in motion . . ." He laughs. He irks me. The avant-garde? Modernity? You want my opinion? Illiterate gibberish . . . Incredibly pretentious . . . Crippling sexual obsessions . . . Scribblings, regurgitations, every kind of stupidity . . . And to top it all, postures! An esoteric mission! Passwords, knowing airs, a prodigious will to know nothing, infinite sloth, unlimited autosatisfaction . . . You have to wonder what establishes and authorizes these people, what keeps them alive and cherishes them like the bungling parasites of a dazed and prostrate world . . . They come and go with their miniscule books, their fatuous journals, their cliques and schemes, always the same, their petty perversities, their pathetic lady poets, their supershitty lady painters, their audacious diarrhea . . . I find S. much too indulgent with this. Complacent . . . Patronizing . . . "No, no, no," he replies, still with his irritating grin, "it's very useful, believe me. —Useful for what? —For confusion. — Why confusion? —Because you have to go forward masked, of course . . . *Larvatus prodeo.* —But why?" A vague gesture . . .

Let's get back to Lutz . . . He had charm . . . But when all was said and done, he was a very sick man . . . Even while he was the intellectual beacon of the revolutionary future, the students' guide, the Party's hope of renewal (and not only in France, but all over the world), he spent half his time in psychiatric clinics . . . Part of the time in analysis (but not with one of Fals's students, which created a rift between them), part of the time in electroshock or lithium therapy . . . Manic depression, queen of the era's psychoses . . . Perhaps the only one, the genuine, the original . . . The one that brings out the lack, in any case . . . "The density of lack." . . . The initial and final Lack no drug could ever dissipate . . . Flora admired Lutz . . . Envied him . . . Fought him . . . Adored him . . . Detested him . . . Kept tabs on him . . . Telephoned him . . . Wrote him . . . Scolded him . . . Invited him . . . Retelephoned him . . . Attacked him . . . Defended him . . . In other words, he counted for her . . . She was obviously in love with him, although it was perhaps less him than his function . . . Guide to revolutionary theory . . . Secretary General of concepts . . . Treasurer of argumentation . . . And yet, Lutz was a very sweet man . . . You realize that, with the division of power on the planet that was still in effect only yesterday, the post of theoretical director of revolutions could take on all its importance at any moment. Lutz was fond of Flora, I think, even though she hounded him . . . She didn't let anything get by . . . She watched his slightest movements, his articles, his initiatives . . . Although she was an anarchist, Flora was still hoping, like all socialists do, and in fact like the left in general does, for a mutation in the Communist parties . . . A purifying transformation . . . A conversion . . . Lutz could have been its author or its occasion, he could have gradually become emperor of Marxovia and she, why not, the red empress, the grey eminence . . . The Tsarina of shock . . . Catherine II and Voltaire . . . Anyway, all that . . . Flora's passionate, naive, wondrous taste for power always fascinated me . . . Because she wanted, she still wants Power to be real, to be what it ought to be . . . That way, she always finds herself more or less in the opposition . . . Which is what defines her quality . . . She wouldn't be able to resist taking an ironic or critical snipe at the absolute Monarch of all universes . . . Just to let him know that in reality he was more or less usurping the place that was rightfully hers . . . A place she doesn't want to assume, however . . . "What does a hysteric want?" said Fals one day . . . "A Master over whom she reigns." This is deep. I was very impressed, I quoted it to Lutz. But Flora is hysteria without hysteria, unadulterated, in broad daylight, the thing itself . . . She's rarely mistaken about people or situations . . . I always pay attention to what she says, even when she horrifies me . . . She senses waves, forces, beginnings, endings . . . I usually do the opposite of what she tells me, but only because, without being aware of it, she actually tells me the opposite of what she's telling me . . . You have to know how to read . . . To hear the other side . . .

We became pretty good friends, Lutz and I. Paradox: my philosophical and political questions annoyed him . . . He would have liked to get away from all that, precisely, away from revolution, Marxism, theory, to cultivate himself, to learn more about the outside he missed while he was imprisoning himself within "scientific" abstraction. The outside: literature, painting, music . . . What's been going on all this time, out there in life? In the end, he would have exchanged one prison for another . . . I noticed that there wasn't even a television at his place . . . For a thinker today . . . And then his illness . . . And his illness's illness: his wife Anne . . . I only saw her once or twice . . . A little dry shape with a beret, older than he, schoolmarmish . . . Extraordinarily antipathetic . . . I think he was scared stiff of her . . . Let's summarize: I've always seen them tremble in front of their wives, these philosophers, these revolutionaries, as if to admit they were in the presence of the real divinity . . . When they say "the masses," they mean their wives . . . At bottom, it's always the same . . . In the doghouse . . . Beaten up at home . . . Policed in bed . . . Lutz lowered his voice when he spoke of Anne . . . I suppose she was obnoxious to him in the usual way . . . Be a man . . . Come on . . . More . . . Get a hold of yourself, please . . . You'll never get any-

where this way . . . You're forgetting who you are . . . What you represent . . . What you believe in . . . I don't understand how you can associ-
ate with people like that . . . When I think that people believe in you, etc.,
etc. She was poisoning him . . . She was smothering him . . . He asphyxi-
ated her . . . One night . . . No doubt he'd been thinking about it for a
long time . . . Ah, the cohabitation of shame and hatred, of revulsion and
contempt, the reversal of earlier idealization, when the other becomes
the unbearable sound of a snore, a running faucet, flushing water, when
the other's body is no more than a scab covered with patches of irritation
that see, and judge! . . . When space itself, and the least gesture, the least
reflection, are electrified by the global, definitive, padlocked refusal of
this alien respiratory body . . . So close . . . Cold as a glacier, advancing
inch by inch . . . When the other's every breath is a torture, and feels as if
it's been torn from one's own integrity . . . From inside one's lungs, one's
throat . . . She's gone to sleep, he's still up . . . He rereads a pointless
article . . . He looks at his books, on the special bookcase, all his works
translated into every language . . . He'd like to burn those books now . . .
At that moment the madness rises, yes, and the madness is nothing other
than the spasm of hyperacute consciousness which allows him to see his
life as an immense little bubble going mad . . . Swelling . . . About to
burst . . . He takes a scarf, he silently approaches this sleeping woman to
whom, after all, he owes so much; this woman who supported him,
helped him, encouraged him, cared for him in his neurosis . . . But who
has also, gradually, become the grimacing mirror of his defeat, of his
failure, of his unreasonable guilt . . . He aspires only to infinite innocence . . . To a great release . . . To loosen the stranglehold of his imaginary obligations . . . The Party . . . The Base . . . The Direction . . . The
Masses . . . Class Struggle . . . The Movement of History . . . Strat-
egy . . . The dance of capital letters on the chessboard of applied
thought . . . All these people who look to him for the correct analysis of
the situation . . . An explanation for the thousandth retreat that has to be
understood as a relative success, one moment in the long process one
should never lose faith in, one doesn't have the right to lose faith . . .
Dialectics . . . Formulae . . . You can demonstrate whatever you want,
it's easy . . . The proper formula can always be found . . . A leap forward . . Elastic retreat . . . Indirect maneuver . . . Deepening of contradictions . . . Transitional period . . . Turning . . . The letters he receives
every day from all over the world, his audience . . . The heroism of the
unknown millions . . .

   Anne is sleeping. She seems settled above her sleep, fragile, light. Her
face is serious. Even asleep, she remains whole, solid, the way women are
when they've managed to latch on to a faith. That's the way it is because
that's the way it has to be . . . She's more of a believer than he is. She was
never contaminated by casuistry . . . She's more pure, at bottom, inpec-

cable . . . And unbearable because she endlessly demands, precisely, the leap, the ramrod back, the intransigence, the fidelity . . . Him and his exhausted body, his belly . . . He's dreaming of long vacations, of sun, of small talk, of walks, of pools and pretty girls . . . He doesn't believe in History anymore. He doesn't believe in anything anymore. He feels tired, death doesn't look as it used to, the way women are obliged to see it, as a negligible detail, as a simple natural formality in a play that *must* go on . . . Why? Because. He's seen it all, censures, condemnations, rehabilitations, new versions just as false as the old ones, corpses you're supposed to forget, screams buried in bookkeeping . . . He's perfectly aware that the clockwork of general, inevitable perversion is well-oiled, down to its tiniest concrete teeth . . . And yet on paper, everything ought to function like he always said, he was never fundamentally wrong, perhaps a nuance here or there . . . But in the essentials, he was always right. In one sense, it's actually reality that's getting side-tracked . . . That never stops getting side-tracked . . . Stalin . . . Stalin, after all . . . Because now, to top it all off, we're living through a return of Opium, yes, of religion itself . . . Where could such a fissure have come from? Such howling senselessness? No one was watching . . . God? No, not quite . . . Anything but that! The Pope's crusade . . . That Pole . . . Islam . . . The Ayatollah . . . Resurgencies, archaisms, the whole black tide still needs to be cleaned, calmly, patiently, to see how and why the irrational reproduces when the conditions of the rational have defaulted in Theory . . . Deviations . . . Regressions . . . And China, which quite predictably went to pieces . . . The great man is mummified, prudently disavowed, his crimes are criticized so they can be adapted to the new period. Basically, they're modernized . . . This is called "Liberalization" . . . Everyone knows the song . . . It's very important of course to make the police less visible, less embarrassing if you want business deals, more efficient, more skillful in fact, more secret . . . Perversion, perversion . . . Everywhere . . . Qiang Jing's trial . . . Everybody's wrong . . . Everybody's a criminal . . . One crime more or less, what's the difference . . . Maybe it was Stalin who was entirely and finally right in laying the foundations of the new universal religion: "In the end, death always wins." . . . Or else death in person can tell you: "In the end, Stalin always wins." Is Stalin the only one who's succeeded? Some new pamphlets are around lately, in Arabic, with his portrait . . . Stalin just keeps on coming . . . His laugh, on the scale of this little clod called earth . . . The earth seen from the cosmos as a point where Stalin's burst of laughter echoes . . . Or is Arthur Baron the one who's right, that narrow-minded, reactionary, American-style social democrat economist, that so-called thinker of the moderate, i.e., the most dangerous right, that smart Jew who's incapable of any real thinking . . . Who sticks to the facts . . . A "factalist," as Lenin would have said . . . Baron took all the honors . . .

And Lutz is still stuck in the miniscule dusty office of a stubborn old man, with an irreproachable, intolerable wife, who tomorrow, at breakfast, will start organizing his daily hell . . . You haven't worked enough . . . You ought to intervene . . . I can't understand how you can meet that vulgar reactionary for lunch . . . That opportunist . . . Working for the CIA, surely . . . And then you're going to meet that scheming woman! That whore! . . .

That night, at the same time, Fals is in a similar frame of mind . . . He knows he won't last much longer . . . He too is looking back, over his long, difficult path, with a tired, disabused inner eye . . . The little men have won everywhere . . . Insects . . . Trash nourished at his expense . . . On his blood . . . Mental ringworms . . . They get the positions . . . The institutions . . . The institutions always win . . . Ultimately it's always death, in other words the institution, that wins . . . The heretic martyr finally accepted, ah what a joke . . . It's dogma that counts, orthodoxy . . . But you can't say that . . . Above all to young people . . . The others don't have the young people with them . . . False profundity, second-hand work . . . Spare a thought for poor Lutz, who interrupted it briefly . . . Lutz, the fool, he never understood . . . These Communists . . . The Communist congregation . . . And to say that their support was necessary . . . To overcome the steely contempt of academic institutions . . . No one understands anything anyway . . . Little men, little men . . . It's hardly half an hour's walk between Lutz's apartment and Fals'. It's three o'clock in the morning. Suppose they were to head toward each other, they'd surely have a few things to talk about, there, under the winter moon, near the Luxemburg Gardens . . . Near the old, frozen, lonely park . . . How they watched, sabotaged, spied on each other . . . How they sent each other false informers, false traitors . . . Top secret! Microrevelations . . . Struggles for hegemony . . . Boy students, girl students . . . Young people . . . Influence on the future . . . How childish! How stupid! And then immediately, they'd get angry . . . Pride . . .

And so they stay at home . . . Watching the night . . . And death comes closer . . . Nothing's left now but classical knowledge, no one else is making any progress at all . . . The Stoics . . . Sartre died this year, after his rather strange autocritique . . . Sartre went only half-way, he too had all the honors . . . But these two had a project on another scale, with a different rigor to its ambition . . . Marxism, Psychoanalysis . . . The outside, the inside . . . You take the outside and I'll take the inside . . . Absolute knowledge . . . At last . . . Who'd have been in charge, that was another question . . . The Question, precisely . . . What's going to happen now . . . Everyone will keep droning on like before . . . People will get back to work without the slightest idea of what happened . . . Philosophers in one corner, priests in the other . . . And no one will remember that the link, the decisive juncture of the new era had been found . . .

Fals isn't sleeping, he's in pain. The greatest pain, after all, is to have been forced to spend your time with imbeciles who always lag behind.

Lutz clenches the scarf in his hands.

He's going to do it. And then he'll do it to himself.

Perhaps.

Anne's neck. Thin and wrinkled. She's breathing softly.

He's got to. Got to get rid of this black spot, there, in front of his eyes, forever blocking the path to fresh air.

He strangles her slowly. There's an unspeakable moment here, a mercurial, supreme, delirious point, after which the act can't be undone. A liquid arc . . . To the end.

And everything falls apart.

Dust.

The next day, Lutz is haggard, prostrate, the police take him away, lock him up, a scandal erupts.

Deliverance.

Fals dies a few months later.

It's only at Anne's funeral that everyone suddenly finds out that she was Jewish. There's a Rabbi, saying Kaddish. The litany is pathetic . . . Jewish. Deported. Communist. Murdered . . . Absolutely antireligious nevertheless . . .

Lutz is declared insane.

Insane as the truth.

TRANSLATED BY PHILIP BARNARD AND CHERYL LESTER

LEONARD R. KOOS

Georges Perec
P or the Puzzle of Fiction

> One will deduce something about it that is without a doubt
> the ultimate truth of the puzzle: despite appearances, it is not a
> solitary game: each gesture that the arranger of the puzzle makes,
> the maker of the puzzle made before him; each piece that he
> takes and takes up again, that he examines, that he caresses,
> every combination that he tries and tries again, every tentative
> movement, every intuition, every hope, every discouragement,
> were decided, calculated, studied by the other.
> —Georges Perec, *La Vie, mode d'emploi*

The untimely death of Georges Perec in 1982 brought to an end a remarkably prolific albeit meteoric writing career. Born in 1936 in Paris to Jewish parents who had emigrated from Poland, Georges Perec directly experienced the upheavals of the 1940s: his father died as the result of a wound received at the front in 1940 and his mother was deported to Auschwitz in 1942. Raised by his aunt, Perec was educated in sociology, a continuing voice in his literary work, and became a researcher for the Centre National de la Recherche Scientifique in the 1960s. At the same time, he began to publish essays in such journals as *Lettres nouvelles, N.R.F., Partisans, Traverses, Esprit*, and *Cause commune*, treating a range of topics including the mass media, writing, fashion, dreams, reading, and games.

If I try to define what I sought to do since I began to write, the first idea that comes to mind is that I never wrote two similar books, that I never wished to repeat in one book a formula, a system or a manner elaborated in a preceding book.
—Georges Perec, "Notes sur ce que je cherche"

Perec created a body of works that can be considered diverse by any standards: novels (*Les Choses*, 1965; *Un Homme qui dort*, 1966; *Quel petit vélo à guidon chromé au fond de la cour*, 1967; *La Disparition*, 1969; *Les Revenetes*, 1972; *W ou le souvenir d'enfance*, 1975; *La Vie, mode d'emploi*, 1978; *Le Cabinet d'amateur*, 1979), poetry (*Ulcerations*, 1974; *La Clôture*, 1976; *Alphabets*, 1976), theater (*L'Augmentation*, 1970; *Le Poche Parmentier*, 1974) and a group of works that have been variously described as autobiography or the sociology of daily life (*La Boutique obscure*, 1973; *Espèces d'espace*, 1974; *Tentative pour l'épuisement d'un lieu parisien*, 1975; *Je me souviens*, 1978; *Récits d'Ellis Island*, 1980).

In the 1960s, as his writing career quickly developed (his first novel, *Les Choses*, received the Prix Renaudot in 1965), Perec became associated with an experimental literary group, Oulipo (Ouvroir de littérature potentielle) which included among its members Raymond Queneau, Italo Calvino, and Harry Mathews. Its influence on Perec proved decisive. The fundamental principle of Oulipo was to demonstrate through experiments the essential ludic nature of literature. Among these experiments were lipograms, palindromes (Perec's contribution runs over five thousand letters), bilingual poetry, poetic anagrams, and similar exercises involving the systematic replacement or manipulation of formal elements.

> . . . in following these main currents, I force myself to realize a project of writing wherein I will never rewrite the same book twice, or rather, in rewriting the same book each time, I will illuminate it with a new light.
> —Georges Perec, in an interview with Jean-Marie Le Sidaner

The notion of formal constraint central to Oulipo experiments came to dominate Perec's work in the 1970s when he wrote his most experimental works: *La Disparition,* a detection story (a genre of major influence on Perec) of over three hundred pages written entirely without using the letter *e;* *Les Revenetes* (sic), a lipogram in *a, i, o,* and *u* (although there are no words in common between *La Disparition* and *Les Revenetes,* Perec felt it necessary to break the rule of the formal constraint of the latter, as the misspelled title indicates); and *Alphabets,* a collection of 176 heterogramic and anagramic poems. Another type of constraint which Perec imposed on himself from the first novel onwards, very much related to his background in sociology, concerns observation and description. Whether in his exercises of pure description (*La Boutique obscure, Espèces d'espace, Je me souviens, Tentative pour l'épuisement d'un lieu parisien*) or in the "hyperrealist" passages of his novels (*Les Choses,* which is an extended description of the material existence of a young, French couple in the 1960s and *La Vie, mode d'emploi,* which is based on the model of the chessboard and resembles a gigantic puzzle consisting of many fragments of description that aim at reconstructing the entire history of an apartment building) a fundamental concern of Perec seems to surface with this mania of observing and describing all, and its unspoken, implied fear of forgetting and disappearing.

> . . . in the beginning, one could only try to name the things, one by one, flatly, to enumerate them, to number them, in the most banal way possible, in the most precise way possible, trying to forget nothing.
> —Georges Perec, *Récits d'Ellis Island*

The dominant feature of description and the possible reasons for it become more apparent in Perec's *W ou le souvenir d'enfance.* Consisting of two alternating narratives which initially seem to have nothing to do with each other, the novel provides some, but not all, of the pieces of the puzzle that it constitutes. The first story (which begins the excerpt below) suggests a detective novel, as the mysterious Otto Apfelstahl contacts an army deserter who has acquired a new identity, Gaspard Winckler (this is also the name of the central character of *La Vie, mode d'emploi* who builds five hundred jigsaw puzzles). This unwelcome visitor who seems to know the intimate details of the deserter's flight from France, his acquisition of a new name, identity, and life, finally persuades the narrator to go in search of the one whose name he was given, a deaf-mute boy presumed dead after a shipwreck in the Tierra del Fuego. In the second part of the novel (ironically announced by three ellipses), however, this tale breaks off and is replaced by a systematic description of the island and city of W, a fascist community devoted entirely to sports. The reader is left to assume that Winckler, the narrator of the first part, came across W while searching for the boy (although this experience has apparently been too traumatic to state it as such), hence, the manner in which it fits into the first part of the novel. In the second set of alternating narratives, the narrator (ostensibly Perec) attempts to reconstruct the story of his past beyond the seemingly emphatic, final beginning, "I have no childhood memories." Using a mix of stories borrowed from relatives, yellowing snapshots and half-forgotten, displaced, and sometimes purely fabricated memories, the narrator searches for the truth of the past but is continually frustrated by his inability to recognize it as such in the labyrinth of memory. The narrator, however, tells the reader that at the age of ten or eleven, he wrote a story entitled W about an olympic phantasm, but he could not recall any of its details. The three separate narratives of the novel, therefore, fit into each other like the pieces of a puzzle.

I do not write to say that I will say nothing. I do not write to say that I have nothing to say. I write: I write because we live together, because I was among them, a shadow among their shadows, a body near their bodies; I write because they left in me their indelible mark and its trace is writing: their memory is dead to writing; writing is the memory of their deaths and the affirmation of my life.

—Georges Perec, *W ou le souvenir d'enfance*

In the elaboration of the structure of *W ou le souvenir d'enfance*, it becomes clear that particular elements in one narrative resemble others in another, seemingly opposing narrative. In the first part, both the fictional and the autobiographical narratives involve the search for an identity, and both are told by narrators who see themselves as the sole witnesses of a forgotten, vanished world. Both narrators hesitate before telling their stories. In the second part of the novel, the first narrative describes the interworkings of the practice and the authority of fascism while the second narrative tries to make some sense out of the question of authority given an individual's experience of fascism. Although these associations permit the pieces of the puzzle to fit more snugly together, they also create a generic tension that serves to problematize the entire novelistic and autobiographical enterprise in which the author is engaged: fiction versus truth; documentary style versus detective-story suspense; imagination versus memory; nonentity versus identity; writing versus silence; life versus death, all of which are magnified at every juncture by the specter of the Holocaust.

. . . the text is not the producer of knowledge, but the producer of fiction, of the fiction of knowledge, of knowledge-fiction.

Georges Perec, in an interview with Jean-Marie Le Sidaner

Fascism and the Holocaust are, indeed, the keys to understanding *W ou le souvenir d'enfance* and, perhaps, all of Perec's work. As the novel demonstrates an increasing fictionalization of reality (which, in the case of the horrors of the fascist regime, seems more like a fiction than reality), there arises a greater inability to understand the past and to create fictions, matched with a greater desire to do so. Story and history become indistinguishable, equally unreliable, for one coming out of the aphasia associated with the personal as well as universal tragedy that the horrors of the Holocaust signify. Hyperrealism, formal exercise, insecure autobiographies that admit their "own" fictiveness, and the conclusion that literature is and should be the result of chance and play, can be seen as attempts to create a neutral and neutered writing that seeks to minimize the dangers of the seduction of fiction. Although these features still always risk the seductiveness of the horror and fascination with the evil fruits of fascism, and always threaten to fall back into the initial void of speechlessness and incomprehension, they represent the only writing possible for one caught in a world somewhere between concentration camps and gulags.

BIBLIOGRAPHY

SELECTED CRITICISM

Colloque de Cerisy: Cahiers Georges Perec, no. 1 (July 12–22, 1984, dir. Bernard Magné). Paris: P.O.L., 1985.
Motte, Warren F. Jr., *The Poetics of Experiment: A Study of the Work of Georges Perec.* Lexington, Kentucky: French Forum, 1984.
Oulipo, *Atlas de littérature potentielle.* Paris: Gallimard, 1981.
Oulipo, *La Littérature potentielle: créations, re-créations, recréations.* Paris: Gallimard, 1973.
Oulipo, *Oulipo: A Primer of Potential Literature.* Trans. Warren F. Motte, Jr. Lincoln: Nebraska University Press, 1986.

In addition to these, special issues of the following journals have been devoted to George Perec:

L'Arc 76 (1979).
Magazine littéraire 193 (March 1983).
Littérature 7 (Spring 1983).

GEORGES PEREC

W ou le souvenir d'enfance*

I

J'ai longtemps hésité avant d'entreprendre le récit de mon voyage à W. Je m'y résous aujourd'hui, poussé par une nécessité impérieuse, persuadé que les événements dont j'ai été le témoin doivent être révélés et mis en lumière. Je ne me suis pas dissimulé les scrupules—j'allais dire, je ne sais pourquoi, les prétextes—qui semblaient s'opposer à une publication. Longtemps j'ai voulu garder le secret sur ce que j'avais vu; il ne m'appartenait pas de divulguer quoi que ce soit sur la mission que l'on m'avait confiée, d'abord parce que, peut-être, cette mission ne fut pas accomplie—mais qui aurait pu la mener à bien?—ensuite parce que celui qui me la confia a, lui aussi, disparu.

Longtemps je demeurai indécis. Lentement j'oubliai les incertaines péripéties de ce voyage. Mais mes rêves se peuplaient de ces villes fantômes, de ces courses sanglantes dont je croyais encore entendre les mille clameurs, de ces oriflammes déployées que le vent de la mer lacérait. L'incompréhension, l'horreur et la fascination se confondaient dans ces souvenirs sans fond.

Longtemps j'ai cherché les traces de mon histoire, consulté des cartes et des annuaires, des monceaux d'archives. Je n'ai rien trouvé et il me semblait parfois que j'avais rêvé, qu'il n'y avait eu qu'un inoubliable cauchemar.

Il y a . . . ans, à Venise, dans une gargote de la Giudecca, j'ai vu entrer un homme que j'ai cru reconnaître. Je me suis précipité sur lui, mais déjà balbutiant deux ou trois mots d'excuse. Il ne pouvait pas y avoir de survivant. Ce que mes yeux avaient vu était réellement arrivé: les lianes avaient disjoint les scellements, la forêt avait mangé les mai-

*W ou le souvenir d'enfance (Paris: Denoël, 1975), 9–29. This passage is reprinted with the kind permission of Denoël.

189

sons; le sable envahit les stades, les cormorans s'abattirent par milliers et le silence, le silence glacial tout à coup. Quoi qu'il arrive, quoi que je fasse, j'étais le seul dépositaire, la seule mémoire vivante, le seul vestige de ce monde. Ceci, plus que toute autre considération, m'a décidé à écrire.

Un lecteur attentif comprendra sans doute qu'il ressort de ce qui précède que dans le témoignage que je m'apprête à faire, je fus témoin, et non acteur. Je ne suis pas le héros de mon histoire. Je n'en suis pas non plus exactement le chantre. Même si les événements que j'ai vus ont bouleversé le cours, jusqu'alors insignifiant, de mon existence, même s'ils pèsent encore de tout leur poids sur mon comportement, sur ma manière de voir, je voudrais, pour les relater, adopter le ton froid et serein de l'ethnologue: j'ai visité ce monde englouti et voici ce que j'y ai vu. Ce n'est pas la fureur bouillante d'Achab qui m'habite, mais la blanche rêverie d'Ishmaël, la patience de Bartleby. C'est à eux, encore une fois, après tant d'autres, que je demande d'être mes ombres tutélaires.

Néanmoins, pour satisfaire à une règle quasi générale, et que, du reste, je ne discute pas, je donnerai maintenant, le plus brièvement possible, quelques indications sur mon existence et, plus précisément, sur les circonstances qui décidèrent de mon voyage.

Je suis né le 25 juin 19 . . . , vers quatre heures, à R., petit hameau de trois feux, non loin de A. Mon père possédait une petite exploitation agricole. Il mourut des suites d'une blessure, alors que j'allais avoir six ans. Il ne laissait guère que des dettes et tout mon héritage tint en quelques effets, un peu de linge, trois ou quatre pièces de vaisselle. L'un des deux voisins de mon père s'offrit à m'adopter; je grandis au milieu des siens, moitié comme un fils, moitié comme un valet de ferme.

A seize ans, je quittai R. et j'allai à la ville; j'y exerçai quelque temps divers métiers mais, n'en trouvant pas qui me plaise, je finis par m'engager. Habitué à obéir et doté d'une résistance physique peu commune, j'aurais pu faire un bon soldat, mais je me rendis bientôt compte que je ne m'adapterais jamais vraiment à la vie militaire. Au bout d'un an passé en France, au Centre d'Instruction de T., je fus envoyé en opérations; j'y restai plus de quinze mois. A V., au cours d'une permission, je désertai. Pris en charge par une organisation d'objecteurs, je parvins à gagner l'Allemagne, où, longtemps, je fus sans travail. Je m'installai pour finir à H., tout près de la frontière luxembourgeoise. J'avais trouvé une place de graisseur dans le plus grand garage de la ville. Je logeais dans une petite pension de famille et je passais la plupart de mes soirées dans une brasserie à regarder la télévision ou, parfois, à jouer au jacquet avec l'un ou l'autre de mes camarades de travail.

II

Je n'ai pas de souvenirs d'enfance. Jusqu'à ma douzième année à peu près, mon histoire tient en quelques lignes: j'ai perdu mon père à quatre ans, ma mère à six; j'ai passé la guerre dans diverses pensions de Villard-de-Lans. En 1945, la sœur de mon père et son mari m'adoptèrent.

Cette absence d'histoire m'a longtemps rassuré: sa sécheresse objective, son évidence apparente, son innocence, me protégeaient, mais de quoi me protégeaient-elles, sinon précisément de mon histoire, de mon histoire vécue, de mon histoire réelle, de mon histoire à moi qui, on peut le supposer, n'était ni sèche, ni objective, ni apparemment évidente, ni évidemment innocente?

« Je n'ai pas de souvenirs d'enfance »: je posais cette affirmation avec assurance, avec presque une sorte de défi. L'on n'avait pas à m'interroger sur cette question. Elle n'était pas inscrite à mon programme. J'en étais dispensé: une autre histoire, la Grande, l'Histoire avec sa grande hache, avait déjà répondu à ma place: la guerre, les camps.

A treize ans, j'inventai, racontai et dessinai une histoire. Plus tard, je l'oubliai. Il y a sept ans, un soir, à Venise, je me souvins tout à coup que cette histoire s'appelait « W » et qu'elle était, d'une certaine façon, sinon l'histoire, du moins une histoire de mon enfance.

En dehors du titre brusquement restitué, je n'avais pratiquement aucun souvenir de W. Tout ce que j'en savais tient en moins de deux lignes: la vie d'une société exclusivement préoccupée de sport, sur un îlot de la Terre de Feu.

Une fois de plus, les pièges de l'écriture se mirent en place. Une fois de plus, je fus comme un enfant qui joue à cache-cache et qui ne sait pas ce qu'il craint ou désire le plus: rester caché, être découvert.

Je retrouvai plus tard quelques-uns des dessins que j'avais faits vers treize ans. Grâce à eux, je réinventai W et l'écrivis, le publiant au fur et à mesure, en feuilleton, dans *La Quinzaine littéraire*, entre septembre 1969 et août 1970.

Aujourd'hui, quatre ans plus tard, j'entreprends de mettre un terme—je veux tout autant dire par là « tracer les limites » que « donner un nom »—à ce lent déchiffrement. W ne ressemble pas plus à mon fantasme olympique que ce fantasme olympique ne ressemblait à mon enfance. Mais dans le réseau qu'ils tissent comme dans la lecture que j'en fais, je sais que se trouve inscrit et décrit le chemin que j'ai parcouru, le cheminement de mon histoire et l'histoire de mon cheminement.

III

J'étais depuis trois ans à H. lorsque, le matin du 26 juillet 19 . . . , ma logeuse me remit une lettre. Elle avait été expédiée la veille de K., une

*ville de quelque importance située à 50 kilomètres à peu près de H. Je
l'ouvris; elle était écrite en français. Le papier, d'excellente qualité, portait en en-tête le nom*

Otto APFELSTAHL, MD

*surmontant un blason compliqué, parfaitement gravé, mais que mon
ignorance en matière d'héraldique m'interdit d'identifier, ou même,
plus simplement, de déchiffrer; en fait, je ne parvins à reconnaître clairement que deux des cinq symboles qui le composaient: une tour crénelée,
au centre, sur toute la hauteur du blason, et, au bas, à droite, un livre
ouvert, aux pages vierges; les trois autres, en dépit des efforts que je fis
pour les comprendre, me demeurèrent obscurs; il ne s'agissait pas pourtant de symboles abstraits, ce n'étaient pas des chevrons, par exemple,
ni des bandes, ni des losanges, mais des figures en quelque sorte doubles,
d'un dessin à la fois précis et ambigu, qui semblait pouvoir s'interpréter
de plusieurs façons sans que l'on puisse jamais s'arrêter sur un choix
satisfaisant: l'une aurait pu, à la rigueur, passer pour un serpent sinuant
dont les écailles auraient été des lauriers, l'autre pour une main qui
aurait été en même temps racine; la troisième était aussi bien un nid
qu'un brasier, ou une couronne d'épines, ou un buisson ardent, ou même
un cœur transpercé.*

*Il n'y avait ni adresse, ni numéro de téléphone. La lettre disait
seulement ceci:*

« Monsieur,
*« Nous vous serions extrêmement reconnaissants de bien
vouloir nous accorder un entretien pour une affaire vous concernant.*
*« Nous serons à l'Hôtel Berghof, au numéro 18 de la Nurmberg-
strasse, ce vendredi 27 juillet, et nous vous attendrons au bar à partir de
18 heures.*
*« En vous remerciant à l'avance et en nous excusant de ne pouvoir
vous donner pour l'instant de plus amples explications, nous vous prions
de croire, Monsieur, à nos sentiments dévoués. »*

*Suivait un paraphe à peu près illisible, et que seul le nom figurant
sur l'en-tête me permit d'identifier comme devant signifier « O. Apfelstahl ».*

*Il est facile de comprendre que, d'abord, cette lettre me fit peur. Ma
première idée fut de fuir: j'avais été reconnu, il ne pouvait s'agir que d'un
chantage. Plus tard, je parvins à maîtriser mes craintes: le fait que cette
lettre fût écrite en français ne signifiait pas qu'elle s'adressait à moi, à
celui que j'avais été, au soldat déserteur; mon actuelle identité faisait de
moi un Suisse romand et ma francophonie ne surprenait personne. Ceux
qui m'avaient aidé ne connaissaient pas mon ancien nom et il aurait
fallu un improbable, un inexplicable concours de circonstances pour*

qu'un homme m'ayant rencontré dans ma vie antérieure me retrouve et me reconnaisse. H. n'est qu'une bourgade, à l'écart des grands axes routiers, les touristes l'ignorent, et je passais le plus clair de mes journées au fond de la fosse de graissage ou allongé sous les moteurs. Et puis même, qu'aurait pu me demander celui qui, par un incompréhensible hasard, aurait retrouvé ma trace? Je n'avais pas d'argent, je n'avais pas la possibilité d'en avoir. La guerre que j'avais faite était finie depuis plus de cinq ans, il était plus que vraisemblable que j'avais même été amnistié.

J'essayais d'envisager, le plus calmement possible, toutes les hypothèses que suggérait cette lettre. Etait-elle l'aboutissement d'une longue et patiente recherche, d'une enquête qui, peu à peu, s'était resserrée autour de moi? Croyait-on écrire à un homme dont j'aurais porté le nom ou dont j'aurais été l'homonyme? Un notaire pensait-il tenir en moi l'héritier d'une fortune immense?
Je lisais et je relisais la lettre, j'essayais d'y découvrir chaque fois un indice supplémentaire, mais je n'y trouvais que des raisons de m'intriguer davantage. Ce « nous » qui m'écrivait était-il une convention épistolaire, comme il est d'usage dans presque toutes les correspondances commerciales, où le signataire parle au nom de la société qui l'emploie, ou bien avais-je affaire à deux, à plusieurs correspondants? Et que signifiait ce « MD » qui suivait, sur l'en-tête, le nom d'Otto Apfelstahl? En principe, comme je le vérifiai dans le dictionnaire usuel que j'empruntai quelques instants à la secrétaire du garage, il ne pouvait s'agir que de l'abréviation américaine de « Medical Doctor », mais ce sigle, courant aux Etats-Unis, n'avait aucune raison de figurer sur l'entête d'un Allemand, fût-il médecin, ou alors il me fallait supposer que cet Otto Apfelstahl, bien qu'il m'écrivît de K., n'était pas allemand, mais américain; cela n'avait rien d'étonnant en soi: il y a beaucoup d'Allemands émigrés aux Etats-Unis, de nombreux médecins américains sont d'origine allemande ou autrichienne; mais que pouvait me vouloir un médecin américain, et qu'était-il venu faire à K.? Pouvait-on même concevoir un médecin, quelle que soit sa nationalité, qui mette sur son papier à lettres l'indication de sa profession, mais remplace les renseignements que l'on serait en droit d'attendre d'un docteur en médecine—son adresse ou l'adresse de son cabinet, son numéro de téléphone, l'indication des heures auxquelles il reçoit, ses fonctions hospitalières, etc.—par un blason aussi suranné que sibyllin?

Toute la journée, je m'interrogeai sur ce qu'il convenait de faire. Devais-je aller à ce rendez-vous? Fallait-il fuir tout de suite, et recommencer ailleurs, en Australie ou en Argentine, une autre vie clandestine, forgeant à nouveau l'alibi fragile d'un nouveau passé, d'une nouvelle identité? Au fil des heures, mon anxiété laissait place à l'im-

patience, à la curiosité; j'imaginais fébrilement que cette rencontre allait changer ma vie.

Je passai une partie de la soirée à la Bibliothèque municipale, feuilletant des dictionnaires, des encyclopédies, des annuaires, avec l'espoir d'y découvrir des renseignements sur Otto Apfelstahl, d'éventuelles indications sur d'autres acceptions du sigle « MD », ou sur la signification du blason. Mais je ne trouvai rien.

Le lendemain matin, pris d'un pressentiment tenace, je fourrai dans mon sac de voyage un peu de linge et ce que j'aurais pu appeler, si cela n'avait été à ce point dérisoire, mes biens les plus précieux: mon poste de radio, une montre de gousset en argent qui aurait très bien pu me venir de mon arrière-grand-père, une petite statuette en nacre achetée à V., un coquillage étrange et rare que m'avait un jour envoyé ma marraine de guerre. Voulais-je fuir? Je ne le pense pas: mais être prêt à toute éventualité. Je prévins ma logeuse que je m'absenterais peut-être quelques jours et lui payai son dû. J'allai trouver mon patron; je lui dis que ma mère était morte et qu'il me fallait aller l'enterrer à D., en Bavière. Il m'octroya une semaine de congé et me paya avec quelques jours d'avance le mois qui finissait.

J'allai à la gare, je mis mon sac dans une consigne automatique. Puis, dans la salle d'attente des deuxième classe, assis presque au milieu d'un groupe d'ouvriers portugais en partance pour Hambourg, j'attendis six heures du soir.

IV

Je ne sais où se sont brisés les fils qui me rattachent à mon enfance. Comme tout le monde, ou presque, j'ai eu un père et une mère, un pot, un lit-cage, un hochet, et plus tard une bicyclette que, paraît-il, je n'enfourchais jamais sans pousser des hurlements de terreur à la seule idée qu'on allait vouloir relever ou même enlever les deux petites roues adjacentes qui m'assuraient ma stabilité. Comme tout le monde, j'ai tout oublié de mes premières années d'existence.

Mon enfance fait partie de ces choses dont je sais que je ne sais pas grand-chose. Elle est derrière moi, pourtant, elle est le sol sur lequel j'ai grandi, elle m'a appartenu, quelle que soit ma ténacité à affirmer qu'elle ne m'appartient plus. J'ai longtemps cherché à détourner ou à masquer ces évidences, m'enfermant dans le statut inoffensif de l'orphelin, de l'inengendré, du fils de personne. Mais l'enfance n'est ni nostalgie, ni terreur, ni paradis perdu, ni Toison d'Or, mais peut-être horizon, point de départ, coordonnées à partir desquelles les axes de ma vie pourront trouver leur sens. Même si je n'ai pour étayer mes souvenirs improbables que le secours de photos jaunies, de témoignages rares et de documents dérisoires, je n'ai pas d'autre choix que d'évoquer ce que trop longtemps j'ai nommé l'irrévocable; ce qui fut, ce qui s'arrêta, ce qui fut clôturé: ce qui fut, sans doute, pour aujourd'hui ne plus être, mais ce qui fut aussi pour que je sois encore.

*

Mes deux premiers souvenirs ne sont pas entièrement invraisemblables, même s'il est évident que les nombreuses variantes et pseudo-précisions que j'ai introduites dans les relations—parlées ou écrites—que j'en ai fait les ont profondément altérés, sinon complètement dénaturés.

Le premier souvenir aurait pour cadre l'arrière-boutique de ma grand-mère. J'ai trois ans. Je suis assis au centre de la pièce, au milieu des journaux yiddish éparpillés. Le cercle de la famille m'entoure complètement: cette sensation d'encerclement ne s'accompagne pour moi d'aucun sentiment d'écrasement ou de menace; au contraire, elle est protection chaleureuse, amour: toute la famille, la totalité, l'intégralité de la famille est là, réunie autour de l'enfant qui vient de naître (n'ai-je pourtant pas dit il y a un instant que j'avais trois ans?), comme un rempart infranchissable.

Tout le monde s'extasie devant le fait que j'ai désigné une lettre hébraïque en l'identifiant: le signe aurait eu la forme d'un carré ouvert à son angle inférieur gauche, quelque chose comme

et son nom aurait été gammeth, ou gammel[1]. La scène tout entière, par son thème, sa douceur, sa lumière, ressemble pour moi à un tableau, peut-être de Rembrandt ou peut-être inventé, qui se nommerait « Jésus en face des Docteurs »[2].

Le second souvenir est plus bref; il ressemble davantage à un rêve; il me semble encore plus évidemment fabulé que le premier; il en existe plusieurs variantes qui, en se superposant, tendent à le rendre de plus en plus illusoire. Son énoncé le plus simple serait: mon père rentre de son travail; il me donne une clé. Dans une variante, la clé est en or; dans une autre, ce n'est pas une clé d'or, mais une pièce d'or; dans une autre encore, je suis sur le pot quand mon père rentre de son travail; dans une autre enfin, mon père me donne une pièce, j'avale la pièce, on s'affole, on la retrouve le lendemain dans mes selles.

1. C'est ce surcroît de précision qui suffit à ruiner le souvenir ou en tout cas le charge d'une lettre qu'il n'avait pas. Il existe en effet une lettre nommée « Gimmel » dont je me plais à croire qu'elle pourrait être l'initiale de mon prénom; elle ne ressemble absolument pas au signe que j'ai tracé et qui pourrait, à la rigueur, passer pour un « men » ou « M ». Esther, ma tante, m'a raconté récemment qu'en 1939—j'avais alors trois ans—ma tante Fanny, la jeune sœur de ma mère, m'amenait parfois de Belleville jusqu'à chez elle. Esther habitait alors rue des Eaux, tout près de l'avenue de Versailles. Nous allions jouer au bord de la Seine, tout près des grands tas de sable; un de mes jeux consistait à déchiffrer, avec Fanny, des lettres dans des journaux, non pas yiddish, mais français.

2. Dans ce souvenir ou pseudo-souvenir, Jésus est un nouveau-né entouré de vieillards bienveillants. Tous les tableaux intitulés « Jésus au milieu des Docteurs » le représentent adulte. Le tableau auquel je me réfère, s'il existe, est beaucoup plus vraisemblablement une « Présentation au Temple ».

V

Il était six heures juste lorsque je passai la porte-tambour de l'Hôtel Berghof. Le grand hall était à peu près désert; négligemment appuyés contre un pilier, trois jeunes grooms vêtus de gilets rouges à boutons dorés bavardaient à voix basse, les bras croisés. Le portier, reconnaissable à sa vaste houppelande vert bouteille et à son chapeau de cocher à plumet, traversait le hall en diagonale, portant deux grosses valises et précédant une cliente qui tenait un petit chien entre ses bras.

Le bar était au fond du hall, à peine séparé de lui par une cloison à claire-voie garnie de hautes plantes vertes. A ma grande surprise, il n'y avait aucun consommateur; la fumée des cigares ne flottait pas en l'air, rendant l'atmosphère presque opaque, un peu étouffante; là où j'attendais un désordre feutré, le bruit de vingt conversations sur un fond de musique fade, il n'y avait que des tables nettes, des napperons bien en place, des cendriers de cuivre étincelants. L'air conditionné rendait l'endroit presque frais. Assis derrière un comptoir de bois sombre et d'acier, un barman à la veste un peu fripée lisait la FRANKFURTER ZEITUNG.

J'allai m'asseoir dans le fond de la salle. Levant un instant les yeux de son journal, le barman me regarda d'un air interrogateur; je lui commandai une bière. Il me l'apporta, traînant des pieds; je m'aperçus que c'était un très vieil homme, sa main considérablement ridée tremblait un peu.

—Il n'y a pas grand monde, dis-je, moitié pour dire quelque chose, moitié parce que cela me semblait tout de même étonnant. Il hocha la tête, sans répondre, puis soudain il me demanda:

—Voulez-vous des bretzels?

—Pardon? fis-je sans comprendre.

—Des bretzels. Des bretzels pour manger en buvant votre bière.

—Non, merci. Je ne mange jamais de bretzels. Donnez-moi plutôt un journal.

Il tourna les talons, mais sans doute m'étais-je mal exprimé ou n'avait-il pas fait attention à ce que je lui avais demandé, car, au lieu de se diriger vers les porte-journaux accrochés au mur, il retourna à son comptoir, posa son plateau, et sortit par une petite porte qui devait donner sur l'office.

Je regardai ma montre. Elle ne marquait que six heures cinq. Je me levai, j'allai chercher un journal. C'était un supplément économique hebdomadaire d'un quotidien luxembourgeois, le LUXEMBURGER WORT, *qui datait de plus de deux mois. Je le parcourus pendant une bonne dizaine de minutes, buvant ma bière, absolument seul dans le bar.*

On ne pouvait pas dire qu'Otto Apfelstahl était en retard; on ne pouvait pas dire non plus qu'il était à l'heure. Tout ce que l'on pouvait dire, tout ce que l'on pouvait se dire, tout ce que je pouvais me dire, c'est que, dans n'importe quel rendez-vous, il faut toujours prévoir un quart d'heure de battement. Je n'aurais pas dû avoir besoin de me rassurer, je n'avais aucune raison d'être inquiet, néanmoins l'absence d'Otto Apfelstahl me mettait mal à l'aise. Il était plus de six heures, j'étais au bar, je l'attendais, alors qu'il aurait dû être lui au bar, en train de m'attendre moi.

Vers six heures vingt—j'avais abandonné le journal et depuis long-temps fini ma bière—je me décidai à partir. Peut-être y avait-il un mes-sage d'Otto Apfelstahl pour moi au bureau de l'hôtel, peut-être m'atten-dait-il dans l'un des salons de lecture, ou dans le hall, ou dans sa chambre, peut-être s'excusait-il et me proposait-il de remettre cet en-tretien à plus tard? Tout à coup, il se fit comme un grand remue-ménage dans le hall: cinq à six personnes firent irruption dans le bar, s'atta-blèrent bruyamment. Presque au même instant, deux barmen surgirent de derrière le comptoir. Ils étaient jeunes et je ne pus m'empêcher de remarquer qu'à eux deux ils devaient tout juste atteindre l'âge de celui qui m'avait servi.

C'est au moment où j'appelai l'un des garçons pour lui régler ma consommation—mais il semblait trop occupé à prendre les commandes des clients récemment attablés pour faire attention à moi—qu'apparut

Otto Apfelstahl: un homme qui, à peine entré dans un endroit public, s'arrête, et regarde tout autour de lui avec un soin particulier, avec un sentiment d'attention curieuse, et reprend sa marche dès que son regard a rencontré le vôtre, ne peut être que votre interlocuteur.

C'était un homme d'une quarantaine d'années, plutôt petit, très maigre, avec un visage en lame de couteau, des cheveux très courts, déjà grisonnants, taillés en brosse. Il portait un costume croisé gris sombre. Si tant est qu'un homme puisse porter sa profession sur sa figure, il ne donnait pas l'impression d'être médecin, mais plutôt homme d'affaires, fondé de pourvoir d'une grande banque, ou avocat.

Il s'arrêta à quelques centimètres de moi.

—Vous êtes Gaspard Winckler! me demanda-t-il, mais en fait la phrase était à peine interrogative, c'était plutôt une constatation.

—Euh . . . Oui . . . répondis-je stupidement, et en même temps je me levai, mais il me retint d'un geste:

—Non, non, restez assis, asseyons-nous, nous serons beaucoup mieux pour bavarder.

Il s'assit. Il considéra un instant mon verre vide.

« Vous aimez la bière, à ce que je vois. »

—Cela m'arrive, dis-je sans trop savoir que répondre.

—Je préfère le thé.

Il se tourna légèrement vers le comptoir, levant à demi deux doigts. Le garçon survint aussitôt.

—Un thé pour moi. Voulez-vous une autre bière! me demanda-t-il. J'acquiesçai.

—Et une bière pour monsieur.

J'étais de plus en plus mal à l'aise. Devais-je lui demander s'il s'appelait Otto Apfelstahl! Devais-je lui demander, tout à trac, à brûle-pourpoint, ce qu'il me voulait! Je sortis mon paquet de cigarettes et lui en offris une, mais il la refusa.

—Je ne fume que le cigare, et encore, seulement après mon repas du soir.

—Etes-vous médecin!

Ma question—contrairement à ce que j'avais naïvement pensé—ne parut pas le surprendre. C'est à peine s'il sourit.

—En quoi le fait que je ne fume le cigare qu'après mon repas du soir vous conduit-il à penser que je puisse être médecin!

—Parce que c'est une des questions que je me pose à votre sujet depuis que j'ai reçu votre lettre.

—Vous en posez-vous beaucoup d'autres!

—Quelques autres, oui.

—Lesquelles!

—Eh bien, par exemple, que me voulez-vous!

—Voilà en effet une question qui s'impose. Désirez-vous que j'y réponde tout de suite!

—Je vous en serais très reconnaissant.
—Puis-je auparavant vous poser une question?
—Je vous en prie.
—Vous êtes-vous déjà demandé ce qu'il était advenu de l'individu
qui vous a donné votre nom?
—Pardon? fis-je sans comprendre.

W ou le souvenir d'enfance

I

I hesitated for a long time before undertaking the account of my journey
to W. I have brought myself to do it today, impelled by an imperious
necessity, persuaded that the events of which I was the witness should be
revealed and brought to light. I did not hide the scruples from myself—I
was going to say, I don't know why, the pretexts—which seemed to be
opposed to publication. For a long time I wanted to keep secret what I had
seen; it wasn't my concern to divulge anything at all about the mission
with which I had been entrusted, first of all, because, perhaps, this mission was never completed—but who could have carried it out?—then
because the one who had entrusted it to me had, he too, disappeared.

For a long time I remained undecided. Slowly I forgot the uncertain
mishaps of that trip. But my dreams were populated by those phantom
cities, by those bloody races from which I still believed I heard a thousand
outcries, by those unfurled banners that the sea wind ripped. Lack of
understanding, horror and fascination were intermingled in these bot-
tomless memories.

For a long time, I searched for the traces of my story, consulting maps
and yearbooks, piles of archives. I found nothing and it sometimes
seemed to me that I had dreamed, that it had only been an unforgettable
nightmare.

It was years ago, in Venice, in a cheap restaurant on the Giudecca, I
saw a man enter whom I thought I recognized. I rushed towards him, but
already mumbling two or three words of pardon. There could not have
been a survivor. What my eyes had seen had actually happened: the lianas
had loosened the connections, the forest had eaten the houses: the sand
had invaded the stadium, the cormorants crashed down by the thousands
and the silence, suddenly the glacial silence. Whatever happens, whatever I do, I was the only trustee, the only living memory, the only vestige

of that world. This, more than any other consideration, made me decide to write.

An attentive reader will understand without a doubt that it is evident from what precedes that in the testimony which I am preparing to make, I was a witness and not an actor. I am not the hero of my story. I am not exactly the singer of it, either. Even if the events that I saw upset the course, up till then insignificant, of my existence, even if they still weigh with all of their weight on my behavior, on my manner of seeing, I would like, for the sake of relating them, to adopt the cold and detached tone of the ethnologist: I visited this swallowed up world and this is what I saw there. It is not the boiling fury of Ahab that inhabits me, but the white reverie of Ishmael, the patience of Bartleby. They are the ones, once again, after so many others, whom I ask to be my guardian shades.

Nevertheless, to satisfy a nearly general rule, which, moreover, I won't discuss, I will now give, as briefly as possible, some indications concerning my existence and, more precisely, the circumstances that decided my trip.

I was born on June 25, 19 . . . , at about four o'clock, in R., a small hamlet with three traffic lights, not far from A. My father owned a small farm. He died as the result of a wound when I was about to be six. He left little else but debts and all of my inheritance consisted of a few effects, some linen, three or four pieces of crockery. One of my father's two neighbors offered to adopt me; I grew up among them, partly like a son, partly like a hired hand.

At sixteen, I left R. and went to the city; there, I worked for some time at various jobs, but not finding one that pleased me, I ended up by enlisting; accustomed to obeying and endowed with uncommon physical endurance, I could have made a good soldier, but I soon realized that I would never really adapt myself to military life. At the end of a year spent in France at the T. Training Center, I was sent to the front; I stayed there more than fifteen months. At V., while on leave, I deserted. Taken care of by an organization of objectors, I managed to reach Germany where, for a long time, I was without work. Finally I settled at H., near the Luxemburg border. I had found a job as a greaser in the biggest garage in the city. I was staying in a small boardinghouse and I would spend most of my nights in a bar watching television or, occasionally, playing backgammon with one or another of my fellow workers.

II

I do not have any childhood memories. Up to about my twelfth year, my story takes up only a few lines: I lost my father at the age of four, my mother at six; I spent the war in different boarding schools in Villard-de-Lans. In 1945, the sister of my father and her husband adopted me.

This absence of a story reassured me for a long time: its objective dryness, its apparent clarity, its innocence, protected me, but from what, if not precisely from my story, my lived story, my real story, my own story that, one can imagine, was neither dry nor objective, nor apparently clear, nor evidently innocent?

"I do not have any childhood memories": I stated that assertion with assurance, with almost a sort of defiance. It was not necessary to ask me that question. It was not written down in my curriculum. I was excused from it: another story, the Great One, History with its big axe, had already answered in my stead: the war, the camps.

At thirteen, I invented, related, and sketched a story. Later, I forgot it. Seven years ago, one night, in Venice, I suddenly remembered that this story was called "W" and that it was, in a certain way, if not the story, at least one of the stories of my childhood.

Beyond the suddenly restored title, I had practically no memory of W. All that I knew about it takes up fewer than two lines: the life of a society exclusively preoccupied with sport, on a small island in the Tierra del Fuego.

Once again, the writing's traps were sprung. Once again, I was like a child who plays hide and seek and does not know what he fears or desires most: staying hidden or being discovered.

I later found some of the drawings that I had done at around thirteen. Thanks to them, I reinvented W and wrote it down, publishing it gradually in installments in *La Quinzaine littéraire*, between September 1969 and August 1970.

Today, four years later, I am trying to put an end—I mean by that just as much the "tracing of limits" as "giving a name"—to this slow deciphering. W no more resembles my olympic phantasm than this olympic phantasm resembles my childhood. But in the network that they weave as in the reading of it that I do, I know that the path I travelled is written down and described, the progress of my story and the story of my slow progress.

III

I had been in H. for three years when, the morning of June 26, 19 . . . , my landlady gave me a letter. It had been posted the day before from K., a city of some importance about fifty kilometers from H. I opened it; it was written in French. The paper, of excellent quality, bore on the heading the name

Otto APFELSTAHL, MD

topping a complicated coat-of-arms, perfectly engraved, but which my ignorance on the subject of heraldry did not permit me to identify, or even, more simply, to decipher; in fact, I only succeeded in clearly recognizing two of the five symbols that formed it; a crenelated tower, at the center, running the entire height of the coat-of-arms, and, at the bottom, on the right, an open book, with blank pages; the three others, despite the efforts I made to understand them, continued to be obscure to me; it wasn't a question, however, of abstract symbols, there weren't chevrons, for example, nor bends, nor diamonds, but figures in some sense double, whose design was at one and the same time precise and ambiguous, open to various interpretations, any one of them never being satisfactory: one figure could, if need be, pass for a winding snake whose scales would have been laurels, the other figure for a hand that would have been at the same time a root, the third figure was as much a nest as a brazier, or a crown of thorns, or a burning bush, or even a pierced heart.

There was neither address nor telephone number. The letter said only this:

"Sir,

"We would be extremely grateful if you would please grant us an interview on a matter of concern to you.

"We will be at the Hotel Berghof, at number 18 on the Nurmberg-strasse, this Friday, July 27, and we will wait for you in the bar from 6:00 P.M. on.

"Thanking you in advance, with our apologies for not being able at the moment to give you more ample explanations, we beg you to believe, sir, in our devoted sentiments."

There followed an almost unreadable flourish, and only the name appearing on the heading allowed me to identify it as signifying O. Apfelstahl.

It's easy to understand that, first of all, this letter frightened me. My first thought was to run away: I had been recognized, it could only mean blackmail. Later, I succeeded in overcoming my fears: the fact that the letter was written in French did not mean that it was addressed to me, to the one I had been, the deserter; my present identity made me French-Swiss and my speaking French didn't surprise anyone. Those who had helped me did not know my former name and an improbable, inexplicable chain of circumstances would have been necessary for anyone who had met me in my previous life to find me again and recognize me. H. was just a small market town, off the main crossroads, the tourists never heard of it, and I spent the greater part of my days at the bottom of a grease pit or stretched out under motors. And even then, what could the one, who by an incomprehensible chance had retraced my steps, ask me? I had no money, I had no possibility of getting any. The war I fought in had been over more than five years; it was more than likely I had even received amnesty.

I was trying to consider, as calmly as possible, all the hypotheses that this letter suggested. Was it the outcome of long and patient research, of an inquest that, little by little, closed in around me? Did someone think he was writing to a man whose name I carried or of whom I would have been the namesake? Did a notary think he had found in me the inheritor of an immense fortune?

I read and reread the letter, I tried to discover an additional clue in it each time, but I only found in it reasons for further perplexity. Was that "we" who was writing to me an epistolary convention, as is used in nearly all commercial correspondence wherein the signature speaks for the name of the company that uses it, or was I dealing rather with two or several correspondents? And what did that "MD" which followed, on the heading, the name of Otto Apfelstahl mean? In principle, as I verified in the common dictionary that I borrowed for a few moments from the secretary of the garage, it could only stand for the American abbreviation "Medical Doctor," but those initials, common in the United States, had no reason to be used on the letterhead of a German, even if he were a doctor, or then I had to suppose that this Otto Apfelstahl, although he wrote to me from K., was not German, but American; there was nothing surprising in that: there are a lot of German emigrés in the United States, numerous American doctors are of German or Austrian descent; but what could an American doctor want with me, and what was he doing in K.? Can one even imagine a doctor of any nationality who might put the indication of his profession on his stationery but omit the information that one would rightly expect of a medical doctor—his address, his telephone number, his office address, the indication of his office hours, his hospital duties, etc.—with a coat-of-arms as old-fashioned as it was sibylline?

All day I asked myself what I should do. Should I go to this meeting? Must I run away immediately, and begin again elsewhere, in Australia or Argentina, another clandestine life, once again inventing the fragile alibi of a new past, a new identity? As the hours passed, my anxiety gave way to impatience, to curiosity; I imagined feverishly that this meeting was going to change my life.

I spent part of the night at the public library leafing through dictionaries, encyclopedias, and yearbooks with the hope of discovering information there about Otto Apfelstahl, eventual indications on other meanings of the initials "MD" or on the significance of the coat-of-arms. But I found nothing.

The next morning, overcome by a stubborn foreboding, I stuffed into my travel bag a little underwear and what might be called, had it not been at that point laughable, my most precious possessions: my radio set, my silver pocket-watch which could well have come to me from my great-grandfather, a little mother-of-pearl statuette bought in V., a strange and rare shell that the lady who used to write to me during the war sent me. Did I want to run away? I don't think so: but to be ready for any eventuality, I warned my landlady that I would perhaps be gone a few days and paid her what I owed. I went to find my boss; I told him that my mother had died and that it was necessary to go bury her at D., in Bavaria. He gave me a week off and paid me a few days in advance for the month that was ending.

I went to the train station, I put my bag in a locker. Then I went to the second-class waiting room, sat nearly in the middle of a group of Portuguese workers bound for Hamburg and waited for six o'clock in the evening.

IV

I do not know where the threads that linked me to my childhood were broken. Like everyone, or nearly everyone, I had a father and a mother, a potty, a crib, a rattle, and later, a bicycle that, it seemed, I never straddled without howling with terror at the simple idea that the two little training-wheels that assured me of my stability were going to be removed. Like everyone, I have forgotten everything about my first years of existence.

My childhood belongs to those things about which I know very little. It is behind me, however, it is the ground on which I grew, it belonged to me, however tenaciously I may affirm that it no longer belongs to me. For a long time I tried to turn away or mask these facts, shutting myself up in the inoffensive status of an orphan, the unbegotten, the son of no one. But childhood is neither nostalgia, nor terror, nor paradise lost, nor the Golden Fleece, but perhaps a horizon, a point of departure, coordinates from which the axes of my life will be able to find their meaning. Even if all I have to support my improbable memories is the assistance of yellowed photographs, rare testimonies, and ridiculous documents, I have no choice other than to evoke that which for too long I named the irrevocable; that which was, that which stopped, that which was terminated: that which was, without a doubt, in order to be no more, but that which was, also, so that I might still be.

My first two memories are not entirely improbable even if it is obvious that the numerous variations and pseudoaccuracies which I introduced into the accounts—spoken or written—that I have made deeply altered them, if not completely distorted them.

The first memory has as a setting the back room of my grandmother's shop. I am three years old. I am sitting in the center of the room, in the middle of some scattered Yiddish newspapers. The family circle completely surrounds me: that sensation of encirclement is not accompanied with any feeling of crushing or menace for me; on the contrary, it is warm protection, love: the whole family, the totality, the wholeness of the family is there, gathered together around the child that has just been born (did I not say a moment ago however that I was three years old?) like an insurmountable rampart.

Everyone is going into ecstasies over the fact that I pointed out a Hebrew letter and identified it; the symbol would have had the form of a square open at the lower left corner, something like

and its name would have been gammeth or gammel.[1] The entire scene, by its theme, its softness, its light, to me resembles a painting, perhaps by Rembrandt or perhaps invented, which would be called "Jesus facing the Doctors."[2]

The second memory is shorter: it is more like a dream; it seems to me even more evidently fabricated than the first one; several variants exist which, by overlapping with each other, tend to render it more and more illusory. Its simplest statement would be: my father returns from work, he gives me a key. In one version, the key is made of gold; in another, it is not a gold key but a gold coin; in yet another, I am on the potty when my father returns from work; finally in another, my father gives me a coin, I swallow the coin, everyone panics and the next day it is found in my stool.

1. Is it this excess of precision that suffices to ruin the memory or in any case loads it with a letter that it did not contain. There exists, in fact, a letter named "Gimel" of which I am pleased to believe that it could be the initial of my first name; it resembles in no way the symbol that I traced and that could, if need be, pass for a "men" or "M." Esther, my aunt, recently told me that in 1939—I was then three years old—my aunt Fanny, the younger sister of my mother, sometimes took me from Belleville to her house. Esther was living on the Rue des Eaux quite near the Avenue de Versailles. We would go to play on the banks of the Seine, very near the great heaps of sand; one of my games consisted in deciphering, with Fanny, letters in newspapers, not Yiddish, but French ones.

2. In this memory or pseudomemory, Jesus is a newborn baby surrounded by benevolent old men. All of the paintings entitled "Jesus facing the Doctors" show him as an adult. The painting to which I am referring, if it exists, is much more likely a "Presentation in the Temple."

V

It was just six o'clock when I passed through the revolving doors of the Hotel Berghof. The big entrance hall was mostly deserted; nonchalantly leaning against a pillar, three young bellboys dressed in red vests with gilt buttons were chatting in low voices, their arms crossed. The doorman, recognizable by his wide, bottle-green overcoat and his feathered coach-man's hat, was crossing the lobby diagonally, carrying two big suitcases and preceding a female client who was holding a little dog in her arms.

The bar was at the end of the lobby, barely separated from it by a partition trimmed with tall, green plants. Much to my surprise, there was not a single customer; cigar smoke did not float through the air, making the atmosphere nearly opaque and a little stifling; there where I had expected muted disorder, the noise of twenty conversations against a background of dull music, there were only clean tables, napkins perfectly in place, glittering copper ashtrays. The air conditioning made the place almost cool. Seated behind a dark wood and steel counter, the bartender in a slightly shabby jacket was reading the *Frankfurter Zeitung*.

I went to sit down at the back of the room. The bartender, raising his eyes for a moment from his newspaper, looked at me inquisitively; I ordered a beer. He brought it to me, dragging his feet; I realized that he was a very old man, his very wrinkled hand was trembling a little.

"There aren't a lot of people," I said, partly to say something, partly because it seemed all the same surprising to me. He nodded his head, without answering, then suddenly asked me:

"Do you want some pretzels?"

"What?" I said without understanding.

"Pretzels. Some pretzels to eat while drinking your beer."

"No, thank you, I never eat pretzels. Instead, give me a newspaper."

He turned tail but without a doubt I had expressed myself poorly or he had not paid attention to what I had requested from him, because instead of heading for the newspaper-racks hung on the wall, he returned to his counter, put down his tray, and left by a small door that must have led to the kitchen.

I looked at my watch. It was only five after six. I got up, I went to get a newspaper. There was a weekly business supplement to a Luxemburg daily, the *Luxemburger Wort*, which was more than two months old. I glanced through it for a good ten minutes, while drinking my beer, completely alone in the bar.

One couldn't say that Otto Apfelstahl was late; one couldn't say either that he was on time. All that one could say, all that one could say to oneself, all that I could say to myself, is that, in any kind of meeting, it is always necessary to plan a quarter hour of waiting. I shouldn't have needed to reassure myself, I had no reason to be uneasy, nevertheless, the absence of Otto Apfelstahl was making me uneasy. It was past six, I was in the bar, I was waiting for him, when he should have been in the bar, busy waiting for me.

At about twenty after six—I had abandoned the newspaper and had long since finished my beer—I decided to leave. Perhaps there was a message from Otto Apfelstahl for me at the hotel desk, perhaps he was waiting for me in one of the reading rooms, or in the lobby, or in his own room, perhaps he was excusing himself and proposing to postpone this conversation until later? Suddenly, a great disturbance occurred in the lobby: five or six people burst into the bar, noisily sat down. At nearly the same second, two bartenders rose up from behind the counter. They were young and I could not help but think that both of them together would nearly reach the age of the one who had served me.

It was at the moment that I called one of the waiters to pay for my drink—but he seemed too busy taking the orders of the recently seated customers to pay attention to me—that Otto Apfelstahl appeared: a man who, as he enters a public place, stops and looks around with particular care, with curiosity, and starts walking in as soon as his glance meets yours, can only be your interlocutor.

He was a man of about forty, rather short, very slim, with a hatchet face, his already greying hair cropped in a crew-cut. He was wearing a dark grey twill suit. If indeed a man can wear his profession on his face, then he didn't give the impression of being a doctor, but rather a businessman, the legal representative of a large bank, or a lawyer.

He stopped a few centimeters from me.

"You are Gaspard Winckler?" he asked me, but in fact his sentence was barely questioning, it was rather a statement.

"Uh . . . Yes . . ." I answered stupidly, and at the same time I got up, but he stopped me with a gesture:

"No, no, stay seated, let's sit down, we will be much more comfortable that way to chat."

He sat down. He looked at my empty glass for a moment.

"You like beer, from what I can see."

"From time to time," I said without really knowing how to answer.

"I prefer tea."

He turned slightly to the counter, halfway raising two fingers. The waiter arrived immediately.

"A tea for me. Do you want another beer?" he asked me.

I agreed.

"And a beer for the gentleman."

I was more and more uneasy. Should I ask him if his name was Otto Apfelstahl? Should I ask bluntly, point blank what he wanted with me? I took out my pack of cigarettes and offered him one, but he refused.

"I smoke only cigars, and then, only after my evening meal."

"Are you a doctor?"

My question—contrary to what I had naively thought—didn't seem to surprise him. He barely smiled.

"What in the fact that I only smoke a cigar after my evening meal leads you to think that I might be a doctor?"

"Because that is one of the questions I have been asking myself about you since I received your letter."

"Are you asking others?"

"Some, yes."

"Which?"

"Well, for example, what do you want from me?"

"That is indeed the question. Do you wish me to answer it right away?"

"I would be very grateful to you."

"May I ask *you* a question first?"

"Please do."

"Have you already asked yourself what happened to the individual who gave you your name?"

"What?" I said without understanding.

TRANSLATED BY LEONARD R. KOOS

FRANÇOISE DUBOR

J. M. G. Le Clézio

Jean-Marie Gustave Le Clézio was born in Nice on 13 April 1940. He spent his childhood in a little village in the south of France, and, except for a year spent after the war in Nigeria with his father (a physician for the English government), he was educated entirely in Nice, receiving the "Licence-ès-lettres" after studying at the Collège Littéraire Universitaire. In 1959–60 he was a student and French teacher in England; in 1966–67 he spent a period in Bangkok and Mexico, doing his military service as a *coopérant*.

Le Clézio has traveled a good deal in Europe, North Africa, the Canary Islands, Thailand, New Mexico (where he taught French literature); he has also repeatedly visited the Embera Indians of Panama. He continues to visit Nice regularly.

The work of J. M. G. Le Clézio, which includes novels, short stories, essays, and translations, is characterized by both a profound unity in the inspiration and the aims of the author, and a distinct evolution that reveals Le Clézio's constant reflection on his position in the world as a writer.

In openly declaring war against a technocratic society and Western Civilization, Le Clézio expresses his insatiable pursuit of Life, in its broadest manifestations as well as in its minutest details. The hero of his first novel, *Le Procès verbal*, a sort of "ontologically desperate person," reemerges in the following novels with a constant dread of death, the symptom of a fundamental dissatisfaction, that leads to endless wandering in which space and time are strongly negated and are only important as setting or context. What is most important is "the adventure of being alive," a major phenomenon on which the author's attention is intensely concentrated. The result is a withdrawal from the ordinary world into the nostalgia of the ideal, ancient, and lost world that is retraced in *Terra amata*. But it is less a question of nostalgia than of reconciliation, a reconciliation revitalized by the natural elements of an environment that is rarely protected from the aggressions of modern civilization such as pollution, war, and various conflicts. The effort to find a suitable place, illustrated in *Désert, Hai, Trois villes saintes, Le Chercheur d'or,* and *Le Journal du voyage à Rodrigues,* is motivated by the search for an absolute purity and a return to a science of cosmic mechanisms such as that proposed by the civilization of the Mayas. Le Clézio looks to the geological formation of Central America, India, and Mauritia in order to transform and redefine a vision of everyday life that would be controlled by the great natural phenomena, in which the ontological essence reappears vigorously and almost exclusively. This attempt to purify, most evident in the metaphors of *Les Voyages de l'autre côté*, is also revealed by Le Clézio through the imaginary world of the child, which is free and detached from any experience exterior to it (*Mondo et autres histoires*).

Fundamentally, the writer sets out to reconcile man with himself. The freedom of his techniques, such as collages, scratched-out texts, typographical games, the substitution of persons in a narrative, and the idiosyncratic tone, in particular the minute accuracy of the description, contribute to a more profound investigation of the depths of being, enigmatic phenomenon that it is. Learning how to see becomes a matter of great urgency, so that one can fully absorb the plenitude of a world offered to man. This results in a growing passivity on the part of each of Le Clézio's "heros," who resist all conventions, artificial by definition. But this passivity permits a better fusion in oneself of the self and the outside world, which enables the heroes at this point to reach an ideal symbiosis. This passivity is not conceived of as detachment from the world implying a refusal to act or even participate in the world, for this itself would constitute an act of violence. It is a passivity conceived in relation to any action—no matter how insignificant—that animates and dynamizes all vital intervention; an action that is not violent but natural and that permits time and space to reintegrate their original importance. They find a place that is identical to that of the "hero," that is, man. Indeed, recognition and reconciliation pass through this breaking-down of barriers, through this experience of otherness which eventually loses its violent and aggressive nature in favor of a general harmony that the work of J. M. G. Le Clézio constantly strives to bring to light.

Writing, then, becomes a way of transcribing in the most accurate manner possible the slightest tremor of an acute sensitivity, in all its unsettling hesitations, in order to capture the most infinitesimal movement of life. But let there be no mistake, purity is not naiveté. Childhood occupies an ideal place in the work of Le Clézio, thanks to its unconscious spontaneity and its very fragility in time and space: Le Clézio's clean style and penetrating thought succeed in preserving its seriousness. Naiveté in its purest state is a goal that can only be reached through a profound understanding of all manifestations of life and a serious acceptance of the importance of the writer.

"To be alive is to be aware," Le Clézio tells us. His essay *L'Extase matérielle* [*Material Ecstasy*], whose title alone is charged with meaning, reveals the double stake of all of his works: man, severed from his original state, carries deep within himself the secret spring of his own primitiveness, and there the principles of discontinuity, rupture, and survival are at work, just as they are in civilization, though in a different mode. Once again, what matters most is seeing and comprehending this "mode." The vivifying spring of the Origin gives rise to the fundamental catharsis of literature that Le Clézio reflects consciously, wisely, and in a poetry that reveals him to be inhabited everywhere by the PASSION OF LIVING.

Translated by Deidre Dawson

BIBLIOGRAPHY

I. SELECTED WORKS

Le Procès-verbal (Paris: Gallimard, 1963, Prix Renaudot).
Le Jour où Beaumont fit connaissance avec sa douleur (Paris: Mercure de France, 1964).
La Fièvre (Paris: Gallimard, 1965).
L'Extase matérielle (Paris: Gallimard, 1966).
Le Déluge (Paris: Gallimard, 1968).
Terra Amata (Paris: Gallimard, 1968).
Le Livre des fuites (Paris: Gallimard, 1969).
La Guerre (Paris: Gallimard, 1970).
Haï (Geneva: Skira, 1971).
Mydriase (Montpellier: Fata Morgana, 1973).
Les Géants (Paris: Gallimard, 1973).
Voyages de l'autre côté (Paris: Gallimard, 1975).
Désert (Paris: Gallimard, 1980).
La Ronde et autres faits divers (Paris: Gallimard, 1982).
Le Chercheur d'or (Paris: Gallimard, 1985).
Journal du voyage à Rodrigues (Paris: Gallimard, 1985).

II. SELECTED CRITICISM

Bersani, Jacques. "Le Clézio sismographe," *Critique* 20, no. 238 (March 1967): 311–21.
——. "Sagesse de Le Clézio," *La Nouvelle Revue Française* 15, no. 175 (1 July 1967): 110–15.
Blot, Jean. "Le Roman et son langage," *La Nouvelle Revue Française* 198 (1 June 1969): 1157–63.
Bollene, Geneviève. "*Le Procès-verbal* ou la folie fiction," *Mercure de France* 12, no. 349 (December 1973): 791–97.
Bosquet, Alain. "*Voyages de l'autre côté*," *La Nouvelle Revue Française* 268 (April 1975): 91–94.
Bourdet, Denise. *Encre sympathique*. Paris: Grasset, 1966, 184–93.
Bureau, Conrad. *Linguistique fonctionnelle et stylistique objective*. Paris: Presses Universitaires de France, 1976, 123–50.
Cagnon, Maurice. "J. M. G. Le Clézio, l'impossible vérité de la fiction," *Critique* 297 (February 1972): 158–64.
——. "J. M. G. Le Clézio, The Genesis of Writing," *Language and Style* 5, no. 3 (Summer 1972): 221–27.
Cagnon, Maurice, and Stephen Smith. "Le Clézio's Taoist Vision," *French Review* 47, special issue no. 6 (Spring 1974): 245–52.
——. "Mors et anima: la dialectique du paradoxe plausible," *Revue du Pacifique* 1, no. 1 (Spring 1975): 33–42.
——. "J. M. G. Le Clézio: Fiction's Double Bind," ed. Raymond Federman, in *Surfiction: Fiction Today and Tomorrow*. Chicago: Swallow Press, 1975.

Foucault, Michel. "Le langage de l'espace, *Le Procès-verbal*," *Critique* 203 (April 1964): 379–80.

Jean, Raymond. *La Littérature et le réel*. Paris: Albin Michel, 1965.

Waelti-Walters, Jennifer R. *J. M. G. Le Clézio*. Boston: Twayne Publications, 1977.

––––––. *Icare ou l'évasion impossible. Etude psychomythique de l'oeuvre de J. M. G. Le Clézio*. Sherbrooke, Québec, Canada: Naaman, 1981.

Zeltner, Gerda. "Jean-Marie Gustave Le Clézio: Le Roman antiformaliste," *Positions et oppositions sur le roman contemporain*. Actes et Colloques 8, ed. Michel Mansuy. Strasbourg: Klincksieck, 1971, 215–28.

J. M. G. LE CLÉZIO

*Désert**

Saguiet el Hamra, hiver 1909–1910

Ils sont apparus, comme dans un rêve, au sommet de la dune, à demi cachés par la brume de sable que leurs pieds soulevaient. Lentement ils sont descendus dans la vallée, en suivant la piste presque invisible. En tête de la caravane, il y avait les hommes, enveloppés dans leurs manteaux de laine, leurs visages masqués par le voile bleu. Avec eux marchaient deux ou trois dromadaires, puis les chèvres et les moutons harcelés par les jeunes garçons. Les femmes fermaient la marche. C'étaient des silhouettes alourdies, encombrées par les lourds manteaux, et la peau de leurs bras et de leurs fronts semblait encore plus sombre dans les voiles d'indigo.

Ils marchaient sans bruit dans le sable, lentement, sans regarder où ils allaient. Le vent soufflait continûment, le vent du désert, chaud le jour, froid la nuit. Le sable fuyait autour d'eux, entre les pattes des chameaux, fouettait le visage des femmes qui rabattaient la toile bleue sur leurs yeux. Les jeunes enfants couraient, les bébés pleuraient, enroulés dans la toile bleue sur le dos de leur mère. Les chameaux grommelaient, éternuaient. Personne ne savait où on allait.

Le soleil était encore haut dans le ciel nu, le vent emportait les bruits et les odeurs. La sueur coulait lentement sur le visage des voyageurs, et leur peau sombre avait pris le reflet de l'indigo, sur leurs joues, sur leurs bras, le long de leurs jambes. Les tatouages bleus sur le front des femmes brillaient comme des scarabées. Les yeux noirs, pareils à des gouttes de métal, regardaient à peine l'étendue de sable, cherchaient la trace de la piste entre les vagues des dunes.

Il n'y avait rien d'autre sur la terre, rien, ni personne. Ils étaient nés du désert, aucun autre chemin ne pouvait les conduire. Ils ne disaient

Désert (Paris: Gallimard, 1980), 7–30. This passage is reprinted with the kind permission of Gallimard.

213

rien. Ils ne voulaient rien. Le vent passait sur eux, à travers eux, comme
s'il n'y avait personne sur les dunes. Ils marchaient depuis la première
aube, sans s'arrêter, la fatigue et la soif les enveloppaient comme une
gangue. La sécheresse avait durci leurs lèvres et leur langue. La faim les
rongeait. Ils n'auraient pas pu parler. Ils étaient devenus, depuis si longtemps, muets comme le désert, pleins de lumière quand le soleil brûle au
centre du ciel vide, et glacés de la nuit aux étoiles figées.

Ils continuaient à descendre lentement la pente vers le fond de la
vallée, en zigzaguant quand le sable s'éboulait sous leurs pieds. Les
hommes choisissaient sans regarder l'endroit où leurs pieds allaient se
poser. C'était comme s'ils cheminaient sur des traces invisibles qui les
conduisaient vers l'autre bout de la solitude, vers la nuit. Un seul d'entre
eux portait un fusil, une carabine à pierre au long canon de bronze noirci.
Il la portait sur sa poitrine, serrée entre ses deux bras, le canon dirigé vers
le haut comme la hampe d'un drapeau. Ses frères marchaient à côté de lui,
enveloppés dans leurs manteaux, un peu courbés en avant sous le poids de
leurs fardeaux. Sous leurs manteaux, leurs habits bleus étaient en lambeaux, déchirés par les épines, usés par le sable. Derrière le troupeau
exténué, Nour, le fils de l'homme au fusil, marchait devant sa mère et ses
sœurs. Son visage était sombre, noirci par le soleil, mais ses yeux brillaient, et la lumière de son regard était presque surnaturelle.

Ils étaient les hommes et les femmes du sable, du vent, de la lumière,
de la nuit. Ils étaient apparus, comme dans un rêve, en haut d'une dune,
comme s'ils étaient nés du ciel sans nuages, et qu'ils avaient dans leurs
membres la dureté de l'espace. Ils portaient avec eux la faim, la soif qui
fait saigner les lèvres, le silence dur où luit le soleil, les nuits froides, la
lueur de la Voie lactée, la lune; ils avaient avec eux leur ombre géante au
coucher du soleil, les vagues de sable vierge que leurs orteils écartés
touchaient, l'horizon inaccessible. Ils avaient surtout la lumière de leur
regard, qui brillait si clairement dans la sclérotique de leurs yeux.

Le troupeau des chèvres bises et des moutons marchait devant les
enfants. Les bêtes aussi allaient sans savoir où, posant leurs sabots sur des
traces anciennes. Le sable tourbillonnait entre leurs pattes, s'accrochait à
leurs toisons sales. Un homme guidait les dromadaires, rien qu'avec la
voix, en grognant et en crachant comme eux. Le bruit rauque des respira-
tions se mêlait au vent, disparaissait aussitôt dans les creux des dunes,
vers le sud. Mais le vent, la sécheresse, la faim n'avaient plus d'importance. Les hommes et le troupeau fuyaient lentement, descendaient vers
le fond de la vallée sans eau, sans ombre.

Ils étaient partis depuis des semaines, des mois, allant d'un puits à un
autre, traversant les torrents desséchés qui se perdaient dans le sable,
franchissant les collines de pierres, les plateaux. Le troupeau mangeait les
herbes maigres, les chardons, les feuilles d'euphorbe qu'il partageait avec
les hommes. Le soir, quand le soleil était près de l'horizon et que l'ombre

des buissons s'allongeait démesurément, les hommes et les bêtes ces-
saient de marcher. Les hommes déchargeaient les chameaux, con-
struisaient la grande tente de laine brune, debout sur son unique poteau
en bois de cèdre. Les femmes allumaient le feu, préparaient la bouillie de
mil, le lait caillé, le beurre, les dattes. La nuit venait très vite, le ciel
immense et froid s'ouvrait au-dessus de la terre éteinte. Alors les étoiles
naissaient, les milliers d'étoiles arrêtées dans l'espace. L'homme au fusil,
celui qui guidait la troupe, appelait Nour et il lui montrait la pointe de la
petite Ourse, l'étoile solitaire qu'on nomme le Cabri, puis, à l'autre extrémité de la constellation, Kochab, la bleue. Vers l'est, il montrait à
Nour le Pont où brillent les cinq étoiles Alkaïd, Mizar, Alioth, Megrez,
Fecda. Tout à fait à l'est, à peine au-dessus de l'horizon couleur de cendre,
Orion venait de naître, avec Alnilam un peu penché de côté comme le
mât d'un navire. Il connaissait toutes les étoiles, il leur donnait parfois
des noms étranges, qui étaient comme des commencements d'histoires.
Alors il montrait à Nour la route qu'ils suivraient le jour, comme si les
lumières qui s'allumaient dans le ciel traçaient les chemins que doivent
parcourir les hommes sur la terre. Il y avait tant d'étoiles! La nuit du
désert était pleine de ces feux qui palpitaient doucement, tandis que le
vent passait et repassait comme un souffle. C'était un pays hors du temps,
loin de l'histoire des hommes, peut-être, un pays où plus rien ne pouvait
apparaître ou mourir, comme s'il était déjà séparé des autres pays, au
sommet de l'existence terrestre. Les hommes regardaient souvent les
étoiles, la grande voie blanche qui fait comme un pont de sable au-dessus
de la terre. Ils parlaient un peu, en fumant des feuilles de kif enroulées, ils
se racontaient les récits de voyages, les bruits de la guerre contre les
soldats des Chrétiens, les vengeances. Puis ils écoutaient la nuit.

Les flammes du feu de brindilles dansaient sous la théière de cuivre,
avec un bruit d'eau qui fuse. De l'autre côté du brasero, les femmes
parlaient, et l'une d'elles chantonnait pour son bébé qui s'endormait sur
son sein. Les chiens sauvages glapissaient, et c'était l'écho dans le creux
des dunes qui leur répondait, comme d'autres chiens sauvages. L'odeur
des bêtes montait, se mêlait à l'humidité du sable gris, à l'âcreté des
fumées des braseros.

Ensuite les femmes et les enfants dormaient sous la tente, et les
hommes se couchaient dans leurs manteaux, autour du feu éteint. Ils
disparaissaient sur l'étendue de sable et de pierre, invisibles, tandis que le
ciel noir resplendissait encore davantage.

Ils avaient marché ainsi pendant des mois, des années, peut-être. Ils
avaient suivi les routes du ciel entre les vagues des dunes, les routes qui
viennent du Draa, de Tamgrout, de l'Erg Iguidi, ou, plus au nord, la route
des Aït Atta, des Gheris, de Tafilelt, qui rejoignent les grands ksours des
contreforts de l'Atlas, ou bien la route sans fin qui s'enfonce jusqu'au
cœur du désert, au-delà du Hank, vers la grande ville de Tombouctou.

Certains étaient morts en route, d'autres étaient nés, s'étaient mariés. Les bêtes aussi étaient mortes, la gorge ouverte pour fertiliser les profondeurs de la terre, ou bien frappées par la peste, et laissées à pourrir sur la terre dure.

C'était comme s'il n'y avait pas de noms, ici, comme s'il n'y avait pas de paroles. Le désert lavait tout dans son vent, effaçait tout. Les hommes avaient la liberté de l'espace dans leur regard, leur peau était pareille au métal. La lumière du soleil éclatait partout. Le sable ocre, jaune, gris, blanc, le sable léger glissait, montrait le vent. Il couvrait toutes les traces, tous les os. Il repoussait la lumière, il chassait l'eau, la vie, loin d'un centre que personne ne pouvait reconnaître. Les hommes savaient bien que le désert ne voulait pas d'eux: alors ils marchaient sans s'arrêter, sur les chemins que d'autres pieds avaient déjà parcourus, pour trouver autre chose. L'eau, elle était dans les *aiun*, les yeux, couleur de ciel, ou bien dans les lits humides des vieux ruisseaux de boue. Mais ce n'était pas de l'eau pour le plaisir, ni pour le repos. C'était juste la trace d'une sueur à la surface du désert, le don parcimonieux d'un Dieu sec, le dernier mouvement de la vie. Eau lourde arrachée au sable, eau morte des crevasses, eau alcaline qui donnait la colique, qui faisait vomir. Il fallait aller encore plus loin, penché un peu en avant, dans la direction qu'avaient donnée les étoiles.

Mais c'était le seul, le dernier pays libre peut-être, le pays où les lois des hommes n'avaient plus d'importance. Un pays pour les pierres et pour le vent, aussi pour les scorpions et pour les gerboises, ceux qui savent se cacher et s'enfuir quand le soleil brûle et que la nuit gèle.

Maintenant, ils étaient apparus au-dessus de la vallée de la Saguiet el Hamra, ils descendaient lentement les pentes de sable. Au fond de la vallée, commençaient les traces de la vie humaine: champs de terre entourés de murs de pierre sèche, enclos pour les chameaux, baraquements de feuilles de palmier nain, grandes tentes de laine pareilles à des bateaux renversés. Les hommes descendaient lentement, enfonçant leurs talons dans le sable qui s'éboulait. Les femmes ralentissaient leur marche, et restaient loin derrière le groupe des bêtes tout à coup affolées par l'odeur des puits. Alors l'immense vallée apparaissait, s'ouvrait sous le plateau de pierre. Nour cherchait les hauts palmiers vert sombre jaillissant du sol, en rangs serrés autour du lac d'eau claire, il cherchait les palais blancs, les minarets, tout ce qu'on lui avait dit depuis son enfance, quand on lui avait parlé de la ville de Smara. Il y avait si longtemps qu'il n'avait pas vu d'arbres. Ses bras un peu desserrés, il marchait vers le bas de la vallée, les yeux à demi fermés à cause de la lumière et du sable.

A mesure que les hommes descendaient vers le fond de la vallée, la ville qu'ils avaient entrevue un instant disparaissait, et ils ne trouvaient que la terre sèche et nue. Il faisait chaud, la sueur coulait abondamment sur le visage de Nour, collait ses vêtements bleus à ses reins, à ses épaules.

Maintenant, d'autres hommes, d'autres femmes apparaissaient aussi, comme nés de la vallée. Des femmes avaient allumé leurs braseros pour le repas du soir, des enfants, des hommes immobiles devant leurs tentes poussiéreuses. Ils étaient venus de tous les points du désert, au-delà de la Hamada de pierres, des montagnes du Cheheïba et de Ouarkziz, du Siroua, des monts Oum Chakourt, au-delà même des grandes oasis du Sud, du lac souterrain de Gourara. Ils avaient franchi les montagnes par le pas de Maïder, vers Tarhamant, ou plus bas, là où le Draa rencontre le Tingut, par Regbat. Ils étaient venus, tous les peuples du Sud, les nomades, les commerçants, les bergers, les pillards, les mendiants. Peut-être que certains avaient quitté le royaume de Biru, ou la grande oasis de Oualata. Leurs visages portaient la marque du terrible soleil, du froid mortel des nuits, aux confins du désert. Certains d'entre eux étaient d'un noir presque rouge, grands et longilignes, qui parlaient une langue inconnue; c'étaient les Tubbus venus de l'autre côté du désert, du Borku et du Tibesti, les mangeurs de noix de cola, qui allaient jusqu'à la mer.

A mesure que le troupeau d'hommes et de bêtes approchait, les silhouettes noires des hommes se multipliaient. Derrière les acacias tordus, les huttes de branches et de boue apparaissaient, telles des termitières. Des maisons en pisé, des casemates de planches et de boue, et surtout, ces petits murs de pierre sèche, qui n'atteignaient même pas le genou, et qui divisaient la terre rouge en alvéoles minuscules. Dans des champs pas plus grands qu'un tapis de selle, les esclaves *harratin* essayaient de faire vivre quelques fèves, du piment, du mil. Les *acéquias* plongeaient leurs sillons stériles à travers la vallée, pour capter la moindre humidité.

C'était là qu'ils arrivaient, maintenant, vers la grande ville de Smara. Les hommes, les bêtes, tous avançaient sur la terre desséchée, au fond de cette grande blessure de la vallée de la Saguiet.

Il y avait tant de jours, durs et aigus comme le silex, tant d'heures qu'ils attendaient de voir cela. Il y avait tant de souffrance dans leurs corps meurtris, dans leurs lèvres saignantes, dans leur regard brûlé. Ils se hâtaient vers les puits, sans entendre les cris des bêtes ni la rumeur des autres hommes. Quand ils sont arrivés devant les puits, devant le mur de pierre qui retenait la terre molle, ils se sont arrêtés. Les enfants ont éloigné les bêtes à coups de pierres, pendant que les hommes se sont agenouillés pour prier. Puis chacun a plongé son visage dans l'eau et a bu longuement.

C'était comme cela, les yeux de l'eau au milieu du désert. Mais l'eau tiède contenait encore la force du vent, du sable, et du grand ciel glacé de la nuit. Tandis qu'il buvait, Nour sentait entrer en lui le vide qui l'avait chassé de puits en puits. L'eau trouble et fade l'écœurait, ne parvenait pas à étancher sa soif. C'était comme si elle installait au fond de son corps le silence et la solitude des dunes et des grands plateaux de pierres. L'eau était immobile dans les puits, lisse comme du métal, portant à sa surface les débris de feuilles et la laine des animaux. A l'autre puits, les femmes se lavaient et lissaient leurs chevelures.

Près d'elles, les chèvres et les dromadaires étaient immobiles, comme si des piquets les maintenaient dans la boue du puits.

D'autres hommes allaient et venaient, entre les tentes. C'étaient les guerriers bleus du désert, masqués, armés de poignards et de long fusils, qui marchaient à grands pas, sans regarder personne. Les esclaves soudanais vêtus de haillons portaient les charges de mil ou de dattes, les outres d'huile. Des fils de grande tente, vêtus de blanc et de bleu sombre, des chleuhs à la peau presque noire, des enfants de la côte, aux cheveux rouges et à la peau tachée, des hommes sans race, sans nom, des mendiants lépreux qui n'approchaient pas de l'eau. Tous, ils marchaient sur le sol de pierres et de poussière rouge, ils allaient vers les murs de la ville sainte de Smara. Ils avaient fui le désert, pour quelques heures, quelques jours. Ils avaient déployé la toile lourde de leurs tentes, ils s'étaient enroulés dans leurs manteaux de laine, ils attendaient la nuit. Ils mangeaient, maintenant, la bouillie de mil arrosée de lait caillé, le pain, les dattes séchées au goût de miel et de poivre. Les mouches et les moustiques dansaient autour des cheveux des enfants dans l'air du soir, les guêpes se posaient sur leurs mains, sur leurs joues salies de poussière.

Ils parlaient, maintenant, à voix très haute, et les femmes, dans l'ombre étouffante des tentes, riaient et jetaient de petits cailloux sur les enfants qui jouaient. La parole jaillissait de la bouche des hommes comme dans l'ivresse, les mots chantaient, criaient, résonnaient gutturalement. Derrière les tentes, près des murs de Smara, le vent sifflait dans les branches des acacias, dans les feuilles des palmiers nains. Mais pourtant ils restaient dans le silence, les hommes et les femmes aux visages et aux corps bleus par l'indigo et la sueur; pourtant ils n'avaient pas quitté le désert.

Ils n'oubliaient pas. C'était au fond de leur corps, dans leurs viscères, ce grand silence qui passait continuellement sur les dunes. C'était le véritable secret. Par instants, l'homme au fusil cessait de parler à Nour, et il regardait en arrière, vers la tête de la vallèe, lá d'où venait le vent.

Parfois un homme d'une autre tribu s'approchait de la tente et saluait en tendant les deux mains ouvertes. Ils échangeaient à peine quelques mots, quelques noms. Mais c'étaient des mots et des noms qui s'effaçaient tout de suite, de simples traces légères que le vent de sable allait ensevelir.

Quand la nuit venait ici, sur l'eau des puits, c'était à nouveau le règne du ciel constellé du désert. Sur la vallée de la Saguiet el Hamra, les nuits étaient plus douces, et la lune nouvelle montait dans le ciel sombre. Les chauves-souris commençaient leur danse autour des tentes, voletaient au ras de l'eau des puits. La lumière des braseros vacillait, répandait l'odeur de l'huile chaude et de la fumée. Quelques enfants couraient entre les tentes, en jetant des cris gutturaux de chiens. Les bêtes dormaient déjà, les dromadaires aux pattes entravées, les moutons et les chèvres dans les cercles de pierres sèches.

Les hommes n'étaient plus vigilants. Le guide avait posé son fusil à l'entrée de la tente, et il fumait en regardant droit devant lui. Il écoutait à peine les bruits doux des voix et des rires des femmes assises près des braseros. Peut-être qu'il rêvait à d'autres soirs, d'autres routes, comme si la brûlure du soleil sur sa peau et la douleur de la soif dans sa gorge n'étaient que le commencement d'un autre désir.

Le sommeil passait lentement sur la ville de Smara. Ailleurs, au sud, sur la grande Hamada de pierres, il n'y avait pas de sommeil dans la nuit. Il y avait l'engourdissement du froid, quand le vent soufflait sur le sable et mettait à nu le socle des montagnes. On ne pouvait pas dormir sur les routes du désert. On vivait, on mourait, toujours en regardant avec des yeux fixes brûlés de fatigue et de lumière. Quelquefois les hommes bleus rencontraient un des leurs, assis bien droit dans le sable, les jambes étendues devant lui, le corps immobile dans des lambeaux de vêtement qui flottaient. Sur le visage gris, les yeux noircis fixaient l'horizon mouvant des dunes, car c'était ainsi que la mort l'avait surpris.

Le sommeil est comme l'eau, personne ne pouvait vraiment dormir loin des sources. Le vent soufflait, pareil au vent de la stratosphère, ôtant toute chaleur de la terre.

Mais ici, dans la vallée rouge, les voyageurs pouvaient dormir.

Le guide se réveillait avant les autres, il se tenait immobile devant la tente. Il regardait la brume qui remontait lentement le long de la vallée, vers la Hamada. La nuit s'effaçait au passage de la brume. Les bras croisés sur sa poitrine, le guide respirait à peine, ses paupières restaient fixes. Il attendait comme cela la première lumière de l'aube, le *fijar*, la tache blanche qui naît à l'est, au dessus des collines. Quand la lumière paraissait, il se penchait sur Nour, et il le réveillait doucement, en mettant la main sur son épaule. Ensemble ils s'éloignaient en silence, ils marchaient sur la piste de sable qui allait vers les puits. Des chiens aboyaient au loin. Dans la lumière grise de l'aube, l'homme et Nour se lavaient selon l'ordre rituel, partie après partie, recommençant trois fois. L'eau du puits était froide et pure, l'eau née du sable et de la nuit. L'homme et l'enfant baignaient encore leur face et lavaient leurs mains, puis ils se tournaient vers l'Orient pour faire leur première prière. Le ciel commençait à éclairer l'horizon.

Dans les campements, les braseros rougeoyaient dans la dernière ombre. Les femmes allaient puiser l'eau, les fillettes couraient dans l'eau du puits en criant un peu, puis elles revenaient, titubant, la jarre en équilibre sur leur cou maigre.

Les bruits de la vie humaine commençaient à monter des campements et des maisons de boue: bruits de métal, de pierres, d'eau. Les chiens jaunes, réunis sur la place, tournaient en rond en jappant. Les chameaux et les bêtes piétinaient, faisaient monter la poussière rouge.

C'était à ce moment-là que la lumière était belle sur la Saguiet el Hamra. Elle venait à la fois du ciel et de la terre, lumière d'or et de cuivre, qui vibrait dans le ciel nu, sans brûler, sans étourdir. Les jeunes filles, écartant un pan de tente, peignaient leurs lourdes chevelures, s'épouillaient, dressaient le chignon où elles accrochaient le voile bleu. La belle lumière brillait sur le cuivre de leurs visages et de leurs bras.

Accroupi dans le sable, immobile, Nour regardait lui aussi le jour qui emplissait le ciel au-dessus des campements. Des vols de perdrix traversaient lentement l'espace, remontaient la vallée rouge. Où allaient-ils? Peut-être qu'ils iraient jusqu'à la tête de la Saguiet, jusqu'aux étroites vallées de terre rouge, entre les monts de l'Agmar. Puis, quand le soleil descendrait, ils reviendraient vers la vallée ouverte, au-dessus des champs, là où les maisons des hommes ressemblent aux maisons des termites.

Peut-être qu'ils connaissaient Aaiun, la ville de boue et de planches où les toits sont quelquefois en métal rouge, peut-être même qu'ils connaissaient la mer couleur d'émeraude et de bronze, la mer libre?

Les voyageurs commençaient à arriver dans la Saguiet el Hamra, caravanes d'hommes et de bêtes qui descendaient les dunes en soulevant des nuages de poussière rouge. Ils passaient devant les campements, sans même tourner la tête, encore lointains et seuls comme s'ils étaient au milieu du désert.

Ils marchaient lentement vers l'eau des puits, pour abreuver leurs bouches saignantes. Le vent avait commencé à souffler, là-haut, sur la Hamada. Dans la vallée, il s'affaiblissait sur les palmiers nains, dans les buissons d'épines, dans les dédales de pierre sèche. Mais, loin de la Saguiet, le monde étincelait aux yeux des voyageurs; plaines de roches coupantes, montagnes déchirantes, crevasses, nappes de sable qui réverbéraient le soleil. Le ciel était sans limites, d'un bleu si dur qu'il brûlait la face. Plus loin encore, les hommes marchaient dans le réseau des dunes, dans un monde étranger.

Mais c'était leur vrai monde. Ce sable, ces pierres, ce ciel, ce soleil, ce silence, cette douleur, et non pas les villes de métal et de ciment, où l'on entendait le bruit des fontaines et des voix humaines. C'était ici, l'ordre vide du désert, où tout était possible, où l'on marchait sans ombre au bord de sa propre mort. Les hommes bleus avançaient sur la piste invisible, vers Smara, libres comme nul être au monde ne pouvait l'être. Autour d'eux, à perte de vue, c'étaient les crêtes mouvantes des dunes, les vagues de l'espace qu'on ne pouvait pas connaître. Les pieds nus des femmes et des enfants se posaient sur le sable, laissant une trace légère que le vent effaçait aussitôt. Au loin, les mirages flottaient entre terre et ciel, villes blanches, foires, caravanes de chameaux et d'ânes chargés de vivres, rêves affairés. Et les hommes étaient eux-mêmes semblables à des mirages, que la faim, la soif et la fatigue avaient fait naître sur la terre déserte.

Les routes étaient circulaires, elles conduisaient toujours au point de départ, traçant des cercles de plus en plus étroits autour de la Saguiet el Hamra. Mais c'était une route qui n'avait pas de fin, car elle était plus longue que la vie humaine.

Les hommes venaient de l'est, au-delà des montagnes de l'Aadme Rieh, au-delà du Yet-ti, de Tabelbala. D'autres venaient du sud, de l'oasis d'el Haricha, du puits d'Abd el Malek. Ils avaient marché vers l'ouest, vers le nord, jusqu'aux rivages de la mer, ou bien à travers les grandes mines de sel de Teghaza. Ils étaient revenus, chargés de vivres et de munitions, jusqu'à la terre sainte, la grande vallée de la Saguiet el Hamra, sans savoir vers où ils allaient repartir. Ils avaient voyagé en regardant les chemins des étoiles, fuyant les vents de sable quand le ciel devient rouge et que les dunes commencent à bouger.

Les hommes, les femmes vivaient ainsi, en marchant, sans trouver de repos. Ils mouraient un jour, surpris par la lumière du soleil, frappés par une balle ennemie, ou bien rongés par la fièvre. Les femmes mettaient les enfants au monde, simplement accroupies dans l'ombre de la tente, soutenues par deux femmes, le ventre serré par la grande ceinture de toile. Dès la première minute de leur vie, les hommes appartenaient à l'étendue sans limites, au sable, aux chardons, aux serpents, aux rats, au vent surtout, car c'était leur véritable famille. Les petites filles aux cheveux cuivrés grandissaient, apprenaient les gestes sans fin de la vie. Elles n'avaient pas d'autre miroir que l'étendue fascinante des plaines de gypse, sous le ciel uni. Les garçons apprenaient à marcher, à parler, à chasser et à combattre, simplement pour apprendre à mourir sur le sable.

Debout devant la tente, du côté des hommes, le guide était resté longtemps immobile à regarder bouger les caravanes vers les dunes, vers les puits. Le soleil éclairait son visage brun, son nez en bec d'aigle, ses longs cheveux bouclés couleur de cuivre. Nour lui avait parlé, mais il n'avait pas écouté. Puis, quand le campement avait été calme, il avait fait un signe à Nour, et ensemble ils étaient partis le long de la piste qui remontait vers le nord, vers le centre de la Saguiet el Hamra. Parfois ils avaient croisé quelqu'un qui marchait vers Smara, et ils avaient échangé quelques paroles:

« Qui es-tu? »

« Bou Sba. Et toi? »

« Yuemaïa. »

« D'où viens-tu? »

« Aaïn Rag. »

« Moi, du Sud, d'Iguetti. »

Puis ils se séparaient sans se dire adieu. Plus loin, la piste presque invisible traversait des rocailles, des bosquets de maigres acacias. C'était difficile de marcher, à cause des cailloux aigus qui sortaient de la terre rouge, et Nour avait du mal à suivre son père. La lumière brillait plus fort, le vent du désert soulevait la poussière sous leurs pas. A cet endroit, la vallée n'était plus ouverte; c'était une sorte de crevasse grise et rouge, qui étincelait par endroits comme du métal. Les cailloux encombraient le lit du torrent sec, pierres blanches, rouges, silex noirs sur lesquels le soleil faisait naître des étincelles.

Le guide marchait contre le soleil, penché en avant, la tête couverte par son manteau de laine. Les griffes des arbustes déchiraient les vêtements de Nour, zébraient ses jambes et ses pieds nus, mais il n'y prenait pas garde. Son regard était fixé devant lui, sur la silhouette de son père qui se hâtait. Tout à coup, ils s'arrêtèrent ensemble: le tombeau blanc était apparu entre les collines de pierres, étincelant dans la lumière du ciel. L'homme restait immobile, un peu incliné comme s'il saluait le tombeau. Puis ils recommencèrent à marcher sur les cailloux qui s'éboulaient.

Lentement, sans baisser les yeux, le guide montait vers le tombeau. A mesure qu'ils approchaient, le toit arrondi semblait sortir des pierres rouges, grandir vers le ciel. La lumière très belle et pure illuminait le tombeau, le gonflait dans l'air surchauffé. Il n'y avait pas d'ombre à cet endroit, simplement les pierres aiguës de la colline, et, au dessous, le lit asséché du torrent.

Ils arrivèrent devant le tombeau. C'étaient juste quatre murs de boue peinte à la chaux, posés sur un socle de pierres rouges. Il y avait une seule porte pareille à l'entrée d'un four, obstruée par une large pierre rouge. Au-dessus des murs, le dôme blanc avait la forme d'une coquille d'œuf, et se terminait par une pointe de lance. Nour ne regardait plus que l'entrée du tombeau, et la porte grandissait dans ses yeux, devenait la porte d'un monument immense aux murailles pareilles à des falaises de craie, au dôme grand comme une montagne. Ici, s'arrêtaient le vent et la chaleur du désert, la solitude du jour; ici finissaient les pistes légères, même celles où marchent les égarés, les fous, les vaincus. C'était le centre du désert, peut-être, le lieu où tout avait commencé, autrefois, quand les hommes étaient venus pour la première fois. Le tombeau brillait sur la pente de la colline rouge. La lumière du soleil se réverbérait sur la terre battue, brûlait le dôme blanc, faisait tomber, de temps à autre, de petits ruisseaux de poudre rouge le long des fissures des murs. Nour et son père étaient seuls près du tombeau. Le silence dense régnait sur la vallée de la Saguiet el Hamra.

Par la porte ronde, quand il a fait basculer la large pierre, le guide a vu l'ombre puissante et froide, et il lui a semblé sentir sur son visage comme un souffle.

Autour du tombeau, il y avait une aire de terre rouge battue par les pieds des visiteurs. C'est là que le guide et Nour s'installèrent d'abord, pour prier. Ici, en haut de la colline, près du tombeau de l'homme saint, avec la vallée de la Saguiet el Hamra qui étendait à perte de vue son lit desséché, et l'horizon immense où apparaissaient d'autres collines, d'autres rochers contre le ciel bleu, le silence était encore plus poignant. C'était comme si le monde s'était arrêté de bouger et de parler, s'était transformé en pierre.

De temps en temps, Nour entendait quand même les craquements des murs de boue, le bourdonnement d'un insecte, le gémissement du vent.

« Je suis venu », disait l'homme à genoux sur la terre battue. « Aide-moi, esprit de mon père, esprit de mon grand-père. J'ai traversé le désert, je suis venu pour te demander ta bénédiction avant de mourir. Aide-moi, donne-moi ta bénédiction, puisque je suis ta propre chair. Je suis venu. »

Il parlait comme cela, et Nour écoutait les paroles de son père sans comprendre. Il parlait, tantôt à voix pleine, tantôt en murmurant et en chantonnant, la tête se balançant, répétant toujours ces simples mots: « Je suis venu, je suis venu.»

Il se penchait en avant, prenait de la poussière rouge dans le creux de ses mains et la laissait couler sur son visage, sur son front, sur ses paupières, sur ses lèvres.

Puis il se levait et marchait jusqu'à la porte. Devant l'ouverture, il s'agenouillait et priait encore, le front posé sur la pierre du seuil. L'ombre se dissipait lentement à l'intérieur du tombeau, comme un brouillard nocturne. Les murs du tombeau étaient nus et blancs, comme à l'extérieur, et le plafond bas montrait son armature de branches mêlées à la boue séchée.

Nour entrait lui aussi, maintenant, à quatre pattes. Il sentait sous les paumes de ses mains la dalle dure et froide de la terre mélangée au sang des moutons. Au fond du tombeau, sur la terre battue, le guide était étendu à plat ventre. Il touchait la terre avec ses mains, les bras allongés devant lui, ne faisant qu'un avec le sol. Il ne priait plus, à présent, il ne chantait plus. Il respirait lentement, la bouche contre la terre, écoutant le sang battre dans sa gorge et dans ses oreilles. C'était comme si quelque chose d'étranger entrait en lui, par sa bouche, par son front, par les paumes de ses mains et par son ventre, quelque chose qui allait loin au fond de lui et le changeait imperceptiblement. C'était le silence, peut-être, venu du désert, de la mer des dunes, des montagnes de pierre sous la clarté lunaire, ou bien des grandes plaines de sable rose où la lumière du soleil danse et trébuche comme un rideau de pluie; le silence des trous d'eau verte, qui regardent le ciel comme des yeux, le silence du ciel sans nuages, sans oiseaux, où le vent est libre.

L'homme allongé sur le sol sentait ses membres s'engourdir. L'ombre emplissait ses yeux comme avant le sommeil. Pourtant, en même temps, une énergie nouvelle entrait par son ventre, par ses mains, rayonnait dans chacun de ses muscles. En lui, tout se changeait, s'accomplissait. Il n'y avait plus de souffrance, plus de désir, plus de vengeance. Il oubliait cela, comme si l'eau de la prière avait lavé son esprit. Il n'y avait plus de mots non plus, l'ombre froide du tombeau les rendait vains. A leur place, il y avait ce courant étrange qui vibrait dans la terre mêlée de sang, cette onde, cette chaleur. Cela n'était comme rien de ce qu'il y a sur la terre. C'était un pouvoir direct, sans pensée, qui venait du fond de la terre et s'en allait vers le fond de l'espace, comme si un lien invisible unissait le corps de l'homme allongé et le reste du monde.

Nour respirait à peine, regardant son père dans l'ombre du tombeau. Ses doigts écartés touchaient la terre froide, et elle l'entraînait à travers l'espace dans une course vertigineuse.

Longtemps ils restèrent ainsi, le guide allongé sur la terre, et Nour accroupi, les yeux ouverts, immobile. Puis, quand tout fut fini, l'homme se releva lentement et fit sortir son fils. Il alla s'asseoir contre le mur du tombeau, près de la porte, et il roula de nouveau la pierre pour fermer l'entrée du tombeau. Il semblait épuisé comme s'il avait marché pendant des heures sans boire ni manger. Mais au fond de lui il y avait une force nouvelle, un bonheur qui éclairait son regard. C'était maintenant comme s'il savait ce qu'il devait faire, comme s'il connaissait d'avance le chemin qu'il devrait parcourir.

Il rabattait le pan de son manteau de laine sur son visage; et il remerciait l'homme saint, sans prononcer de paroles, simplement en bougeant un peu la tête et en chantonnant à l'intérieur de sa gorge. Ses longues mains bleues caressaient la terre battue, saisissant la fine poussière.

Devant eux, le soleil suivait sa courbe dans le ciel, lentement, descendant des l'autre côté de la Saguiet el Hamra. Les ombres des collines et des rochers s'allongeaient, au fond de la vallée. Mais le guide ne semblait s'apercevoir de rien. Immobile, le dos appuyé contre le mur du tombeau, il ne sentait pas le passage du jour, ni la faim et la soif. Il était plein d'une autre force, d'un autre temps, qui l'avaient rendu étranger à l'ordre des hommes. Peut-être qu'il n'attendait plus rien, qu'il ne savait plus rien, et qu'il était devenue semblable au désert, silence, immobilité, absence.

Quand la nuit a commencé à descendre, Nour a eu peur et il a touché l'épaule de son père. L'homme l'a regardé sans rien dire, en souriant un peu. Ensemble ils se sont mis à redescendre la colline vers le lit du torrent desséché. Malgré la nuit qui venait, leurs yeux avaient mal, et le vent chaud brûlait leurs visages et leurs mains. L'homme titubait un peu en marchant sur le chemin, et il dut s'appuyer sur l'épaule de Nour.

En bas, au fond de la vallée, l'eau des puits était noire. Les moustiques dansaient dans l'air, cherchaient à piquer les paupières des enfants.

Plus loin, près des murs rouges de Smara, les chauves-souris volaient au ras des tentes, tournaient autour des braseros. Quand ils arrivèrent devant le premier puits, Nour et son père s'arrêtèrent encore, pour laver soigneusement chaque partie de leur corps. Puis ils ont dit la dernière prière, tournés vers le côté d'où venait la nuit.

Desert

Saguiet el Hamra, winter 1909–1910

They appeared, as in a dream, at the summit of the dune, half-hidden by the cloud of sand that their feet were raising. Slowly, they went down into the valley, following the almost invisible trail. At the head of the caravan were the men enveloped in their wool cloaks, their faces masked by the blue veil. With them walked two or three dromedaries, then the goats and sheep harassed by the young boys. The women brought up the rear. They were heavy silhouettes, weighted down by the heavy cloaks, and the skin of their arms and of their forearms seemed even more dark in the indigo veils.

They walked soundlessly in the sand, slowly, without looking where they were going. The wind blew steadily, the desert wind, hot during the day, cold at night. The sand flew around them, between the legs of the camels, whipped the faces of the women who pulled the blue cloth down over their eyes. The children ran, the babies cried, wrapped up in the blue cloth on the backs of their mothers. The camels snorted, sneezed. No one knew where they were going.

The sun was still high in the naked sky, the wind swept away sounds and smells. Sweat ran slowly down the faces of the travelers and their dark skin had taken the reflection of indigo, on their cheeks, on their arms, the lengths of their legs. The blue tattoos on the foreheads of the women shone like scarabs. Dark eyes, like drops of metal, hardly looked at the expanse of sand, sought the tracks of the trail between the waves of the dunes.

There was nothing else on earth, nothing, no one. They had been born of the desert, no other path could lead them. They said nothing. They wanted nothing. The wind passed over them, through them, as if there were no one on the dunes. They had been walking since the first light without stopping, fatigue and thirst enveloped them like a gangue. The dryness had hardened their lips and tongue. Hunger gnawed at them.

They would not have been able to speak. They had become, since so long ago, silent as the desert, full of light when the sun burns at the center of the vacant sky, and icy from the night of frozen stars.

They continued to go slowly down the slope toward the bottom of the valley, zigzagging when the sand caved in under their feet. The men chose without looking the place where they would put down their feet. It was as though they were traveling on invisible tracks which were leading them toward the other end of solitude, toward the night. Only one of them carried a gun, a flint-lock with a long muzzle of blackened bronze. He carried it on his chest, held tight between his two arms, the muzzle pointed upwards like a flagpole. His brothers walked beside him enveloped in their cloaks, slightly bent forward under the weight of their burdens. Under their cloaks their blue clothes were in tatters, ripped by thorns, worn thin by sand. Behind the exhausted flock, Nour, the son of the man with the gun, walked ahead of his mother and sisters. His face was sombre, darkened by the sun, but his eyes sparkled and the light of his gaze was almost supernatural.

They were men and women of the sand, of the wind, of the light, of the night. They had appeared, as in a dream, at the top of a dune, as if they had been born of the cloudless sky and had in their limbs the harshness of space. They carried with them the hunger, the thirst that makes lips bleed, the harsh silence where the sun gleams, the cold nights, the glimmer of the Milky Way, the moon. They had with them their giant shadow at sunset, the waves of virgin sand which their spread open toes touched, the inaccessible horizon. They had above all the light of their gaze which shone so clearly in the sclera of their eyes.

The flock of sheep and greyish-brown goats walked ahead of the children. The animals also went without knowing where, setting down their hooves on ancient tracks. The sand swirled between their legs, clung to their dirty fleece. A man led the dromedaries using only his voice, snorting and spitting as they did. The hoarse sound of breathing mingled with the wind, disappeared immediately in the hollows of the dunes toward the south. But the wind, the dryness, the hunger no longer mattered. The men and the flock fled slowly, descended toward the bottom of the waterless, shadowless valley.

They had been gone for weeks, months, going from one well to another, traversing the dried up streams that vanished in the sand, crossing the hills of stones, the plateaux. The flock ate the sparse grasses, the thistles, the spurge leaves which they shared with the men. In the evening, when the sun was near the horizon and the shadow of the bushes lengthened disproportionately, the men and animals stopped walking. The men unloaded the camels, pitched the large brown wool tent on its single cedarwood post. The women started the fire, prepared the millet mash, the curdled milk, the butter, the dates. The night came very quickly; the immense and cold sky opened up over the extinguished earth. Then the stars came out, thousands of stars stopped in space. The man with the gun, the one who led the band, called Nour and showed him the tip of the Little Bear, the solitary star which is called *Cabri*, then, at the other extremity of the constellation, *Kochab*, the blue one. Toward the east he showed Nour the bridge where the five stars, *Alkaïd*, *Mizar*, *Alioth*, *Megrez*, and *Feda* shine. All the way to the east, barely above the ash-colored horizon, Orion had just come out, with *Alnilam* leaning a bit to one side like the mast of a ship. He knew all the stars, he sometimes gave them strange names which were like the beginnings of stories. Then he showed Nour the route they would follow the next day, as if the lights which lit up in the sky traced the paths men must travel on earth. There were so many stars! The desert night was full of these fires which throbbed gently while the wind came and went like a breath. It was a country outside of time, far from the history of men, perhaps, a country where nothing could ever again appear or die, as if it were already separated from the other countries at the summit of earthly existence. The men often looked at the stars, the great white way which is like a bridge of sand over the earth. They spoke a little while smoking rolled kif leaves. They told each other travel stories, the rumors of the war against the Christian soldiers, acts of revenge. Then they listened to the night.

The flames of the twig fire danced beneath the copper teapot with a sound of spurting water. On the other side of the brazier, the women talked, and one of them sang to her baby who was falling asleep on her breast. Wild dogs yelped, and it was the echo in the hollow of the dunes that answered them like other wild dogs. The smell of the animals rose, mingled with the dampness of the grey sand, with the bitterness of the fumes from the braziers.

Afterwards, the women and children slept under the tent and the men bedded down in their cloaks around the extinguished fire. They disappeared on the expanse of sand and stone, invisible, while the black sky glowed even more radiantly.

They had walked thus for months, for years, perhaps. They had followed the routes of the sky between the waves of the dunes, the routes which come from the Draa, from Tamgrout, from the Erg Iguidi, or, even more to the north, the route of the Aït Atta, of the Gheris, of Tafilelt which connect the great *ksours* of the Atlas foothills, or even the endless road which disappears into the very heart of the desert beyond the Hank, toward the great city of Timbuctoo. Some had died along the way, others had been born, had married. The animals too had died, their throats opened to fertilize the depths of the earth, or else stricken by the plague and left to rot on the hard soil.

It was as though there were no names here, as though there were no words. The desert cleansed everything in its wind, obliterated everything. The men had the freedom of space in their look, their skin was like metal. The sunlight burst forth everywhere. The ochre, yellow, grey, white sand, the light sand glided along, showed the wind. It covered all the tracks, all the bones. It repelled light, it drove away water, life, far from a center that no one could recognize. The men knew well that the desert wanted nothing to do with them; so they walked without stopping on the paths which other feet had already traveled to find something else. Water was in the *aiuns*, the sky-colored eyes, or else in the damp beds of the old mud streams. But the water was neither for pleasure nor for refreshment. It was barely the trace of a bead of sweat on the surface of the desert, the parsimonious gift of a dry God, the last motion of life. Heavy water wrung from the sand, dead water from the crevices, alkaline water that caused diarrhea, that made one vomit. They had to go even further, bent slightly forward, in the direction which the stars had given.

But it was the only, the last free country perhaps, the country where the laws of men were no longer important. A country for stones and for the wind as well as for scorpions and jerboas, those that know how to hide and run away when the sun burns and when the night freezes.

Now they had appeared above the valley of the Saguiet el Hamra; they went slowly down the slopes of sand. At the bottom of the valley traces of human life began: earth fields surrounded by walls of dry stone, enclosures for the camels, groups of huts made of dwarf palm leaves, large tents of wool like overturned boats. The men descended slowly, sinking their heels into the falling sand. The women slowed their pace and remained far behind the group of animals suddenly driven wild by the scent of the wells. Then the immense valley appeared, opened up beneath the plateau of stone. Nour looked for the tall dark green palm trees springing up from the ground in close rows around the lake of clear water. He looked for the white palaces, the minarets, everything they had said to him since his childhood when they had told him about the city of Smara. It had been such a long time since he had seen trees. His arms slightly unclenched, he walked toward the bottom of the valley, his eyes half-closed because of the light and the sand.

As the men went down toward the bottom of the valley, the city they had glimpsed for an instant disappeared and they found only the dry and naked earth. It was hot, the sweat ran copiously down Nour's face, stuck his blue clothing to his back, to his shoulders.

Now other men, other women also appeared, as if born of the valley. The women had lit their braziers for the evening meal, the children, the men motionless in front of their dusty tents. They had come from all points of the desert, beyond the Hamada of stones, from the mountains of the Cheheïba and from Ouarkziz, from Siroua, from the Oum Chakourt mountains, beyond even the great oases of the South, from the subterranean lake of Gourara. They had crossed the mountains by way of Maider

Pass towards Tarhamant, or, further down where the Draa meets the Tingut, by way of Regbat. They had come, all the peoples of the South, the nomads, the merchants, the shepherds, the looters, the beggars. Perhaps some had left the kingdom of Biru, or the large oasis of Oualata. Their faces bore the mark of the terrible sun, of the deathly cold nights, at the ends of the desert. Some of them were of an almost reddish black, tall and lanky and spoke an unknown language. They were the Tubbus from the other side of the desert, from Borku and from Tibesti, the eaters of cola nuts who were going all the way to the sea.

As the flock of men and animals approached, the black silhouettes of the men multiplied. Behind the twisted acacias, huts of branches and mud appeared like so many termitaria. Houses made of clay, block houses of boards and mud, and especially, those little walls of dry stone that hardly rose as high as the knee and divided the red earth into miniscule cells. In fields no larger than a saddle blanket, the *harratin* slaves tried to keep alive a few broad beans, some peppers, some millet. The *acéquias* thrust their sterile furrows through the valley to tap the slightest bit of moisture.

It was there they were arriving now, toward the great city of Smara. The men, the animals, all moved forward over the parched earth at the bottom of that great wound, the Saguiet Valley.

There had been so many days, hard and sharp as flint, so many hours they had waited to see that. There was so much suffering in their bruised bodies, in their bleeding lips, in their scorched gaze. They hurried toward the wells, without hearing the cries of the animals or the sound of the other men. When they arrived in front of the wells, before the stone wall which held back the soft earth, they stopped. The children shooed away the animals by throwing stones while the men kneeled to pray. Then each one plunged his face into the water and drank for a long time.

That is how it was: eyes of water in the middle of the desert. But the tepid water still held within it the force of the wind, of the sand, and of the great frozen night sky. As he drank, Nour felt the emptiness which had sent him from well to well entering him. The turbid, insipid water turned his stomach, did not manage to quench his thirst. It was as though it planted in the depths of his body the silence and the solitude of the dunes and the big plateaux of stones. In the wells the water was still, smooth as metal, carrying on its surface the debris of leaves and wool from the animals. At the other well the women washed themselves and smoothed their hair.

Near them, the goats and dromedaries were immobile as if stakes were holding them in the mud of the well.

Other men came and went among the tents. They were the blue warriors of the desert, masked, armed with daggers and long rifles, who walked with long strides and looked at no one. The Sudanese slaves

wearing rags carried loads of millet or dates, goatskins of oil. Sons of big
tents dressed in white and dark blue, *chleuhs* with almost black skin,
children from the coast with red hair and freckled skin, men without
race, without names, leprous beggars who did not come near the water.
All of them walked on the ground of stone and red dust. They were going
toward the walls of the holy city of Smara. They had fled the desert, for a
few hours, a few days. They had opened out the heavy canvas of their
tents. They had wrapped themselves up in their wool cloaks. They were
waiting for the night. They ate, now, millet porridge drenched in curdled
milk, bread, dried dates tasting of honey and pepper. Flies and mosquitoes
danced around the hair of the children in the evening air, wasps lit on
their hands, on their cheeks dirtied with dust.

They spoke, now, very loudly, and the women in the stifling shadow
of the tents laughed and threw small pebbles at the playing children.
Speech spurted from the mouths of the men as in drunkenness, the words
sang, cried, resonated gutturally. Behind the tents, near the walls of
Smara, the wind whistled in the branches of the acacias, in the leaves of
the dwarf palms. But, nevertheless, they remained in the silence, the men
and women with faces and bodies turned blue by indigo and sweat.
Nevertheless, they had not left the desert.

They did not forget. It was in the depths of their bodies, in their inner
organs, this great silence that passed continually over the dunes. It was
the real secret. At times, the man with the rifle stopped talking to Nour
and looked behind him toward the head of the valley whence the wind
was coming.

Occasionally, a man from another tribe approached the tent and held
out his two open hands in greeting. They barely exchanged a few words, a
few names. But they were words and names that were immediately
erased, simple, light traces that the wind of sand was going to bury.

When night came here, over the water of the wells, it was once again
the reign of the star-studded desert sky. Over the valley of the Saguiet el
Hamra, the nights were milder and the new moon rose in the dark sky.
The bats began their dance around the tents, flitting level with the water
of the wells. The light of the braziers flickered, gave off the odor of hot oil
and smoke. A few children ran among the tents letting out guttural dog
cries. The animals were already asleep, the dromedaries with their legs
fettered, the sheep and goats inside the circles of dry stones.

The men were no longer watchful. The guide had placed his rifle at
the entrance to the tent, and he smoked while staring straight ahead. He
barely listened to the soft sounds of the voices and the laughter from the
women sitting near the braziers. Perhaps he was dreaming of other evenings, other trails, as if the burning of the sun on his skin and the ache of
thirst in his throat was only the beginning of another desire.

Sleep passed slowly over the city of Smara. Elsewhere, to the south, on the great Hamada of stones, there was no sleep in the night. There was the numbness of cold when the wind blew over the sand and laid bare the base of the mountains. One could not sleep on the desert trails. One lived, one died, always staring unblinkingly, with eyes burned by fatigue and light. Sometimes the blue men came across one of their own, sitting very straight in the sand, his legs stretched out in front of him, his body immobile in tatters of clothing that fluttered. On the grey face black eyes stared at the shifting horizon of the dunes, for it was thus that death had surprised him.

Sleep is like water; no one could really sleep far from the springs. The wind blew, like the wind of the stratosphere, taking away all warmth from the earth.

But here, in the red valley, the travelers were able to sleep.

The guide woke before the others; he stood motionless in front of the tent. He watched the mist which slowly went back up the length of the valley towards the Hamada. The night faded with the lifting of the mist. Arms folded across his chest, the guide scarcely breathed, his eyelids remained unblinking. He waited this way for the first light of daybreak, the *fijar*, the white spot which is born in the east above the hills. When the light appeared, he bent over Nour and he woke him gently by putting his hand on his shoulder. Together they withdrew in silence, they walked on the slope of sand that went toward the wells. Dogs barked in the distance. In the grey light of dawn the man and Nour washed themselves according to the ritual order, part after part, starting over again three times. The water from the well was cold and pure, water sprung from the sand and from the night. The man and the child again bathed their faces and washed their hands, then they turned towards the East to make their first prayer. The sky began to light up the horizon.

In the camps the braziers glowed red in the last shadow. The women went to draw water. The little girls ran into the water of the well shouting a little. Then they returned, staggering, the earthenware jar balanced on their slender necks.

The sounds of human life began to rise from the camps and from the mud houses: sounds of metal, of stones, of water. Yellow dogs, assembled at the center of the camp, turned in circles yelping. The camels and animals stamped their feet, made the red dust rise.

It was at this moment that the light was beautiful over the Saguiet el Hamra. It came at once from the sky and from the earth, a light of gold and copper that vibrated in the naked sky without burning, without making one's head spin. The girls, pulling back a panel of the tent, combed their heavy hair, deloused themselves, made the chignon on which they attached the blue veil. The beautiful light shone on the copper of their faces and arms.

Crouched down in the sand, motionless, Nour also watched the day that was filling the sky above the camps. Flocks of partridges slowly crossed the void, went back up the red valley. Where were they going? Perhaps they would go as far as the head of the Saguiet, as far as the narrow valleys of red earth, between the Agmar mountains. Then, when the sun would go down, they would return toward the open valley, above the fields, there where the houses of men resemble the houses of termites.

Perhaps they knew Aaiun, the city of mud and boards, where the roofs are sometimes made of red metal. Perhaps, even, they knew the emerald and bronze-colored sea, the open sea?

Travelers were beginning to arrive in the Saguiet el Hamra, caravans of men and animals that came down the dunes raising clouds of red dust. They went in front of the camps without even turning their head, still distant and alone as though they were in the middle of the desert.

They walked slowly toward the water of the wells in order to wet their bleeding mouths. The wind had begun to blow up on top of the Hamada. In the valley it died down over the dwarf palms, in the thorn bushes, in the mazes of dry stone. But, far from the Saguiet, the world sparkled before the eyes of the travelers: plains of sharp rocks, jagged mountains, crevices, sheets of sand that reverberated in the sun. The sky was without limits, of a blue so harsh that it burned the face. Further still, men walked in the network of the dunes, in an unfamiliar world.

But it was their real world. This sand, these stones, this sky, this sun, this silence, this pain, and not the cities of metal and cement, where one heard the sound of fountains and human voices. It was here, the empty order of the desert, where everything was possible, where one walked shadowless on the verge of one's own death. The blue men proceeded over the invisible track toward Smara, free as no being in the world could be. Around them, as far as the eye could see, were the shifting crests of the dunes, the waves of space that one could not know. The bare feet of the women and children came down on the sand leaving a faint impression that the wind immediately erased. In the distance, mirages floated between the earth and sky, white cities, fairs, caravans of camels and donkeys loaded with provisions, busy dreams. And the men were themselves like mirages that hunger, thirst and exhaustion had brought forth on the desert. The routes were circular, they always led to the point of departure, tracing ever-narrower circles around the Saguiet el Hamra. But it was a journey that had no end, for it was longer than human life.

The men came from the east, beyond the Aadme Rieh mountains, beyond the Yetti, from Tabelbala. Others came from the south, from the el Haricha oasis, from the Abd el Malek well. They had walked toward the west, toward the north, as far as the shores of the sea, or else through the big salt mines of Teghaza. They had come back, laden with provisions and ammunition, as far as the holy ground, the great valley of the Saguiet el Hamra, without knowing where they were going to start out for next.

They had traveled, looking at the paths of the stars, avoiding the winds of sand when the sky becomes red and the dunes begin to shift.

The men, the women lived this way, walking without finding rest. They died one day, surprised by the light of the sun, struck by an enemy bullet, or else sapped by fever. The women bore children, simply crouched in the shadow of the tent, supported by two women, their belly held tight by the big cloth belt. From the first minute of their life, the men belonged to the limitless expanse, to the sand, to the thistles, to the snakes, to the rats, to the wind above all, for it was their real family. The little girls with coppery hair grew up, learned the never-ending gestures of life. They had no other mirror than the fascinating expanse of gypsum plains under the even sky. The boys learned to walk, to speak, to hunt and to fight, simply in order to learn how to die on the sand.

Standing in front of the tent beside the men, the guide had remained motionless watching the caravans move toward the dunes, toward the wells. The sun shone down on his brown face, his hooked nose, his long curly copper-colored hair. Nour had spoken to him, but he had not heard. Then, when the camp had calmed, he had signaled to Nour and together they had set out along the trail that rose up toward the north, toward the center of the Saguiet el Hamra. Occasionally they met someone who was walking toward Smara and they had exchanged a few words:

"Who are you?"

"Bou Sba. And you?"

"Yuemaïa."

"Where are you from?"

"Aaïn Rag."

"I'm from the South, from Iguetti."

Then they separated without saying farewell to one another. Further along, the almost invisible trail cut through rocky ground, groves of scraggy acacias. It was difficult to walk because of the sharp stones that came out of the red earth, and Nour had trouble following his father. The light shone more brightly, the desert wind lifted the dust under their steps. In this place, the valley was no longer open; it was a kind of grey and red crevice that gleamed in places like metal. Stones littered the dry stream bed, white stones, red ones, black flints on which the sun made sparks.

The guide walked against the sun, bent forward, his head covered by his wool cloak. The claws of the bushes tore at Nour's clothing, striped his legs and his bare feet, but he took no notice. His gaze was fixed ahead of him on the silhouette of his father who hurried along. All of a sudden, they came to a halt together: the white tomb had appeared between the hills of stones, sparkling in the light of the sky. The man remained still, leaning forward a little as though he were greeting the tomb. Then they started walking again over the unsteady stones.

Slowly, without lowering his eyes, the guide climbed toward the tomb. As they approached, the rounded roof seemed to emerge out of the red stones, to grow toward the sky. The very beautiful pure light illuminated the tomb, swelled it in the overheated air. There was no shadow in this place, merely the sharp stones of the hill, and beneath, the dried up stream bed.

They arrived in front of the tomb. It was just four walls of white-washed mud set on a base of red stones. There was a single door similar to the entrance of an oven, blocked by a broad red stone. Above the walls, the white dome was shaped like an eggshell and ended in a spear point. Nour no longer looked at anything but the entrance of the tomb, and the door grew bigger in his eyes, became the door of a vast monument with walls like chalk cliffs, with a dome as big as a mountain. Here stopped the wind and the heat of the desert, the solitude of the day. Here ended the faint trails, even those where lost men, mad men, defeated men tread. This was the center of the desert, perhaps, the place where everything had begun, in the past, when the men had come for the first time. The tomb shone on the slope of the red hill. The sunlight reverberated on the hard-packed surface, burned the white dome, caused, from time to time, little streams of red powder to trickle down the length of the cracks in the walls. Nour and his father were alone next to the tomb. Dense silence reigned over the valley of the Saguiet el Hamra.

Through the round door, when he tipped over the broad stone, the guide saw the powerful and cold darkness, and it seemed to him to feel like a breath on his face.

Around the tomb there was an area of red earth packed hard by the feet of visitors. That is where the guide and Nour settled themselves first to pray. Here, on top of the hill, near the tomb of the holy man, with the valley of the Saguiet el Hamra stretching its parched bed out as far as the eye could see, and the vast horizon where other hills, other rocks, appeared against the blue sky, the silence was even more poignant. It was as if the world had stopped moving and speaking, had turned into stone.

Every now and again, Nour nevertheless heard the cracking of the mud walls, the buzzing of an insect, the groaning of the wind.

"I have come," said the man kneeling on the hard-packed earth, "Help me, spirit of my father, spirit of my grandfather. I have crossed the desert. I have come to ask your blessing before I die. Help me, give me your blessing, for I am your own flesh. I have come."

That is how he spoke, and Nour listened to his father's words without understanding. He spoke, now in a full voice, now murmuring and singing to himself, his head swaying, always repeating these simple words: "I have come, I have come."

He leaned forward, took some the red dust in the hollow of his hands and let it run down his face, over his forehead, over his eyelids, over his lips.

Then he got up and walked as far as the door. In front of the opening, he knelt and prayed again, his forehead placed on the stone threshold. The darkness lifted slowly inside the tomb, like a nocturnal mist. The walls of the tomb were bare and white like the exterior, and the low ceiling showed its framework of branches mixed with dried mud.

Nour entered also, now, on all fours. He felt the hard, cold slab of earth mixed with the blood of sheep under the palms of his hands. At the far end of the tomb, on the hard-packed earth, the guide was stretched flat on his stomach. He touched the earth with his hands, his arms extended in front of him, making himself one with the ground. He was no longer praying, at present, he was no longer singing. He was breathing slowly, his mouth against the earth, listening to the blood pulse in his throat and in his ears. It was as though something foreign was entering him through his mouth, through his forehead, through the palms of his hands and his stomach, something which was going deep inside of him and changing him imperceptibly. It was the silence perhaps, come from the desert, from the sea of dunes, from the mountains of stone under the moonlit clearness, or else from the great plains of pink sand where the sunlight dances and trips like a sheet of rain; the silence of the holes of green water that stare at the sky like eyes, the silence of the sky without clouds, without birds, where the wind is free.

The man stretched out on the ground felt his limbs grow numb. The darkness filled his eyes as before sleep. Yet, at the same time, a new energy was entering through his stomach, through his hands, radiating in each one of his muscles. Deep inside him everything was changing, coming to fruition. There was no longer any suffering, any desire, any vengeance. He forgot those things, as if the water of the prayer had cleansed his spirit. There were no longer any words either, the cold darkness of the tomb rendered them vain. In their place there was this strange flow of energy that vibrated in the earth mixed with blood, this wave, this warmth. It was like nothing on earth. It was a direct power, without thought, that came from the depths of the earth and went on toward the furthermost part of space, as though an invisible bond were uniting the body of the stretched out man and the rest of the world.

Nour hardly breathed, watching his father in the shadow of the tomb. His spread open fingers touched the cold earth and it swept him along through space in a vertiginous flight.

They remained this way for a long time, the guide stretched out on the ground and Nour squatting, his eyes open, not moving. Then, when it all was over, the man got up slowly and made his son go out. He went to sit down against the wall of the tomb near the door, and he rolled the stone again to shut the entrance to the tomb. He seemed worn out as if he had been walking for hours without drinking or eating. But deep inside him there was a new strength, a joy that lit up his look. It was now as though he knew what he had to do, as though he already knew the path he had to travel.

He pulled a piece of his wool cloak down over his face, and he thanked the holy man without uttering words, simply by moving his head a little and by singing in the back of his throat. His long blue hands stroked the hard-packed earth, grasping the fine dust.

Before them, the sun was following its curve in the sky, slowly, going down on the other side of the Saguiet el Hamra. The shadows of the hills and rocks were lengthening at the bottom of the valley. But the guide seemed not to notice anything. Motionless, his back leaning against the wall of the tomb, he was aware neither of the passing day, nor of hunger and thirst. He was full of another force, of another time, which had made him a stranger to the order of men. Perhaps he no longer expected anything, no longer knew anything, and had become like the desert, silence, stillness, absence.

When the night began to fall, Nour became frightened and he touched his father's shoulder. The man looked at him without saying anything, smiling a little. Together they began to go back down the hill toward the dried up stream bed. In spite of the night that was coming, their eyes ached and the hot wind burned their faces and hands. The man staggered a little while walking on the path, and he had to lean on Nour's shoulder.

Below, at the bottom of the valley, the water of the wells was black. The mosquitoes danced in the air, tried to bite the children's eyelids. Further away, near the red walls of Smara, the bats flew low over the tents, circling round the braziers. When they arrived in front of the first well, Nour and his father stopped again to carefully wash each part of their body. Then they said the last prayer, turned toward the direction from which the night was coming.

TRANSLATED BY KATRINE PFLANZE

DEIDRE DAWSON

Danièle Sallenave: The Writer as Archaeologist

Born in 1940, Danièle Sallenave has been preoccupied with the "ethics of literature" since she began teaching in the midsixties. Firm in her conviction that a novel should be an experimental process, a constant rediscovery of the world, she is perplexed by post-*Nouveau Roman* efforts to deconstruct the narrative tradition in western fiction. Influenced from an early age by writers as diverse as Flaubert, Simone de Beauvoir, Milan Kundera and Claude Simon, she was the first writer to defend Simon publicly when an outraged academician protested against his receiving the Nobel Prize for Literature in 1985. At this time Sallenave had already completed her most recent novel, *La Vie fantôme* (P.O.L. Hachette, 1987), praised by certain critics as an encouraging return to literary realism and traditional values, and criticized by others as a trivial tale of adultery in a provincial French village constituting a step backwards for the *avant-garde*. Refusing to take sides in a polemic that seems like a contemporary version of the *Querelle des anciens et des modernes*, Sallenave believes that literature must above all fulfill an ethical responsibility to present the reader with a world vision, so that he may reevaluate his own existence and better understand himself. The writer should not be forced to choose between a philosophy of *"littérature engagée"* and "art for art's sake"; literature is both artistic and political because it necessarily poses the problem of individual freedom. Sallenave sees herself as diverging from the modernists in her integration of philosophical reflections into the novel. For literature to be of value to society, it must present certain values: this is the novelist's task.*

A professor of literature and film at l'Université Paris X-Nanterre, Danièle Sallenave is a novelist, dramatist, translator, and essayist, with a particular interest in poetics, narratology, and textual semiotics. In 1973 she cofounded *Diagraphe*, a review dedicated to the renewal of fictional writing that has published studies of Althusser, Barthes, Derrida, and Freud, as well as Sallenave's *Paysage de ruines avec personnages* (1975), *Le Voyage d'Amsterdam ou les règles de la conversation* (1977) and her translation of Pasolini's *La Divine mimesis*. Her third novel, *Les Portes de Gubbio*, (P.O.L. Hachette, 1980) was awarded the Prix

*These ideas were discussed by Sallenave in "Danièle Sallenave et l'éthique de la littérature," entretien avec Jean-Pierre Salgas, in *La Quinzaine Littéraire* 478 (January 1987).

Renaudot for literature. Since then Sallenave has published *Un Printemps froid: récits* (1983), which she describes as a "a narrative containing eleven narratives— not a 'collection of short stories,'" a novel, *La Vie fantôme* (1986) that is currently being translated into English, translations of works by Calvino and Calasso, and the introduction to a book on the Hungarian photographer André Kertesz. She also writes regularly for *L'Art du Théâtre*, a contemporary theater journal.

Sallenave's first two books are long reflections on the finality of death conquered by the eternity of art, the fleeting passage of time curtailed by the recuperative power of memory. As the title of her first novel, *Paysage de ruines avec personnages* suggests, Sallenave's universe is composed of ancient artifacts, landscaped with ruins left behind by those whose anguish and joy would have long been forgotten if the indomitable human yearning for immortality had not engraved them in the collective memory of man. Like sections of an archaeological site, Sallenave's work is divided into Tombs, Inscriptions, Excavations, Porticos, Crypts. The reader is guided through the remains of these ancient cities, whose inhabitants have neither faces nor names. Here and there one discerns the traces left by a specific individual: the footprint of a slave on a path in a Roman village; the marks left by a heretic in the rough stone of a Venetian prison. Only art endures: the Pyramids still stand, though the slaves crushed beneath them have dissolved into the sand. Cathedrals, photographs, newspapers, sculptures are all reminders of both the ephemeral and the eternal nature of man, of ". . . the fleeting joy of a man doomed to an irremediable death who gently poses his hand on the abdomen of a woman . . . a couple engraved in stone that embraces each other for all eternity . . ." captured in a medieval miniature on a column of San Marco cathedral. (*Paysages*, 92) The characters of this universal history are nameless: they drift and meld into the architecture of the cities of Man, becoming signs themselves for future generations to interpret.

An element of the *Nouveau Roman* that has always interested Sallenave is the relationship between fragmented and continuous discourse. In *Le Paysage de ruines*, narrative authority is expressed in a single chorus of many voices: the "je" of the first-person narrative is replaced by a collective "nous" that speaks for generations past, present, and future. The absence of punctuation permits the fragments to blend into the whole, in a continuous narration of human culture and creativity. In *Le Voyage d'Amsterdam*, two distinct discourses appear: the voice of memory, and the continuous voice of the present. A woman lies alone in her bed one night, unable to sleep; photographs, shadows, street noises trigger a mental process that projects her mind through time and space. Her thoughts are revealed as they occur, uninterrupted by the formalities of punctuation and syntax. For these are dreams, memories, and fantasies; images reappear, phrases repeat themselves, one sequence melds into the next in an unending flow of recollections and reflections. In this netherworld of semiconsciousness, the dreamer and her imaginary partner are transformed into the archetypal lovers; like Chagall's eternal newlyweds, they float through the night over rooftops and fields, they become one with the structures of the city as they drift down the centuries-old streets. The contours, passageways, angles of their own bodies are caressed and explored: "it is thus," she thought, "that man's body is comparable to a huge urban landscape . . . " (*Voyage*, 103). These bodies, like the buildings they inhabit, will crumble and return to dust. With each step they touch the remains of hundreds of generations that have loved, toiled, and died before them; there hardly seems room for the living in the midst of such a cluttered past. And yet bodies make love anew, the human chain continues: " . . . immobile, man, woman, in the profound patience of time . . . " (63, 73). The resurgence of symbols, the echoing of phrases, the recurrence of universal themes throughout the text all converge in a hymn to *l'éternel retour* of mankind.

Sallenave's characters all carry a world within them. "In each person there is a dead city, full of ruins that were once inhabited by we know not what" (*Portes*, 241). In the archaeology of the human psyche, the most obscure passages of mind and memory are explored by the writer's tool. Les *Portes de Gubbio* is the testimony of one man's path to self-discovery through the long and painful excavation of the past. In this highly philosophical work, Sallenave chose the journal form to resolve the tension between *continuité-discontinuité*. Excerpts from letters and journals are linked together in a montage of different voices, times, and styles. For Sallenave, *Les Portes de Gubbio* is a turning point, the first of her works in which the narrator is distinct from the author; she sees in it a change in her writing rather than a return to any literary tradition. The *journal intime*, the epistolary mode, and a "Préface du Traducteur" presenting the entire work as a translation of an authentic document are reminiscent of narrative techniques used in eighteenth-century fiction; at the same time, they permit a multiplicity of perspectives and a liberty of expression favored by contemporary French fiction.

The journal of S., a composer and professor of music at a state conservatory, was written in five plain notebooks between October 1966 and June 1967. Names of cities, streets, and most of the characters are indicated only by first initial, which suggests a need to protect the narrator and his acquaintances from persecution. No specific historical references are given, but the general climate is one of military oppression and political unrest: the mounting violence is a prelude to the "Prague Spring" of 1968, season of the definitive Soviet takeover of Czechoslovakia. S. is asked to compose nationalistic propaganda hymns and subliminal music to improve the productivity of factory workers; if he refuses, his career will be jeopardized. Claiming poor health, he obtains a leave of absence so that he can rest and compose; instead, he begins researching the life of Egon Kaerner, a composer who died insane in 1937. Like S., Kaerner had refused to collaborate with a repressive regime and compromise his artistic integrity.

As a result, his music was officially banned by the state, though it continued to receive international acclaim. Kaerner represents the artist's total sacrifice to his art; the musician's vocation is especially painful because it demands a separation from the self: the composer is unable to hear the music as he works, and he writes and plays for an invisible audience. Music underlines the tragic duality between body and soul, between the necessity of death and the eternity of the human spirit. It is the proof that there is something in man that refuses to die; as such, music affirms man's immortality at the cost of his individuality. The composer risks losing himself through his complete sacrifice to the universal human soul. Slowly sinking into madness, tormented by a single musical note that resounds in his head, Kaerner had attempted to preserve his identity and halt the progression of illness and time through writing, an introspective and egocentric art.

As S. sifts through Kaerner's newspaper clippings, letters, and journals, his memory is set into motion; rather than write a biography of Kaerner, he begins exploring his own thoughts and recording his daily activities. Several times a week, he visits F., an old friend and famed archaeologist who is slowly dying. Unlike the composer who strives to triumph over death, the archaeologist studies death's triumph over man: the dusty remains he digs up will again return to dust. Yet this study of dead civilizations permits the present generation to confront the future. Individuals die, but new ones are born, and the great human cycle is never broken.

As the soul needs the body, and the present is determined by the past, the composer cannot exist without the archaeologist: man's dual nature, his strong physical attachment to the earth and insatiable longing for a transcendent existence, is incarnated in F. and Kaerner respectively. Their struggles and sufferings help S. put his own life in perspective. In his journal, the tormented composer unearths past passions and pain, examines them, analyzes them, and buries them again. S. does not take complete control of the narrative; he permits phantoms from the past to speak for themselves as they appear before him, sometimes pasting clippings from their writings next to his own. The nonlinear progression of memory is reflected in the lack of transition between the entries, which record distant childhood memories, an analysis of a recent love affair, and brief accounts of daily events. Writing is both a cathartic and generative process. For the first time, S. confronts and comprehends his turbulent and destructive affair with Béatrice, a married woman he once loved. When his present lover Anne eventually leaves him, when F. finally dies, when the conservatory refuses to take him back, he goes his way with the calm reassurance that "there is no misfortune . . . only the continuity of life" (298).

BIBLIOGRAPHY

NOVELS

Paysage de Ruines avec personnages. Paris: Flammarion, Collection Diagraphe, 1975.
Les Portes de Gubbio. Paris: P.O.L. Hachette, 1980.
Un printemps froid: Récits. Paris: P.O.L. Hachette, 1983.
La Vie fantôme. Paris: P.O.L. Hachette, 1986.
Le Voyage d'Amsterdam ou les règles de la conversation. Paris: Collection Diagraphe, 1977.

DANIÈLE SALLENAVE

Les Portes de Gubbio*

18 mars.

Tout se passe comme si la tenue régulière de ce journal avait ouvert
en moi des voies que je croyais obstruées: il me semble qu'il suffit que
j'attende, comme quelqu'un qui est resté assis sur la terrasse longtemps
après le coucher du soleil, et ne mesure pas, au ciel toujours clair que ses
yeux habitués à la pénombre parviennent encore à percer, que la nuit est
tout à fait venue. Soudain la porte du fond s'entrebaîlle en grinçant un
peu: celle que mon père n'ouvrait jamais qu'avec de grandes difficultés
lors de nos retours à B., parce que les plantes grimpantes s'y étaient
prises, et quand il avait enfin huilé ses gonds et la serrure et dégagé le
pourtour à la faucille, c'était vraiment le signe que les vacances étaient
là.

Alors, à la porte du fond une tête se montre et quelqu'un dit: « Je ne
dérange pas? La porte était ouverte, je passais. » Je fais oui de la tête, et ils
entrent, l'un après l'autre, et commencent à me parler.

Et il en est ainsi chaque soir derrière ma table, comme au fond de ce
jardin que je n'ai jamais revu (je vendis la maison aussitôt, en 59): visages,
mémoires, figures, mon père, ma mère, le temps d'avant, Bétrice.

. . . « mais vous, Dormeurs, vous veillez dans mon cœur, dans mon
âme parente repose votre image enfuie . . . »

19 mars.

Il y a deux portes aux maisons de Gubbio: l'une est large, l'autre
étroite, légèrement plus haute que le niveau de la rue; l'une sert de passage aux vivants, l'autre de passage aux morts.

Ma mémoire est semblable aux maisons de Gubbio, parfois cependant elle confond les deux portes.

Les Portes de Gubbio (Paris: P.O.L-Hachette, 1980), 228–40. This passage is reprinted
with the kind permission of P.O.L-Hachette.

(Tard, le soir.)

C'était à Pâques, j'avais laissé mes parents partir seuls à la campagne pour mettre au point, avec quelques camarades avec qui j'étais très lié (et dont j'ai oublié aujourd'hui jusqu'au nom) un projet très complexe, visant à créer une nouvelle échelle harmonique. C'était vers le milieu d'avril, tout était calme ici, depuis qu'à la Faculté on avait renvoyé deux étudiants pour avoir rédigé une profession de foi absurde et enflammée dans notre journal. Nous les avions soutenus: nous pensions qu'on ne pouvait mieux le faire qu'en liant leur sort à celui de la musique nouvelle en quoi nous avions placé notre foi, et auprès de laquelle la musique sérielle faisait figure de vieillerie. Pour le reste, je ne me souviens de rien: sauf de l'intensité de notre conviction et de la fougue de nos débats. A vrai dire, moi-même je n'y croyais pas vraiment: il y avait quelque chose d'artificiel, et de forcé, qui me choquait dans cette alliance contre nature d'un projet artistique et de la « grande réforme » politique: mais je m'y tenais, pour quelque temps encore, afin de garder l'estime et l'amitié de mes camarades, et de ne pas être coupé du « petit groupe ».

Nous dînions chaque soir dans un restaurant de mariniers, non loin de l'endroit où je me suis récemment promené avec Anne. On disait que les serveuses y étaient gentilles, et cela me tenait éveillé, la nuit. Nous venions de transformer le monde, et c'était bien le moins qu'il vînt nous offrir en retour du vin rouge et de la friture d'anguilles et qui sait, un peu plus tard, le corps doux et complaisant d'une fille.

Le cabaret mettait en guise d'enseigne un bouquet de fleurs fraîches au-dessus de sa porte quand le vin nouveau était arrivé. Un soir, il y avait beaucoup de monde et de mouvement sur la berge qui descendait en pente douce vers le fleuve: on se penchait sur une barque, un marinier parlait avec de grands gestes. Une fille était sortie du cabaret, les joues rouges, et s'appuyait sur mon épaule. Le petit attroupement s'écarta, on portait quelqu'un par la tête et par les pieds: c'était une femme en sarrau, les cheveux défaits, le visage horriblement gonflé, il me sembla qu'il lui manquait une joue. « C'est l'hélice », dit quelqu'un. De sa poche sortait une pâte de biscuits détrempés. On crut la reconnaître, un gros homme s'avança, l'air contrarié, le crayon derrière l'oreille. Non, ce n'était pas sa mère. La fille était revenue du cabaret et me tendait un verre de vin chaud. Les gens se dispersaient, on emmena le corps. Il fallait dégager le chenal où la péniche s'était mise en travers quand son hélice avait été coincée.

Notre projet s'arrêta là. De toute façon c'était la rentrée. Je n'allais pas à B., mais je revis deux ou trois fois la fille du cabaret.

20 mars.

Lettre à Clara, sans date:

« Il n'est donné à aucun d'entre nous de mourir *son œuvre faite.* Si tard qu'elle arrive, la mort est toujours une rupture, jamais un achèvement.

Lorsque quelqu'un meurt, la route s'arrête, le paysage ne change pas. Comme ces voies que le caprice d'un despote ou le rêve d'un conquérant avait voulu percer à travers un désert, des montagnes: et brusquement, parce que le despote est mort, parce que le conquérant a été défait, les travaux ont été suspendus, et la route s'est arrêtée au milieu des pierres. A quelques mètres c'est de nouveau la nature sauvage où l'on discerne encore, mais pour peu de temps, la marque et le reste des projets inachevés: un soubassement, des arbres abattus, un défrichage commencé, des mètres de cailloux alignés, des jalons plantés. Car si limité que soit l'avenir d'un homme—et réduit parfois à l'espace qui sépare son fauteuil de son lit—il ne peut s'empêcher de continuer le tracé de sa route (. . .) »

Ma tâche à moi, dont la mémoire se nourrit de celle des autres, c'est de dresser la carte de ces tracés, de ces projets interrompus. De là où je regarde, le temps m'apparaît comme un grand territoire d'où émerge entre les taches blanches des régions inconnues, la butée que font sous le sable les villes disparues. Comment cela s'est-il fait? Qu'y avait-il en moi qui me disposait à ce rôle d'archiviste? Quelle angoisse, et devant quelle disparition?

Je ne suis la source d'aucun récit: j'en suis le confluent. *Je ne prends pas la parole; je la donne.*

21 mars.

« J'aime bien que nous soyons là », dit Anne en montrant un point au centre de l'Europe, tout en retenant le jouet qui grinçait et tentait de lui échapper. C'est un petit chat grossièrement figuré qui tient entre ses pattes une boule où sont vaguement dessinés la silhouette des continents, la mer bleue, les chaînes de montagnes marron, et de grandes plaines vert clair. Quand on remonte le mécanisme, le chat se livre autour de la boule à toute sorte de cabrioles. « Un peu plus haut tout de même », dis-je. « Si près de ses griffes? » Anne était toute songeuse: « Mais ses dents et ses yeux sont encore pires. » Ses dents sont très blanches, aiguës, au-dessus des babines rouges.

Nous ne nous sommes pas rhabillés, nous avons passé tout l'après-midi au lit, sans ouvrir les rideaux, mais on voyait bien que le ciel était clair et que ce n'était pas la nuit.

« Je vais passer la soirée avec mon père, m'a dit Anne un peu tristement, lui non plus, il n'ouvre jamais les volets. »

(Plus tard, dans la nuit)

J'ai mis ce soir à la boîte les deux transcriptions, accompagnées d'une étude brève sur leur origine, et leur évolution.

Quelque part dans cette ville où il me semble que nous sommes seuls à veiller, F. a éteint les lumières, il s'est couché, mais il ne parvient pas à dormir. La ville l'éclaire, le ciel est uniformément rouge, et je ne peux pas franchir cet espace qui nous sépare pour aller lui offrir du secours. Mais quel secours? Et l'accepterait-il? Sa main cherche à tâtons quelque chose sur la table de nuit, ses doigts s'attardent sur le marbre frais.

Maintenant, il dort, mais sa paupière n'est pas entièrement baissée, et elle laisse voir un fragment blanc et luisant de son œil. Je ne dors pas, je suis à ma table, il est très tard.

L'air est d'une grande douceur pour la saison: peut-être est-ce l'effet de la fatigue, de la nuit, du manque de sommeil et d'un peu de « cognac français ». J'ai entrouvert la fenêtre, rien ne bouge. Un bourdonnement traverse la nuit, comme celui d'un avion volant à bas régime. Ce n'est pas la première fois que j'entends cela: hier c'étaient des sirènes de police, ou d'ambulance. Et une lueur rouge, au couchant, bien après la disparition du soleil.

En écrivant ces mots: « tard dans la nuit », il me revient que je commençais ainsi mes lettres à Béatrice chaque fois qu'il ne me suffisait pas de l'avoir vue, de l'avoir tenue contre moi quelques heures et que, ne pouvant m'endormir, je commençais une lettre comme pour abolir symboliquement l'espace qui nous séparait et, en lui réaffirmant ma tendresse et mon désir, exorciser l'angoisse que son absence avait fait naître. En général, je n'allais pas loin, une sorte de lassitude m'envahissait, une somnolence brutale. J'éteignais la lumière, et je retrouvais le lendemain dans les draps le billet interrompu, que je déchirais avec un sentiment de honte.

Je restais souvent des jours sans la voir autrement que dans un café où elle m'avait fixé rendez-vous quelques heures auparavant par téléphone, avec dans la voix une nuance impérieuse et un tremblement que je prenais pour l'exigence de la passion. Elle se tenait dans un angle, à demi cachée derrière le col relevé de son manteau, les mains dans ses manches, et pourtant je la voyais tout de suite: je ne voyais qu'elle, dans la foule la plus épaisse, dans la fumée des cigarettes et le bruit des voix, entre les plateaux des garçons. Isolée, marquée d'un signe noir, cernée d'un trait invisible, m'étant destinée, et refusée, implacablement.

Elle buvait à petits coups son thé noir et presque froid, jetant des regards par-dessus mon épaule vers la grosse pendule du café, et elle me quittait, désespérée, sombre, après m'avoir violemment baisé les lèvres. Elle devait rentrer plus tôt chez elle ce soir-là, pour recevoir des amis de son mari, ou bien c'était sa fille qui donnait un goûter d'enfants. « Tu vois bien, disait-elle, je fais tout ce que je peux. » Mais la semaine suivante, le libraire chez qui elle travaillait la gardait trois soirs de suite pour l'inventaire de fin d'année, et c'en était fait de notre soirée hebdomadaire.

Je ne la suivais pas, je restais un moment après elle dans le café. Il me semblait qu'il y avait, tout près de moi et à portée de la main, une vie tranquille et humble dont je ne voulais pas et qui cependant reprenait son cours doucement, dès que la portière de la rue était retombée sur elle. Dehors la ville était recouverte d'un brouillard épais, ou bien il avait neigé. Je rentrais chez moi afin de retrouver le travail où je m'étais plongé pour oublier son absence et que ce bref rendez-vous avait interrompu, le rendant dérisoire. J'allais et venais dans la pièce, ranimant le feu, je regardais les portées couvertes de notes sans signification, l'élan était tombé, et je restais comme debout sur une terre gelée. J'allais me coucher. J'ai vécu ces mois-là dans une chasteté absolue, et désespérée, entrecoupée de ses visites trop brèves, qui me laissaient insatisfait.

22 mars.

Quelque chose s'est levé en moi hier, que je ne peux maintenant écarter, et qui a trait à la nature de mon amour pour Béatrice. Le souvenir d'un détail de jalousie absurde me fait mesurer à quel degré de folie j'en étais arrivé. Je lui avais donné une petite aquarelle italienne, et je ne peux concevoir maintenant dans quelle fureur d'anxiété ce cadeau m'avait plongé. Elle l'avait accroché au mur du salon, m'avait-elle dit, comme une provocation muette. Cela contrastait si vivement avec les précautions dont elle entourait nos rencontres que je ne l'avais crue qu'à demi. Parfois, dans des accès de ressentiment injustes, j'imaginais au contraire qu'elle l'avait roulée dans un journal et jetée au fond d'une penderie. « Et ça, dirait un jour son mari, qu'est-ce que c'est donc? » « Oh, ce n'est rien, un truc réclame. » « Comment cela? » « Mais oui, avec le réabonnement à la *Revue d'Art,* tu te souviens bien? » « Mais c'est très joli! Pourquoi ne le fais-tu pas encadrer? » « Penses-tu! » dirait-elle. Et lui: « Au fond, tu as raison, c'est un peu mou comme dessin. » « Mais, mon chéri (une sueur froide me baignait alors le corps: quand je le lui avais demandé, elle m'avait dit: comment pourrais-je! Ces mots-là me resteraient en travers de la gorge) mais, mon chéri, c'est une aquarelle, le dessin passe en second. » Lui: « Au fond tu as raison, je n'y entends rien, mais ces bleus sont très jolis, etc. »

. . . Quelques heures plus tôt, je l'avais retenue contre moi, distraite et fâchée. « Non, je t'assure, laisse-moi, il faut que je rentre, Caroline a la grippe. » « Mais je croyais qu'elle était en vacances d'hiver? » Et je la laissais descendre du lit, et se rhabiller seule. « Non, ne fais pas la tête », disait-elle. Mais je ne faisais pas la tête. J'allumais la lampe, je me rhabillais à mon tour, et je me préparais à une nouvelle semaine d'attente.

23 mars.

Durant cette cruelle époque, je savais pourtant qu'un jour j'aurais cessé de l'aimer: mais, loin de me consoler—occasion plutôt et motif d'une douleur nouvelle—cette idée n'était pas plus un réconfort pour moi que ne l'est pour un malade celle que la mort va bientôt le délivrer de ses maux. Dans ces moments-là, tout s'obscurcissait en moi; je me mettais à préférer toutes les formes de la souffrance que Béatrice m'infligeait (retards, mauvaise humeur, indifférence) à la perspective terrifiante d'un avenir où ces absences mêmes ne me feraient plus souffrir. Un jour viendrait, que je n'envisageais pas sans terreur, où j'aurais cessé de la voir à travers ce voile de flammes et de fumée qui me brouillait la vue: où elle n'aurait plus pour moi ce visage ardent qui me brûlait le cœur. Mais cette idée ne pouvait pas m'apaiser. Car elle me faisait sentir que le jour où je pourrais vivre sans l'attendre, et la voir sans souffrir, c'est que sa présence comme son absence me seraient devenues indifférentes: en d'autres termes, que je ne l'aimerais plus. Le rêve fou que je poursuivais de l' « aimer moins » afin de « moins souffrir », était une utopie. Dès lors que ses absences me seraient tolérables, cela signifierait que sa présence ne m'était plus nécessaire.

Et c'est en effet ce qui se produisit. Comme si le trajet de l'amour devait s'accomplir deux fois: car, même dans les ruptures brutales, il est des étapes par où l'on repasse nécessairement. Et je les reconnaissais au passage, comme des stations de chemin de fer ou des villages qui, au retour de vacances, ont un air familier, nostalgique, et semblent déjà reflétés dans le triste miroir du souvenir. Je rencontrais Béatrice un peu moins souvent; mais loin de me faire souffrir, ce relâchement était lui-même le signe de ma guérison. De sorte qu'au début et à la fin de cette passion, l'époque des rencontres espacées ne fut jamais une période douloureuse: à l'aller, tout attentif que j'étais de parvenir à mon but—qui était de la posséder et, ensuite, de multiplier nos rencontres et les occasions de la voir—je prenais chacune de ses échappées hors de la librairie ou de son domicile, pour des concessions merveilleuses de la Providence. Au retour, quoique je l'eusse ainsi voulu afin de moins souffrir, de mieux me protéger, puis de me guérir tout à fait, le souvenir des débuts de mon amour et l'allusion constante à cette période ascendante, rendaient l'espacement de nos rencontres un peu mélancolique, mais ils ne me donnaient pas la douleur que le moindre contretemps me causait trois ans plus tôt. Et je me persuadais que ma guérison était l'œuvre de ma volonté, alors que je ne faisais que subir une des lois les plus exactes dans l'histoire d'une passion et de son développement, qui est que la douleur, par suite d'un réflexe quasi biologique de survie et de conservation, est la cause du refroidissement des sentiments, et non comme on le croit généralement de leur exaspération.

Et puis il y eut une troisième étape, qui suivit de près le départ de Béatrice. Lorsque j'eus donc tout à fait cessé de la voir, et de l'aimer—en admettant qu'on cesse d'aimer, ce qui n'est pas sûr: il se peut que le sentiment nuisible et douloureux soit seulement mis hors d'état de nuire, et comme placé en réserve sur une voie secondaire—je devrais donc dire: lorsque j'eus tout à fait cessé de souffrir de l'amour que m'inspirait Béatrice, il m'arriva d'entendre qu'elle avait autrefois beaucoup fréquenté Un tel, et connu tel autre dans les périodes les plus vives de mon amour pour elle. Et je me disais d'abord avec soulagement: comme j'aurais souffert d'apprendre cela quelques mois plus tôt—comme c'est bien d'être guéri et de pouvoir entendre cela sans un affreux serrement de cœur. Or c'était une illusion: car si j'avais appris cette nouvelle au plus fort de ma passion, et cela s'était sans doute produit sans que j'en aie gardé le souvenir, l'amour menacé, comme un poisson aveugle au fond de son creux de roche, aurait aussitôt enveloppé l'ennemi du puissant jet d'encre d'une explication rassurante, afin d'en dissoudre les aspérités, et de rendre telle rencontre, ou tel dîner dont on m'avait parlé, sinon anodin, du moins explicable. Car ce n'est pas seulement à la jalousie que je suis particulièrement sujet: c'est à une forme extraordinaire de la capacité de se rassurer, de se faire illusion, de nier les évidences les plus criantes et les faits les mieux avérés. Ainsi, loin de souffrir, j'aurais échafaudé des arguments, parfois contradictoires, contre toute vraisemblance. En y songeant bien, c'était aujourd'hui que « je ne l'aimais plus » que je souffrais, car l'amour n'étant plus là pour déposer autour du fait gênant sa gomme protectrice, je découvrais dans toute leur nudité et dans toute leur horreur les preuves que Béatrice ne m'aimait pas ou du moins qu'elle en aimait d'autres dans le même moment que moi.

24 mars

Jeudi dernier (le 19), j'étais sorti dans la fin de l'après-midi sans but précis, il faisait déjà très sombre car la pluie n'avait cessé de tomber. Peu après dans la rue G., j'ai vu de petits groupes se former, qui me semblaient se diriger tous dans la même direction. Des hommes le plus souvent, quelques femmes aussi, et des enfants dont la présence pouvait avoir pour but de donner à cette rencontre une allure pacifique, et d'éviter que la police ne s'en mêle trop tôt.

La pluie s'était arrêtée. J'ai suivi la foule, par curiosité ou par désœuvrement: toute ma force s'était trouvée absorbée ces jours-ci dans le souvenir de Béatrice, et le balancement entre le temps passé et le temps présent m'avait laissé douloureusement flottant, la tête vide et bourdonnante comme après un long voyage en bateau lorsqu'on pose le pied sur le quai.

Des enfants jouaient encore dans une petite rue. Une voix de femme tomba de l'étage: « David! David, tu montes ou c'est moi qui descends! » Une charcuterie était restée ouverte; un garçon brun et court, en tablier, sortit en voyant le petit groupe et abaissa le rideau de fer avec une longue perche. Puis il rentra en se courbant. Nous avions franchi le pont V. et cette fois il n'y avait plus de doute, les petits groupes convergeaient, sans un mot. Je me séparai d'eux un instant pour acheter des cigarettes et du chocolat. Le vieil homme qui me servit coinça le tiroir-caisse en rendant la monnaie: « Oh ça va mal, ça va mal! » disait-il. Je ne savais pas s'il parlait de la situation générale, de la manifestation qui se préparait, ou plus simplement de sa maladresse et des maux de la vieillesse. Une odeur de veau rôti venait de l'arrière-boutique d'où sortit une vieille femme, l'air méfiant, suivie d'un chat qui se frottait à ses jambes. « Votre chocolat, dit le vieux, excusez-moi, il faut que je ferme. »

Il rabattit le rideau derrière moi d'un coup sec.

Je retrouvai le groupe deux rues plus loin: un gros jeune homme qui tentait de prendre des photos disparut au premier geste de menace. Nous avions atteint la place H., grande, entourée de beaux bâtiments en demi-cercle, que la foule traversa sans s'arrêter, sûre apparemment de son but. A droite s'ouvraient les grilles de l'ancienne usine à gaz, maintenant désaffectée; on avait jeté des planches sur le sol défoncé où de grandes flaques d'eau renvoyaient l'image du ciel sombre et des lourds portails. Sur une grande palissade, des affiches déchirées montraient des coureurs à pied franchissant la ligne d'arrivée.

Le groupe s'engageait maintenant dans la petite rue qui contournait l'usine en direction du quartier interdit. Il arrivait des gens de partout, on commençait à piétiner, les premiers devaient être au mur. Un chien aboya, un autre lui répondit. Puis le silence se fit, et j'entendis la musique. Tout au bout de la longue rue qui longeait le mur, un peu en avant des barbelés, un petit orchestre s'était installé sur des caisses empilées. Il y avait un accordéon, deux violons et une petite flûte. Personne ne disait mot, une pluie légère recommença de tomber, au loin on entendit une sirène, puis une autre. Puis plus rien. La foule applaudit. Et comme de nouveau les sirènes se faisaient entendre, le flûtiste esquissa le début de *L'entrée des gladiateurs*: on applaudit encore et on commença à se disperser. Les musiciens avaient remballé leurs instruments. Aucun soldat, aucun policier ne s'était montré: je suis rentré sans avoir parlé à personne.

25 mars.

« Vous êtes fou, m'a dit F., qui vous demande de faire le moraliste? » « C'est tout de même mieux que de faire danser Jules et Marie. » Il s'est tu. « Je ne sais pas. » Et en me quittant: « Souvenez-vous que vous ne devez rien à personne. A personne. »

Dans les journaux, rien, comme toujours.

26 mars.

Devant moi, derrière moi: ma vie. Comme un projet qui se formerait à mon insu, et presque en mon absence.

Ce corps à corps de chaque jour avec le langage, la mémoire et le temps produit des effets que je ne soupçonnais pas: de même que j'avais sans doute sous-estimé la puissance de la machine du souvenir. Une fois

mise en branle, rien ne l'arrête; mais sa marche est capricieuse, imprévisible. Et le progrès que je fais dans la redécouverte de mon passé, n'aug-
mente pas à proprement parler la connaissance que j'en ai: les causes, les
conséquences, les liaisons me demeurent obscures. J'observe, comme s'il
ne s'agissait pas de moi, la montée d'un personnage énigmatique.

Ainsi par exemple: je pense en ce moment aux étés que nous passions, mes parents et moi, peu avant la guerre dans la petite maison de B.
Mais il ne m'est pas possible de dire ce qui a fait reparaître un souvenir si
longtemps enfoui. Il est là, il flotte et je le saisis, comme un bloc de glace
errant sur une mer dont j'ignore les contours et la profondeur. Ce sont des
images libres qui surgissent, et que j'apparie librement. Mais leur fré-
quence est si grande, ces temps derniers, qu'elles relèguent au second
plan tout ce qui n'est pas leur capricieuse apparition.

Le temps se recompose—dans une unité qu'il n'avait peut-être jamais eue.

Mais c'est la musique encore: à tout le moins, des inflexions com-
parables à celles qu'elle m'avait enseignées.

(Comme ceux de la matière, les états de la pensée sont au nombre de
trois: connaître, se souvenir, imaginer. Mais la mémoire est comme la
matière en fusion: sans cesse elle invente de nouvelles formes.)

Les Portes de Gubbio

18 March
Everything is happening as if the regular keeping of this journal had
opened in me passages I thought were blocked: it seems as if I only have to
wait; like someone sitting on the porch long after sunset whose eyes,
accustomed to shadows, are still able to penetrate the dwindling light of
the sky, and who doesn't notice that night has fallen. Suddenly the back
door opens half-way with a light squeak: the one my father was never able
to open without great difficulty every time we returned to B., because
clinging vines had overtaken it; when he had finally oiled the hinges and
the lock and cleared off the frame with a sickle, it was the sign that
vacation had begun.

Then, at the back door a head pops in and someone says: "Am I
bothering you? The door was open, I was just passing by." I nod, and they
come in, one after the other, and begin to talk to me.

And so it is every evening behind my writing table, just like in the back of the garden that I never saw again (I sold the house soon after, in '59): faces, memories, shapes, my father, my mother, the past, Béatrice.

". . . but you who sleep, you keep vigil in my heart, in my kindred soul your buried image lies . . . "

19 March

There are two doors to each house in Gubbio: one wide, the other narrow, slightly above street level; one serves as a passage for the living, the other as a passage for the dead.

My memory is like the houses of Gubbio; sometimes, however, it confuses the two doors.

(Late evening.)

It was Easter; I had let my parents leave for the countryside without me so that I could complete, along with a few friends with whom I was very close (and whose names I can't even remember today), a very complex project aimed at creating a new musical scale. It was around mid-April, everything had been calm here since the University had expelled two students for drawing up an absurd and inflammatory profession of faith in our newspaper. We supported them: we thought that the best way to do so was to link their fate with that of the new music in which we had placed our faith, and next to which serial music appeared obsolete. As for the rest, I remember nothing: nothing except the intensity of our conviction and the passion of our debates. To tell the truth, I myself didn't believe in it completely: there was something artificial and forced in this unnatural alliance of an artistic vision and the "great political reform" that shocked me: but still I stuck to it for some time, if only to keep the respect and friendship of my comrades, to avoid being cut off from the "little group."

We dined every night in a restaurant frequented by sailors, not far from the place where I recently went walking with Anne. People said that the waitresses were nice there, and this thought kept me awake at night. We had just transformed the world; certainly the least it could offer us in return was red wine, fried eels, and who knows, perhaps a little later, the soft and complaisant body of a young girl.

To signal that the new wine had arrived, the cabaret put a bouquet of fresh flowers above its door. One evening there was a crowd and a lot of commotion on the bank that sloped gently towards the river: we were leaning against a boat and a sailor was gesticulating wildly as he spoke. A girl had come out of the cabaret, her cheeks flushed, and was leaning on my shoulder. The little gathering stood back; somebody was being carried by the head and feet: it was a woman wearing a smock, her hair disheveled, her face horribly bloated; it seemed to me one of her cheeks was missing. "It's the propeller" someone said. A mass of soggy cookies was hanging our of her pocket. Someone thought they recognized her; a fat man with a pencil behind his ear who seemed annoyed came up. No, it wasn't his mother. The girl had come back from the cabaret and offered me a glass of warm wine. The people dispersed, the body was carried away. The channel where the barge had gone sideways when its propeller jammed had to be cleared out.

That was the end of our project. Anyway, it was the start of a new term. I didn't go to B., but I saw the girl from the cabaret a few more times.

20 March

Letter to Clara, undated:

"None of us are ever permitted to die having completed our life's work. No matter how late it arrives, death is always a rupture, never a completion.

When someone dies, the road stops; the scenery doesn't change. Like those paths that a despot's whim or a conqueror's dream had wanted to pierce through the desert or the mountains—abruptly, because the despot has died, because the conqueror has been defeated, the work is interrupted, the road stops in the middle of a rocky terrain. A few yards away is untamed nature where one can still discern, but only for a short time, the trace and the remains of unfinished projects: a foundation, chopped-down trees, the beginning of a clearing, rows of neatly arranged stones, alignments. For no matter how limited the future of a man may be—sometimes reduced to the space that separates his armchair from his bed—he cannot keep himself from continuing the plotting of his path."

The task left for me, whose memory is nourished by others' memories, is to draw up the map of these plottings, of these interrupted plans. From my perspective, the past seems to me a vast territory where the mounds of cities that have disappeared under the sands emerge between the blank spots of unknown regions. How did this happen? What was there in me that inclined me to accept the role of an archivist? What anguish, in the face of what disappearance?

I am the source of no narrative: I am its confluence. *I do not speak, I allow others to speak.*

21 March

"I like the fact that we're right here," Anne said, pointing to a dot in the center of Europe while holding the squeaky toy that was trying to get away from her. It's a roughly modeled little cat with a ball between its paws on which the outline of the continents, the blue sea, the brown mountain chains, and the great bright green plains are roughly sketched. When the toy is wound, the cat performs all sorts of stunts around the ball. "Just a little higher," I say. "So close to his claws?" Anne was in a thoughtful mood: "But his teeth and his eyes are even worse." His teeth are stark white, sharp, above red chops.

We didn't put our clothes back on, we spent all afternoon in bed, without opening the curtains, but we could tell the sky was light and it wasn't yet dark.

"I'm going to spend the evening with my father," Anne said a bit sadly, "he never opens the shutters either."

(Later, in the evening)

This evening I dropped the two musical arrangements in the mail-box, alone with a brief study of their origin and evolution.

Somewhere in this city where it seems we are the only ones still awake, F. has turned out the lights, gone to bed, but is unable to sleep. The city lights shine on him, every corner of the sky is red, and I can't cross the space that separates us to offer him help. But what help? And would he accept it? His hand is groping for something on the night stand, his fingers linger on the cool marble.

Now he is asleep, but his eyelid is not completely shut; it reveals a gleaming white fragment of his eye. I can't sleep, I'm at my table, it's very late.

The air is very mild for the season: maybe it's the effect of fatigue, of the night, of lack of sleep and a little "French cognac." I've opened the window a crack; nothing is stirring. A buzzing sound pierces the night, like that of an airplane flying close to the ground. This isn't the first time I've heard it: yesterday there were police sirens, or ambulances. And a red glow, at dusk, long after the sun had disappeared.

In writing these words: "late in the night," I recall that I began my letters to Béatrice that way every time when it was not enough for me to have seen her, to have held her against me for several hours; not being able to fall asleep, I would start a letter as if to abolish the space that separated us symbolically; to exorcize by reaffirming my tenderness and desire the anguish that her absence had given birth to. In general, I didn't get very far; a sort of weariness overtook me, a brutal drowsiness. I would put out the lights, and the next morning I would find the interrupted letter in the sheets, and I would tear it up with a feeling of shame.

I often went for days without seeing her except in a café where she had arranged to meet me by phone a few hours earlier, with a trembling and imperious tone to her voice which I took for the urgency of passion. She would be sitting in a corner, half-hidden behind the turned-up collar of her coat, her hands in her pockets, and nevertheless I would spot her immediately: I saw only her, in the thickest crowd, amidst the smoke of the cigarettes and the din of the voices, between the waiters' trays. Iso-lated, marked with a black dot, encircled with an invisible line, destined for me, refused to me, implacably.

She would be sipping her black, nearly cold tea, glancing over my shoulder toward the big café clock, and desperate, somber, she would leave me, after having kissed me violently on the lips. She had to go home earlier that evening, to receive her husband's friends, or perhaps her daughter was giving a children's tea party. "You can see for yourself," she'd say, "I'm doing everything I can." But the next week, the bookseller she worked for kept her three evenings in a row to do year-end inventory, and that was it for our weekly outing.

I wouldn't follow her, I would stay behind her for a moment in the café. It seemed to me that, right next to me and within my reach, there was a tranquil and simple life that I didn't want and that nevertheless gently continued its course, as soon as the café door had closed behind her again. Outside, the city was once again covered with a thick fog, or perhaps it had snowed. I went home in order to take up the work into which I had thrown myself in an effort to forget her absence and which this brief rendezvous had interrupted and made ludicrous. I paced up and down the room, stirring up the fire, I looked at the staves covered with notes that had no meaning; the ardor had died out, I was left standing cold on a frozen terrain. I went to bed. I lived those months in an absolute and desperate chastity, interrupted by her visits, which were always too brief and left me unsatisfied.

22 March

Something stirred in me yesterday that I can't dismiss now, and that is related to the nature of my love for Béatrice. The recollection of a detail of absurd jealousy makes me realize how completely irrational I had become. I had given her a little Italian watercolor, and I can't even conceive now the furor of anxiety into which this gift had plunged me. She had hung it on the living room wall, she told me, in a silent act of defiance. This contrasted so vividly with the precautions with which she normally cloaked our meetings that I had only half believed her. Sometimes, in unfair resentful outbursts, I imagined on the contrary that she had rolled it up in a newspaper and thrown it in the bottom of a wardrobe. "And this," her husband would say one day, "what's this?" "Oh, it's nothing; an advertising gimmick." "What do you mean?" "You remember, when we renewed our subscription to the *Revue d'Art*?" "But it's really very pretty! Why don't you have it framed?" "Do you really think so?" she would say. And he: "No, you're right. The design is a little weak." "But my dear," (a cold sweat broke out over my body at this moment: when I asked her about it, she had said, 'How could I?' These words would remain stuck in my throat) "but, my dear, it's a water color, the design is secondary." "I guess you're right. I don't understand art, but those blues really are very pretty, etc."

. . . A few hours earlier, I had held her, distracted and angry, against me. "No, I mean it, let me go, Caroline has the flu." "But I thought she was on winter vacation?" And I let her get down from the bed, and get dressed alone. "No, don't sulk." But I wasn't sulking. I lit the lamp, got dressed, and prepared myself for another week of waiting.

23 March

During this cruel period, I knew nonetheless that one day I would stop loving her: but, far from consoling me—rather an occasion and cause for new grief—this idea was no more a comfort to me than a sick person's knowledge that death will soon relieve him of his suffering. In these moments, a cloud of confusion crept over me; I began to prefer all the forms of suffering that Béatrice inflicted upon me (delays, bad moods, indifference) to the terrifying perspective of a future where even the absences would no longer make me suffer. The day would come, which I could not envision without terror, when I would have stopped seeing her through this veil of flames and smoke that obscured my view: when she would no longer have for me that ardent face which seared my heart. But this idea could not appease me; it made me realize that the day when I could live without waiting for her, and see her without suffering, her presence, like her absence, would leave me completely indifferent: in other words, I would no longer love her. My mad dream of "loving her less" in order to "suffer less" was a utopia. As soon as I could bear her absence, that would mean that her presence was no longer necessary to me.

And this is in fact what happened. As if one had to retrace each step of love's journey: for even in brutal partings there are stages which one necessarily goes through more than once. And I recognized them in passing, like the train stations or villages that have a familiar, nostalgic air as one is returning from vacation, and seem to be already reflected in the sad mirror of remembrance. I met with Béatrice a little less often; but far from making me suffer, this letting go was itself the sign of my cure. So that at the beginning and at the end of this passion, the period of occasional meetings was never a painful time: at the outset of my journey, as attentive as I was to arrive at my goal—which was to possess her and then to multiply our meetings and the opportunities to see her—I viewed every one of her escapes from the bookstore or from her home as a marvelous concession of Providence. On the way back, the memory of the beginnings of my love and the constant allusion to this period of rising passion rendered the infrequency of our meetings a little melancholic—even though I wanted it that way in order to suffer less, better to protect myself, and finally to cure myself altogether—but didn't cause me the pain that the least disappointment had caused me three years earlier. And I persuaded myself that my recovery was the result of my will power, though I was merely acting according to one of the most exact laws in the history of a passion and its development, which is that pain, owing to an almost biological reflex of survival and conservation, is the cause of a cooling of the passions, and not, as is generally believed, of their exacerbation.

And then I went through a third stage, which followed closely on the departure of Béatrice. When I had thus completely stopped seeing her, and loving her—that is, if one ever stops loving, which is questionable: it is possible that the destructive and painful passion simply becomes incapable of doing any more harm, as if placed in reserve on a side-track—I should say then: when Béatrice's love no longer made me suffer, I heard that she had seen quite a bit of this or that man, and known another during the most ardent periods of my love for her. And at first I said to myself with relief: how I would have suffered upon learning that a few months ago—how good it is to be healed and to be able to hear this without my heart sinking frightfully! But it was an illusion: for if I had learned the news at the height of my passion, and this no doubt must have happened without my remembering it, I would have reacted like a blind fish hidden in a cave who envelops his enemies with an inky spray to shield himself from attack. My love would have fabricated reassuring explanations to justify a certain dinner, a certain meeting I was told of, and soothe the sting of the truth. For I am not only particularly susceptible to jealousy, but also to an extraordinary ability to reassure myself, delude myself, deny the most flagrant evidence and the most established facts. And so, instead of suffering, I would have constructed arguments, sometimes contradictory ones, against every probability. Thinking carefully, it was today when "I no longer loved her" that I suffered, for without love to surround the disturbing fact with its protective coating, I discovered today, in all its nakedness and horror, the proof that Béatrice no longer loved me, or at least that she had loved others at the same time as me.

24 March

Last Thursday (the 19th), I had gone out in the late afternoon for no particular purpose; it was already very dark; the rain hadn't stopped falling. Shortly afterwards on G. street, I saw small groups forming that all seemed to be moving in the same direction. Mostly men, some women too, and a few children whose presence might have been intended to give this meeting a peaceful look and keep the police from getting involved too soon.

The rain had stopped. I followed the crowd, out of curiosity or idleness: all my strength was absorbed during those days with the memory of Béatrice; and the wavering between the past and the present had left me floating painfully, my head empty and buzzing, as when one first sets foot on the dock after a long sea voyage. Some children were playing on a little street. A woman's voice fell from an upper story: "David! David, you come up here or I'm coming down!" A delicatessen was still open; upon seeing the little group, a short, dark boy wearing an apron came out and pulled down the iron safety curtain with a long pole. Then he stooped to go back in. We had crossed the V. bridge and this time there was no doubt that the small groups were converging, without a word. I broke away from them for an instant to buy some cigarettes and chocolate. The old man waiting on me jammed the cash register when he made change for me: "It's getting bad," he said. I didn't know if he was speaking of the general situation, of the impending demonstration, or simply of his clumsiness and the pains of old age. A smell of roast veal drifted in from the back room, from which an old woman with a distrustful air came out, followed by a cat that began rubbing itself against her legs. "Here's your chocolate," said the old man, "Excuse me, I have to close up." He jerked the curtain shut behind me abruptly.

I caught up with the group two streets further down: a fat young man trying to take pictures disappeared at the first menacing gesture. We had reached H. place, a large square surrounded by a semicircle of beautiful buildings, which the crowd crossed without stopping, apparently sure of its destination. On the right the iron gates of the abandoned gas-works gaped open; wooden planks were thrown over the rutted soil, where big puddles of water reflected the image of the overcast sky and the heavy gateway. On a tall fence, torn posters depicted runners crossing a finish line.

The group was now entering the little street that curved around the factory in the direction of the forbidden district. People were arriving from everywhere, they started stamping their feet; the first ones had already reached the wall. A dog barked, another answered him. Then there was silence, and I heard music. All the way at the end of the long street that ran along the wall, a little before the barbed wire, a small orchestra was set up on stacked boxes. There were an accordion, two violins and a piccolo. Nobody said a word; it started to drizzle again; in the distance a siren was heard, then another. Then nothing. The crowd applauded. And since the sirens were blaring once again, the flutist ran through the beginning of *L'Entrée des gladiateurs*: everyone applauded again and the crowd began to disperse. The musicians packed up their instruments. Not one soldier, not one policeman had appeared: I went home without having spoken to anyone.

25 March

"You're crazy," F. said to me, "Who's asking you to play the moralist?" "It's better than playing dance music for Jules and Marie." He fell silent. "I don't know." And then, upon leaving, "Remember that you don't owe anything to anyone. To anyone."

In the newspapers, nothing, as usual.

26 March

Before me, behind me: my life. Like a project that would take shape without my knowledge, and almost in my absence.

This daily hand-to-hand combat with language, memory, and time produces effects I never dreamed of: just as I had, without doubt, under-estimated the power of the memory machine. Once set into motion, nothing stops it, but its course is capricious, unpredictable. And the progress I make in the rediscovery of my past, does not, strictly speaking, enhance my knowledge of it: the causes, the consequences, the connec-tions, remain obscure to me. I observe the emergence of an enigmatic character, as if it had nothing to do with me. Like this, for example: I'm thinking at this moment about the summers that we spent shortly before the war, my parents and I, in the little house at B. But it is impossible for me to say just what made this memory, buried for so long, reappear. It's there, it's floating and I seize it, like an iceberg drifting on a sea whose depth and contours I am unaware of. They are free images that spring up, and that I pair together freely. But they've been occurring so frequently these past few days that they push everything that is not their capricious apparition into the background.

Time reconstructs itself—in a unity that perhaps it never had.

But that, again, is music: at the very least, inflections comparable to the ones that music taught me.

(Like the different states of matter, there are three states of thought: to know, to remember, to imagine. But memory is like the fusion of matter: it constantly invents new forms.)

TRANSLATED BY DEIDRE DAWSON

VICTORIA BRIDGES

Patrick Modiano: *Quartier perdu*

In the tradition of André Pieyre de Mandiargues, Patrick Modiano did not follow the usual academic cursus; instead, "there was a kind of urgency" (*Le Monde*, 4 January 1985; all translations are mine [a translation of *Quartier perdu* under the title *A Trace of Malice* will be published by David R. Godine of Boston].) which led him to begin to write, to publish at twenty-three in 1968. But the urgency of his writing does not seem to have its origin in that particular political moment: "I was almost ashamed. I had the impression that it was almost vulgar to write" (*Libération*, 4 January 1985). One might suggest that it stemmed from the conditions of his childhood, which he refers to as "an accident of the Occupation" (*Le Monde*), but one might better start with the epigraph of his first novel, *La Place de l'etoile* (1968, prix Roger-Nimier, prix Fénéon) which stands as an emblem of his work. It is anecdotal, an instant's detail, seemingly a dialogue overheard and later recorded; it is attached to a historic place at a historic moment; it concerns the "Sojourner," he who is there as a consequence of the diaspora, speaking a language which is his by accident, and whose part in the dialogue is somehow already written; it is a fictional literary construct playing with word associations: a Paris intersection, *la Place de l'Etoile*, and the place over their hearts where Jews wore a star during the Occupation, *la place de l'étoile*; it is called "a story," if you will, a short version of the novel, Patrick Modiano's chosen genre:

> In the month of June 1942, a German officer came up to a young man and said: "Excuse me, Sir, where is the Place of the Star [*la Place de l'Etoile*]?"
> The young man indicated the left side of his chest.
>
> [A Jewish Story]

At a casual first glance, his works are reminiscent of the best detective stories or mystery novels. (If I ran the experiment of asking a fellow traveler on a French train who by chance is reading one of his novels, that is/was the characterization given . . . at least once). And his most classical of styles also suggests the comparison. However, when one reads his comments on writing, it becomes evident that something else is at stake: "The pleasure of speech or of writing does not excuse what it can, at a given moment, contain of the criminal" (P. Modiano, E. Berl, *Interrogatoire* [Paris, Gallimard, 1976], 128); "each sentence must be definitive [but it is only] when a character says 'I' that all begins to become clear" (J.-L. de Rambures, *Comment travaillent les écrivains*, "P. Modiano. Apprendre à mentir" [Paris, Flammarion, 1978], 126); "one must deform, concentrate, go looking for the significant details through the fog of what happened and then amplify it in an exaggerated fashion . . . it is a lie . . . but at the same time, it is truth itself, pushed to its ultimate consequences" (Rambures, 130); "I write to know who I am, to find an identity" (J.L.-Ezine, *Les Ecrivains sur la sellette* [Paris, Seuil, 1981], 22).

These reflections on writing, when considered with the epigraph quoted above, point to the question central to his work, a question which leads him to incorporate into a traditionally fictional genre, anecdotal/archival, biographical, and finally autobiographical writing. We shall call that central question a *figura*, the "Sojourner." If it is at first readable as a figuration of the Jewish people after the diaspora, it also invites being read as the "sojourner in time," or more precisely, as a figure of the present in relation to (hi)story, as an "Everyman" in relation to a collective or an individual memory. Such at least is suggested by the epigraph to *Livret de famille* (1977): "*Vivre, c'est s'obstiner à achever un souvenir*" [To live is to insist on putting an end to/on realizing a memory]—René Char.

What might it mean to remember in writing, to "accomplish" the figure of a memory in writing a novel? If Adorno has written, "After Auschwitz, to write a poem is barbaric," if Tadeusz Borowski seems to have answered, "Write, in order that a portion of the sad fame of Auschwitz may belong to you as well" (I. Howe, "Writing and the Holocaust" [*The New Republic*, 27 October 1986], with thanks to Professor Stephen Murphy) the writings of P. Modiano concern the moment of the Occupation, but also the place of the past, as memory, in the present.

The figuration of memory as a "Sojourner" is realized in three modes: first, as a fatality independent of human choice, persistent and sometimes unwanted. One work best exemplifies this: *Les Boulevards de ceinture* (1972, *Grand Prix du roman de l'Académie française*), whose principal character begins a search for his father only to interrupt the narrative to say,

I stop to consider these displaced marginal people in order to find through them the fleeting image of my father. I know virtually nothing of him. But I will invent. . . . Today these people have either disappeared or been shot. I suppose they no longer interest anyone. Is it my fault if I am the prisoner of my memories? [and to close the "story"] Well, after all . . . yes . . . if I want this photo, he'll give it to me. But I am young, he says, and I would do better to think about the future.

The figuration of memory as a "Sojourner" is realized in a second mode as (hi)story, with the concomitant injunction to become the author of the "story" which is our heritage. *Villa Triste* (1975, *Prix des libraires*) opens with what is gone: "They have destroyed the Verdun Hotel. Nothing is left of the wonderful café, of its chandeliers, of its mirrors, of the umbrella'd tables overflowing onto the street," to then integrate into this memory, authorship: "It is my turn, I must introduce myself: Victor Chamara. It's the name I chose to fill out the registration cards at The Lindens hotel," then to undermine words themselves, which, like places and people, seem also to be "gone": "So her name was Yvonne. But her last name? I have forgotten it. . . . But what has become of her? What makes the

disappearance of someone dear all the more painful, are the passwords that existed between him and yourself and which suddenly become useless, empty." What
remains to be remembered, to be written are "dull places, precarious way stations
which must always be evacuated before the Germans arrive and which keep no
trace of you."

Memory's figure is finally portrayed as the "Sojourner" who by listening
saves people and their stories from falling away into the forgotten. In the novel
Rue des boutiques obscures (1978, *prix Goncourt*) a young amnesiac begins a
search to find out who he is. In his attempt to (re)write his own (auto)biography
out of phone numbers, names, vague impressions, it becomes necessary to invent
connections between the pieces, if any "memory" is to be (re)constructed out of
the forgotten.

I dial ANJOU 15-28. . . . Is there any trace left of my passing in the deserted apartment. . . . She returned, holding something in her hand. Two books. An agenda. . . .
An impression passes through me, like the bits and pieces of a fleeting dream that you
try to keep hold of as you wake up so as to put the entire dream back together. . . .
Something continues to vibrate after their passing, the waves evermore feeble, but that
one can still catch if one listens attentively.

Characters in other works perceive recording as a "vocation," but leave ironically
only an impression of the meaninglessness, the illegibility of what they record, as
in *La Ronde de nuit* (1969): "I wanted to leave several memories: to at least
transmit to posterity the names of Coco Lacour and Esmeralda. This night I am
watching over them but for how much longer? What will become of them without
me? . . . I've got to give these details since everyone has forgotten them . . . "

If from a question central to his writings in general one then raises the question of
what is particular to an individual work, to *Quartier perdu* (1984), another aspect
becomes apparent: the novel's very careful construction, a construction which
would seem to turn, to play on several images: "to descend," "to enter or to
open," "to come (back) to." In this, his is an incessantly evocative, if not symbolic
writing, where the seemingly most trivial of events—or even most common of
words—becomes suddenly decisive, reminiscent of Walter Benjamin's reflections on the "flaneur," on the "chiffonnier" of Baudelaire. But let us follow one
such word's roll through the work: as the novel opens, the second sentence reads
(A ma *descente* de l'avion), marking his return to France . . . (que nous *descendions* en roue libre), describing his first motion in relation to what had been
stopped by his exile in England. . . . "Eyes wide open, I lay very still. Little by
little I shed the thick shell of the English writer which I had hidden behind for the
past twenty years. Not moving. Waiting for the fall through time to be over"
[Attendre que la *descente* à travers le temps soit achevée] "to descend" changes
register from the geographic and spatial to the temporal . . . (*descendre* au fond
d'un puits pour chercher), where "to descend" becomes the metaphor of a search
within oneself, if not of a "self-analysis." . . . (Je m'assieds sur un banc, là où
vient mourir la pente du boulevard Sérurier. Je pense à Maillot qui me disait: la
montée sera dure, mais après, vous verrez . . . Quel plaisir de *descendre*) indicating first a "dead end" to his "descent," to his "search" and announcing prophet-

ically its resolution. . . . [Et maintenant, je vois une silhouette qui *descend* la pente du boulevard Sérurier] closing the story with "descending" having become again, as at the beginning, a simple mode of spatial displacement.

It would be equally possible to follow at length the imagery which turns around "ghost," "death," "shadow," "deserted," and which pivots suddenly at one point, to change the narrator's specular window into a mirror: "I had never known such heat at night in Paris, and it heightened the unreality I was feeling in the middle of this ghost town. And what if I were the ghost?" [au milieu de cette ville fantôme. Et si le fantôme, c'était moi?].

The third determining image "to enter or to open" becomes synonymously symbolic of displacement, whether it concerns opening or entering streets, hotel rooms, apartments, doorways, an old notebook, files, phone books, phone numbers, or finally writing itself:

only a pretext: after all these years, I wanted to return to this city which meant so much to me, to see it one last time. I'm staying another two weeks, the time it will take to write about all the things that Paris evokes for me, things which are for me the beginnings of my life. . . . When I returned to the apartment I began to write. . . . Now that I've got to the point of admitting things to myself, I must immerse myself in a distant past.

The first part of this passage is taken from a letter, with which he finally begins to write; it is a pre-text to the book that he "must" write, which itself "is like a letter that I would have addressed to you. A very belated letter." And it would seem that the word "pretext" invites that reading, the "descent" into Paris having been also the pre-text of his beginning to write, his coming *back* having been also a "coming *to* the point of admitting things," of writing. "Writing about evocations" is "entering or opening" into/onto where they lead, a "beginning" and a displacement: writing becomes not so much a *re*tracing as a tracing, such that a confusion occurs between "real" autobiography, fictional (auto)biography, and fiction. But the slippage does not stop here, as the book/letter continues: "you had kindly explained to me that there are two kinds of people in the world: those who write books, and those about whom the books are written and who have no reason to read them. They live them," which is also what the detective story writer turned autobiographer finally *does* as the slope/road/book ends, closing what its beginning had opened:

maybe it's all that remains from one of those accidents in which everything that went before disappears, for life. Beginning today, I too don't want to remember anything, anymore.

Little critical writing has as yet been done in English on P. Modiano's works even though many of them have been translated; one writer suggested that this was in large part due to their French specificity. Nonetheless, two articles worth mentioning appeared, one in the *Times Literary Supplement* (25 August 1985, 856), as a general comment on his work and as a specific review of *De si braves garçons* (1982). Anne Duchêne calls attention to "the extraordinary, fulgurant energy of his first books . . . on the Jewish experience of the war" and to the quite distinct "elegiac, admiringly cool and rueful . . . sense of loss and dispossession" of his more recent works; the second appeared in the *Australian Journal of French Studies* (May-August, 1984, 21:213–23) as a review of *Livret de famille* (1977). C. W. Nettleback remarks on the novel's tight structure, which has the same number of chapters as a *livret de famille* has pages, and then notes the nature, both persistent and ephemeral, of remembered experience, "a suicidal rebelliousness on the one hand, and impotent resignation on the other."

As a brief comment on French criticism of his work, on the most salient questions raised there: from Claude Dix (NRF, April 1985) the notion of writing as the settling of a debt with the past, be it a specific, haunting memory or that of still-wandering souls in search of refuge in a fixed point; from Jacques Bersani (NRF, Nov. 1977) P. Modiano's identification with the image of the Jew so as to become the author of his own image: "an absurd and rigorous project"; from Marc Lambron (NRF, May 1981) the description of "an uninhabited interiority . . . of this indifference to time, which is the other name of misfortune"; from Francine de Martinoire (NRF, Nov. 1978) the suggestion that all writing be writing on the ruins of the Book, which is to say the Bible, as the Cabbalist exegetes . . . raising the question of what it might mean to record in postdiaspora time the experience of the "chosen people."

BIBLIOGRAPHY

Works by the author

La Place de l'étoile. Paris: Gallimard, 1968.
La Ronde de nuit. Paris: Gallimard, 1969.
Les Boulevards de ceinture. Paris: Gallimard, 1972.
Lacombe, Lucien. Film scenario written with Louis Malle. Paris: Gallimard, 1974.
Villa Triste. Paris: Gallimard, 1975.
Emmanuel Berl, Interrogatoire. Paris: Gallimard, 1976.
Livret de famille. Paris: Gallimard, 1977.
Rue des boutiques obscures. Paris: Gallimard, 1978.
Une Jeunesse. Paris: Gallimard, 1981.
Memory Lane. Illustration by Pierre Le-Tan. Paris: Editions P.O.L., 1981.
De si braves garçons. Paris: Gallimard, 1982.
Poupée blonde. Illustrations by Pierre Le-Tan. Paris: Editions P.O.L., 1983.
Quartier perdu. Paris: Gallimard, 1984.
Dimanches d'août. Paris: Gallimard, 1986.

PATRICK MODIANO

*Quartier perdu**

C'est étrange d'entendre parler français. À ma descente de l'avion, j'ai senti un léger pincement au cœur. Dans la file d'attente, devant les bureaux de la douane, je contemplais le passeport, qui est désormais le mien, vert pâle, orné de deux lions d'or, les emblèmes de mon pays d'adoption. Et j'ai pensé à celui, cartonné de bleu marine, que l'on m'avait délivré jadis, quand j'avais quatorze ans, au nom de la République française.

J'ai indiqué l'adresse de l'hôtel au chauffeur de taxi et je craignais qu'il n'engageât la conversation car j'avais perdu l'habitude de m'exprimer dans ma langue maternelle. Mais il est resté silencieux tout le long du trajet.

Nous sommes entrés dans Paris par la porte Champerret. Un dimanche, à deux heures de l'après-midi. Les avenues étaient désertes sous le soleil de juillet. Je me suis demandé si je ne traversais pas une ville fantôme après un bombardement et l'exode de ses habitants. Peut-être les façades des immeubles cachaient-elles des décombres? Le taxi glissait de plus en plus vite comme si son moteur était éteint et que nous descendions en roue libre la pente du boulevard Malesherbes.

À l'hôtel, les fenêtres de ma chambre donnaient sur la rue de Castiglione. J'ai tiré les rideaux de velours et je me suis endormi. À mon réveil, il était neuf heures du soir.

J'ai dîné dans la salle à manger. Il faisait encore jour mais les appliques des murs diffusaient une lumière crue. Un couple d'Américains occupaient une table voisine de la mienne, elle, blonde avec des lunettes noires, lui, sanglé dans une sorte de smoking écossais. Il fumait un cigare et la sueur dégoulinait le long de ses tempes. J'avais très chaud moi aussi. Le maître d'hôtel m'a salué en anglais et je lui ai répondu dans la même

---

Quartier perdu (Paris: Gallimard, 1984), 9–13, 28–29, 86–89, 125–27, 154–56, 158–59, 180–82. These passages are reprinted with the kind permission of Gallimard.

264

langue. À son attitude protectrice, j'ai compris qu'il me prenait pour un Américain.

Dehors, la nuit était tombée, une nuit étouffante, sans un souffle d'air. Sous les arcades de la rue de Castiglione, je croisais des touristes, américains ou japonais. Plusieurs cars stationnaient devant les grilles du jardin des Tuileries, et sur le marchepied de l'un d'eux, un homme blond en costume de steward accueillait les passagers, micro à la main. Il parlait vite et fort, dans une langue gutturale et s'interrompait, d'un éclat de rire qui ressemblait à un hennissement. Il a fermé lui-même la portière et s'est assis à côté du chauffeur. Le car a filé en direction de la place de la Concorde, un car bleu clair au flanc duquel était écrit en lettres rouges: DE GROTE REISEN ANTWERPEN.

Plus loin, place des Pyramides, d'autres cars. Un groupe de jeunes gens, sac de toile beige en bandoulière, étaient vautrés au pied de la statue de Jeanne d'Arc. Ils faisaient circuler entre eux des baguettes de pain et une bouteille de Coca-Cola dont ils versaient le contenu dans des gobelets en carton. À mon passage, l'un d'eux s'est levé et m'a demandé quelque chose en allemand. Comme je ne comprenais pas cette langue, j'ai haussé les épaules en signe d'impuissance.

Je me suis engagé dans l'avenue qui coupe le jardin jusqu'au pont Royal. Un car de police était à l'arrêt, feux éteints. On y poussait une ombre en costume de Peter Pan. Des hommes encore jeunes, qui portaient tous les cheveux courts et des moustaches, se croisaient, raides et lunaires, dans les allées et autour des bassins. Oui, ces lieux étaient fréquentés par le même genre de personnes qu'il y a vingt ans et pourtant la vespasienne, à gauche, du côté de l'arc de triomphe du Carrousel, derrière les massifs de buis, n'existait plus. J'étais arrivé sur le quai des Tuileries, mais je n'ai pas osé traverser la Seine et me promener seul sur la rive gauche, où j'avais passé mon enfance.

Je suis resté longtemps au bord du trottoir, à regarder le flot des voitures, le clignotement des feux rouges et des feux verts, et, de l'autre côté du fleuve, l'épave sombre de la gare d'Orsay. À mon retour, les arcades de la rue de Rivoli étaient désertes. Je n'avais jamais connu une telle chaleur la nuit, à Paris, et cela augmentait encore le sentiment d'irréalité que j'éprouvais au milieu de cette ville fantôme. Et si le fantôme, c'était moi? Je cherchais quelque chose à quoi me raccrocher. L'ancienne parfumerie lambrissée de la place des Pyramides était devenue une agence de voyages. On avait reconstruit l'entrée et le hall du *Saint-James et d'Albany*. Mais, à part ça, rien n'avait changé. Rien. J'avais beau me le répéter à voix basse, je flottais dans cette ville. Elle n'était plus la mienne, elle se fermait à mon approche, comme la vitrine grillagée de la rue de Castiglione devant laquelle je m'étais arrêté et où je distinguais à peine mon reflet.

Des taxis attendaient, et j'ai voulu en prendre un pour faire une grande promenade à travers Paris et retrouver tous les lieux familiers. Une appréhension m'a saisi, celle d'un convalescent qui hésite à se livrer à des efforts trop violents les premiers jours.

Le concierge de l'hôtel m'a salué en anglais. Cette fois-ci, j'ai répondu en français et il en a paru surpris. Il m'a tendu la clé et une enveloppe bleu ciel.

—Un message téléphonique, monsieur . . .

J'ai ouvert les rideaux de velours et les deux battants de la porte-fenêtre. L'air était encore plus chaud dehors que dans la chambre. Si l'on se penchait au balcon on voyait, à gauche, la place Vendôme noyée de pénombre et tout au fond les lumières du boulevard des Capucines. De temps en temps un taxi s'arrêtait, les portières claquaient et des bribes de conversations en italien ou en anglais montaient jusqu'à moi. De nouveau, j'ai eu envie de sortir et de me promener, au hasard. À cette même heure quelqu'un arrivait à Paris pour la première fois et il était ému et intrigué de traverser ces rues et ces places, qui, à moi, ce soir, semblaient mortes.

J'ai déchiré l'enveloppe bleue du message. Yoko Tatsuké avait téléphoné à l'hôtel en mon absence et, si je voulais le joindre, il serait demain, toute la journée, au *Concorde-Lafayette* de la porte Maillot.

J'ai été soulagé qu'il me donne rendez-vous très tard pour le dîner, car le perspective de traverser Paris de jour, sous ce soleil de plomb, m'accablait. À la fin de l'après-midi j'ai fait quelques pas dehors mais sans quitter l'ombre des arcades. Rue de Rivoli, je suis entré dans une librairie anglaise. Au rayon « detective-stories », j'ai remarqué l'un de mes livres. Ainsi on trouvait à Paris la série des *Jarvis* d'Ambrose Guise. Et comme la photographie de l'auteur qui ornait la jaquette de ce livre était très sombre, je me suis dit que personne, ici, en France, parmi ceux qui m'avaient rencontré jadis, ne saurait jamais que cet Ambrose Guise c'était moi.

J'ai feuilleté le livre avec l'impression d'avoir abandonné Ambrose Guise de l'autre côté de la Manche. Vingt années de ma vie étaient, d'un seul coup, abolies. Ambrose Guise n'existait plus. J'étais revenu au point de départ, dans la poussière et la chaleur de Paris.

. . . .

Je me suis allongé sur le lit. À cause de la chaleur, il fallait éviter de faire le moindre geste, mais j'ai tendu le bras vers la table de nuit en direction de mon vieux cahier. Je l'ai posé près de l'oreiller. Je n'avais pas vraiment envie de le consulter. Couverture verte, bords usés, spirales, triangle dans le coin gauche, au sommet duquel était écrit « Clairefontaine ». Un simple cahier d'écolier que j'avais acheté un jour dans une papeterie de l'avenue de Wagram et sur lequel j'avais noté des adresses, des numéros de téléphone, quelquefois des rendez-vous: l'un des seuls vestiges de ma vie antérieure à Paris, avec mon passeport français périmé et un porte-cigarettes en cuir, inutile aujourd'hui puisque je ne fumais plus.

Je pouvais déchirer ce cahier, page après page, mais il était inutile que je me donne cette peine: les numéros de téléphone qu'il contenait ne répondaient plus depuis longtemps. Alors pourquoi rester à Paris, sur le lit d'une chambre d'hôtel, en essuyant du poignet de ma chemise la sueur qui dégoulinait de mon menton dans mon cou? Il suffisait de prendre le premier avion du matin et de retrouver la fraîcheur de Rutland Gate . . . .

J'ai éteint la lampe de chevet. La fenêtre était ouverte, et dans la lumière bleue et phosphorescente de la rue de Castiglione tous les objets de la chambre se détachaient nettement: armoire à glace, fauteuil de velours, table circulaire, appliques des murs. Un reflet en forme de treillage courait au plafond.

Immobile, les yeux grands ouverts, je me dépouillais peu à peu de cette carapace épaisse d'écrivain anglais sous laquelle je me dissimulais depuis vingt ans. Ne pas bouger. Attendre que la descente à travers le temps soit achevée, comme si l'on avait sauté en parachute. Reprendre pied dans le Paris d'autrefois. Visiter les ruines et tenter d'y découvrir une trace de soi. Essayer de résoudre toutes les questions qui sont demeurées en suspens.

J'écoutais claquer les portières, les voix et les rires monter de la rue, les pas résonner sous les arcades. Le cahier faisait une tache claire à côté de moi et, tout à l'heure, je le feuilletterais. Une liste de fantômes. Oui, mais qui sait? Quelques-uns hantaient encore cette ville écrasée de chaleur.

Sur ma table de nuit la carte rouge que m'avait donnée le concierge. Ce nom inscrit en caractères noirs: Hayward m'évoquait quelque chose. Mais oui. Hayward . . .

. . . .

Et cela m'a paru naturel de composer le 01 13 24 à Klosters dans cet appartement de Rocroy qui était associé pourtant à toute une partie, déjà si ancienne, de ma vie. Oui, naturel. Peut-être à cause du soleil qui entrait à flots dans la chambre, ce matin-là. Ou de la résolution que j'avais prise. Je me sentais le cœur léger. Et si le passé et le présent se mêlaient? Pourquoi n'y aurait-il pas, à travers les péripéties en apparence les plus diverses d'une vie, une unité secrète, un parfum dominant?

—Madame dort.

J'ai reconnu la voix ensommeillée de Miss Mynott.

—Je vous réveille, Miss?

—Non . . . non . . . pas du tout, Monsieur.

—Comment vont les enfants?

—Très bien, Monsieur. Ils ont une mine magnifique.

—Et ma femme?

—Comme toujours, elle est ravie d'être à Klosters.

—Elle ne s'ennuie pas trop?

—Non . . . non . . . Elle voit vos amis. Ils sont tous là. M. Irwin Shaw va venir déjeuner tout à l'heure.

—Vous le saluerez de ma part.

Shaw était le seul confrère avec lequel j'entretenais des liens d'amitié.

—Vous direz à ma femme que je reste encore une quinzaine de jours à Paris. Et que je vais lui écrire une lettre pour lui en expliquer les raisons.

—C'est dommage, Monsieur. Il fait si beau à Klosters . . . Et les enfants s'ennuient un peu de vous.

—Ne vous inquiétez pas. Je serai là dans quinze jours.

—Mais je ne m'inquiète pas, Monsieur . . .

En quittant la chambre de Ghita Wattier, j'ai rencontré mon visage dans une glace. Je ne m'étais pas rasé depuis longtemps. Peu importait si, au cours des jours qui allaient venir, je prenais l'apparence d'un clochard. Il faisait beau à Klosters, mais moi, je devais maintenant descendre au fond d'un puits pour chercher, à tâtons, quelque chose, dans l'eau noire.

Je suis sorti et j'ai suivi la rue de Courcelles. Le soleil tapait fort, mais loin de m'accabler, ses rayons me donnaient du courage. J'ai bu un café à une terrasse déserte du boulevard Haussmann. Par chance, j'ai trouvé une papeterie, à quelques pas de là. J'ai acheté trois blocs de papier à lettres grand format sans rayures. Et un stylo. Un simple feutre bleu floride.

Paris, le 9 juillet

Chère Katy,

Je préfère t'envoyer un mot que de te téléphoner. Peut-être n'aurais-je jamais dû donner rendez-vous à ce Japonais à Paris . . . Mais il ne s'agissait que d'un prétexte : après tant d'années, je voulais retourner dans cette ville qui a compté pour moi et la voir une dernière fois . . . J'y reste encore une quinzaine de jours, le temps d'écrire sur toutes les choses que Paris évoque pour moi et qui sont mes débuts dans la vie . . . Que tout cela ne t'attriste pas, ma chère Katy. Je t'embrasse. Embrasse les enfants de ma part. Et transmets mes amitiés aux Irwin Shaw.

Je t'aime

Ambrose.

De retour à l'appartement, j'ai commencé à écrire, les jambes repliées sur le canapé du salon, le bloc de papier contre mes genoux. J'ai laissé la porte-fenêtre ouverte. Il fait très chaud. Peu importe. Maintenant que j'en suis venu aux aveux, il faut que je replonge dans ces années lointaines.

Avant de devenir le romancier anglais Ambrose Guise, j'ai débuté

dans la vie, en qualité de bagagiste. Oui. Bagagiste. C'est le seul métier—
exception faite de celui d'écrivain—que j'aurai jamais exercé.

J'avais vingt ans et je passais quelques jours de vacances en Haute-
Savoie dans une station de sports d'hiver, vacances qu'il me faudrait
bientôt interrompre: il me restait à peine de quoi payer mon ticket de
retour. Pour quelle destination, j'aurais été bien incapable de le dire.

. . . .

Un jour, j'étais venu le chercher chez lui, rue de Courcelles. Nous
avions rendez-vous avec Carmen et il y aurait, comme d'habitude, cette
attente interminable dans le salon avant qu'elle se réveille. Rocroy était
allongé sur le canapé. Ghita Wattier répondait au téléphone, et chaque
fois il agitait son index d'un geste négatif pour qu'elle dise qu'il n'était pas
là.

—Amoureux de Carmen, hein? m'avait-il demandé brusquement.

J'avais dû rougir ou hausser les épaules. Alors, d'une voix douce et
paternelle, il m'avait tenu des propos qui—si j'ai bonne mémoire—corre-
spondaient à peu près aux termes employés dans sa lettre : « Tous ces
gens qui ont été les témoins de vos débuts dans la vie vont peu à peu
disparaître. Vous les avez connus très jeune, quand c'était déjà le crépuscule pour eux . . . »

Puis il s'était retourné:

—Tu lui donnes un bloc, Gyp, . . . et un stylo . . .

Ghita m'avait tendu un petit bloc jaune. Le stylo, Rocroy lui-même
l'avait sorti de la poche intérieure de sa veste.

—Prenez note, mon vieux.

Et il m'avait dicté une foule de détails: des noms de gens, des dates,
des noms de rues que je notais sur les feuilles du bloc jaune. J'ai perdu le
bloc mais cela n'a aucune importance: tout ce qu'on vous dit, à cet âge-là,
vous n'avez pas besoin de le noter. Cela s'inscrit, d'une manière indé-
lébile dans votre tête, pour la vie.

Avait-il donc le pressentiment que j'écrirais quelque chose sur cette
période et sur toutes ces personnes de mon entourage? Lui ai-je confié que
je voulais écrire plus tard? Je ne crois pas. Parlions-nous, lui et moi, de
littérature? Mais oui. Il me prêtait ses romans policiers et m'avait fait
découvrir pêle-mêle Earl Biggers, Rufus King, Phillips Oppenheim, Saint-
Bonnet, Dornford Yates et tant d'autres dont les œuvres sont toujours
rangées dans sa bibliothèque. Avec les miennes.

Mon cher Rocroy, ce livre est comme une lettre que je vous adres-
serais. Une lettre bien tardive. Vous n'aurez jamais l'occasion d'en prendre connaissance. Seule, Ghita . . . Les autres ont disparu. De toute manière, ni Carmen ni Georges Maillot ne lisaient jamais rien. Nous en
avions parlé tous les deux et vous m'aviez expliqué gentiment qu'il existe

deux sortes de gens: ceux qui font les livres, et ceux sur qui les livres se
font, et qui n'ont pas besoin de les lire. Ils les vivent. C'est bien cela,
Rocroy? Je ne me trompe pas? Carmen et Georges appartenaient à la
seconde catégorie.

J'aurai trente-neuf ans à la fin du mois de juillet et j'espère terminer
mon livre à ce moment-là. Je devrais vous le dédier, Rocroy. Et le dédier à
Carmen, à Maillot, qui ont été avec vous les témoins de mes débuts dans
la vie—selon votre expression.

. . . .

Dans ma chambre, je me suis assis en bordure du lit. « Hayward. Sté
location automobiles de luxe. Auto grande remise avec chauffeur. Itiné-
raires touristiques. Paris By Night/2 avenue Rodin (XVIᵉ). TRO 46-26. »

C'était bien leur ancienne adresse. J'ai composé le numéro.

—Allô . . . Agence Hayward . . . m'a annoncé une voix d'homme.

Avait-il décroché le téléphone dans le salon? Je me souvenais du large
balcon de ce salon d'où l'on pouvait accéder, par un petit escalier en fer, à
la terrasse, sur le toit.

—Je vous téléphone pour une location de voiture.

—Avec chauffeur?

—Oui. Avec chauffeur.

Etait-ce lui qui me parlait? Ou l'un de ses employés?

—Et pour quand, monsieur?

—Pour aujourd'hui, à neuf heures du soir.

—À quelle adresse?

—*Hôtel Lotti.*

—Pour combien de temps?

—Deux heures au maximum. Juste le temps de faire une promenade
touristique à travers Paris.

—Très bien. Je demande monsieur . . .

—M. Guise. Ambrose Guise.

—Très bien. À ce soir, monsieur, au *Lotti*, à neuf heures.

Il a raccroché brutalement, sans me laisser le temps de lui demander
si c'était bien à Philippe Hayward lui-même que j'avais l'honneur de
parler.

—Le chauffeur vous attend à la réception, monsieur . . .

J'ai voulu mettre mes vieilles lunettes de soleil d'il y a vingt ans, en
hommage à la Société de location d'automobiles Hayward, et j'ai choisi,
en définitive, celles à verres miroir, que je portais d'ordinaire.

C'était lui. Le visage soufflé, les cheveux gris. Mais je l'avais reconnu
à une certaine allure juvénile qu'il conservait encore. Costume d'alpaga
bleu marine. Cravate bordeaux.

—Bonjour, monsieur, m'a-t-il dit avec la réserve et la lassitude d'un
homme qui vit au-dessous de sa condition. Mais peut-être me trompais-je
et Hayward avait-il toujours exercé ce métier de chauffeur, même à

l'époque de Carmen. Je me souvenais de la vision fugitive que j'avais eue de lui en uniforme de steward. Il m'avait jeté un regard indifférent. Non, il ne semblait pas me reconnaître. Nous sommes sortis dans la nuit étouffante. Pas un souffle d'air. La voiture était garée au coin de la rue de Castiglione et de la rue Saint-Honoré. Une américaine de taille imposante. Noire.

—J'espère qu'elle vous convient, monsieur.

—Tout à fait.

Il m'a ouvert la portière et je me suis assis sur la banquette, du côté droit.

—Où désirez-vous que je vous conduise?

—Oh . . . une simple promenade dans Paris . . . Tour Eiffel . . . Invalides . . . Champs-Elysées . . . Pigalle . . .

—Très bien, monsieur. Par où voulez-vous que je commence?

—Tour Eiffel . . .

J'avais ôté mes lunettes.

Il m'observait dans le rétroviseur.

—Vous connaissez Paris?

—Je n'y étais pas revenu depuis presque vingt ans. Paris a beaucoup changé en vingt ans?

—Beaucoup.

À travers ce mot, perçait une pointe d'amertume. Si Paris avait beaucoup changé, Hayward, lui, sentait la même odeur qu'il y a vingt ans, odeur qui me parut surannée: celle de l'eau de toilette Acqua di Selva dont je revoyais les flacons vert sombre sur la tablette de la salle de bains de son appartement, avenue Rodin.

. . . .

—Et maintenant, monsieur? Je vous emmène où?

Je me suis penché vers lui, et mon menton touchait presque son épaule.

L'odeur d'Acqua di Selva augmentait mon vertige. Je lui ai dit, en articulant bien toutes les syllabes :

—Nous allons rentrer à l'hôtel. Mais avant, je voudrais que vous vous arrêtiez un instant, place de l'Alma, à un endroit que je vous indiquerai.

De nouveau, il a fait demi-tour; il a suivi le quai et puis il a traversé le pont de l'Alma.

Beaucoup de monde à la terrasse de *Chez Francis*. Les tables débordaient sur la chaussée. Un car bleu ciel attendait, au flanc duquel était écrit en grosses lettres rouges: PARIS-VISION.

—Vous vous arrêterez à droite . . . juste au début de la rue Jean-Goujon . . .

—Là?

—Oui.

Nous étions devant l'entré de l'immeuble où habitait Carmen.

Il a coupé le contact et s'est retourné vers moi.

Ses yeux s'étaient agrandis et me fixaient dans une expression atten-tive qui le vieillissait brusquement. À moins que ce ne fût la demi-pénombre: elle lui creusait le visage.

—Je me demande si quelqu'un habite encore cet appartement . . .

Et je lui désignais les volets fermés des fenêtres de l'appartement de Carmen, celles qui donnaient sur la rue Jean-Goujon.

—Vous pourriez peut-être me renseigner?

Il me dévisageait d'un regard inquiet et mon vertige augmentait en-core. J'avais envie de lui demander des nouvelles de sa femme. Et même d'évoquer certains détails que je connaissais à cause des soirées un peu particulières où tous les deux ils nous avaient entraînés, Carmen et moi. Martine Hayward avait-elle toujours à la hauteur de la taille, du côté gauche, un grain de beauté?

—Nous avons dû nous rencontrer ici, il y a très longtemps . . . Chez une Mme Blin, n'est-ce pas? m'a-t-il dit sur le ton de la conversation mondaine.

—Oui . . . Je crois . . .

—Elle est morte il y a cinq ans.

Morte. Je ne sais pas pourquoi, la grosse figure rose de Tintin Carpen-tieri m'est revenue en mémoire, de façon si nette qu'un instant j'ai cru que ce n'était pas Hayward accoudé à la banquette, devant moi, mais Carpentieri lui-même qui me parlait.

. . . .

J'ai respiré un grand coup.

—Dites, Ghita . . .

—Oui?

—Vous allez encore me reprocher de remuer le passé mais . . . Com-ment pourrais-je faire pour retrouver la trace . . .

—La trace de quoi?

—Rien, Ghita. Vous savez . . . Toutes ces choses d'il y a vingt ans me remontent à la gorge . . .

—C'est malsain, Jean . . .

Il y a eu un moment de silence.

—Vous n'avez rien trouvé d'intéressant dans les dossiers de De Rocroy?

—Si, Si, Ghita . . .

—Écoutez, mon petit Jean. Vous savez ce que me répétait toujours de Rocroy?

—Non.

—Il me disait qu'on trouve tout ce qu'on cherche dans les annuaires. À condition de savoir les consulter.

J'ai retrouvé son nom, entre les pages de mon vieux cahier, sur le bout de papier où elle l'avait écrit avec son adresse à Saint-Maur. Et le même nom figure dans l'annuaire de cette année: 76, boulevard Sérurier, XIXᵉ arrondissement, 208-76-68. Il n'y a qu'un seul nom comme le sien. Décidément Rocroy avait raison. Il connaissait bien la vie.

Neuf heures du matin. L'air n'est pas encore trop étouffant bien que le soleil brille dans un ciel sans nuages. Pas de brume de chaleur. Le rouge brique du grand immeuble du 76 boulevard Sérurier se détache sur le vert du parc, dont les pelouses dévalent jusqu'au périphérique.

Un café est ouvert, beaucoup plus loin sur le boulevard Sérurier, et je compose pour la cinquième fois au cadran du téléphone 208-76-68. Mais personne ne répond. Je sors du café. Le boulevard est désert. Là-bas, vers la banlieue, un bâtiment ocre—une église sans doute—se dresse au milieu d'un terrain vague. Je m'assieds sur un banc, là où vient mourir la pente du boulevard Sérurier. Je pense à Maillot qui me disait: « La montée sera dure, mais après, vous verrez . . . Quel plaisir de descendre. » Avenue Carnot. Rue Anatole-de-la-Forge. Rue de l'Arc-de-Triomphe. Avenue Mac-Mahon. Boulevard Sérurier. L'avenue du Nord, elle aussi, glissait en pente douce. Jusqu'à la Marne.

Et maintenant, je vois une silhouette qui descend la pente du boulevard Sérurier, une valise à la main, une valise de fer-blanc, dont les reflets me font cligner les yeux. Mirage? Elle se rapproche, peu à peu. C'est elle. Je reconnais la démarche indolente. Elle est vêtue d'un imperméable mais ce n'est plus l'imperméable de Ludo. Beaucoup plus foncé, celui-ci. Vert émeraude.

Elle est presque arrivée à ma hauteur et je me lève. Nous sommes seuls, tous les deux, sur ce boulevard perdu, écrasé de soleil et de silence. Je lui propose de porter sa valise.

—Merci.

—Vous revenez de vacances?

—Oui. Ce n'est pas pratique. La station de métro est trop loin de chez moi.

Nous marchons côte à côte vers l'immeuble de brique du 76 boulevard Sérurier. Nous ne parlons pas. Il commence à faire très chaud, et pourtant elle garde son imperméable. Elle n'a pas beaucoup changé en vingt ans. Les mêmes cheveux noirs, mais coiffés un peu plus court. Les yeux bleus. Taille moyenne. Le teint pâle . . .

—Vous revenez d'où?

—Du Midi.

—Vous n'êtes pas très bronzée pour quelqu'un qui revient du Midi.

Elle revient de plus loin encore. Carmen. Rocroy. La Varenne-Saint-Hilaire. Paris. Toutes ces rues en pente . . . Sa valise ne pèse pas lourd. Je la regarde à la dérobée. Une grande cicatrice lui barre le front. La marque du temps, peut-être. Ou bien la trace que vous laisse l'un de ces accidents

qui vous ont fait perdre la mémoire pour la vie. Moi aussi, à partir d'aujourd'hui, je veux ne plus me souvenir de rien.

Quartier perdu

It's odd to hear French. Getting off the plane I had a lump in my throat.
Waiting in line at customs I studied the passport that would be mine for
the rest of my life—pale green, embossed with two golden lions, em-
blems of my adopted country. Then I thought about the other one, the one
they gave me a long time ago in the name of "La République française"
when I was fourteen—a stiff little navy blue one.

I gave the taxi driver the address of the hotel, afraid that he might try
to make conversation; I wasn't used to expressing myself in my native
tongue. But he didn't say a thing the whole way.

We came into Paris through Porte Champerret. It was Sunday at two
o'clock in the afternoon. The avenues lay deserted in the July sun. I
wondered if I were not riding through a ghost town after a bombing when
everyone else had left. What if there were nothing but ruins behind these
facades? The taxi cruised along faster and faster, as if the motor had been
shut off and we were careening downhill on Boulevard Malesherbes.

At the hotel, the windows of my room looked out onto Rue Castiglione. I drew the velvet drapes and fell asleep. When I woke up, it was
nine in the evening.

I ate in the dining room of the hotel. It wasn't dark out yet, but the
wall lamps gave off a harsh light. An American couple was at the table
next to mine—she, a blond with dark glasses; he, done up in some kind of
plaid dinner jacket. He was smoking a cigar as sweat dripped down his
temples. I was also very hot. The head waiter greeted me in English and I
answered him in kind. I knew by his patronizing manner that he took me
for an American.

Outside, night was falling, sweltering, without a breath of air. Under
the arches on Rue de Castiglione I passed tourists, American or Japanese.
Several tour buses were parked in front of the gates leading into the
Tuileries, and a blond man in a steward's uniform stood in the door of one
of them, welcoming the passengers, microphone in hand. He was speaking a guttural language very quickly and in a loud voice, and he kept
interrupting his monologue with bursts of laughter that made him sound
like a whinnying horse. Then he closed the door and sat down next to the

driver. The bus took off and headed for Place de la Concorde, a bright blue bus with red letters printed on the side: DE GROTE REISEN ANTWERPEN.

A little further on, Place des Pyramides, and more buses. A group of young people were sprawled out at the foot of the statute of Jeanne d'Arc, beige canvas shoulder bag on the ground. They were passing around loaves of bread and a bottle of Coca-Cola, pouring it into paper cups. One of them got up and asked me something in German as I passed. I didn't speak German, so I shrugged my shoulders to show I couldn't understand.

I turned into the avenue that cuts through the garden and leads to Pont Royal. A police van had stopped, lights off. They were pushing a shadowy figure dressed like Peter Pan into the van. Other men, still young, with short hair and moustaches passed one another along the paths, around the basin, stiffly, like moon walkers. Ah yes, these places were still frequented by the same kind of people as twenty years ago, and yet the urinal behind the boxwood on the left, on the Carousel Arch side was no longer there. I had reached the quai of the Tuileries, but didn't dare cross the Seine and walk alone on the Left Bank where I had spent my childhood.

I stayed a long time at the edge of the sidewalk, watching the continual flow of cars, the blinking lights, red and green, the dark wreck of the Orsay station. When I returned to Rue de Rivoli, the arches were empty. I had never known such heat at night in Paris, and it heightened the feeling of unreality of this ghost town. And what if I were the ghost? I was looking for something to hold on to. The old, wainscoted *parfumerie* at Place des Pyramides had become a travel agency. And they had remodeled the door and the foyer of *Saint-James et d'Albany*. But nothing had changed. Nothing. No matter how often I repeated it to myself under my breath, I was still adrift in this city. It wasn't my city any more; it seemed to close up as I approached, like the shop window with its grill pulled down on Rue de Castiglione where I stopped and could only barely make out my reflection.

There were taxis waiting on the street, and I wanted to hire one to drive me around Paris so I could find the familiar places. But a sudden apprehension came over me, something like what a convalescent must feel who's afraid to do too much the first few days he's up.

The concierge at the hotel greeted me in English. This time I answered him in French and he looked surprised. He handed me the key and a light blue envelope.

"A telephone message for you, monsieur."

I opened the velvet drapes and the French doors leading onto the balcony. It was even hotter outside than in the room. If you leaned over the balcony, you could see Place Vendôme on the left, bathed in shadows, and beyond that the lights of Boulevard des Capucines. Once in a while a taxi pulled up in front of the hotel; the doors would slam and snatches of conversation in Italian or English drifted up to where I was. And again, I had an urge to go out for a walk, to wander around aimlessly. At that very moment, someone was probably arriving in Paris for the first time, excited and intrigued by the thought of walking down these streets and crossing these squares which seemed so dead to me that evening.

I tore open the blue envelope. Yoko Tatsuké had telephoned while I was out, and if I wanted to meet him, he would be at the *Concorde-Lafayette* at Porte Maillot all day tomorrow.

I was relieved that he had arranged for us to meet very late for dinner—just the thought of going from one end of Paris to the other during the day, in this oppressive heat, overwhelmed me. By the end of the afternoon I had taken a few steps outside, but I stayed close to the shade of the arcades. On Rue de Rivoli I went into an English language bookshop. I noticed one of my books in the section marked "Detective Stories." So. . . , you could find the *Jarvis* series by Ambrose Guise in Paris. The photograph of the author which adorned the jacket of the book was so dark that I told myself no one here in France whom I used to know would ever guess that *I* was Ambrose Guise.

I leafed through the book with the feeling that I had left Ambrose Guise on the other side of the Channel. Twenty years of my life were wiped out just like that. Ambrose Guise no longer existed. I had returned to where it all began, in the heat and dust of Paris.

. . . .

I lay down on the bed. Because of the heat, I refrained from even the smallest gesture, but I did reach over to the bedside table and my old notebook. I put it next to the pillow. I really had no desire to look through it. Green cover, worn edges, spirals, triangles in the left corner, at the top the word "Clarefontaine." I had bought it one day in a stationary shop on Avenue Wagram, just a school notebook where I had written addresses and telephone numbers, occasionally the time and place to meet someone; all that remained of my former life in Paris, except for my expired French passport and a leather cigarette case no use to me now that I don't smoke any more.

I could tear up the notebook, page by page, but it wasn't worth the effort: the telephone numbers it contained hadn't been in service for some time. So why should I stay in Paris, on some bed in a hotel room, wiping sweat with my shirt sleeve as it dripped from my chin to my neck? All I had to do was take the first morning plane and return to the cool air of Rutland Gate. . . .

I turned off the lamp. The window was open and all the objects in the room stood out sharply in the blue, phosphorescent light of Rue de Castiglione: the mirrored armoire, the velvet armchair, the round table, the wall lamps. A latticed shadow danced on the ceiling.

Eyes wide open, I lay very still. Little by little I shed the thick shell of the English writer I had been hiding behind for the past twenty years. Not

moving. Waiting for the fall through time to be over, like someone drop-
ping though the air in a parachute. Stepping into a Paris of long ago.
Visiting the ruins, looking for a trace of oneself. Trying to tie together all
the loose ends that had been left dangling.

I listened to car doors slamming, voices and laughter floating up from
the street, footsteps echoing in the arcades. The notebook glowed next to
me; I knew I would leaf through it in a while. A list of ghosts. Maybe, but
who knows? Some of them were still haunting this city, overwhelmed by
the heat.

On my night table the red card the concierge had given me. That
name inscribed in black letters: Hayward. It reminded me of something.
But of course, Hayward . . .

. . . .

Even though I associated Rocroy's apartment with an entire part of
my life that was far in the past, it seemed somehow so natural to be there,
dialing the number at Klosters, 01-13-24. Yes, natural. Maybe because of
the sunshine streaming into my room that morning. Or maybe it was the
resolution I had made. I felt lighthearted. And what if the past and present
became confused? In spite of the apparently diverse turns life takes, why
wouldn't there be a hidden unity, a predominant scent that held it all
together?

"Madame is sleeping."

I recognized Miss Mynott's drowsy voice.

"Did I wake you, Miss?"

"Oh no . . . not at all, sir."

"How are the children?"

"They're fine, sir. They look wonderful."

"And my wife?"

"She's delighted to be at Klosters, as she always is."

"She's not getting bored?"

"No . . . no . . . She's been seeing your friends. They're all here. Mr.
Irwin Shaw is coming for lunch later on."

"Please say hello to him for me."

Shaw was my only colleague who was also a friend.

"Will you please tell my wife that I will be staying another fortnight
in Paris? And that I will write her a letter explaining the reasons?"

"That's unfortunate, sir. The weather is beautiful at Klosters . . . and
the children miss you."

"Don't worry. I'll be there in a fortnight."

"I won't worry, sir . . . "

Leaving Ghita Wattier's room, I spotted my face in a mirror. I hadn't
shaved for quite a while. It hardly mattered if I started looking like a bum
for a few days. The weather was beautiful at Klosters, but now I had to go
down to the bottom of a well to grope for something in the dark water.

I went out and followed Rue de Courcelles. The sun was still beating down, but instead of overwhelming me its rays gave me courage. I had coffee on the deserted terrace of a café on Boulevard Haussmann. I happened to find a stationary shop close by. I bought three large note pads, no lines. And a pen. A simple felt-tipped pen, Florida blue.

Paris, 9 July

Dear Katy,

I'd rather send you a note than ring you up. Maybe I should never have arranged a meeting with the Japanese in Paris. But that was only a pretext: after all these years, I wanted to return to this city which meant so much to me, to see it one last time. . . . I'm staying another two weeks, the time it will take to write about all the things that Paris evokes for me, things which are for me the beginnings of my life. . . . I hope that this doesn't make you sad, Katy dear. I send you my love. Kiss the children for me. And give my best to the Shaws.

I love you,
Ambrose

When I returned to the apartment I began to write, my legs curled up on the couch in the living room, the pad of paper on my knees. I've left the French doors open. It is very hot. But who cares. Now that I've come to the point of facing up to things, I must immerse myself in a distant past.

Before becoming the English novelist Ambrose Guise, I began as a porter. Yes, that's right, a porter. It is the only thing—besides writing—that I have ever done.

I was twenty and I spent a few days on holiday in Haute Savoie at a ski resort. This vacation had to be cut short: I hardly had enough money left to buy a return ticket. Where was I going? I could not have said.
. . . .
One day I had come to look for him [Rocroy] at his place. We had a date with Carmen, and there would be the usual, interminable wait in the living room while she woke up. Rocroy was stretched out on the couch. Ghita Wattier was answering the phone, and each time she looked at him to see if he would take the call, he would wave his index finger in the air to tell her to say he wasn't there.

"In love with Carmen, are you?" he asked me bluntly.

I must have blushed or shrugged my shoulders. Then in a soft, fatherly voice he gave me a little talk which, if I remember it right, sounded a lot like his letter: "All those who witnessed the beginnings of your life are going to disappear one by one. You knew them when you were very young, but those were the twilight years for them . . . "

Then he turned to Ghita:

"Give him a pad of paper, Gyp, . . . and a pen . . . "

Ghita had handed me a little yellow pad. Rocroy pulled out a pen from his inside coat pocket.

"Take this down, old man."

So he dictated a lot of facts: people's names, dates, street names, and I took it all down on the yellow pad. I've lost the pad, but that doesn't matter: with all the things they tell you at that age, you really don't have to take it down. It's written indelibly in your head, for life.

Did he have an idea then that I would write something about those days and all those people in my group? Did I mention to him that I wanted to write? I don't think so. Did we talk about literature? That, yes. He loaned me his detective novels and introduced me to the lot of them: Earl Biggers, Rufus King, Phillips Oppenheim, Saint-Bonnet, Dornford Yates, and so many others whose works are on the shelves of his library. With my own.

My dear Rocroy, this book is like a letter that I might have addressed to you. A very belated letter. You'll never know about it. Only Ghita. . . . The others have disappeared. And anyway, neither Carmen nor Georges Maillot ever read anything. We had talked about that together, and you had kindly explained to me that there are two kinds of people in the world: those who write books, and those about whom the books are written and who have no reason to read them. They live them. Isn't that what you said, Rocroy? Have I got it right? Carmen and Georges, they were in the second group.

I'll be thirty-nine at the end of July, and that's when I want to have the book finished. I should dedicate it to you, Rocroy. And to Carmen, to Maillot, who like you, witnessed the beginnings of my life—as you put it.

. . . .

Back in my hotel room I am sitting on the edge of the bed. "Hayward. Luxury cars for hire. Special price with chauffeur. Sightseeing. Paris By Night/2 Avenue Rodin (XVIème). TRO 46-26."

That was their old address. I dialed the number.

"Hello . . . Agence Hayward . . . " a man's voice informed me.

Had he answered the telephone in the living room? I remembered a large balcony off the living room which led to a fire escape where you could climb onto a rooftop terrace.

"I'm calling to hire a car."

"With a chauffeur?"

"Yes, with a chauffeur."

Was I talking to him? Or was it one of his employees?

"When would you like it, Monsieur?"

"Today, nine o'clock this evening."

"And your address?"

"Hotel Lotti."

"For how long would you like the car?"

"No more than two hours. Just enough for a sightseeing trip around Paris."

"That'll be fine. I'll ask for Monsieur . . . "

"Monsieur Guise. Ambrose Guise."

"All right. I'll see you then, Monsieur, at the Lotti at nine o'clock."

He hung up so quickly that I didn't have a chance to ask him if I had had the honor of speaking with Philippe Hayward himself.

"The chauffeur is waiting for you at the desk, Monsieur . . . "

I wanted to put on my old sunglasses from twenty years ago, to show my respects for the Hayward automobile rental agency, but I finally chose the mirrored ones I always wore.

It was he. Puffy face, grey hair. I recognized him by the kind of youthful air, which he still had. Navy blue wool suit. Maroon tie.

"Good evening, Monsieur," he said to me with the reserve and weariness of a man living below his station. But maybe I was wrong and Hayward had always been in this business, even during the days with Carmen. I remembered the fleeting glance I had had of him once in a waiter's uniform. Now he looked at me with an air of indifference. No, he didn't seem to recognize me. We went out into the stifling night air. Not even a hint of a breeze. The car was parked at the corner of Rue de Castiglione and Rue Saint-Honoré. An imposing American model. Black.

"I hope this will suit you, Monsieur."

"Absolutely."

He opened the door for me and I sat in the back seat on the right side.

"Where would you like me to me to take you?"

"Oh . . . just make a tour of Paris . . . The Eiffel Tower . . . Invalides . . . Champs-Elysées . . . Pigalle . . . "

"All right, Monsieur. Where would you like to begin?"

"The Eiffel Tower . . . "

I had taken off my glasses.

He looked at me in the rearview mirror.

"Do you know Paris?"

"I haven't been back here for nearly twenty years. Has it changed much in twenty years?"

"A lot."

He said it with a note of bitterness. Even if Paris had changed a lot, Hayward himself still had the same smell of twenty years ago, and now it seemed very out-of-date: Acqua di Selva shaving lotion, I could still see the dark green bottles on the shelf in the bathroom of his apartment on Avenue Rodin.

· ·

"And now where would you like me to take you, Monsieur?"

I leaned forward, my chin almost touching his shoulder.

The odor of Acqua di Selva was making me more and more dizzy. I said to him, enunciating every word carefully:

"We'll go back to the hotel. But first, I'd like you to stop a moment at Place de l'Alma, I'll show you where."

He made another U-turn; he followed the quai and then crossed the Pont de l'Alma.

There were a lot of people on the terrace of Chez Francis. The tables were spilling into the street. A bright blue tour bus was waiting, large red letters on its side: PARIS-VISION.

"Please stop up there on the right . . . just where Rue Jean-Goujon begins . . . "

"Here?"

"Yes."

We were in front of the building where Carmen used to live.

He shut off the car and turned around to face me.

His eyes widened and he stared at me fixedly, which suddenly made him look older. Unless it was the shadow in the car: something seemed to change his face.

"I'm wondering if someone still lives in this apartment. . . ."

And I pointed at the closed shutters on the windows of Carmen's apartment, the ones that looked out over Rue Jean-Goujon.

"Perhaps you could tell me."

He stared at me uncomfortably. I was getting dizzier and dizzier. I felt like asking him about his wife. And even mentioning certain details that I knew because of those somewhat peculiar evenings when they would take us out, Carmen and me. Martine Hayward, did she still have the beauty mark on her left side, near her waist?

"We must have met here, a long time ago. . . . At the home of a Mme. Blin, wasn't that it?" he said, trying to be casual.

"Yes, I believe it was. . . ."

"She died five years ago."

Died. I don't know why, but the huge pink face of Tintin Carpentieri emerged from somewhere in my memory; I saw the image so clearly that it wasn't Hayward resting his elbow on the seat in front of me, but Carpentieri himself who was talking.

· ·

I took a deep breath.

"Ghita, tell me. . . ."

"Yes?"

"I know you're getting tired of my stirring up the past like this. . . . But how could I find a trace of . . . "

"A trace of what?"

"Oh, nothing, Ghita. But you know. . . . All those things which have been stuck in my throat for the past twenty years. . . ."

"It's not healthy, Jean. . . ."

There was a moment of silence between us.

"Haven't you found anything interesting in de Rocroy's papers?"

"Yes, of course I have, Ghita. . . ."

"Now listen to me, Jean. You know what de Rocroy always used to say to me?"

"No."

"He used to tell me that you can find anything in the phone book. If you know how to look."

I found her name stuck between the pages of my old notebook on a slip of paper where she had written it with her address at Saint-Maur. And that was the same name that could be found in the phonebook that year: 76 Boulevard Sérurier, XIXème, 208-76-68. There was only one entry under that name. There was no doubt about it, Rocroy knew what he was doing. He knew what life was about.

Nine o'clock in the morning. Even though the sun is shining brightly in a cloudless sky, it isn't too hot. No heat haze yet. The red brick building at 76 Boulevard Sérurier stands out against the green of the park, its grasses slope all the way down to the ring road.

A café is open much further down the boulevard, and I dial the number for the fifth time, 208-76-68. But no one answers. I leave the café. The boulevard is deserted. In the distance, toward the suburbs, an ochre-colored building rises up in the middle of an empty lot, a church no doubt. I sit down on a bench where the slope of the boulevard comes to an end. I think about Maillot, who used to say to me: "The climb will be hard, but afterwards you'll see. . . . The pleasure of the descent." Avenue Carnot. Rue Anatole de la Forge. Rue de l'Arc-de-Triomphe. Avenue Mac Mahon. Boulevard Sérurier. L'Avenue du Nord, it also slips into a gentle descent. All the way to the Marne.

And now I see a silhouette coming down the hill of Boulevard Sérurier carrying a suitcase, a shiny tin suitcase; its reflection makes me blink. Is it a mirage? She's coming closer and closer. It's she. I recognize the lazy walk. She's wearing a raincoat, but it's not Ludo's. This one's much darker. Emerald green.

She's almost level with me now and I stand up. We are alone, just the two of us on this lost boulevard, overwhelmed by the sun and the silence. I offer to take her suitcase.

"Thank you."

"Just coming back from vacation?"

"Yes. It's not very convenient. The métro stop is too far from my house."

We walk side by side toward the brick building at 76 Boulevard Sérurier. We don't say anything. It's starting to get very hot but she doesn't take off her raincoat. She hasn't changed much in twenty years. The same black hair, a little shorter. Blue eyes. Medium build. Pale skin. . . .

"Where have you been?"

"In the Midi."

"You're not very tanned for someone who's just coming back from the Midi."

She's coming back from even farther than the Midi. Carmen. Rocroy. La Varenne-Saint-Hilaire. Paris. All those sloping streets. . . . Her suitcase isn't heavy. I look at her out of the corner of my eye. A deep scar breaks the line of her forehead. The mark of time perhaps. Or maybe it's all that remains from one of those accidents in which everything that went before disappears, for life. Beginning with today, I too don't want to remember anything, anymore.

TRANSLATED BY SARAH BARBOUR

PIERRE FORCE
DOMINIQUE JULLIEN

Renaud Camus

Renaud Camus was born in 1946 in Chamalières, near Clermont-Ferrand. He studied law, political science, and philosophy. He spent a year at Oxford and lived in the USA as a lecturer in two universities, in New York (CUNY) and in the South (Hendricks College). He recently spent two years in Italy, as a fellow of the French Academy in Rome (Villa Medici). Renaud Camus lives in Paris, rue du Bac. Unlike most young writers, he has chosen to make his living by his writings.

Renaud Camus is not famous yet, although his last two novels (*Roman Roi*, 1985, *Roman Furieux*, 1987) have begun to attract a wider audience. Very little criticism is available on him. Roland Barthes wrote a preface to *Tricks*; Gérard Genette mentions him several times in his latest book, *Seuils* (1987), as an example for his use of pseudonyms, footnotes, and other aspects of the literary "*liminaire.*"

Roman roi was the first of Renaud Camus's novels to receive wide critical attention. While the French press unanimously agreed in proclaiming the remarkable originality of Camus's work, most critics attempted to constitute lists of authors to whom Renaud Camus owed something.[1] A comparison between those lists shows they have very few names in common: if we merge them, we come to a total of at least three dozen names. This total list, however, seems short if we compare it to the one provided by Camus himself in a previous work, *Eté*, where sixty-four titles of films, cartoons, novels, criticism, and other sorts of written material are listed. As far as *Eté* is concerned, speaking of literary influence would be a misunderstanding. The main writing technique of *Eté* is plagiarism: we read on page 383: "Here is the most original novel ever published: its author hasn't written a single line of it." In the postface of *Passage*, Renaud Camus's first novel, thirty-four authors are given credit for a quarter of the book, the rest consisting of "passages taken from the author's previous writings."[2]

---

1. Here are a few examples: Abel Hermant, Jean d'Ormesson, Maurice Donnay, Alphonse Daudet, Musil (*Le Figaro*); Arsène Lupin rewriting *Les Mémoires d'outre-tombe* (*Quinzaine littéraire*); Albert Camus's *La Chute* (Gai-pied hebdo); Stendhal, Jules Verne. Michelet, Roussel, Walter Scott, Hergé's *Le Sceptre d'Ottokar* (*Le Nouvel observateur*). The same magazine characterizes the novel as u. l. o., Unidentified Literary Object.
2. *Passage* (Paris: Flammarion, 1975), 207.

It is fairly easy to give a critical account of Camus's work, since most of the information necessary for such a purpose is already contained in the work itself. In that respect, a key to Camus's idea of literature can be found in the now canonical chapter 21 of Barthes's *S/Z* (Irony, parody); although this particular chapter is not mentioned, one other chapter to which it is intimately related (chapter 59 on Flaubert's irony) is quoted in *Eté*. In chapter 21, Roland Barthes, stating that irony acknowledges the origin of quoted sentences, defines modern writing as an attempt to go one step beyond ironical discourse. On the contrary, "*Ecriture* refuses all claims to property and, therefore, can never be ironical." According to Barthes, the quick obsolescence of literary forms leads literature to parody; forms are reused in an ironical manner. Previous authors are quoted ironically. Since nothing new can be invented, the modern text cannot avoid being a sequence of quotations from existing literature. The task left to the modern writer is "to abolish quotation marks." This is exactly what Renaud Camus does in a work like *Eté*.

Not all of Camus's works, however, belong to the category of polyphonic writing. Several essays and chronicles combine autobiographical elements with reflections on the interpretation of signs in everyday life. The *Journal d'un voyage en France* (1981), following the tradition of nineteenth-century travel diaries, offers critical additions to the *Guide bleu*, detailed descriptions of provincial cities, meticulous accounts of the author's sexual encounters, health problems, financial difficulties, a comparative study of the quality of service in French hotels, and numerous digressions of all kinds. *Tricks* (1979), *Notes achriennes* (1982) and *Chroniques achriennes* (1984) deal with homosexuality from the point of view of an author who believes that homosexuality should be a topic of no more and no less interest than any other topic related to human behavior. Camus writes in his foreword to *Tricks*, "if this books helps to make its subject banal as *subject*, it will not have been written in vain." In so saying, Camus renews the classical doctrine according to which literature has both the power and the duty to influence moral behavior.[3] This moral purpose is also clear in *Notes sur les manières du temps* (1985), which deals with manners in everyday life. Through a subtle analysis of real-life situations, Camus tries to overturn the widespread Rousseauist ideology which values sincerity and spontaneity in social behavior. His praise of rules and conventions is based on the assumption that civilization is a set of arbitrary rules which must be accepted as such. In a social context, spontaneous behavior means a diminished civilization and more brutality. Therefore, convention has a higher moral value.

Such statements could easily be translated into the vocabulary of Pascal's *Pensées*. In *Buena Vista Park* (1980), Camus quotes Pascal's thought on the hierarchy of opinions in society, which ranges from the opinion of the "populace" to that of the "clever," with an intermediate step, the "half-clever."[4] This clearly shows that Camus's praise of convention, although very difficult to distinguish from traditional, conservative discourse, is to be understood as a step beyond the questioning of convention, that is to say, in Camus's vocabulary, a third-degree

3. The forging of the word *achrien,* an arbitrary, and therefore unconnotated neologism for *homosexual,* is based on this assumption.

4. *Buena Vista Park* (Paris: Hachette, 1980), 56.

position. Camus makes a universal use of *bathmology* (Barthes's neologism for the science of degrees in speech). *Bathmology* is a key to all of Camus's productions: its applications range from considerations on manners to statements on literature itself.

Novelists born after 1968 must be divided into two families. Those who continue to repeat their lessons in Freudolinguistics and wonder about the birth of the text in the depth of their ego. And those who more modestly accept the use of the inherited language to tell intelligible stories, which is far more difficult.[5]

This statement on contemporary French literature could be a quotation from the literary supplement of *Le Figaro*. However, what is relevant is not its origin but its bathmological status. If we consider it as a third-degree opinion, it explains why Camus moved away from polyphonic writing in *Roman roi* (1983) and *Roman furieux* (1987), which belong unambiguously to the novelistic *genre*. Indeed, his allegiance to *genre* leads him to reactivate the conventional stance "this is not fiction" which characterizes eighteenth-century novels. In a television presentation of *Roman roi*, Renaud Camus boldly asserted that *Roman roi* was the true story of Roman, kind of Caronia, born in 1920 and dethroned by the Communists in 1948.[6] From this perspective, one is tempted to retrace Camus's career as a progression from criticism to fiction, in a French literary tradition which considers that, after *Bouvard et Pécuchet*, writing has become impossible.[7]

It seems, however, that such an itinerary (from sterile criticism to creation) has little to do with Camus's personal history as a writer. Camus, who published twelve books in twelve years, never felt the anxiety of the blank page. On the contrary, what strikes us is a remarkable fecundity and an obvious pleasure in writing. This is the reason why works like *Eté* do not seem to be an experimental step toward a more conventional form of fiction. One should first take into account that some passages of *Eté* contain characters and situations that are later developed in *Roman roi* and *Roman furieux*. Secondly, *Eté* is a part of *"Les Eglogues*, a trilogy in four books and seven volumes," of which three volumes are still to come. Therefore, Camus's novelistic cycle could just as well be considered a by-product of this more ambitious project, which will end with an appendix entitled *Lecture (comment m'ont écrit certains de mes livres).*[8]

Camus is not likely to abandon polyphonic writing because, even though he knows what must come after them, works like *Eté* and the *Eglogues* in general are still facing indifference and misunderstanding. As one would say in bathmological terms, a vast majority of readers are still used to first-degree novels (traditional nineteenth-century writing, perpetuated by most of today's authors), while polyphonic writing and the *Nouveau Roman* are popular among academics (second degree) and have become *cliché* in *avant-garde* circles. Therefore, according to Renaud Camus, statements like the following should be strongly supported:

5. *Eté* (Paris: Hachette, 1982), 233.
6. The book itself provides us with a map of Caronia and a genealogical tree of the royal family. A publisher's note on the back cover insists that the story is true.
7. This does not mean that people will stop writing novels, any more than Hegel meant, when he said art was a thing of the past, that there would be no more works of art.
8. A parodic reference to Raymond Roussel's famous *Comment j'ai écrit certains de mes livres.*

Literature is running late: painters are, fortunately, seldom asked what their paintings represent, but when it comes to writers, the majority of the public still wants to know what the *subject* of their novels is and *what it is about.*[9] The idea that the subject of a work should be only itself, its composition, the arrangement of its elements is now more or less admitted by the *doxa* when it comes from artists, but it is rejected if one talks about novelists.[10]

This throws light on the titles Camus gave to his polyphonic writings: *Passage, Echange. Travers, Eté (Travers II)* and those to come, (*Travers III, Travers Coda & Index, Lecture*). More than information about the contents of the books, these titles refer to a certain kind of writing. Therefore, they could well be interchangeable. *Passage, Echange, Travers*, refer to relations between meanings, not to meanings themselves. Of course, these relations become meaningful in their turn; if Camus actually wrote a text entirely made of quotations, he could reject the accusation of plagiarism by quoting Pascal: "Do not tell me I have said nothing new: the arrangement of the matter is new."[11]

In his polyphonic writings, Camus gathers sentences that are powerless, banal or *cliché* in their original context, because of the obsolescence of literary forms. As they become a part of Camus's text, these meanings play and interact in many unexpected ways. They come back to life. The reader is swiftly carried from one voice to another, from one style to its parody, from one time to another, from criticism to fiction, and vice versa. Of course, in these wanderings, the crossings of borders are so complex that the reader never exactly knows where he is. In *Eté*, Camus uses up to twelve levels of footnotes, making the distinction between note and main text irrelevant. This technique and others of the same kind lead to what we can only call a Balkanization of writing.

In fact, saying that these heterogeneous fragments of meanings are gathered to become Camus's text is already saying too much. Modern writing, says Barthes, abolishes the notion of literary property. Camus, in a move that reminds us of some very ancient conceptions of literature, tends to abolish the notion of author. Camus's use of pseudonyms does not aim at hiding a personality or a private life. The opposition usually made between literary confession and impersonal literature is irrelevant in his case. There is not even a clear distinction between Camus's own name and the various pseudonyms he uses. These form a continuum that goes from slight alterations of the author's officially registered name (Renaud Camus) to names which are totally different (Jean-Renaud Camus, J. R. G. Le Camus, Renaud Camus & Tony Duparc, Jean-Renaud Camus et Tony Duvert, Denise du Parc, etc.). Not included in this list are those pseudonyms to be found in the text itself: anagrams, such as Duane Markus.

The meaning of all these games is clear. Renaud Camus (the author), in the way Borges once wrote a story called *Borges and I*, is a character, if not several

9. In English in the original.
10. *Eté*, 123. Camus immediately gives the antithesis of this statement in a footnote: "Of course; this because language is, by nature, and intrinsically, representative. On the other hand, a literature that would give up speaking of the world and would refer only to itself, would, in that meaningless specularity, encounter only derision and death."
11. Quoted in *Eté*, 231.

characters, in his own books. Therefore, it is not surprising to find sentences like this one in *Eté*: "Ronald, Duane, Renaud, and I took a taxi with Markus to go to his house.[12]

It may seem paradoxical to assert that, in total, Camus's ultimate goal is simplicity. But as Barthes says, "speaking *simply* belongs to a higher art, writing."[13] One may also be surprised by Barthes's assessment of Camus's writing:

> Our period interprets a great deal, but Renaud Camus's narratives are neutral, they do not participate in the game of interpretation. They are surfaces without shadows, *without ulterior motives.*[14]

Obviously, there is a great deal of interpretation in Camus's writing. The *Voyage en France* and *Notes sur les manières du temps* are entirely hermeneutic. *Buena Vista Park* is a treatise on interpretation. But those works may not be interpreted in the usual way because they are based on a virtue which belongs both to ethics and hermeneutics: good will. Common interpretation is forever in search of hidden motives and intentions. Its favorite tool and highest value is supicion.[15] Renaud Camus, on the contrary, one step beyond sarcastic distance, considers meaning with kindness. The way he reports the sometimes naive words of his sexual partners, and the way he quotes texts of various origins, show the same absence of irony. What common interpretation would consider ridiculous, pedantic, naive, impossible to say, boring, too difficult to understand, or *passé* finds its place in Camus's writing.

Camus's slogan on interpretation could be: less is more. Meaning dissolves itself in commentary. Therefore, Camus chose silent ways of interpretation. Rearranging old material is already all the interpretation we need. It is also all we need to produce new meaning.

BIBLIOGRAPHY

Eglogues (Unfinished trilogy in four books and seven volumes:
    Passage, by Renaud Camus (Paris: Flammarion, 1975).
    Echange, by Denis Duparc (Paris: Flammarion, 1976).
    Travers, by Renaud Camus & Tony Duparc (Paris: Hachette, 1978).
    Eté (Travers II), by Jean-Renaud Camus & Denis Duvert (Paris: Hachette, 1982).

NOVELS

Roman roi (Paris: P.O.L., 1983).
Roman furieux, by Jean-Renaud Camus (Paris: P.O.L., 1986).

12. *Eté*, 307.
13. Preface to *Tricks*, trans. Richard Howard (New York: St. Martin's Press, 1981), vii.
14. Op. cit., viii.
15. A literary expression of this attitude would be Nathalie Sarraute's *L'Ere du soupçon*.

290 Yale French Studies

AUTOBIOGRAPHY

Tricks (Paris: Hachette, 1979).
Jounal d'un voyage en France (Paris: Hachette, 1981).
Journal romain (Paris: P.O.L., 1987).

MISCELLANEOUS

Buena Vista Park (Paris: Hachette, 1980).
Notes achriennes (Paris: Hachette, 1982).
Chroniques achriennes (Paris: P.O.L., 1984).
Notes sur les manières du temps (Paris: P.O.L., 1985).

RENAUD CAMUS

*Buena Vista Park**

Le Bandeau du Maréchal Ney

J'ai pour la première fois eu le sentiment que sur la plupart des points il n'y avait que deux positions possibles, mais qu'il importait de distinguer des *niveaux* à l'intérieur de chacune, lorsque j'avais quatorze ou quinze ans et lisais une *Histoire des Deux Restaurations,* probablement celle du vicomte de Vaulabelle. Il s'agissait de l'exécution du maréchal Ney. Le maréchal, au moment d'être fusillé, avait refusé le bandeau qu'on lui proposait. Et c'est sur cette figure du condamné à mort et du bandeau que s'était greffée ma réflexion, ou ma rêverie. Le condamné à mort ne peut qu'accepter ou refuser le bandeau. Mais il peut prendre l'une ou l'autre décision pour des raisons tout à fait différentes:

1) Le condamné à mort accepte le bandeau, parce qu'on le lui propose et qu'il ne songe pas à le refuser.

2) Le condamné à mort refuse le bandeau, parce qu'il est courageux et veut voir la mort en face (Ney, *etc.*).

3) Le condamné à mort accepte le bandeau parce que la position *2* lui parait ridiculement banale, er fastidieuse cette tradition éculée du condamné à mort qui refuse le bandeau pour montrer qu'il est courageux et peut regarder la mort en face.

4) Le condamné à mort refuse le bandeau, bien qu'il soit tout à fait d'accord avec la position *3,* parce que ça l'intéresse de voir ce qui se passe.

Buena Vista Park (Paris: Hachette, 1980), 14–16. This passage is reprinted with the kind permission of Hachette.

5) Le condamné à mort accepte le bandeau, parce qu'il craint que la position qu'il aurait eu tendance à adopter, la quatrième, ne soit confondue avec la seconde, et que sa simple préférence pour une absence de bandeau ne passe pour une démonstration ridicule à ses yeux d'héroïsme codifié.

6) Le condamné à mort refuse le bandeau, parce que la position 5, au moment où il va s'y ranger, lui parait témoigner d'un souci exagéré de l'opinion des observateurs, et qu'il lui est indifférent que ceux-ci, et l'Histoire éventuellement, confondent sa simple préférence avec une démonstration de courage stéréotypé.

7) et II. *1)* Le condamné à mort accepte le bandeau, parce que toutes les précédentes tergiversations, auxquelles il s'est rapidement livré, lui paraissent absurdes, et vulgaire leur affectée subtilité, qu'on lui propose le bandeau et que le plus simple est de l'accepter.

II. *2)* Le condamné à mort refuse le bandeau parce que, revenu à II. *1)*, il n'en préfère pas moins affronter la mort sans bandeau, et qu'il n'a pas l'intention de négliger sa simple préférence pour le seul souci de démontrer, ne serait-ce qu'à ses propres yeux, qu'il est bien au-delà des banales subtilités de la bathmologie avant la lettre.[1]

---

1. Sur la *méta-bathmologie,* dont relèverait II.*1)* et la suite, *cf.* infra, *Vuitton.*

Buena Vista Park

Marshal Ney's Blindfold

The first time I had the feeling that on most points there are only two possible positions, but that it was important to distinguish levels within each one, was when I was fourteen or fifteen years old and was reading a *History of the Two Restorations,* probably the one by the Viscount of Vaulabelle. It was about Marshal Ney's execution. At the moment he was to be shot, the marshal refused the blindfold he had been offered. And it was on the face of the condemned man and the blindfold that my reflection (or my daydream) hung. The condemned man can only accept or refuse the blindfold. But he can make one or the other decision for quite different reasons:

1) The condemned man accepts the blindfold, because it is offered to him and he doesn't think of refusing it.

2) The condemned man refuses the blindfold, because he is courageous and wants to look death in the face (Ney, etc.).

3) The condemned man accepts the blindfold because position #2 seems ridiculously banal to him, and the worn-out tradition of the condemned man who refuses the blindfold to show that he is courageous and can look death in the face seems tiresome.

4) The condemned man refuses the blindfold, even though he is in complete agreement with position #3, because he's interested in seeing what's happening.

5) The condemned man accepts the blindfold, because he's afraid that the position he might have tended to adopt, the fourth one, will be confused with the second, and that his simple preference for the absence of a blindfold will pass for a ridiculous (in his eyes) demonstration of codified heroism.

6) The condemned man refuses the blindfold, because position #5, at the moment he's going to adopt it, seems to him to display an exaggerated concern for the opinion of the observers, and because it is indifferent to him that these people and History (eventually) confuse his simple preference with a display of stereotyped courage.

7) and II.1) The condemned man accepts the blindfold, because all the preceding tergiversations in which he has quickly engaged seem absurd to him, and their affected subtlety vulgar, because he is being offered the blindfold and the simplest thing is to accept it.

II. 2) The condemned man refuses the blindfold because, going back to II.1), he nonetheless prefers to confront death without a blindfold, and he has no intention of disregarding his own simple preference just so as to demonstrate, even if only in his own eyes, that he is far above the banal subtleties of bathmology before its time.[1]

TRANSLATED BY CHRISTOPHER RIVERS

---

1. On meta-bathmology, on which II.1, etc., cf., infra, Vuitton.

RENAUD CAMUS

Journal d'un voyage en France*

[18 octobre: *je me lève ici pour chercher ce livre et relire encore le même chapitre. Au passage, je pousse le bouton de France-Musique: deuxième sonate de Fauré. Pas le courage de couper. Puis, voix familiè- res: Claude Maupomé, qui était toujours au premier rang du séminaire, au Collège de France, reçoit dans son émission « Comment l'entendez- vous? » Romaric Sulger-Büel, grand ami de Barthes. Je retrouve mieux celui-ci dans ce hasard que dans des lignes d'une agressivité que je ne lui ai pas connue. J'encourrai d'ailleurs bien davantage cette ire, et ma façon de voyager, et ce livre, que le malheureux Guide Bleu, qui pro- cédait déjà, à l'époque, « d'une mythologie dépassée par une partie de la bourgeoisie elle-même ». Vingt-cinq ans plus tard, il est frappé carré- ment d'archaïsme. Le discours qu'il soutient (qu'il soutenait, car aux rédacteurs des nouvelles éditions on a fait lire le texte de Barthes: je préfère les anciennes) n'est plus, loin de là, le discours en place. Ren- versé, comme on le dit très justement d'une autorité, il n'est pas inno- cent de pouvoir, mais il n'en est pas gros. Que le sens n'a ici qu'une importance secondaire, bien sûr; c'est la situation qui compte. Si je trouve obscène et menaçant le discours sur le voyage comme moyen de « se trouver » et sur le rapport « authentique » avec les gens du pays, tu vois, en vivant exactement comme eux, ce n'est pas parce qu'il est naïf ou faux, c'est parce qu'il est empoissé d'approbation générale. Je l'habi- terai sans doute avec plaisir quand il sera passé. En attendant, il m'ins- pire la même espèce d'écœurement que cette femme dans une librairie très animée, hier, qui feuilletant des livres à la table des nouveautés criait très fort, à l'adresse d'un ami assez éloigné, en lui montrant « le dernier Yourcenar »: « Ça, tu vois, c't' un truc que j'lirais bien. J' suis sûre qu' c'est formidable. Elle est géniale cette bonne femme. » Qui parle là, et à si grand bruit! De qui est-ce l'opinion! Quelle importance qu'elle*

*Journal d'un voyage en France (Paris: P.O.L.-Hachette, 1981), 106–07. This passage is reprinted with the kind permission of P.O.L-Hachette.

294

soit juste ou non? Elle est oppressante parce qu'elle a l'insolence et la complaisance grasse d'une année de campagne publicitaire réussie. Ceux qui ont aimé tout seuls Yourcenar, en dehors des programmations médiatisées, ne le proclament pas d'un bout à l'autre des librairies.

Tandis que d'aller voir la maison natale de la mère de Félix Arvers me touche. Je suis l'ami de tout ce qui est tombé. Le shah d'Iran que j'avais tellement haï, j'ai tremblé qu'il ne fût livré aux sévices de ses successeurs. Et la culture bourgeoise du début du siècle, si niaise et bouvard-et-pécuchetesque qu'elle ait pu être, je lui trouve des qualités maintenant qu'elle est effondrée. Absurde, il arrivait qu'elle ignorât les œuvres mêmes au profit de leur aura. On s'émouvait d'une villa ridicule où René Boylesve avait écrit un roman qu'on n'avait pas lu mais qu'une cousine avait reçu en premier cadeau d'un jeune officier de marine, aujourd'hui son fiancé (mais non, c'était Claude Farrère). On apposait consciencieusement des plaques de marbre sur telle demeure de Nietzsche dont toute la pensée vous riait au nez. Et tout récemment encore, à faire le pèlerinage d'Illiers, on se croyait dispensé de lire Proust. Mais l'erreur, l'oubli, les rapprochements abusifs, les incursions aventurées, une curiosité formidable et le désir créaient un espace heureux du savoir, immense à la fois et intime, chaleureux, où le monde et les livres, à force d'échanges périlleux, indéfendables et réussis, finissaient par ne constituer plus qu'un Eden de phrases où promener une âme romanesque, mortelle et policée. Les noms de rues, les villages, un paysage qu'avait peint Daubigny sur un petit tableau dont je me demande bien ce qu'il est devenu, par exemple, une aïeule un peu légère (« Oui, mais elle, au moins, c'était avec le duc d'Aumale! » dit son petit-fils), un souvenir inexact attribué à un personnage erroné, ces fils inégaux tissaient une tapisserie familière, trop grande pour les appartements d'aujourd'hui. Qu'ont-ils de français, ces lycéens qui ne connaissent pas le prénom de leur grand-père et pour qui le futur général Drouot n'a jamais appris ses leçons à la lueur du four de boulanger paternel? A-t-on finalement jeté aux orties le vase de Soissons, sous prétexte qu'il n'avait jamais été brisé? Cambre la tête, vieux si courbe! Si vous ne voulez garder d'une culture que ses vérités, vous n'aurez plus rien.]

Journal d'un voyage en France

18 October: I get up to go get the book and reread the same chapter again. On the way, I push the button on the radio for France-Musique: Fauré's Second Sonata. I don't have the heart to turn it off. Then, familiar voices: Claude Maupomé, who was always in the first row at the seminar at the Collège de France, is welcoming Romaric Sulger-Büel, great friend of

Barthes's, on his program "What do you think of it?" I recognize Suger-Büel much better in this happenstance than in some writings of an aggressivity I hadn't known him to have. Furthermore, I'd much sooner incur this wrath, and my way of travelling, and this book, than the wretched *Guide Bleu*, which already functioned in its day on the basis of "a mythology abandoned by a part of the bourgeoisie itself." Twenty-five years later, it is unquestionably archaic. The discourse that it sustains (that it sustained, because they made the editors of the new editions read Barthes's text: I prefer the old ones) is no way near the present discourse (far from it). Overthrown, as is said aptly about authority, it is not entirely without power, but it's not rife with it either. Certainly, meaning here has only a secondary importance; it's the situation that counts. If I find obscene and threatening the discourse on travel as a means of "finding oneself" and on the "authentic" relations with the people of the country, you know, by living exactly like them, it's not because it's naive or false, it's because it's been stuck with general approval. I will no doubt live in it with pleasure when it's passé. In the meantime, it inspires in me the same sort of nausea as that woman in a very crowded bookstore yesterday who, while leafing through books on a table of new releases, screamed very loudly to a friend at some distance, showing him "the latest Yourcenar": "You know, here's something I could really get into. I bet it's first rate. This dame is great." Who is speaking here, and so loudly? Whose opinion is this? What does it matter if it's right or not? It's oppressive because it has all the insolence and fatuous complaisance of a year-long successful publicity campaign. Those who loved Yourcenar all by themselves, outside of mediatized schemes, don't proclaim it from one end to the other of bookstores.

Whereas I am moved by going to see the house in which the mother of Felix Arvers was born. I am the friend of all that's fallen. I trembled that the shah of Iran, whom I had hated so much, would be given over to the cruelties of his successors. And, as foolish and bouvard-et-pecuchet-esque as it might have been, I find certain good qualities in the bourgeois culture of the turn of the century now that it has collapsed. Absurdly, it happened that this culture was unaware of the works themselves in favor of their aura. They were moved by a ridiculous villa where René Boylesve had written a novel they hadn't read but which their cousin had received as her first gift from a young naval officer, now her fiancé (but no, that was Claude Farrère). They conscientiously placed marble plaques on such-and-such a residence of Nietzsche, whose entire thought laughed in their faces. And still quite recently, making the pilgrimage to Illiers dispensed one from reading Proust. But error, oblivion, extravagant comparisons, hazardous expeditions, a formidable curiosity, and desire created a blissful space for knowledge, at once immense and intimate, warm, where the world and books, by dint of many perilous, indefensible and

successful exchanges, finally constituted nothing but an Eden of sentences in which a romantic, mortal, and refined soul could wander. Street
names, villages, a landscape painted by Daubigny in a little picture which
seems to be lost, damn it, a slightly flighty ancestress ("Yes, but at least in
her case it was with the duke d'Aumale!" says her grandson), an inaccurate memory attributed to an erroneous character, these unequal threads
wove a familiar tapestry, too large for today's apartments. How are they
French, these teenagers who don't know their grandfather's first name
and for whom the future General Drouot never learned his lessons by the
light of his father's bakery oven? Have we finally thrown out the Soissons
vase with the rubbish, on the pretext that it was never broken? Hang your
head, gnarled old man! If you want to retain only the truths of a culture,
you'll have nothing left.

TRANSLATED BY CHRISTOPHER RIVERS

RENAUD CAMUS

Eté†

*De 16 à 19 ans, j'ai été parfaitement mythomane. A Oxford, j'arborais un nom très aristocratique. Il arriva que les animateurs d'une petite revue vaguement poétique me demandent quelques pages. Je n'avais rien à leur offrir, malgrès mes assurances. J'étais certain, pourtant, qu'ils ne connaissaient rien de Levet, et je décidai de m'approprier quelques poèmes de lui, choisis parmi les *Cartes postales*. Mais je m'en souvenais mal et la mince plaquette, là-bas, était bien sûr introuvable. N'importe. J'ai ainsi débuté dans les lettres en publiant sous un faux nom des textes fautifs qui n'étaient pas de moi.

Cet épisode a longtemps fait ma honte. J'avoue qu'il m'enchante aujourd'hui, et d'avoir atteint d'emblée à une telle perfection dans l'apocryptie.
. . . .

*On s'appuiera avec profit, pour la lecture des *Eglogues*, sur:
—*Les Eglogues.*
—L'ensemble de l'œuvre de Roland Barthes, et particulièrement *Roland Barthes par Roland Barthes, S/Z,* ou encore la préface à un roman de Loti, parue d'abord en italien et reprise dans les *Nouveaux Essais critiques.*

DÈS LA PAGE 13 DU RAPPORT, C'EST-À-DIRE DÈS LE PREMIER ÉNONCÉ DES « FAITS », NOUS SOMMES INFORMÉS QU'« IL ESSAYA DE TUER LE MAJOR-GÉNÉRAL EDWIN A. WALKER (DÉMISSIONNAIRE, *U.S. ARMY*) EN UTILISANT LE FUSIL QU'IL AVAIT COMMANDÉ PAR LA POSTE UN MOIS PLUS TÔT SOUS UN FAUX NOM.

—L'ensemble de l'œuvre de Robbe-Grillet, et particulièrement *La Ja-*

†*Eté (Travers II)* (Paris: P.O.L.-Hachette, 1982), 102–03, 352–54. These passages are reprinted with the kind permission of P.O.L.-Hachette.

lousie, L'Année dernière à Marienbad, La Maison de rendez-vous, Projet pour une révolution à New York, Souvenirs du Triangle d'or.

—L'ensemble de l'œuvre de Simon, et particulièrement *La Bataille de Pharsale, Orion aveugle* ou *Les Corps conducteurs.*

—Les travaux théoriques de Jean Ricardou, *Problèmes du Nouveau Roman, Pour une théorie du Nouveau Roman,* etc., ainsi que, par exemple, *L'Observatoire de Cannes* ou *Révolutions minuscules.*

—Les textes des différents colloques de Cerisy, tels qu'ils ont été publiés dans la collection 10/18, sur le Nouveau Roman en général, Simon, Robbe-Grillet ou Roland Barthes.

—Le « cycle indien » de Duras: *Le Vice-consul, India Song, La Femme du Gange,* etc., et *Le Ravissement de Lol V. Stein.*

—Les biographies de Proust, de Roussel, de Mallarmé, de Joyce, de James, de Pessoa, de Loti, de George Sand, de Levet, de Mahler, de Matisse, de Wagner, de Duparc, d'Hugo Wolf, etc., etc.

—*Pale Fire, Lolita, Ada, Indiana, Bouvard et Pécuchet, A la Recherche du temps perdu, Ulysse, Le Mariage de Loti, Le Journal d'un fou, Le Nez, Lionnerie, William Wilson, La Mort à Venise, Tristan, Le Horla, L'Aleph, Le Sentiment géographique, Journal d'un Voyage en France, Buena Vista Park,* etc.

—Des textes et essais critiques tels que *Le Schizo et les langues,* de Wolfson, *La Tour de Babil,* de Michel Pierssens, *La Seconde main,* d'Antoine Compagnon, *La Fourche, Le Récit spéculaire, Prénoms de Personne, Le Nom et le corps, Glas, Scribble, Folle vérité, Chercher le monstre,* etc.

GESTURES, THE POSITION OF HANDS, LEGS, BODY, LANGUAGE, WHICH BECAME THE GREATNESS OF LANGE'S PHOTOGRAPHS, BEGIN TO SHOW IN THE WORK SHE DID IN THE STUDIO. GUSTAVE III LE MAGNIFIQUE, L'AMI DES ARTS, EST ASSASSINÉ EN SORTANT DE L'OPÉRA. CE FAISANT, L'ÉCRITURE SE RÉVÈLE A-CAUSALE, BÂTARDE OU PARRICIDE.

—Les différents rapports d'Amnesty International sur la torture dans le monde.

—Tout ce qui a été écrit sur les crimes politiques dont les Etats-Unis ont été le théâtre depuis 1963.

—Les films noirs américains des années trente ou quarante tels que *Dark Passage* ou *Key Largo; Histoire immortelle, l'Immortelle, Prima della Rivoluzione, Senso, La Mort à Venise, Ludwig, Les Trois jours du Condor,* etc.

—*Il Ritorno d'Ulysse in patria, Orfeo, Orlando, Rinaldo, Tristan et Isolde, Parsifal,* etc., et la littérature les concernant.

Etc. On pourra s'appuyer sur *Les Eglogues* pour lire, voir ou entendre *Les Eglogues* et toutes les œuvres ci-dessus mentionnées, feuilleter journaux et magazines, regarder la télévision, rêver, écouter sa famille, ses amis, les gens de la rue, les hommes politiques ou « l'inconnu que le hasard a placé à côté de vous ».

Eté

*From 16 to 19 years old, I was a perfect liar. At Oxford, I sported a very aristocratic name. It happened that the promoters of a small and vaguely poetic journal asked me to submit a few pages. In spite of my assurances, I had nothing to offer them. I was certain, however, that they knew nothing of Levet's, and I decided to appropriate a few of his poems, chosen from *Cartes postales.* But I didn't remember them very well and the slim volume was of course impossible to find over there. No matter. I thus made my literary debut by publishing under a false name faulty texts that weren't even my own. This episode was my shame for a long time. I confess that I now find it enchanting, having attained from the beginning such perfection in apocrypty.

. . . .

*It would be worthwhile, for reading the *Eclogues,* to read the following:

—*The Eclogues.*
—The Complete Works of Roland Barthes, and particularly *Roland*

Barthes par Roland Barthes, S/Z, or even the preface to a novel by Loti, first published in Italian and reprinted in *New Critical Essays.*

AS OF PAGE 13 OF THE REPORT, I.E., AS OF THE FIRST ANNOUNCEMENT OF THE "FACTS," WE ARE INFORMED THAT "HE TRIED TO KILL MAJOR-GENERAL EDWIN A. WALKER (U.S. ARMY, RESIGNED) USING THE GUN HE HAD ORDERED BY MAIL A MONTH EARLIER UNDER A FALSE NAME.

—The Complete Works of Robbe-Grillet, and particularly *La Jalousie, L'Année dernière à Marienbad, La Maison de rendez-vous, Projet pour une révolution à New York, Souvenirs du Triangle d'or.*

—The complete works of Simon, and particularly *La Bataille de Pharsale, Orion aveugle* or *Les Corps conducteurs.*

—The theoretical works of Jean Ricardou, *Problèmes du Nouveau Roman. Pour une théorie du Nouveau Roman,* etc., as well as, for example, *L'Observatoire de Cannes* or *Révolutions miniscules.*

—The texts of the various Cerisy colloquia, as they were published in the *10/18* series, on the New Novel in general, Simon, Robbe-Grillet, or Roland Barthes.

—Duras's "Indian cycle": *Le Vice-consul, India Song, La Femme du Gange,* etc., and *Le Ravissement de Lol V. Stein.*

—The biographies of Proust, Roussel, Mallarmé, Joyce, James, Pessoa, Loti, George Sand, Levet, Mahler, Matisse, Wagner, Duparc, Hugo Wolf, etc., etc.

—*Pale Fire, Lolita, Ada, Indiana, Bouvard et Pécuchet, A la recherche du temps perdu, Ulysses, Le Mariage de Loti, Le Journal d'un fou, Le Nez, Lionnerie, William Wilson, La Mort à Venise, Tristan, Le Horla, L'Aleph, Le Sentiment géographique, Journal d'un Voyage en France, Buena Vista Park,* etc.

—Texts and Critical essays such as *Le Schizo et les langues* by Wolfson, *La Tour de Babil* by Michel Pierssens, *La Seconde main* by Antoine Compagnon, *La Fourche, Le Récit spéculaire, Prénoms de Personne, Le Nom et le corps, Glas, Scribble, Folle vérité, Chercher le monstre,* etc.

—GESTURES, THE POSITION OF HANDS, LEGS, BODY, LANGUAGE, WHICH BECAME THE GREATNESS OF LANGE'S PHOTOGRAPHS, BEGIN TO SHOW IN THE WORK SHE DID IN THE STUDIO. GUSTAVE III THE MAGNIFICENT, FRIEND OF

THE ARTS, IS ASSASSINATED COMING OUT OF THE OPERA. IN DOING THIS, WRITING REVEALS ITSELF TO BE ACAUSAL, SPURIOUS, OR PARRICIDAL.

—The various Amnesty International reports on torture in the world.

—Everything written on political crimes in the United States since 1963.

—The American "films noirs" from the thirties and forties such as *Dark Passage*, or *Key Largo*; *Histoire immortelle*, *L'Immortelle*, *Prima della Rivoluzione*, *Senso*, *La Mort à Venise*, *Ludwig*, *Les Trois jours du Condor*, etc.

—*Il Ritorno d'Ulysse in patria*, *Orfeo*, *Orlando*, *Rinaldo*, *Tristan et Isolde*, *Parsifal*, etc., and the literature concerning them.

Etc. One could also rely on *The Eclogues* to read, see, or hear *The Eclogues* and all the above-mentioned works, to leaf through newspapers and magazines, watch television, dream, listen to one's family, friends, people in the street, politicians or "the stranger whom chance has placed next to you."

TRANSLATED BY CHRISTOPHER RIVERS

RENAUD CAMUS

Roman Roi*

Roman néglige les fauteuils à hauts dossiers, noirs autour d'une bande de tapisserie aux couleurs qui furent vives. Il aime s'asseoir sur la plus haute marche de l'escalier de fer. De là, au pied des clairs vitraux, il peut tout voir, les arrivées et les départs, le jardin, la prairie, l'avenue qui descend vers Hörst, le fleuve, son île, la vallée, la forêt, la montagne, le ciel. Sa chienne Vanya est assise à côté de lui. Il ouvre sur ses genoux de grands volumes, recueils semestriels des numéros hebdomadaires de *L'Illustration*, par exemple, ou de *Lectures pour tous*, dont certaines images lui sont plus familières que celles de sa propre vie; atlas, encyclopédies, *Gazette des Beaux-Arts*, reproductions monochromes des plus fameux tableaux du monde. Le temps est suspendu comme le lieu.

Mais l'année ne se passe pas tout entière au manoir d'Arkel. La Russénie, pour marquer son rattachement au royaume, a offert à la famille royale un immense domaine, Toreev, ancienne propriété d'une famille russe, les princes Otchakovsky. Le château est un grand bâtiment rectangulaire, néo-classique, tel qu'il en abonde dans les plaines russes, et assez peu différent, au fond, des aristocratiques demeures du Sud, aux Etats-Unis. Il est précédé d'un péristyle, dont le fronton triangulaire est soutenu par dix colonnes doriques, blanches. Autour de lui s'étendent des bâtiments d'exploitation, des champs de blé ou de maïs, des forêts de bouleaux, des étangs.

Roman, sa mère et sa grand-mère, passent là, chaque année, un mois au moins, au printemps, et quelquefois reviennent pour quelques semaines en automne. Le soir, paysans et paysannes viennent offrir des concerts champêtres. Au-dessus de leurs longues et larges jupes et de leurs pantalons bouffants, très blancs, leurs blouses, blanches également, sont rehaussées de gilets richement brodés, éclatants. Ils dansent autour

Roman Roi (Paris: P.O.L.-Hachette, 1983), 87–90, 182–84. These passages are reprinted with the kind permission of P.O.L.-Hachette.

d'un grand feu, au son d'un violon suraigu, endiablé, et ils chantent dans une langue incompréhensible.

Le séjour d'été à Sibor, sur la mer Noire, a eu aussi, tout d'abord, des raisons politiques. Il s'agissait de témoigner de l'intérêt de la dynastie pour une autre province nouvelle, l'Esthénie. On en profita pour s'offrir une résidence balnéaire. Ce ne fut pas chose aisée. La côte esthénienne est basse, marécageuse, dépourvue d'ombrage. N'importe. Le Régent décida, dès 1920, d'y établir, autour d'un minuscule hameau de pêcheurs, Sibor, une station de bains de mer. Sa famille contribuerait au lancement. On fit les plans de la ville nouvelle, on asséna tant bien que mal le site choisi, on traça même, sur le sol, des avenues que ne bordèrent longtemps aucun bâtiment. Toutes convergeaient vers la villa royale, qui commença à s'édifier en 1921. La princesse Marie, dans un effort pour sortir de la neurasthénie qui la rongeait, accepta la responsabilité de l'entreprise. Contrainte entre la nécessité de marquer la prééminence de la villa sur ses voisines et les exigences d'une discrétion de bon aloi et d'une modestie qui lui était naturelle, elle adopta un parti singulier, dont le résultat ne cessa jamais d'étonner les visiteurs, même ceux qui l'avaient contemplé déjà souvent. La configuration générale était celle d'une maison bourgeoise telle qu'aurait pu en faire bâtir une famille de gros commerçants raisonnablement modernistes de Back ou de Bucarest, mais toutes les proportions avaient été pour le moins doublées. Il n'y avait pas un très grand nombre de fenêtres, par exemple, mais elles étaient d'une taille vertigineuse, et un homme normal avait du mal à en atteindre, de la main, le loquet. Le trouble qu'on éprouvait à observer la maison à partir de la longue perspective qui y menait était multiplié, on l'imagine, pour ses habitants, dont toutes les perceptions étaient soumises à des remises en cause d'autant plus singulières que tous les matériaux employés à la construction, ou la décoration, s'ingéniaient à dissimuler leur somptuosité pour se donner l'apparence de leurs propres imitations.

Néanmoins la famille royale commença en 1925 à passer là une partie des mois d'été. Des terrasses à balustrades blanches, trop élevées, comme tout le reste, dominaient une vaste plage en pente très douce, et bien entendu fermée au public, dont la protégeaient, à chaque extrémité, de hauts grillages de fer plongeant dans la mer, et de nombreux policiers.

La reine Amélie avait toujours déploré l'isolement intellectuel de la Caronie, et que les principales phases du développement culturel de l'Europe ne s'y fussent jamais fait sentir que de manière feutrée, ou diluée. A Sibor, elle crut trouver matière à un rapprochement audacieux, mais selon elle parfaitement légitime, de ces rivages dénudés avec la littérature la plus classique. Ils étaient, soutenait-elle, le lieu véritable de l'exil d'Ovide. C'était là qu'il avait écrit *Les Tristes*. Les érudits sont à peu près unanimes, certes, à placer la Tomes antique sur le site de l'actuelle Constanza roumaine, et le séjour d'Ovide au sud du Danube. Mais ils se sont toujours étonnés, c'est vrai, et jusqu'à Wilamowitz-Mollendorf, de la rigueur des conditions climatiques hivernales que décrit le poète, et des menaces constantes dont il fait état d'invasions barbares, les unes et les autres peu vraisemblables à la latitude de Constanza. L'explication la plus généralement proposée, en particulier par les latinistes roumains, c'est qu'Ovide voulait faire plaindre son sort et qu'il en a exagéré la cruauté. L'explication de la reine Amélie, c'était que Tomes devait être identifiée avec Sibor, où les hivers sont effectivement rigoureux et où la présence romaine, attestée par quelques maigres vestiges, ne fut jamais que précaire. Aussitôt que cette conviction se fut emparée de son esprit, tout, pour la vieille souveraine, devint signe et l'étaya, que ce fût des lieux ou du livre. Elle ne doutait pas d'occuper le rivage des *Tristes*. Et pour les habitants de la villa royale, l'espace qui les entourait, et qui ne fut long-temps qu'un vaste chantier assez morne, frémissait des ïambes mélan-coliques de l'illustre exilé.

. . . .

Le 7 décembre, le père et le fils sont à Nemheïd, en Vésanie. On respire. Nemheïd est une cité éminemment « pierriste », elle l'a montré en s'offrant la première à l'exilé lors de son retour de France. Le Roi lui en est reconnaissant. On est entre amis. Le service d'ordre peut se relâcher un peu. Les terroristes n'ont jamais tenté ici aucune action, la folie meur-trière des derniers mois n'a pratiquement pas touché la province. Le soleil est éclatant. Pierre et Roman, précédés du gouverneur de la Vésanie, se rendent à l'hôtel de ville en voiture découverte, malgré le froid, pour mieux s'offrir aux acclamations de la population, très dense le long de l'avenue de l'Armistice. Plusieurs fois des hommes ou des femmes s'a-vancent près des portières pour montrer au Roi des enfants, ou pour leur montrer le Roi, ou pour mieux le voir eux-mêmes. On les repousse sans brutalité. L'ambiance est chaleureuse et cordiale. Pierre sourit, de son irrésistible sourire. Il est toujours l'enfant chéri du pays, celui à qui l'on pardonne toujours tout. Rien de grave ne peut arriver aussi longtemps qu'il est là.

Un des curieux s'est approché davantage. Il est même monté sur le marchepied de la voiture et il s'agrippe d'une main à la carrosserie. Il est jeune, il a un visage agréable et carré, ses cheveux sont séparés par une raie au milieu du front, il a une moustache épaisse et très noire. Lui n'a aucun enfant à présenter au Roi. Il est fort, il s'accroche à la portière, d'une seule main, quand déjà un garde du corps le ceinture. Roman n'est pas sûr de l'ordre exact des événements, il ne se souvient que d'une paradoxale impression d'extrême lenteur, et même d'une espèce de si-multanéité, hallucinante, des causes et des effets. Le revolver, avant, après, il ne saurait dire. Mais le revolver, très présent, énorme, béant, son trou noir, un coup part, la détonation formidable, le Roi est blessé dans la région du cœur mais il semble surtout, oui, c'est exactement le mot, « estomaqué ». Des cuisses il s'est reculé dans son siège, il se penche en avant. Un deuxième coup, en plein visage. L'invraisemblance de la chose. L'homme paraît n'avoir peur de rien, il ne doit pas tenir à sauver sa vie, il n'espère pas fuir, il a tout son temps. Mais comment ne l'arrache-t-on pas à la portière? Toute la scène a dû se passer plus vite que Roman ne la vit. Le haut du corps de son père est cette fois-ci reparti vers l'arrière, contre le dossier du siège, et il penche vers la gauche, vers l'endroit où il est assis lui. Un troisième coup, tiré maintenant tandis que le canon est tout contre la tempe du Roi. La tête achève d'éclater. Roman est éclaboussé de sang, de débris de cervelle qui glissent lentement le long de son uniforme, et surtout cet objet qui a giclé avec ses filaments sur son ventre puis entre ses cuisses c'est un œil, un œil de son père.

Il craint d'écraser cette chose qu'il ne veut pas voir, qu'il ne voudrait pas toucher mais dont il ne peut pas supporter un instant de plus la présence entre ses cuisses, il s'en saisit pour l'éloigner au plus vite, tant pis, il en a une horreur plus grande que du canon du pistolet, il la touche, une seconde, trois secondes, pour s'en débarrasser il l'a prise dans sa main, il la jette le plus loin qu'il le peut, dans la foule, il est maintenant dressé en arrière, jambes tendues, arc-bouté contre le dossier du siège, il a toujours aimé cette odeur de cuir bien entretenu, ce n'est pas la peur, c'est pour échapper à ce corps gigantesque qui tombe sur lui et dont la tête n'est plus une tête mais un magma de chairs en lambeaux, d'os brisés, de matière grise liquide qu'il sent contre sa hanche, il va tomber de la voiture, il est dans des bras qui le tirent, des conjurés, des policiers, des badauds qui le déposent à terre, il n'a rien, il ne voit plus que la voiture, noire, luisante, et son image à lui renvoyée par les flancs astiqués, brillants, mais il se lève, il tient à peine sur ses jambes, il voit encore un grand tumulte, une bagarre, un homme au visage ouvert, en sang, un coup de sabre l'a frappé en pleine face, c'est l'assassin, la foule veut le dépecer, des policiers le battent encore tandis que d'autres le protègent, tout cela dans un silence complet, le corps du Roi est étendu de côté sur la banquette de la voiture, il la recouvre tout entière, encore plus grand mort que vivant, des soldats à cheval distribuent des coups dans la foule pour l'empêcher de tuer l'homme à la moustache noire, encore une fois les choses ne se sont pas passées ainsi, dans cet ordre, il n'y avait pas d'ordre, c'est invraisemblable, comment a-t-il pu tirer trois coups sans qu'on y mette obstacle, tout a dû se dérouler beaucoup plus vite, le temps était arrêté, je serais un très mauvais témoin, alors que personne n'était aussi près que moi, évidemment, de la victime et de l'assassin, je ne me suis pas évanoui, je tremblais, je n'entendais rien, rien depuis la troisième détonation, la troisième balle était entrée dans le dossier du siège à peu près à l'endroit où s'était trouvée ma nuque, en tout cas il n'a pas voulu me tuer, il aurait pu le faire facilement, je ne sais pas pourquoi vous voulez que je vous

raconte tout cela, c'était dans les journaux, c'est dans cinquante livres. Je
ne l'avais jamais fait.

Roman Roi

Roman passes over the high-backed armchairs, black around a band of
embroidery in what were once vivid colors. He likes to sit on the top step
of the iron staircase. From there, at the foot of the transparent windows,
he can see everything, arrivals and departures, the garden, the prairie, the
avenue that descends toward Hörst, the river, its island, the valley, the
forest, the mountain, the sky. His bitch Vanya sits next to him. He opens
on his knees great volumes, biannual collections of the weekly editions
of *L'Illustration*, for example, or of *Lectures pour tous*, of which certain
images are more familiar to him than those of his own life; atlases,
encyclopedias, *Gazette des Beaux-Arts*, monochromatic reproductions
of the most famous paintings in the world. Time is suspended, as is place.

But the whole year is not spent entirely at the Arkel manor. To mark
its attachment to the kingdom, Russenia gave the royal family an immense domain, Toreev, former property of a Russian family, the Otchakovsky princes. The chateau is a large neoclassical rectangular building,
such as abound on the Russian plains, and basically not very different
from the aristocratic residences of the South of the United States. In
front, it has a peristyle, the triangular pediment of which is supported by
ten white Doric columns. Around it extend outbuildings, fields of wheat
or corn, forests of birch-trees, ponds.

Roman, his mother, and his grandmother spend at least a month in
the spring, and sometimes several weeks in the fall, there each year. In
the evening, peasants give pastoral concerts. Above their long, wide
skirts and their baggy, very white pants, their blouses, also white, are set
off by dazzling, richly embroidered vests. They dance around a great fire,
to the sound of high-pitched, frenzied violin, and they sing in an incomprehensible language.

The summer sojourn at Sibor, on the Black Sea, was also at the
beginning for political reasons, which had to do with showing the interest
of the dynasty in another new province, Esthenia. They took advantage of
this to acquire a seaside residence. It was not an easy thing. The Esthe-
nian coast is low, marshy, without any shade. Never mind. The Regent
decided, as early as 1920, to establish Sibor, a beach resort, around a tiny
fishing village. His family would contribute to its launching. Plans for the

new city were drawn up, the chosen site dried out as well as possible, avenues were even traced on the ground which would not be bordered by any buildings for a long time. All the avenues converged towards the royal villa, the construction of which began in 1921. Princess Marie, in an effort to overcome the neurasthenia gnawing away at her, accepted responsibility for the enterprise. Caught between the necessity of marking the preeminence of the villa over its neighbors and the demands of genuine discretion and a modesty which came naturally to her, she adopted a peculiar course of action, the result of which never ceased to amaze visitors, even those who had already seen it many times. The general configuration was that of a middle-class house such as a family of important, reasonably modern merchants from Back or Bucarest might have built, but all the proportions were doubled in size. There weren't very many windows, for example, but they were of a dizzying size, and a normal man had trouble reaching the latch with his hand. The vague unrest one felt observing the house from the long drive leading up to it was multiplied, one imagines, for its inhabitants, whose every perception was constantly challenged by the most peculiar fact that all the materials used in the construction and decoration of the house contrived to hide their sumptuousness by creating the appearance of being their own imitations.

Nonetheless the royal family began to spend part of the summer months there in 1925. Terraces with white balustrades, too high like everything else, rose over a vast, gently sloping beach. This was of course closed to the public and protected at either end by tall iron railings plunging into the sea, and by numerous policemen.

Queen Amelia had always deplored the intellectual isolation of Caronia, as well as the fact that the most important stages of the cultural development of Europe had always been celebrated in a muffled, diluted way. In Sibor, she thought she had found a reason for making an audacious (according to her, perfectly legitimate) association between its bare shores and the most classical literature. They were, she maintained, the true site of Ovid's exile. It was there that he wrote the *Tristia*. Scholars are certainly more or less unanimous in placing the ancient Tomes on the site of the present-day Rumanian Constanza, and Ovid's residence south of the Danube. But it's true that they've always (even Wilamowitz-Möllendorf) been amazed at the rigor of the wintry climate described by the poet and by the constant threats of barbarian invasions he talks about, both of which are rather unlikely at the latitude of Constanza. The most generally proposed explanation, particularly by Rumanian Latinists, is that Ovid wanted to arouse pity for his lot and that he exaggerated its cruelty. Queen Amelia's explanation was that Tomes should be identified with Sibor, where the winters are indeed rigorous and where the Roman presence, attested to by a few meager vestiges, was never anything but precarious. As soon as her mind had latched on to this conviction, everything, about the place or the book, became a sign for the old sovereign and supported her theory. She didn't doubt that she occupied the shore of the *Tristia*. And for the inhabitants of the royal villa, the space which surrounded them, and which was but a vast, rather dismal construction site, quivered with the melancholy iambs of the illustrious exile.

. . . .

On 7 December, the father and son are in Nemheid, in Vesania. They breathe freely. Nemheid is an eminently "Pierrist" city, demonstrated by its being the first to offer refuge to the exile when he returned from France. The king is grateful for this. They are among friends. The guards can relax a bit. The terrorists have never attempted any action here; the murderous folly of the last months has hardly touched the province. The sun is dazzling. Pierre and Roman, preceded by the governor of Vesania, go to the city hall in an open car, in spite of the cold, in order better to offer themselves before the acclamations of the people densely lining the Avenue of the Armistice. Several times men or women approach the car doors, in order to show the King their children, or their children the King, or to see him better themselves. They are pushed away without brutality. The ambiance is warm and cordial. Pierre smiles his irresistible smile. He is still the country's darling, the one who is always forgiven everything. Nothing serious can happen as long he's there.

One of the curious has gotten even closer. He's even climbed up on the running board of the car and he's holding on to the body of the car with one hand. He is young, he has a pleasant, square face, his hair is parted in the middle of his forehead, he has a thick, very black moustache. He has no child to present to the King. He's strong, he is hanging on to the car door with one hand when already a bodyguard has grabbed him around the waist. Roman isn't sure of the exact order of events, he only remembers a paradoxical impression of extreme slowness and even a kind of hallucinatory simultaneity of causes and effects. The revolver, before, after, he couldn't say. But the revolver, very present, enormous, gaping, its black hole, a shot goes off, the fearful detonation, the King is wounded in the area of his heart but he seems above all "disheartened". With his thighs he pushes himself back into his seat, he leans forward. A second shot, right in the face. The improbability of the thing. The man seems to fear nothing, he must not care about saving his life, he is not trying to escape, he has plenty of time. But why don't they pull him off the car door? The whole scene must have happened more quickly than Roman saw it. His father's torso has gone back in the seat, and he's leaning to the left, towards the spot where he himself is sitting.

A third shot, fired now that the barrel is right next to the King's temple. The head finishes exploding. Roman is splattered with blood, with bits of brain which slide slowly down his uniform, and especially this thing that spurts out with its filaments on his belly then between his thighs it's an eye, his father's eye.

He's afraid of crushing this thing that he doesn't want to see, that he wouldn't want to touch, but whose presence between his thighs he can't stand another instant, he grabs it to get it away as soon as possible, too bad, he's more horrified of it than of the barrel of the pistol, he touches it, one second, three seconds, to get rid of it he's taken it in his hand, he throws it as far as he can, into the crowd, he's arching backwards now, legs stiff, propped on the back of the seat, he always liked that smell of well cared-for leather, it's not fear, it's to get away from this gigantic body falling on him whose head is no longer a head but a confusion of shredded flesh, broken bones, liquid gray matter that he feels against his hip, he's going to fall from the car, he is in arms that are pulling him, conspirators, policemen, rubberneckers who place him on the ground, nothing's wrong with him, he sees nothing but the shining black car, and his image sent back to him by the polished sides, shining, but he gets up, his legs are shaking, he sees another great fracas, a fight, a man with his face cut open, bloody, he's been hit by a sabre right in the face, it's the killer, the crowd wants to tear him to pieces, some policemen are still beating him while others protect him, all of this in complete silence, the King's body is stretched out on its side on the seat of the car, he completely covers it, even larger in death than in life, soldiers on horseback strike out into the crowd to stop them from killing the man with the black moustache, once again things didn't happen this way, in this order, there was no order, it's unbelievable, how could he fire three shots without being stopped, everything must have happened much more quickly, time was stopped, I would be a very bad witness, although no one was as close as I, obviously, to the victim and the killer, I didn't faint, I was trembling, I heard nothing, nothing after the third detonation, the third ball entered the back of the seat just about where my neck had been, in any case he didn't want to kill me, he could have done it easily, I don't know why you want me to tell you all this, it was in the papers, it's in fifty books. I hadn't ever told it before.

TRANSLATED BY CHRISTOPHER RIVERS

RENAUD CAMUS

Notes sur les manières du temps*

LE TRIOMPHE D'ALCESTE

Il faut dire qu'il m'avait d'emblée mal disposé, celui-là. Il m'avait donné pour certain jour un rendez-vous dans un café, en me précisant que son « ami », à cette date, serait en voyage. J'ai beau m'en être moi-même rendu coupable, en mon temps, les mesquineries des petits ménages me répugnent un peu.

Il m'avait envoyé une photographie: nous nous reconnaissons, nous nous rapprochons, nous commençons à bavarder. L'une de ses premières phrases est celle-ci:

« En tout cas il y a un point sur lequel je suis tout à fait d'accord avec toi: Tony Duvert est un meilleur écrivain que toi . . . »

Boum!

Il est bien vrai que j'ai pu exprimer, par écrit, de quoi impliquer, chez moi, une telle opinion. Par exemple: « Le ton de Duvert n'est qu'à lui, je serais bien incapable de l'imiter, et de sa violence. » (1) Ou bien, l'ayant cité: « Je ne saurais mieux dire, certes. » (2) Etc. Qu'il soit un « meilleur écrivain » que moi, ça me paraît parfaitement vraisemblable et ça ne me cause aucune espèce de souci. Je puis me laisser aller à des polémiques, éventuellement, mais je n'ai pas le moindre sentiment de ce que peut être la rivalité littéraire. Et je me souviens avec stupéfaction d'un jeune auteur, mort depuis, qui, comme on lui demandait s'il m'avait lu, répondait devant moi: « Je ne lis jamais mes rivaux. » Ce terme en ce contexte n'a pour moi aucun sens. Mais encore une fois, il ne s'agit pas ici du sens, du fond, mais de « rôles » sociaux. Que je dise, moi, que Duvert est un

---

(1) *Notes Achriennes, op. cit.*, p. 55.
(2) *Id.*, p. 90.
Notes sur les manières du temps (Paris: P.O.L.-Hachette, 1985), 360–62. This passage is reprinted with the kind permission of P.O.L.-Hachette.

meilleur écrivain que moi, ça n'a rien que de très normal, c'est même, si je puis dire, dans mon rôle. Mais il n'est pas dans celui d'un quidam qui m'a proposé un rendez-vous plutôt intime, apparemment, de relever d'emblée, avec tant d'enthousiasme, ce propos-là. Ce garçon n'est pas un critique dans l'exercice de son métier; il ne m'a pas convié à un débat littéraire; il ne m'a invité, pour autant que j'en ai pu juger, qu'à une soirée amoureuse clandestine. Je ne veux pas insinuer que ce qu'il dit soit faux, mais seulement relever que c'est déplacé.

Seulement l'idéologie petite-bourgeoise (qui, rappelons-le, n'est nullement une affaire de classe: le Jockey Club et Billancourt sont pleins de petits-bourgeois) ne veut pas de ce concept-là. Elle ne connaît que le vrai et le faux, et elle juge, comme Alceste, que le vrai, ou ce qu'elle prend pour tel, est toujours bon à dire.

Un lecteur de province, qui m'avait envoyé plusieurs lettres très aimables, m'écrit soudain, après une interruption que je n'avais pas remarqué, ceci:

« Mon silence est l'effet d'un embarras certain devant *Roman Roi* dont je vous avais promis[!] de vous dire quelques mots, l'ayant lu. Malgré mes efforts répétés, je ne l'ai toujours pas lu—en entier. Que je l'aborde par le commencement, par la fin ou par le milieu, je ne parviens pas à m'y intéresser. C'est un livre . . . égoïste: je me sens exclu de ce jeu qui vous a donné, j'imagine, du plaisir (. . .). Pastiches, clins d'œil et anagrammes m'ont fait sourire parfois; mais l'impression constante était celle-ci: dieu, que tout cela est vain! A qui s'adresse-t-il? A son éditeur, à quelques confrères qui œuvrent dans le même sens que lui, à deux ou trois critiques. Même pas: à lui-même. Le meilleur lecteur possible de ce roman, c'est vous. »

Sauf quand elles ont pour base de manifestes erreurs, je suis toujours plus ou moins convaincu par toutes les opinions qu'on m'exprime sur mes travaux. Il se peut très bien que cette personne ait tout à fait raison. Mais ce ton-là n'est pas de bonne compagnie. Je n'ai pas sollicité de ce monsieur un jugement objectif. Il a pris l'initiative d'une correspondance entre nous, de caractère amical. Il n'est pas un illustre vieillard qui me prodiguerait généreusement ses conseils. Il aime un livre, il n'en aime pas un autre, c'est la moindre des choses. Je ne vois aucune objection à ce qu'il me le fasse comprendre, et me donnes ses raisons. Mais ce détachement de juge n'est pas de mise dans des échanges polis.

Je m'avise que mon correspondant se trouve être critique, en fait, dans un grand journal régional. Il aurait pu exposer sa désapprobation dans un article. Elle m'y aurait semblé parfaitement légitime. Mais ce n'est pas le critique, en ses fonctions professionnelles, qui m'a envoyé cette lettre. Et l'on en revient toujours à la question des rôles: on ne saurait, dans la vie quotidienne, la dissocier du problème de la vérité.

Ce qui me frappe chez les champions de la sincérité, outre leur dogmatisme, c'est leur vanité. Qu'est-ce qui leur donne à croire que le fond de leur pensée soit si précieux? On n'a pas acheté leurs sentences, ni quêté leurs arrêts. Et pourtant ils continuent de les prodiguer, et même ils les multiplient.

L'horrible, c'est qu'on est contre eux sans défense. Car, sauf accès de fureur, on ne peut pas leur répliquer sur le même ton. Le démon de la sincérité, l'incube de l'agression, ils vous possèdent ou non. Et s'ils ne sont pas en vous, vous aurez beau vous entendre dire bien en face que vous avez une mine de déterré, que vos livres sont exécrables ou vos mœurs infâmes, jamais vous ne pourrez répliquer, même si vous le ressentez au fond de l'âme, que votre agresseur est ignare, que ses cravates sont révoltantes, son haleine fétide ou son français une poubelle. Ça ne passe pas. Vous n'avez, fors la patience ou la divine sagesse, aucun recours; sauf, peut-être, d'écrire *Manières du Temps*.

Notes sur les manières du temps

THE TRIUMPH OF ALCESTE

I must say that guy had made an unfavorable impression on me from the start. He had made a date with me for a certain day in a café, specifying that his "friend" would be away at that point. Even though I myself have been guilty of them in my time, the couple's petty little affairs repel me a bit.

He had sent me a photograph: we recognize each other, we approach each other, we start to chat. One of his first sentences is this:

"In any case, there's one thing I completely agree with you about: Tony Duvert is a better writer than you." . . .

Boom!

It is indeed true that I might have written something to imply that I had such an opinion. For example: "Duvert's tone is his own, I would be incapable of imitating it and its violence." (1) Or, having quoted him: "I certainly couldn't say it any better myself." (2) Etc. That he might be a "better writer" than I seems perfectly plausible to me and this causes me

(1) *Notes Achriennes, op. cit.*, p. 55.
(2) *Id.*, p. 90.
Notes sur les manières du temps (Paris: P.O.L.-Hachette, 1985), 360–62. This passage is reprinted with the kind permission of P.O.L.-Hachette.

314   *Yale French Studies*

no worry of any kind. I can let myself get into polemics on occasion, but I haven't the slightest sense of what literary rivalry might be. And I remember with stupefaction a young author, since dead, who, when asked if he had read me, answered in front of me: "I never read my rivals." That term in that context makes absolutely no sense to me. But once again, it's not a question of sense here, of substance, but of social "roles." The fact that I say that Duvert is a better writer than I is completely normal, it's even my role, so to speak. But it's not the role of an unknown someone who has made an apparently rather intimate date with me to reveal, with such enthusiasm, that particular observation. The boy is not a critic exercizing his profession; he didn't summon me to a literary debate; he only invited me, as far as I could tell, to a clandestine romantic evening. I don't mean to insinuate that what he said is false, but only make the point that it's inappropriate.

Only petit-bourgeois ideology (which, let's remember, isn't at all a question of class: the Jockey Club and Billancourt are full of petits-bourgeois) doesn't accept that concept. It only knows the true and the false, and it deems, like Alceste, that the true or what it considers as such, is always a good thing to say.

A reader from the provinces, who had sent me several very amiable letters, writes me suddenly, after an interruption in the correspondence that I hadn't noticed, the following:

"My silence is the result of a certain perplexity over *Roman roi* about which I had promised [!] to say a few words after I had read it. In spite of my repeated efforts, I still haven't read it—in its entirety. Whether I start it at the beginning, the end, or the middle, I can't get interested in it. It's a . . . selfish book: I feel excluded from this game which, I imagine, gave you pleasure. . . . Pastiches, winks and anagrams made me smile a few times, but my constant impression was the following: God, all this is futile! Who is he speaking to? To his editor, to a few colleagues who work in the same area as he, to two or three critics. Not even them: to himself. The best possible reader for this novel is you."

Except when they are based on manifest errors, I am always more or less convinced by all the opinions expressed about my work. It is quite possible that this person is completely right. But his tone is not well-bred. I didn't solicit an objective opinion from this gentleman. He initiated a correspondance between us, of a friendly nature. He is not an illustrious old man who lavishes his advice on me. He likes one book, he doesn't like another, so what? I have no objection to his telling me, and giving me his reasons. But this judgelike detachment is uncalled for in polite exchanges.

I realize myself that my correspondant happens to be a critic, in fact, for a large regional newspaper. He could have expressed his disapproval in an article. It would have seemed perfectly legitimate to me there. But it wasn't the critic in his professional capacity who sent me that letter. And we always come back to the same question of roles: we can't, in everyday life, dissociate it from the problem of truth.

What strikes me about the champions of sincerity, aside from their dogmatism, is their vanity. What leads them to believe that the content of their thought is so precious? No one bought their judgments or sought their verdicts. Yet, they continue to pour them forth profusely, and in fact are even multiplying them.

The horrible thing is that one is defenseless against them. Because, barring a fit of fury, one cannot respond in kind. The demon of sincerity, the incubus of aggression either possess you or they don't. And if they're not in you, you will in vain be told to your face that you look like someone who's just been dug up, that your books are execrable or your lifestyle disgraceful, because you will never be able to retort, even if you feel its impact to the depths of your soul, that your aggressor is illiterate, that his neckties are revolting, his breath fetid or his French a pile of garbage. It doesn't work. Aside from patience or divine wisdom, you have no recourse; except, perhaps, to write *Manières du temps*.

TRANSLATED BY CHRISTOPHER RIVERS

MARTINE REID

Jeanne Hyvrard

> L'écriture est mémoire. Pour qu'augmente la connaissance.
> —*La Meurtritude.*

Jeanne Hyvrard is intent on preserving her anonymity. She has chosen to reveal only a name and a written trace, the inscription of her voice. No face, no habits, no places, no friends, and no opinions will be associated with her other than the ones she expressly puts on paper, for she scornfully rejects the "biographical" for the sole benefit of the textual matter. "I live outside of myself," she says straight-away, anxious to designate with a quasi-oxymoronic formula the *atopia* from which she writes, a symbol of all the differences she plays on and claims as a woman, as a Creole, and as a madwoman (ill, she was once considered mad).[1]

In 1975, Jeanne Hyvrard published her first novel, *Les Prunes de Cythère.* Accumulating the usual descriptive terms, critics said that the book was "upset-ting," "embarrassing," "truthful." These were the many ways for them to assimi-late the new into the known and to reduce the event to the news item. Hyvrard repeats her offense a little later with *Mère la mort* and with a two-part work: a "roman" entitled *La Meurtritude,* followed by *Les Doigts du figuier,* a text de-fined by her as "parole." This strange gesture can hardly be identified with any existing literary posture: poetry mingled with prose, or to be more exact, the metaphoric demands of her prose, subject to the convulsions of rebellion, natu-rally seems to give "birth" to a second language. This decanted language would reiterate the same violence, would resume the same imperious narrative, but differently. In fact, one cannot read one version without the other. "Parole" and "roman" stick together like the two sides of a page. ln 1982, Hyvrard published *Le Corps défunt de la comédie,* called simply "littérature." This text, a kind of poeticopolitical essay, assembles the tragic record of all the "follies," "horrors," and forms of oppression, in daily life as well as in peoples' destiny. Since then the author has primarily written poetic prose, both in the form of "short stories" and "novels," pursuing the model itinerary she set for herself.

In the beginning, Hyvrard says in most of her texts, was oppression. Let us not be deceived by the familiarity of the word: it is not the author's intention to take up again the well-known notion, duly defined in political terms and contained in its geographical and social limits, which has found a place—a way to neutralize its effects—in the various epistemological discourses. There is more, the author says from the outset, much more. There is an even more radical form of oppres-

---

1. Her name appears in the J. P. Beaumarchais, Daniel Coutis and Alain Rey *Diction-naire des littératures* (Bordas, 1984) under the rubrique "Caraïbes et Guyane."

sion, a constituent and original oppression which resides in the flesh and mind, unthinkable, unnameable, and unlivable. In the beginning, and from the furthest reaches of memory, is this *ill-being*, a symbol of all the others. If, in this context, writing appears to be a "duty" (one which consists in expressing this ill-being, in giving voice to it), that is to say responsibility, it is in order to *witness*, to remind everyone, to contribute to the construction of a certain understanding of the world. How?

There is something like "femininity of writing," Hélène Cixous observed, and we must first look for it in the "privilege of the *voice*: writing and *voice* get intertwined and interwoven, and by being interchangeable, the continuity of writing and the rhythm of the voice take each other's breath away. They cause the text to pant or compose it with suspense, silences, they break its voice or tear it with screams." And she added: "she [the woman] does not 'speak', she throws her shivering body in the air, lets go of herself, flies, puts herself entirely in her voice, and vitally supports the 'logic of her discourse' with her body: her flesh speaks the truth."[2]

To speak in the feminine, one must, however, face a great obstacle which has been amply debated: which language are we to speak which was not created to serve ends contrary to our own, how do we "make a niche for ourselves," and name the difference in a discourse in which it is by definition ignored?

Jeanne Hyvrard consistently deals with this question, and tries all means at hand to answer it. Creating a new language is out of the question: "If I invent a new language, I escape them completely. But there is no other one available. It is our common tongue. I don't know any other."[3] Thus, it is from within this very language and *from* it that we will have to speak, cost what it may.

Hyvrard recalls an initiation (the teaching of reading and writing) and an endless feeling of discomfort (due to the difficulty of situating herself in this learned language, and of finding a place within it to signify difference). This feeling is echoed by the frightening constraints of "normality" she experienced in medical discourse when she was institutionalized. The author painfully remembers first of all her experience at school which she describes as "linguistic breaking in": school, which France imposes from afar without considering the difference between the metropolis and the overseas territories, fights without patience the accent, the family lexicon, the colloquialisms, the children's idioms and those of the imaginary. "Who are those who correct? Who are those who scratch my skin every time they underline my verbs? . . . Do they know how to conjugate the imaginary when the hands of the trees seize my ankles? Who are those who annotate us? Can they conjugate assimilation while I am disintegrating?"[4]

In fact, what the writer is asking for, contrary to "logic" (yet, coming close to Luce Irigaray's preoccupations),[5] is a language that would cease to separate, differ-

2. *La Jeune née*, avec C. Clément (Paris: UGE, 1975), 170.
3. *Mère la mort* (Paris: Minuit, 1976), 75.
4. Ibid., 54.
5. In *Ce sexe qui n'en est pas un* (Paris: Minuit, 1977), 73, Irigaray proposes to "listen to the processes of repression [of knowledge, grammar and philosophy], to the structures underlying the representation(s) of language, identifying truth from falsity, sanity from insanity, etc."

entiate or create opposite terms. Rather, this language would name in harmony, it would *fuse*. Remembering "a very old language deep down in my body. A language where words also mean their opposite,"[6] Hyvrard accuses the "separators,"[7] particularly the school teachers and the doctors, who impose repressive forms of knowledge and whose power relies precisely on what she calls "the refusal to contrarize":[8] "They have separated things from their opposites. They said that reason was born whole from the creator's thigh. They wove wreaths of conjunctions around it. They perverted language. They invented the pronouns and the articles. They fabricated the tenses of oblivion."[9] Language appears, then, as a warlike machine founded on separation and amnesia which performs vivi-*section* on the speaker. This murderous tongue scratches, hurts, cuts, leaves its marks on the flesh until "enmaddening," it imposes an identity upon the body, a pronoun upon the voice, *I*, a true death threat for those who pay for it: "They deny our imaginations and call theirs reality. They appropriate us. And we have nothing to say to them. We will die of it. They are killing us. They are driving us crazy. . . . They cannot accept reality or imagination. We will die because of not fitting in their narrow limits. Because we can't stay within their small molds. Because they can't put us through the mill."[10]

To respond to this aggression, Hyvrard talks, again and again, of her refusal to *differentiate* in any way and of her quest for new linguistic properties. Refusal of identity, first of all, because refusal of an assigned place, the mark imposed by a differentiating power, and because it is the inacceptable separation from the whole: "Identity is a trap. Only the perceptible other. Changing power into strength. Being born to oneself to be reborn with it. I am nobody anymore. I escape from them. I don't look for identity";[11] "I have no identity. I am separation and fusion. . . . I am just a pronoun calling you and me together. I and She. We and me. The indefinite pronoun. The infinite pronoun. The pronoun of unity."[12] She refuses the rules of a language and of an imprisoning grammar: Hyvrard asks for "a language with three modes. The real. The imaginary. The fusional. And doubtless many others. A language spare enough to express at last the cosmic. A language without tenses or pronouns."[13] She also refuses a congealed lexicon: "They say that 'to gob' never existed. What do they know? After all there is 'gobbler'. 'To gobble'. 'Gobbling'. 'Gobblying'. 'Gobblation.' No, death."[14] Hyvrard calls for the rebellion of words: "Words are like anger which has been contained for too long. They are like a cage letting its hornets go free. They are like a smashed crate, yielding its weapons. . . . Our colorful parachutes jumping from the planes. Our battleships of light drawing alongside in their harbors. Our mines sinking their

6. *Mère la mort*, 59.
7. "They say that we can't say death and life at the same time. Their language can say the contrary without saying the negation. It is the language of the separators." *La Meurtritude*, 96.
8. Ibid.
9. *Mère la mort*, 60.
10. Ibid., 68–69.
11. *Mère la mort*, 99.
12. *La Meurtritude*, 130.
13. Ibid., 60.
14. Ibid., 78.

good conscience. We will succeed. We will not die. Tear. Tearing. Tearingness. Tearance. Tearitude."[15]

We see that the writer returns the violence, whose many forms of oppression she was invested with, to its source. She returns blow for blow. Far from accepting the violence of images (and in some way, her writing, her argument remind us of Aimé Césaire in *Cahier d'un retour au pays natal*), she attacks language itself, its syntax which falls prey too easily to reasonings, and its narrow lexicon. With blackouts, ellipses, anacolutha, Hyvrard purposely chooses images which break, stab, tangle up. The words, known and forged for what needs to be said, acquire a disquieting sense of the "uncanny." They are violence: after scratching the mouth of the woman who speaks, they seem to have been laid on paper in order to scratch the eyes of those who will attempt to read them. Through repetition, juxtaposition of terms, short sentences, entirely devoid of grammatical or linguistic artifice, Jeanne Hyvrard proposes, poles apart from the classical period, a singular rhythm and claims its incantatory and "wild" characteristic as well as its "archaic" dimension.

If Jeanne Hyvrard's writing beckons to Hélène Cixous's, Catherine Clément's, Monique Wittig's, Viviane Forrester's and many other women of her generation, it also contains the anguished lucidity and the painful resplendence one finds in Nerval, Rimbaud, and Artaud. The radicality of Jeanne Hyvrard's questions, asked in a very original language, makes her one of the great writers of our time.

BIBLIOGRAPHY

I. Selected Works

Les Prunes de Cythère. Paris: Minuit, 1975.
Mère la mort. Paris: Minuit, 1976.
Les Doigts du figuier. Paris: Minuit, 1977.
La Meurtritude. Paris: Minuit, 1977.
Le Corps défunt de la comédie, Traité d'économie politique. Paris: Seuil, 1982.
Le Silence et l'obscurité (Requiem littoral pour corps polonais). Paris: Montalba, 1982.
Auditions musicales certains soirs d'été. Paris: Editions des Femmes, 1984.
La Baisure, suivi de Que se partagent encore les eaux. Paris: Editions des Femmes, 1984.

II. Selected Criticism

Le Clézio, M. "Mother and Motherhood: The Daughter's Quest for Origins," *Stanford French Review* 5, no. 3 (1981): 381–89.
———. "Jeanne Hyvrard: The Writing of the Night," *Revue de l'Université d'Ottowa* 54, no. 4 (1984): 117–23.

15. Ibid., 122.

Juris, S. "Beyond Historicity. The Middle Passage in the Writings of Contemporary Francophone Carribbean Authors," *Studies in Honor of Reino Virtanen*. Ann Arbor: Society of Spanish and Spanish American Studies, 1978, 269–79.

Moscovici, M. "Un langage décolonisé," *Critique* 347 (1976): 375–80.

Pétillon, M. "La Parole convulsée de Jeanne Hyvrard," *Le Monde* (30 December 1977): 13–15.

Waelti-Walters, J. "He Asked for her Hand in Marriage—or the Fragmentation of Woman," *New York Literary Forum* 8–9 (1981): 211–22.

———. " 'Ils ont fait de moi la mort': la mère dans l'oeuvre de Jeanne Hyvrard," *Etudes Littéraires* 17, no. 1 (1984): 117–29.

JEANNE HYVRARD

*Mère la mort**

Ils disent que je dois guérir. Ils m'ont enfermée au mouroir. Ils m'écrivent quelquefois. Les lettres s'accumulent au bas de l'escalier de pierre. Le chien demeure couché dans l'ombre. Le discours monocorde de la rivière. La ligne du plateau. Je ne suis plus que le rebord de la montagne qui me protège de l'angoisse. C'est l'été immobile qui m'ouvre tout grand les bras. Je ne parviendrai pas à casser la langue pour dire enfin l'osmose dans le monde. Je ne réussirai pas. Ils ne me laisseront pas partir. Ils vont me renvoyer à l'hôpital. La maison de repos rouvre sur l'asile. Le lit de fer. Les sangles de chanvre. Les piqûres de coma. Les soleils qu'ils m'envoient dans la tête. Cherchant la maladie qu'ils n'ont pas sur leurs fiches. La mémoire. La révolte. Le refus. Mille soleils dans mon crâne pour localiser la tumeur de l'amour. Tant de piqûres pour me faire oublier les jours où je courais sur les galets. Tant de drogues pour forcer mon consentement. Tant d'interrogatoires pour brouiller les pistes.

Rien n'y fait. Je ne parviens pas à oublier. Mon bras matriculé. Mes cheveux tondus. Mes chevilles enchaînées. Ils cherchent sur leurs fiches le nom de ma maladie. Elle s'appelle la mémoire. Ils pansent mes blessures dans des couvertures de cartons. Mais le sang coule toujours du ventre de la montagne. Ils rangent mes membres paralysés sur leurs rayons de bibliothèque. Mais elle m'étouffe toujours dans son ventre. Ils dissèquent mes phrases pour établir un diagnostic. Mais la fleur véné-neuse ronge mes chairs. Ils cherchent dans leurs fiches le nom de ma maladie. Elle s'appelle la mémoire. Ma perdition. Elle s'appelle ton corps. Ma rassurance. Ton corps me nourrissant et m'abritant. Ma sauvegarde. Ton corps me paralysant et me dévorant.

Mère la mort, ils cherchent le nom de ma maladie. La gestation. La gestance. Le gestement. La gestude. La mémoire des eaux bleues de son

*Mère la mort (Paris: Minuit, 1976), 48–55. This passage is reprinted with the kind permission of Editions de Minuit.

ventre quand elle les assèche pour me perdre. La formation des acides rouges. Dans le four de quel alchimiste, la liqueur d'immortalité? Si je trouve, ils me laisseront partir. Je suis ensemble elle et moi. C'est moi qui me dévore et me détruis. Les acides rouges. Si je consens à être elle. Je survis. La formation de la conscience. L'apprentissage d'un comportement. Si je suis elle, je survis. Le début de l'osmose. Le consentement de la victime au bourreau. Je vais mourir. Si je consens à être elle. Je ne meurs pas. La symbiose. La perte de l'identité. L'apprentissage d'un comportement. La nuit. La maladie. La déportation. Je m'identifie à eux. Ils ne peuvent plus me faire de mal. Ils me possèdent mais je survis en eux. Les pas tournants. Les aboiements. La mutité. La survie. Je leur donne ce qu'ils demandent. Mais ils n'ont plus dans les bras qu'un bois mort. La maladie me sauve. Ils croient m'avoir nommée. Je n'ai plus de nom. Ils m'identifient. Je deviens autre. Ils veulent me faire marcher. Je paralyse mes jambes. Ils veulent me faire parler. Je deviens muette. Ils veulent me faire enfanter. J'étouffe à mon tour mes propres enfants.

Les hirondelles sur le rebord du balcon. La citerne qui se vide peu à peu. L'orage entre les chênes et les buis. Le causse rouge. A cause du sang. A cause du sang coulant du ventre de la terre. A cause du sang qu'ils ont sur les mains. Ils parlent de nécessité historique, de raison d'état, d'accords diplomatiques. Le causse rouge. A cause des acides qui paralysent ma tête et mes membres. Il n'y a personne. Des heures de marche durant. Mais les racines, le thym, les immortelles. Ils disent que ce sont les fleurs dans la cour du mouroir. La fin du repos. Je n'ai pas trouvé la pièce qui manque. Tu demandes à me reprendre avec toi, mais ils disent que ce n'est pas possible. Que je suis dangereuse. Que je suis folle. Qu'il faut me ramener à l'hôpital.

Nous marchons sous l'orage. Les éclairs et la foudre. Les pierres rouges sanglotent de plus en plus fort, tout autour de nous. Elle tricote une couverture pour abriter mon corps paralysé. Écru, bisé, grisé, burel. Les couleurs de ma peine. Cela ne sert à rien puisque je vais mourir. Je n'ai rien trouvé. Les éclairs tout autour de nous. La borie au milieu des champs. Au bout des pierres rouges, la borie dans les avoines coupées. Ma chemise est trempée. Elle va appeler la garde. Elle avait pourtant bien dit de ne pas m'agiter. Ils disent qu'il est temps que je retourne à l'hôpital. Ils disent qu'ils vont de nouveau m'attacher, puisque je ne suis pas raisonnable. Mais la pièce qui manque. La pièce qui reconstruirait tout le jeu. La pièce qui me délivrerait enfin. Tu me tiens par le bras. Tu me tires en avant. Les éclairs autour de nous. La foudre. La garde et son aiguille de coma. Tu ne veux pas la laisser faire. Mais les oiseaux-pieuvres voltigent autour de moi. Mes enfants morts sanglotent dans l'écorce des arbres. Tu veux me reprendre à la maison. Mais l'aigle noir dans mon crâne. Il ne faut pas rester sous les arbres mais ils me tendent leurs mains ouvertes. La garde appelle les infirmiers pour qu'ils m'attachent. Tu me prends dans tes bras. Tu me tires vers la borie. La terre rouge et les avoines coupées. Sang et or le désastre. Quelle liqueur dans le creuset de l'alchimiste? Revoilà entre les arbres tordus la femme en mauve qui parade. Revoilà qu'elle me prend dans ses filets de mots que je ne connais pas. Revoilà qu'elle tricote des pièges au coin de la syntaxe. Revoilà qu'elle exige une orthographe impossible à mettre. Elle est là sur la chaise près de mon lit. Elle me tient le front. Tu me tiens le bras. Nous avançons sous l'orage. La borie dans les avoines coupées. Les éclairs et la foudre. Tu me serres contre toi. Le vent pousse l'orage. Je suis trempée. Le lit est trempé. Tu m'essuies avec ton mouchoir. Ils m'ont attachée. Ils disent qu'il n'y a que des relations de pouvoir. Mais l'orage sur le causse. Le consentement. L'abandon au monde. Les forces cosmiques. Le vent et les étoiles. Le consentement à la mort. Les mains tendues des arbres. Les sanglots des pierres mouillées. La plainte du chemin raviné. Le causse rouge. A cause de mon sang. Ou à cause de ta peine. Ils ne veulent pas me laisser partir. Ils disent qu'ils vont me ramener à l'hôpital. Je n'ai pas trouvé la pièce qui manque. Ils continuent à dire. Le pouvoir. Le pouvoir. Trouver son identité. Mais la borie dans les avoines coupées. Ils vont me ramener à l'hôpital. Mais nos corps l'un à l'autre, dans l'abri du berger.

Elle est assise au bord du lit. Elle exige que j'accorde les participes. Les oiseaux dans la falaise. La rivière qui baisse. Elle va m'étouffer. La règle des participes. Ils s'accordent dans un cas et pas dans l'autre. Qu'en savent-ils? Que savent-ils de mon corps abandonné dans la lumière? L'accord du participe. S'il est placé avant ou après. Avant ou après quoi, au juste? Elle crie dans mes oreilles. Le complément. Le sujet. Je ne vois pas la différence. Le complément et le sujet participent ensemble à l'invariable. Que veulent-ils que j'accorde? Pourquoi ne me tend-elle pas les bras? Si les participes s'accordent, pourquoi pas les mères et les filles? Mais oui, je la connais la règle des participes. Les marécages de mon crâne. Les oiseaux et les serpents quand ils gestent dans mon ventre. Mais les jactants séparent les personnes et les genres. Mais les envahisseurs nous courbent le front. Mais les mères attachent les carcans de leurs filles. Ils veulent que je corrige mes fautes. Mais je ne les connais pas.

Je ne parviens pas à embrasser leur langue qui me demeure étrangère. Elle dit que je n'arriverai jamais à rien. Ils disent que j'invente des mots. Pourtant, je ne fais qu'appliquer leurs règles. Ils disent que j'invente des mots. Pourtant, il me semble qu'ils y étaient déjà. Ils les avaient seulement oubliés. Ils dissèquent la chair de mes suffixes. Ils y voient le signe certain de ma maladie. Ils prennent mes conjugaisons. Ils y voient des symptômes. Ils prennent une phrase et ils la nomment. Ils prennent une autre phrase et ils la nomment encore. Ils croient que je n'entends pas qu'ils disent que je suis folle. Ils sont sûrs que je ne peux pas guérir. Et ils croient refermer ma tombe ouverte. Mais je parle la même langue qu'eux. Ils ne savent pas que c'est à son corps mutilé que je fais l'amour. Ils ne savent pas qu'elle a mille bras et qu'ils les ont coupés. Ils ne savent pas qu'elle est notre langue commune mais qu'elle est mon amour. Ils découpent mes phrases comme ils découpent mon corps. Ils fondent leurs diagnostics sur des lambeaux de chair. Ils donnent un nom aux soleils immobiles. Ils disent, elle invente des mots. Ils les citent comme des symptômes. Ils croient que je n'entends pas qu'ils disent que je suis folle. Mais je parle la même langue qu'eux.

Ils prétendent que je fais des fautes et qu'il faut distinguer le futur du conditionnel. Ils mettent du sang plein mes copies. Ils éructent que je ne laisse pas de marge. Ils me mettent des zéros tous les jours de grammaire. Dictée. Dictée. Dictée. Rédaction. Dissertation. Composition. Analyse logique. Dans quelle langue le même temps pour dire le futur et le passé? Dans quelle langue un temps sacré, un temps profane? Dans quelle langue une forme qui dure et une qui ne dure pas? Ils disent que je suis folle, mais je parle la même langue qu'eux. Qui sont-ils ceux-là qui mettent du rouge sur mes copies? Qui sont-ils ceux-là qui corrigent? Qui sont-ils ceux-là qui griffent ma chair en soulignant mes verbes? Qui sont-ils ceux-là qui nous raturent? Savent-ils conjuguer l'imaginaire, quand les mains des arbres saisissent mes chevilles? Qui sont-ils ceux-là qui nous annotent? Savent-ils conjuguer le fusionnel quand je me dissous dans le monde?

Mère la mort, dans quelle langue les mots signifient-ils aussi leur contraire? Dans quelle langue l'absence de conjonction? Dans quelle langue ne peut-on lire les phrases que si on en connaît le sens? Mais non. Ils disent que je suis folle et ils croient que je ne les entends pas. Ils se servent du langage pour mentir et de l'orthographe pour nous soumettre. Ils ont tué les mots et ils disent que je suis malade parce que je m'en souviens. Ils ont choisi les formes qui nous déportent et ils disent que nous ne savons pas parler. Ils attachent des grelots à nos cous et disent, voyez les fous qui passent. Ils veulent que j'emploie les auxiliaires. Être et avoir, disent-ils. Mais ils ne savent plus les auxiliaires de quoi.

Le pouvoir et l'identité. Avoir et être. Les verbes qui se conjuguent avec être et ceux avec avoir. Les temps avec être. Les temps avec avoir. Pourquoi pas les deux formes? Pourquoi ne pas choisir? Les conjugaisons du pouvoir. Les conjugaisons de l'identité. Courir chercher la grammaire. Pour quoi faire, elle a son air impassible. Elle tricote l'écheveau de ma peine. Elle crochète les irrégularités. Elle élimine sournoisement les mots invariables. Écru, bisé, grisé, burel. Les couleurs de ma peine. Elle a son air impassible. Elle fait semblant de ne pas comprendre ce que je dis. Elle regarde dans son panier d'osier. Elle me propose les pelotes des temps composés. Il faudrait faire des fiches. Mais l'infirmière ne veut pas m'aider. Elle dit que je ne dois pas travailler. Elle dit qu'il faut que je me repose si je veux guérir. J'en mourrai. Je lui ai dit que je n'étais pas malade. Elle dit que nous disons tous cela. Ce n'est pas vrai puisqu'il y en a qui remercient d'être guéri. La rivière continue à baisser. C'est le soir. Le soir quand il prend la rivière à la gorge pour l'étouffer pour plus d'amour encore. La femme en mauve traverse maintenant les vignes et les murets. Les amandiers aussi peut-être ou le noyer. Le même carré de fenêtre que rien jamais ne peut faire basculer. S'y rassemblent tout le temps et tout l'espace. Je l'entends. Je la connais. Je la reconnais. Elle dit que nous disons tous cela. Mais ce n'est pas vrai.

Mother Death

They say that I should get better. They put me away in the dying place. They write to me sometimes. The letters accumulate at the bottom of the stone stairway. The dog stays lying down in the shadows. The monochord discourse of the river. The line of the plateau. I am no longer anything but the rim of the mountain that protects me from anguish. It is the immobile summer that opens its arms wide to me. I will not manage to break language to finally say the osmosis in the world. I won't succeed. They won't let me leave. They are going to send me back to the hospital. The rest home opens out into the asylum. The iron bed. The hempen straps. The coma injections. The suns that they send into my head. Looking for the disease that they don't have on their charts. Memory. Revolt. Refusal. A thousand suns in my skull to localize the love-tumor. So many injections to make me forget the days when I ran on the stones. So many drugs to force my consent. So many interrogations to muddy the waters.

Nothing works. I can't manage to forget. My numbered arm. My shorn hair. My chained ankles. They are looking for the name of my disease on their charts. It's called memory. They staunch my wounds in cardboard covers. But the blood still flows out of the mountain's belly. They arrange my paralyzed limbs on their library shelves. But it still chokes me in its belly. They dissect my sentences to establish a diagnosis. But the venomous flower gnaws at my flesh. They look for the name of my disease on their charts. It's called memory. My perdition. It's called your body. My assurance. Your body nourishing me and sheltering me. My safeguard. Your body paralyzing me and devouring me.

Mother Death, they are looking for the name of my disease. Gestation. Gestancy. Gesting. Gestitude. The memory of the blue waters of her belly when she dries them out to finish me off. The formation of red acids. In the oven of what alchemist, the liquor of immortality? If I guess, they will let me leave. I am together she and I. It is I who devour and destroy myself. Red acids. If I consent to be her. I survive. The formation of consciousness. Apprenticeship to a way of behaving. If I am her, I survive. The beginning of osmosis. The victim's consent to the executioner. I am going to die. If I consent to be her. I'm not dying. Symbiosis. Loss of identity. Apprenticeship to a way of behaving. Night. Disease. Deportation. I identify with them. They can't do me any harm. They possess me but I survive in them. Pacing. Barking. Mutism. Afterlife. I give them what they ask for. But they have nothing on their hands but dead wood. The disease saves me. They think they have named me. I no longer have a name. They identify me. I become other. They want to make me walk. I paralyze my legs. They want to make me talk. I become mute. They want to make me have a baby. So I in turn smother my own children.

Swallows on the edge of the balcony. The cistern emptying out little by little. The storm among the oaks and the hedges. The chalky-red plain. Because of the blood. Because of the blood flowing from the belly of the earth. Because of the blood that they have on their hands. They speak of historical necessity, of reasons of state, of diplomatic agreements. The chalky-redness. Because of the acids that paralyze my head and my limbs. There is no one. For hours of walking. But the roots, the thyme, the everlasting flowers. They say that these are the flowers in the courtyard of the hospice. The end of rest. I haven't found the missing piece. You ask if you can take me back with you, but they say that it isn't possible. That I am dangerous. That I am crazy. That they'll have to take me back to the hospital.

We are walking in the storm. Thunder and lightening. The red stones sob more and more loudly, all around us. She is knitting a cover to shelter my paralyzed body. Off-white, dark gray, light gray, mottled gray. The colors of my pain. This doesn't serve any purpose since I'm going to die. I haven't found anything. Lightning all around us. The shepherd's stone shelter in the middle of the fields. At the end of red stones, the stone shelter among felled oats. My shirt is soaked. She's going to call the attendant. She had warned that I should not get excited. They say it is time that I return to the hospital. They say that they will tie me up again because I'm not good. But the missing piece. The piece that would reconstruct the whole game. The piece that would deliver me at last. You hold me by the arm. You pull me forward. The flashes of lightning around us. The bolts of lightning. The attendant and her coma needle. You don't want to let her do it. But the devilfish birds dart around me. My dead children sob in the bark of the trees. You want to take me back home. But the black eagle in my skull. I must not stay under the trees but they extend their open hands to me. The nurse calls the attendants to tie me up. You take me in your arms. You pull me towards the shelter. Red earth and cut oats. Blood and gold the disaster. What liquor in the alchemist's crucible? There she is again, the woman in purple who struts among the twisted trees. There she goes again, taking me in her nets of words that I do not know. There she goes again, knitting snares in the syntax corner. There she goes again, asking for a spelling impossible to put down. She is there on the chair next to my bed. She holds my forehead. You hold my arm. We advance in the storm. The shelter among felled oats. Flashes and lightning bolts. You hold me tight against you. The wind pushes the storm on. I am soaked. The bed is soaked. You wipe me off with your handkerchief. They tied me up. They say that there are only power relationships. But the storm on the chalk-plain. Consent. Abandonment to the world. Cosmic forces. Wind and stars. Consenting to die. The extended hands of trees. The sobs of damp stones. The cry of the ravaged path. The chalky-red plain. Because of my blood. Or because of your sorrow. They don't want to let me leave. They say that they are going to take me back to the hospital. I haven't found the missing piece. They continue to say. Power. Power. Find its identity. But the shelter in the felled oats. They are going to take me back to the hospital. But our bodies each for the other, into the shepherd's shelter.

She is seated on the edge of the bed. She insists that I make participles agree. The birds in the cliff. The falling river. She is going to suffocate me. The rule on participles. They agree in one case and not in another. What do they know? What do they know about my body abandoned in the light? The agreement of participles. If it is placed before or after. Before or after what, exactly? She screams in my ears. The object. The subject. I don't see the difference. The object and the subject participate together in the invariable. What do they want me to make agree? Why does she not hold out her arms to me? If participles can agree, why not mothers and daughters? Yes, of course! I do know the rule on participles. The swamps in my skull. The birds and the snakes when they gestate in my belly. But the ejaculants separate person and gender. But the invaders lower our foreheads. But the mothers fasten up their daughters' neck-irons. They want me to correct my mistakes. But I don't know them.

I can't seem to learn their tongue, which remains foreign to me. She says that I will never come to anything. They say that I invent words. Yet, I only apply their rules. They say that I invent words. Yet, it seems to me that they already were. Only they forgot them. They dissect the flesh of my suffixes. They see there the sure sign of my sickness. They take my conjugations. They see symptoms in them. They take a sentence and they name it. They take another sentence and they name it too. They think that I don't hear that they say I am crazy. They are sure that I can't get better. And they think they are closing my open tomb. But I speak the same tongue as they. They don't know that it is to its mutilated body that I am making love. They don't know that it has a thousand arms and that they have cut them off. They don't know that it is our common tongue, but that it is my love. They cut up my sentences like they cut up my body. They found their diagnoses on shreds of flesh. They give a name to immobile suns. They say she invents words. They cite them as symptoms. They think that I don't hear them say I am crazy. But I speak the same language as they do.

They claim that I make mistakes and that one must distinguish the future from the conditional. They put blood all over my papers. They belch that I didn't leave a margin. They give me zeros on every grammar day. Dictation. Dictation. Dictation. Composition. Essay. Logical analysis. In what language is there the same tense to say the future and the past? In what language a sacred tense, a profane tense? In what language is there one form that lasts and one that does not last? They say that I am crazy, but I speak the same language as they do. Who are those people who put red on my papers? Who are those people who correct? Who are those people who claw my flesh by underlining my verbs? Who are those who scratch us out? Do they know how to conjugate the imaginary, when the hands of the trees seize my ankles? Who are those who annotate us? Do they know how to conjugate assimilation while I am disintegrating?

Mother Death, in what language do words also signify their opposite? In what language the absence of conjunctions? In what language can one read the sentences only if one knows the meaning? But no. They say that I am crazy and they think that I don't hear them. They use language to lie and spelling to bring us into line. They have killed words and they say that I am sick because I remember it. They chose the forms that deport us and they say that we don't know how to speak. They tie bells to our necks and say look at the crazy people passing by. They want me to use auxiliaries. To be and to have, they say. But they no longer know auxiliaries of what.

Power and identity. To have and to be. The verbs conjugated with to be and those with to have. The tenses with to be. The tenses with to have. Why not both forms? Why not choose? The conjugations of power. The conjugations of identity. Run and get the grammar book. Why bother, she's back to her impassive self. She is knitting the skein of my pain. She is crocheting irregularities. She slyly eliminates invariable words. Beige, dark gray, light gray, mottled. The colors of my pain. She's her old impassive self. She pretends not to understand what I say. She looks into her straw basket. She suggests balls of past tenses. You'd have to make the charts. But the nurse doesn't want to help me. She says that I shouldn't work. She says that I have to rest if I want to get better. I will die of it. I told her that I wasn't sick. She says that we all say that. That isn't true since there are some who are grateful to be cured. The river keeps falling. It is night. The night when he takes the river by the throat to smother it for yet more love. The woman in purple is now coming through the vines and the stone walls. Perhaps the almond trees as well or the walnut tree. The same window pane that nothing can ever knock over. All time and space gather there. I hear it. I know it. I recognize it. She says that we all say that. But it isn't true.

TRANSLATED BY LAUREN DOYLE-MCCOMBS

JEANNE HYVRARD

*Le Corps défunt de la comédie**

Leçon 3: Les femmes

Tout a été dit. Ne disez plus. Faisez. Marcher. Marcher encore.
Marcher boulevard de l'Hôpital. Marcher jusqu'à pouvoir dire. Quoi
donc? Le reste. Le petit reste qui n'a pas été dit. Le petit reste par quoi tout
renaît. Le petit reste de l'espérance. La marche. Le chant d'oiseau au
milieu des immeubles. La palpitation de la rue. L'imperceptible qui permet de continuer. Ce que je ne sais pas nommer. Ce qu'il ne faut pas
nommer. Ce qui ne peut être nommé. Ce qui échappe à la langue. L'in-
nommable. Le transmis pourtant à travers les failles du langage. Cette
faute. Faute de grammaire. Faute de français. Ne disez plus. Faisez. Oser.
Oser enfin. La faute. La faute de frappe. La faute de conjugaison. La faute
de grammaire. La faute professionnelle. La faute de goût. La faute de
temps. La faute de courage. La faute de détermination. La faute d'amour.
   Boulevard de l'Hôpital. La Pitié. La Salpétrière. Le craquement de la
langue. La dislocation de la parole. La fissure de l'ordre ancien. La faute.
La faute toujours la même. Je n'arrive plus à maîtriser le flot. La charpie
des verbes ne pansent plus la déchirure. Les bandages des mots ne retien-
nent plus les chairs. Les plâtres des conjugaisons n'empêchent plus la
confusion. La lésion grossit. La tumeur enfle. La malformation geste. Une
grossesse de cauchemar. Un accouchement mortel. Une gestation d'horreur. Quand vous disez. Quand vous dites. Lequel des deux. Comment
savoir? Au nom de quoi? L'usage rien d'autre. L'ordre. Le maintien de
l'ordre. Le maintien de l'ordre à peine de mort. Quand vous disez. Quand
vous dites quoi donc accoudés au comptoir: Les ratons. Les crouilles. Les
sidis ben basculante dans quel chantier du désespoir.

Le Corps défunt de la comédie (Paris: Seuil, 1982), 26–30. This passage is reprinted
with the kind permission of Editions du Seuil.

Leçon 4: La presse

Le Trou dans le Mur. Le café le long du boulevard. Le café dans la digue. Le comptoir. En inox. Les hommes accoudés. Le Parisien. Le Meilleur. Minute. L'Aurore. France-Soir. Le papier ruisselant d'encre. Le gros titre. La photo. Comment dites-vous? Qu'est-ce qu'ils out encore fait les ratons? Le journal passé de main en main. Les moustaches. Les musettes. Les salopettes. L'indignation. La colère. La haine. Les cafés noirs sur le zinc. Les trois hommes. Le patron du Trou dans le Mur. Son tablier blanc. Son gilet de satin. Sa moustache aussi. Sa moustache noire. Très noire. Vous avez vu les bougnoules? Les parasites. La vermine. La lie. Le déchet. La honte de la planète. Sans sommation, moi je vous dis. Je me demande ce qu'on attend. Vous disez? Vous dites on dit. On ne dit pas tirer dans le tas de bougnoules. On dit condamner à mort les terroristes qui mettent en cause la sécurité de l'État. Quand vous disez. Quoi donc? Faute. Objection de conscience? La conscience n'est pas un concept grammatical. L'usage. L'usure. L'usurpation. Quand vous disez vous avez tous les droits. Pour dire et redire. Tous les droits pour ces deux-là seulement. Vous médisez. Vous contredisez. Vous interdisez. Vous prédisez. Morphologie du français page 198 nota bene. Le verbe dire et son composé redire forment irrégulièrement la deuxième personne du pouvoir. Non. La deuxième personne du pluriel au présent de l'indicatif et de l'impératif. Cette voix que dit-elle. Tais-toi mais tais-toi donc. Cette voix que dit-elle au présent de mon désespoir.

Leçon 4: La presse. La Cour de cassation rejette le pourvoi du Canard enchaîné dans l'affaire dite des micros.

Gare d'Austerlitz. Le ferraillement du métro aérien. L'effort de respiration du corps souterrain. Jardin des Plantes.

L'impossibilité de rejoindre le corps du matin. La pensée éclatée. La chair fatiguée. L'être écartelé. L'impossibilité d'aller une fois encore. Et pourtant si. Une fois encore l'arrachement à la nuit. Une fois encore la séparation. Une fois encore la réunion au corps des errants. Au flot des agonisants. Au corps du monde. Dans les arbres et dans les pierres. Dans les grilles et dans l'asphalte. Dans la désespérance et le mensonge. Dans la détresse et l'absurde. Dans l'interrogation et l'habitude. Dans la nécessité et le renouvellement. Dans l'obstination et le refus. Être avec eux toujours. La ville gigantesque. La commune demeure. Le lieu. Le lien. Le partage. L'entassement. Le chantier et le charnier. La ville de broyage quotidien. La ville d'oiseaux en cages. Des pigeons sur les toits. De moineaux dans les cours. De fourmis. De blattes. De termites. D'insectes renaissants. De rats majuscules. De chats cloîtrés. De chiens impotents. De batraciens aux aquariums minuscules. De volailles aussi par endroits. De lapins de petites filles. De cobayes héréditaires. De hamsters complaisants. De souris consentantes. L'impossibilité de rejoindre le corps du matin. 18 février—à Vitry—Kader 15 ans est abattu par un gardien. Rechercher cette pierre au-dessus de la cheminée. Cet oiseau à l'arrière du bateau. Cet homme qui a frappé. On ne dit pas vous disez. Rechercher la tache de sang au milieu de la peinture. On dit vous dites. La tache sur le vêtement. La trace sur la pierre. Ce corps écrasé entre les tôles. Cette chair déchirée dans le fossé. Ces élytres broyées sur la pierre. Marcher dans la ville. Marcher vers le travail. Marcher vers les retrouvailles. Marcher vers le temps. Marcher vers le recommencement de toute chose. Marcher vers la fin de l'éternité. Le doigt dans la digue n'a pas suffi. Les secours ne sont pas venus. Les femmes-oiseaux ont enterré le Roi Forgeron. Je ne saurai jamais la grammaire.

Pont d'Austerlitz. Tes ailes grandes ouvertes au-dessus du fleuve. Ma chair blessée dans le trou du rocher. Tu m'apportes à vivre. Tu m'apprends à survivre. Tu n'entends pas les craquements. Les marguerites défoliées tentant de survivre. La traversée de la mort. Les temps nouveaux. La renaissance. L'eau boueuse. Fétide. Puante. Tenir quand même. L'eau du fleuve entre tes mains tremblantes.

The Deceased Body of Comedy

Lesson 3: The Women

All has been said. Says no more. Does. Walk. Walk some more. Walk on Hospital Boulevard. Walk until you are able to say. What, then? The rest. The little bit that hasn't been said. The little bit from which everything is reborn. The little bit of hope. The step. The bird's song in the middle of buildings. The palpitation of the street. The imperceptible that allows to continue. What I don't know how to name. What must not be named. What cannot be named. What escapes language. The unnameable. The transmitted for all that through the cracks in language. This error. Grammatical error. Error in French. Says no more. Duz. Dare. So dare. The error. The typo. The error in conjugation. The grammatical error. The professional error. The error of taste. The error of tense. The error of courage. The error of determination. The error of love.

Hospital Boulevard. Pity Hospital. Saltpeter Hospital. The cracking of the language. The dislocation of the word. The fissure of the old order. The error. Always the same error. I can't seem to master the flow anymore. The shreds of verbs no longer dress the wound. The bandages of words no longer hold the flesh together. The sticking plaster of conjugations no longer deters confusion. The lesion grows. The tumor swells. The disformity gestates. A nightmarish pregnancy. A fatal delivery. A gestation of horror. When you says. When you say. Which of the two. How do we know? In the name of what? Usage, nothing else. Order. Maintaining order. Maintaining order on pain of death. When you says. When you say so what leaning on the counter: The coons. The niggers. The wogs good and falling over in some pit of despair.

Lesson 4: The Press

The Hole in the Wall. The café on the boulevard. The café in the dike. The counter. In stainless steel. Men leaning. The Parisian. The Best. Up To The Minute. The New Dawn. Evening France. The newsprint streaming with ink. The headline. The photo. How do you say? So what have the coons done now? The newspaper passed from hand to hand. Moustaches. Bagpipes. Overalls. Indignation. Anger. Hate. Black coffees on the bar. Three men. The boss of the Hole in the Wall. His white apron. His satin vest. His moustache too. His black moustache. Very black. You seen the darkies? The parasites. The vermin. The dregs. The refuse. The shame of the planet. I don't need to be asked, I'll tell you. I wonder what they're waiting for. You says? You say one says. One doesn't say shoot into a pile of niggers. One says condemn to death terrorists who threaten the security of the State. When you says. So what? Error. Objection of conscience? The conscience is not a grammatical concept. Usage. Usury. Usurpation. When you says you has all the rights. To say and to say over. All the rights for these two only. You slander. You contradict. You interdict. You predict. N. B., Morphology of French on page 198. The verb to say and its composite to resay form the second person of power irregularly. No. The second person plural in the present indicative and in the imperative. This voice what says it? Shut up, just shut up. This voice, what says it in the present of my despair.

Lesson 4: The press. The Court of Appeals rejects the *Canard enchaîné*'s appeal in the so-called mike affair.

Austerlitz Station. Reinforcing the metal of the aerial metro. The effort of the subterranean body's breathing. The botanical garden.

The impossibility of catching up with the body of morning. The shattered thought. The tired hide. The quartered being. The impossibility of going one more time. And yet, yes. Tearing away from the night one more time. Separation once more. The reunion of wandering bodies once more. In the flood of the dying. In the body of the world. In the trees and the stones. In the fences and the asphalt. In despair and lying. In distress and absurdity. In interrogation and habit. In necessity and renewal. In stubbornness and refusal. To be with them always. The gigantic city. The common dwelling. The locale. The link. The division. The overcrowding.

The construction pit and the open grave. The city of daily crushing. The city of birds in cages. Of pigeons on the roofs. Of sparrows in the courtyards. Of ants. Of cockroaches. Of termites. Of regenerating insects. Of capital rats. Of cloistered cats. Of impotent dogs. Of frogs with miniscule aquariums. Of fowl, too, in places. Of little girls' rabbits. Of hereditary guinea pigs. Of complaisant hamsters. Of consenting mice. The impossibility of catching up with the body of morning. 18 February—in Vitry— Kader, fifteen years old, is struck down by a janitor. Look for that stone over the fireplace. That bird at the back of the boat. That man who struck. One doesn't say you says. Look for the spot of blood in the middle of the painting. One says you say. The spot on the clothes. The trace on the stone. This body crushed between sheets of metal. This torn flesh in the ditch. These elytra ground into the stone. Walk in the city. Walk to work. Walk towards reunions. Walk towards time. Walk towards the new beginning of every thing. Walk towards the end of eternity. The finger in the dike was not enough. Help didn't come. The bird-women buried the Blacksmith King. I will never know grammar.

Austerlitz Bridge. Your widespread wings over the river. My wounded flesh in the hole in the rock. You bring me things to live on. You teach me how to survive. You don't hear the cracking. Defoliated daisies trying to survive. Death's crossing. New times. Renaissance. Muddy water. Fetid. Stinking. Hold on just the same. The river's water in your trembling hands.

TRANSLATED BY LAUREN DOYLE-MCCOMBS

DOMINIQUE JULLIEN

Jean Echenoz

Jean Echenoz was born after World War II, grew up in southern France, and lives in Paris, where he works in a press agency. His three novels (*Le Méridien de Greenwich*, 1979, *Cherokee*, 1983, *L'Equipée malaise*, 1986) have been published by Les Editions de Minuit. A collection of short stories is in print. Articles published on him in several magazines and newspapers portray him as a shy and reticent personality, and biographical information is scarce. We do know, however, that although his novels often take place in exotic countries (*L'Equipée malaise* in Malaysia, *Le Méridien de Greenwich* on a tiny coral island off the coast of Australia), he has not traveled there himself, but has collected very thorough information through books and maps—an interesting concern, not unlike Flaubert's, for historical and geographical realism, in novels otherwise so full of fantasy:

> It's not a question of vagueness. Only the accumulation of multitudinous small details makes lying possible. . . . I know neither Malaysia nor Le Havre. I bought maps. I remembered conversations. I read loads of technical books on the cultivation of rubber. I took a lot of notes. After starting the engine at this point of truth, I engaged the gears of fiction. [Interview with Yann Plougastel, *L'Evénement*, 5 to 11 February 1987.]

Although the Médicis prize awarded to him for his second novel, *Cherokee*, has begun to familiarize the public with his work, Jean Echenoz is still a new name in contemporary French fiction. No critical studies are available on him yet, but a number of short articles can be found in different periodicals. One of the best is Patrick MacCarthy's presentation of *Cherokee*, which also offers very perceptive insights on his other works ("Playing with the parrot," *Times Literary Supplement*, 14 October 1983): so overwhelming, moreover, are the similarities between the three novels, that they may appear as variations on a theme.

Jean Echenoz's first two novels, *Le Méridien de Greenwich* and *Cherokee*, are an obvious parody of detective stories, and more specifically of the American *roman noir* of the fifties. *L'Equipée malaise* owes more to the adventure novel. Another major influence is, not surprisingly, cinematography. To motion pictures Jean Echenoz owes his visual presentation of characters ("Il y a maintenant Justine Fischer dans une chambre grise" [*L'Equipée malaise*, 17]) as well as numerous ironic references to cinematographical *clichés*. Paul is boarding the ship which will take him to Malaysia: "Paul descendit sur le pont. Classique bande-son d'appareillage" (*L'Equipée malaise*, 162). *Le Méridien de Greenwich* ends in Hollywoodian apotheosis:

> They remain thus, almost immobile. We rise in the air. Without taking our eyes off them—they become smaller—we rise slowly until we encompass the entire ship, and the sea all around, in the rectangular space of our gaze. Music can be added to this spectacle. Can also be retained the natural sound of the ocean which decreases during our ascension until it becomes silence. The image freezes. [*Le Méridien de Greenwich*, 255–56]

The novels combine strong realistic elements (portrayal of the underworld, accurate descriptions of Paris and its suburbs) with a dreamlike quality generated by a certain arbitrariness in the characters' behavior, and above all by the lack of any satisfactory solution of the entangled mysteries that form the plots. Any attempt to summarize the novels would be hopeless: they offer a confusing network of murders, blackmail, and manhunt, among which the reader easily becomes lost.

In *Cherokee*, the unheroic but mildly sentimental Georges Chave, who works for a private detective agency, becomes involved in an increasingly complex network of criminal interactions through his search for the beautiful Jenny Weltman, whom he met at the Bibliothèque Nationale. As we meet Georges Chave's criminal cousin (the sinister Fred Shapiro), a lunatic sect that worships the Sister-in-Law and practices human sacrifices, a colossal Mexican fortune whose heirs have died out, a pair of imbecilic gangsters chased by another pair of imbecilic policemen, the story bounces on, from missed appointments to inane pursuits, until the protagonist is finally reunited with his cousin, simultaneously recovering both Jenny Weltman and his lost version of Charlie Parker's *Cherokee*: "Bon, dit Fred. Qu'est-ce qu'on fait, maintenant?" (*Cherokee*, 247). The book ends, leaving the reader to wonder if it is in a reconciliation or a last murder.

In *Le Méridien de Greenwich* we come across a scientist held prisoner on a tiny Australian island in order to construct a mysterious machine for an international gang. As the characters proliferate (a blind contract killer, a secret militia of Australian rebels, two or three ladies) we even lose track of who the main character may be: is it Paul, the unwilling accomplice, forced into a last contract by blackmail, and absurdly killed as he is about to be reunited with his lover? Or Byron Caine the scientist, who coolly blows up the island and falls asleep while awaiting death? Or the two survivors Theo and Rachel, whose final kiss puts an arbitrary end to the novel?

In *L'Equipée malaise*, the paths of Charles Pontiac and Jean-Luc Pons, who loved the same Nicole Fischer thirty years earlier but were rejected by her, cross again, as the former helps the latter stir up a rebellion on his Malaysian rubber plantation, with the inefficient help of Pons's nephew Paul, a small-scale arms dealer, who turns out to be in love with Nicole's daughter Justine, and is also tracked down by a rival gang of Belgian dealers. Uniting all these spicy components is the *Boustrophédon*, the Cypriot freighter used for shipment of the weapons to the Malaysian rebels. Like the ancient Greek writing that reads alternatively from left to right and right to left, it sails back and forth between Le Havre and Malaysia and carries the characters through a plot overflowing with mutinies, rebellions, useless kidnappings, vanishing ladies, cold-hearted adventurers, an underground network of Parisian *clochards*, and so forth.

All the traditional ingredients of detective and adventure genres, all the *clichés*, are thrown together; parody is generated in the excess of their accumulation. Indeed, suspense, the major element of detective novels, seems to be deliberately misused. The kidnapping of Degas's wife flatly annihilates all potential suspense, as Georges Chave discovers the hideaway in less than a page and frees the victim without a fight (*Cherokee*, 54). This wholly undramatic episode is deliberately unexploited, as if by an ironic mishandling of the model genre.

For none of these extravagant schemes ever comes to any clear issue. The useless abduction of Justine by the Belgian gansters is a good example of these empty quests which are the substance of the narration. They kidnap the girl in the vain hope that she will lead them to Paul; uncertain of the next step to take under such circumstances, they decide to send a message to the family, but do not know how to phrase it. " 'This message is violent,' Plankaert stated, while giving it back to Van Os. 'It is extremely threatening. Isn't it excessive?' " (*L'Equipée malaise*, 235). Finally the message is written but never sent.

The principle of the novels is that everything happens but nothing goes on. While in the detective story every detail eventually finds its place in the solution, here on the contrary we are given too many pieces of the puzzle, so that we feel the uneasiness (a pun obviously encouraged by the French title, *L'Equipée malaise*) of a story both overcrowded and vacuous. The characters are frantically busy yet strangely inactive. Paul, sent on a secret mission to the island of Greenwich, does not seem to have any clear duty to perform. The task assigned to Abel is hopelessly obscure:

If we thus mobilize these people around a gamble, if we set them against each other for the sake of this gamble, they will all kill each other—this is the reason for the operation—without taking the time to verify if this gamble truly exists. . . .
—But who *are* these people? Abel asked without really expecting an answer. Why should they kill each other?
—Some of them are potential trouble makers. But let's come to the point concerning your involvement. Since the object is to pull into this operation as many individuals as possible, it is a good idea to have as many false clues as possible—they are all fake anyway, therefore in one sense all true. But I am wandering. [*Le Méridien de Greenwich*, 243–44]

In *Le Méridien de Greenwich*, the scientist spends his captivity working on jigsaw puzzles; instead of a new puzzle he is offered a woman, an extra character, who naturally does not fit into the story but rather adds another loose end to it, further puzzling the reader.

The funny thing is that the other is still waiting for his puzzle and it's a woman who will be offered to him instead.
Yes, said Tristano.
But that's not the same thing at all.
Maybe, said Tristano. [*Le Méridien de Greenwich*, 163]

Loose ends become the very principle of the narration. Even the minutely descriptive realism is paradoxically used to distort the story (in this respect Echenoz is not far from the Nouveau Roman): "Les objets décrits précisément, en un sens c'est réaliste, mais à force de précisions cela devient imaginaire" (Interview with Anne Théron, *Libération*, 13 october 1983). The accurate depiction of Malaysian plantations, the story of Marguerite-Elie Ferro's Mexican fortune (the other detailed biography in *Cherokee* being that of the parrot), for all their historic verisimilitude, serve no other purpose than to lead astray from the "main" story. Another exemplary case is the useless character of Odile Otéro, to whom *L'Equipée malaise* devotes four pages, while she is only accidentally connected to the story, as a victim of the bank robbery. The author abruptly breaks off this fascinating biography, as if suddenly realizing that it is beside the point.

The portrayal of characters shows the same slightly irrelevant features. Their presentation is both abrupt and arbitrary; they are not introduced as much as dropped into the story: "Voici donc Fred. Fred est assis" (*Cherokee*, 21). The description singles out arbitrary features which convey a sense of utter shallowness:

Jouvin, who had no shoulders, parted his hair on the right flank of his skull, was always raising his eyebrows over washed-out eyes, like Luce he wore size forty shoes. [*L'Equipée malaise*, 12]

Such characters are unlikely to have a psychology.

I don't like psychology. So to dwell on the psychology of the characters does not interest me. But to write how they sit, drive, or drink allows me in fact to reveal more about their mood. [Interview with Yann Plougastel, *L'Evénement*, 5 to 11 February 1987.]

Even the futile precision of their appearance cannot be taken as an indication of interiority, but rather as an ironic short-circuit of the conventional novelistic portrait:

Once upon a time, there were two men whose names were Ripert and Bock. The latter sported a wide, cream-colored tie on a chocolate polyester shirt, which gave him simultaneously the ambiguous appearance of a pimp and breakfast. [*Cherokee*, 12.]

This voluntarily unconvincing portrayal falls short of any attempt to suggest psychological depth. The characters live and die, but always remain to some extent unconcerned. After a courteous and unemotional torture scene, the gangsters and their victim proceed to drink together in a very civil fashion (*Le Méridien de Greenwich*, 111). Love, likewise, is underplayed. In the same novel, Paul, although in love with Vera, lacks the energy to see her, almost regrets her coming to the island, while she, upon learning that he is dead, essentially resents being left in the middle of the story that he was telling her. The characters are insufficiently gifted for love as for life, doomed to that loneliness which comes from lack of passion. Human relationships are precarious and accidental.

Death is both bloody and undramatic, a radical rejection of the tragic dimension:

One characteristic of the Astro 400 being to absorb and expel indifferently all kinds of projectiles, three bullets of different sizes crossed the air one after the other before lodging in the body of Paul, who, flailing about, fell and died without any apparent suffering, almost instantaneously, but not before the idea crossed his mind that the ground and he were about to meet in an unusual way. [*Le Méridien de Greenwich*, 166]

A few pages later, the death of the blind killer Russel gives way to a comparison between his brain and the cauliflowers on which it is spilled (204). The cruelty with which the author abuses and discards these shallow characters leaves little room for emotion. Their deaths are as meaningless as their lives, a bungled improvisation. The novels lack the tenderness which we find in another model, Queneau. Like Queneau's, these characters are banal and unheroic, like them they often lead humble, suburban lives. Charles Pontiac the *clochard*, like the character in *Le Chiendent* who spends his life alternatively defacing and painting his own front gate, convey the same conviction that all lives are equal. The novel arbitrarily singles them out in the crowd: "La silhouette d'un homme se profila; simultanément, des milliers" (*Le Chiendent*).

But Queneau's characters, although he does not take them seriously, are endearing because they are subject to change (one has only to remember Zazie's famous last sentence): they are, in a way, two and a half dimensional. Echenoz's world is a harder one, perhaps closer in this respect to its model genre of the *roman noir*, and one in which the characters, for all the extravagant events which take place, are static. The lack of humanity is even more perceptible in *L'Equipée malaise*, where characters and events form couples, a peculiarity which gives them a comic, mechanical aspect, ironically summarized by the fortune-teller's prediction: "C'est tout à fait clair, tout ira par deux, toujours plus ou moins par deux" (*L'Equipée malaise*, 49).

Echenoz's novels are self-destroying devices. They make use of all the elements of adventure and mystery, but play them against one another. The structure of their plots is closer to vaudeville than to the detective novel; each character or group of characters is presented in short, autonomous narrative units, interact with increasing complexity until the final clash which brings them together, leaving the mystery not only unresolved, but unexposed. "On ne trouve rien, d'accord, mais au moins qu'on ait l'air de chercher" (*Cherokee*, 34).

But whereas the success of a vaudeville comedy consists of the final tying together of all the situations, here, although the links are present, the story falls to pieces, so that not even the emblematic reel of catgut sitting on Pons's table in a chaos of heteroclite objects could sew it together.

Drama is deprived of its catastrophe; the detective genre is deprived of its *raison d'être*, the solution. The reader, constantly tantalized by a whirlwind of events leading nowhere, is left to experience the uneasiness, the *malaise*, whose symbol is Caine's monstrous machine in *Le Méridien de Greenwich*:

As to the related machine, which was supposed to represent the application of his theory, supposed to show the extent of his speculations—it did it: it was anything at all. Caine had put together a kind of collage, a conglomeration of accumulated junk which he assembled according to the arbitrary but rigorous principle of random selection. It was a mere technological trompe l'oeil with just the right number of motors and mysteries. . . . [*Le Méridien de Greenwich*, 222]

BIBLIOGRAPHY

NOVELS

Le Méridien de Greenwich. Paris: Minuit, 1979.
Cherokee. Paris: Minuit, 1983.
L'Equipée malaise. Paris: Minuit, 1986.

JEAN ECHENOZ

*L'Equipée malaise**

—Elle a dit non. Ça ne me dit rien. C'est ce qu'elle a dit, mais je ne
suis pas tout à fait sûr que. Tu es gentil, tu cesses de ricaner, tu veux?

—Je connais ça, dit Bob en agitant les mains pour suggérer une esca-
drille de bêtes volantes au-dessus de lui, j'ai tellement connu ça. Ensuite?

Ensuite Paul avait essayé de se rappeler au souvenir de Justine. Il
avait évoqué le film de l'autre soir, le premier film, du soir qu'elle avait
son chapeau —spécialement certaines scènes qu'à son dam elle paraissait
avoir moins aimées que lui —, sans oser faire allusion au chapeau. Il avait
proposé d'aller prendre quelque chose quelque part, mais elle avait argué
d'amis qu'elle devait retrouver autre part. C'était un refus léger, sans
hauteur, Paul ne s'était pas senti rejeté vertigineusement: elle avait bien
voulu noter son numéro de téléphone sur un calepin de cuir, à fermoir de
cuivre, qu'elle dut chercher longuement dans le fond de son grand sac
plein d'objets. Elle accepta même de lui donner le sien, son propre numéro, quoique du bout de ses lèvres rouges et sans dévoiler son prénom,
sans même songer à s'inventer un faux prénom, c'est juste qu'elle ne
voulait pas dire le sien, va savoir pourquoi.

Mais une semaine s'était passée sans qu'elle appelât Paul, qu'on
retrouve encore solitaire et défait au fond du même fauteuil, dans le
même coin sombre du studio de Bob, les pieds posés sur une incomplète
collection du magazine *Penthouse*, une main accrochée au rebord du bar
où s'emplissent d'anciens contenants de moutarde et d'anchois. Certains
de ces contenants sont un peu ébréchés, d'autres n'ont pas encore ôté leur
étiquette, des pellicules d'alcool y poissent, durcissent, brunissent. Le bar
est encastré dans la cloison, à angle droit, mais la saignée demeure ina-

---

L'Equipée malaise (Paris: Minuit, 1986), ch. 8, 44–51. This passage is reprinted with
the kind permission of Editions de Minuit.

chevée: le plâtre y parait brut, pulvérulent sans enduit protecteur. Ce n'est pas terminé, ce n'est pas net. Chez Bob, presque tout est ainsi. Le visage de Paul exprime un tiers de renoncement, deux d'amertume avec un trait de secret contentement de soi. Il regarde son verre au fond duquel, dans sa haute cour translucide, le cube de glace a repris son lent parcours de détenu à l'heure de la promenade.

—Ça n'a pas de sens, je ne sais même pas son nom. J'ai le numéro mais je n'ai pas le nom. (Paul considère maintenant l'ongle, à distance, de son pouce gauche.) Je ne peux pas l'appeler dans ces conditions. (Paul ronge l'ongle.) Ça n'a pas de sens.

—Tu ne peux pas rester comme ça, rappelle Bob. Tu ne veux pas voir quelqu'un? (Paul hausse l'épaule en recrachant l'arc d'ongle.) On va voir quelqu'un, viens.

Foin du tarot sempiternel, fi du globe de cristal où l'être aimé danse les sept voiles tel un poisson chinois dans son bocal: Bob, dans le quartier, connaissait quelques spécialistes aux techniques rares, experts dont les pratiques se fussent éteintes sans eux. Les récents Africains par exemple, masse fraîche sur le marché mantique, disposaient d'un réseau d'hiéra-tiques agents commerciaux, hommes de haute taille en vaste boubou clair, sous toque léopardée, distribuant des bristols aux croisements de grande circulation. Bob avait pris langue avec certains d'entre eux qui tous lui avaient parlé de monsieur Brome, marabout absolu, le plus extra-lucide en sa branche. Allons le voir, proposa Bob. Paul était toujours d'accord pour qu'on s'occupât de lui.

Monsieur Brome était absent, on le supposait chez son beau-frère qui n'était pas chez lui non plus. Dans la cuisine d'un voisin de palier du beau-frère, toutes portes ouvertes, quatre sujets nattés disputaient en idiome toucouleur; Bob s'en fut aux renseignements. Paul attendit seul dans un petit living tapissé de rouge et vert, moquetté d'orange, avec un jeté de lit également vif sur le divan et un gros récepteur Téléavia sur son meuble de tubulure et de verre fumé. A l'étage inférieur du meuble, un magnétoscope de la première heure se patinait de poussière gluante— hormis sur les touches de commande où les index avaient poli d'ovales luisances, nettes comme du réglisse frais.

Paul s'assit sur le divan, fouilla dans le tas de cassettes formé au pied du meuble, lisant les étiquettes sans reconnaître aucun titre, aucun nom, sans les comprendre tous. Au hasard, il choisit une de ces cassettes qu'il enfonça dans le ventre de l'appareil: la bande à moitié dévidée fit soudain paraître une scène d'amour sous les cocotiers, beaucoup de cocotiers, énormément de cocotiers aux branchages mollement mus par un sirop de zéphyr. Bob ressortit de la cuisine, arrêtant son œil embué par la conver-sation sur toute cette palmeraie. On y va, dit-il, allons-y.

Dehors s'affirmait le crépuscule. Rue de l'Orillon se promenaient d'autres Africains, leurs dents arrachaient de petits bouts de nuit mâchés comme de la gomme, de la cola, un collier vert phosphorait autour du cou de l'un, le front d'un autre était biffé d'un trait de sparadrap rose, aucun d'entre eux ne savait où monsieur Brome était passé. A l'angle du passage Piver, Bob se souvint d'un ami géomancien qui exerçait là, nommé Bouc Bel-Air et rencontré chez Félix Potin. On y va? Attends, fit Paul en arrêt devant un magasin de chaussures. J'aime bien ça, dit-il en désignant une paire exposée, j'aime bien ce genre. Toi non?

Bob grimaça devant le modèle: son empeigne s'ornait d'une espèce de revers, d'une manière de col de part et d'autre du laçage qui avait ainsi l'allure d'un nœud texan, serré comme autour d'un cou à la base de la cheville. Ils entrèrent, la vendeuse était humble, timide en blouse lavande, aimable par résignation. Paul plongea son pied dans le soulier, qui d'abord lui parut trop grand. Puis trop petit, quoique en même temps toujours trop grand. Testée, chaque taille adjacente accentuait l'un de ces défauts sans jamais tout à fait résoudre l'autre. Il essaya, plusieurs fois, toutes les demi-pointures dans les deux sens, incertain de son inconfort, sans pouvoir faire appel à d'autres témoins que ses propres pieds, et le sentiment de la solitude à nouveau le submergeait. Il éleva l'œil vers la chausseuse: touchez mon pied, supplia-t-il, juste le bout, est-ce que ça va? Est-ce que je suis bien dedans? Elle ne sut, ne voulut répondre. Il renonça. On s'enfonça dans le passage Piver.

Bouc Bel-Air était un homme normal qui vivait proprement dans un petit logement. Ses vêtements n'étaient pas boutonnés de travers, quoique sa barbe et ses cheveux fussent hirsutes, presque perpendiculaires à la peau. Sur toute sa joue, parallèlement à l'arc du maxillaire, cette barbe était traversée par une longue balafre transamazonienne à plusieurs voies, marque des dents d'une petite fourche ou des griffes d'un moyen lion. Aucune table, aucune chaise en vrai bois n'étaient visibles ici, nulle pièce pesante de mobilier. L'ameublement consistait en matériel de camping assez ancien, fleurant la récupération: un lit pliant, des fauteuils en tube tendus de forte toile aux rayures ternies, aux couleurs diluées, pochées par l'usage. Le géomancien pria ses hôtes autour d'une table en isorel plastifié bleu, au pourtour tigré de souvenirs de mégots, puis il passa dans ce qui devait être l'office, où se distinguaient une glacière en tôle, un deux-feux au butane monté sur acier cadmié, un garde-manger sous du tulle de nylon. Il revint avec une bouteille ainsi que des quarts d'alu bossu; on but. On but en silence, après quoi Bouc Bel-Air considéra Bob interrogativement.

—C'est pour lui, dit Bob en désignant Paul.

Bouc Bel-Air se tourna donc vers Paul, parut l'étudier un moment puis se pencha vers un bac de sable posé par terre près de la table, tout à fait semblable aux garde-robes qui servent à l'exonération des chats. Le principe, dit-il, est le suivant.

Il souleva le bac pesant, le posa sur la table, égalisant sa surface blonde du bout des doigts. Le principe est le suivant, dit-il encore en extrayant de sa poche un sachet de plastique fort d'où s'écoulèrent au creux de sa paume une demi-douzaine de chevrotines. Il les examina, les fit rebondir dans sa main tout en répétant que le principe était le suivant, paraissant hésiter sur la meilleure façon d'exposer ce principe. Puis il dut renoncer à ses vues didactiques, car tout à trac il fit sauter ses projectiles sur la petite plage close.

Le grand silence, tout de suite, fut dans l'appartement; le monde extérieur même l'observait, immédiatement représenté par le passage Piver. Quelques secondes une grappe d'enfants le troubla, l'un d'eux criait distinctement que c'est comme ça, Pascal, c'est comme ça.

Bouc Bel-Air considéra les plombs ensablés, l'un après l'autre, puis l'ensemble de leur arrangement. Paul et Bob le virent amener sa main ouverte par-dessus le dispositif, la déplacer comme s'il prenait des mesures dans l'air, ouvrant divers compas avec ses doigts sur lesquels, ensuite, il parut compter. Puis il se recula d'un cran comme pour gagner de la perspective, tout en se massant longtemps l'extérieur puis l'intérieur du nez. Il se leva enfin, passa dans l'autre pièce, on l'entendit tirer de l'eau à l'évier, boire et se gargariser, se moucher entre ses doigts qu'il rinça. Qu'est-ce qu'il fout, murmura Paul.

Bob ne lui exposa pas comment l'autre venait de tirer les points, former les figures, définir l'horoscope, comment il devait à présent réfléchir activement, remonter comme à la source d'un fleuve vers l'axe de tout un éventail de déductions partielles. Tais-toi, grogna-t-il seulement, tu vas le déconcentrer. Bouc Bel-Air revenait de la cuisine, s'essuyant les mains dans un torchon bleu. C'est très clair, dit-il en reprenant place devant Paul, qui jeta sur Bob un regard à peine inquiet.

—C'est clair, répéta-t-il. Juste je vérifie.

—Vous n'êtes pas sûr? osa Paul dans le silence maintenu.

—Je suis sûr, dit l'autre, je suis sûr. Juste que ma confiance n'exclut pas le contrôle.

D'une main sûre il chercha sous sa chaise une épaisse brochure congestionnée de chiffres minuscules, tassés sur mauvais papier entre des marges étroites, et qui devaient constituer une sorte de calendrier stellaire. Il le feuilleta par à-coups, se référant par coups d'œil aux écarts entre les chevrotines, puis le referma quoique hésitant à s'en défaire, et tout compte fait le glissa entre son siège et son séant, comme son corps se penchait plus avant vers le tableau géomantique:

—C'est tout à fait clair, tout ira par deux, toujours plus ou moins par deux. Voilà ce qui va se passer. Vous allez rencontrer un homme actif, cheveux blonds grisonnants, portant lunettes. Lunettes, Mars dans le Bélier, n'est-ce pas. Il devrait vous, attendez un instant.

Déjà plus détaché, Bouc Bel-Air régla l'angle du pouce et de l'index par-dessus deux plombs, par-dessus deux autres, comparant les écarts en levant ses doigts à hauteur d'œil mi-clos, laborantin devant l'éprouvette, hochant un crâne professionnel.

—Solliciter pour un placement, compléta-t-il, quelque chose comme un investissement, affaire d'outillage semblerait-il. Machines-outils. Naturellement, à ce degré de précision il peut toujours y.

Mimique évasive, genre garagiste ou chirurgien. Mais quand même en cinquième maison, Vénus conjointe, en principe ça ne faisait pas un pli. Quant à déterminer quand se produirait cette rencontre, on ne le pouvait pas. La question, d'ailleurs, n'était pas là.

—Où est la question, Bouc? voulut savoir Bob.

—La question n'est pas dans les faits, dit le géomancien, mais dans leurs conséquences.

—Alors, demanda Paul, qu'est-ce que je devrais faire?

—M'est avis que cet homme, exprima Bouc après une réflexion, vous ne devriez pas accepter son offre (je vous dis ça, vous faites comme vous voulez), il me semble qu'il vaut mieux refuser. Je ne pourrais pas dire pourquoi, par exemple.

—Rien d'autre?

—Un homme encore, estima Bouc Bel-Air. Je le verrais plus proche de vous, plus vieux que l'autre, plus maigre aussi (je vous ai dit qu'il serait maigre, l'autre?), outillage également.

—D'accord, dit Paul, donc je refuse.

—Non, fit Bouc, cette fois vous marchez. C'est ce que je préconise, naturellement c'est à vous de voir. Avis tout personnel.

Il traça dans l'air un geste plus expéditivement arrondi que les autres, comme s'il y signait une décharge. L'amour, dit Paul, l'amour maintenant. Bouc Bel-Air observa ses genoux. Bon, dit Paul, vous acceptez les chèques?

L'Equipée malaise

The following is an excerpt from Jean Echenoz's novel *L'Équipée malaise*. The hero, Paul, has spotted the attractive Justine, who is wearing a fedora, in line for a movie. He follows her into the theater—unnoticed, imagining she is the perfect woman for him—but doesn't dare introduce himself. When he sees her again several nights later, bareheaded and in front of another movie house, he works up the courage to ask if she remembers him. The attempted pick-up, predictably, falls flat, and Paul is now seeking solace from his best friend, Bob.

—Translator's note

"She said no. Doesn't ring a bell. That's what she said, but I'm not entirely sure she's—Would you mind not snickering?"

"I've been there," said Bob, waving his hands above his head as if to ward off a squadron of flying insects. "Man, have I been there. So then what?"

Then Paul had tried to recommend himself to Justine's memory. He had alluded to the film from the evening when she'd been wearing her hat—especially certain scenes that, to his dismay, she seemed to have enjoyed less than he—without daring mention the hat itself. He had suggested they go somewhere to get something, but she had pleaded friends that she had to meet somewhere else. It was a casual rejection, without haughtiness; Paul had not felt too let down. She had seemed quite willing to jot his phone number in her leather-bound address book with copper clasp, which she sought at length at the bottom of a large bag chock-full of objects. She had even agreed to give him hers, her own phone number—although in a murmur that barely made it past her red lips, and without revealing her name. She hadn't thought to make up a false name; she just didn't want to tell him her real one, go figure why.

But a week had gone by without her calling Paul, whom we still find lonely and unkempt in the hollow of the same armchair, in the same dark corner of Bob's studio. His feet are resting on an incomplete collection of *Penthouse* magazines. One hand clutches the edge of the bar, on which rests a collection of former mustard and anchovy jars. Some of these jars are chipped; others have not yet shed their labels. Rings of alcohol become sticky, harden, tarnish. The bar is embedded in the wall at a right angle, but the juncture remains unfinished; without a protective coat, the plaster appears naked, pulverulent. It's not complete, it's not clean. At Bob's, almost everything is like this. Paul's face expresses one part renunciation, two parts bitterness, with a dash of hidden self-satisfaction. He looks at his glass, at the bottom of which, in its tall translucent courtyard, the ice cube has resumed its slow course, like a jailbird at recess.

"It doesn't make any sense, I don't even know her name. I know her number but I don't know her name." (Paul now considers, at a distance, his left thumbnail.) "I can't call her under these conditions." (Paul gnaws at the nail.) "It doesn't make any sense."

"You can't stay like this," Bob advises him. "Don't you want to see someone?" (Paul shrugs his shoulders while spitting out the crescent of nail.) "Come on, let's go see someone."

Scornful of the sempiternal tarot, disdainful of the crystal ball in which the loved one does the dance of the seven veils like a Chinese fish in its jar, Bob knew several neighborhood specialists in rare techniques, experts whose practices would have become extinct were it not for them. The most recent crop of Africans, for example, a fresh load on the divination market, commanded a network of hieratic sales representatives—

men of large stature wearing enormous, light-colored *boubous* and leop-
ard-skin toques, distributing business cards in heavily trafficked crossroads. Bob had broken the ice with several among them, who had all
spoken of a certain Mr. Brome, the ultimate Marabout, the most extra-
lucid in his field. "Let's go see him," suggested Bob. Paul was always
willing for someone to take care of him.

Mr. Brome was out, said to be visiting his brother-in-law, who was
not at home either. In the kitchen of a next-door neighbor of the brother-
in-law's, four plaited subjects were quarrelling in Tukulor idiom; Bob
went to reconnoiter. Paul waited alone in a narrow living room with red
and green wallpaper, and orange carpet, with an equally vibrant bed-
spread on the sofa. A large television perched on a table made of metal
tubing and smoked glass. On the table's lower shelf, a primitive VCR
displayed a patina of sticky dust—except on the control buttons, which
fingers had polished into gleaming ovals, shiny as fresh licorice.

Paul sat on the sofa, flipped through the pile of cassettes at the foot of
the table, read the labels without recognizing a single title, a single name,
without even understanding all of them. He chose one of the cassettes at
random and slid it into the belly of the machine. Abruptly the half-
rewound tape brought forth a love scene under coconut palms, many
coconut palms, an incredible number of coconut palms, their branches
limply swayed by a syrupy zephyr. Bob returned from the kitchen, resting
his conversation-clouded eye on all those palms. "Come on," he said,
"let's go."

Outside the dusk asserted itself. On Rue de l'Orillon other Africans
walked. Their teeth tore off small bits of night which they chewed like
gum, like cola. A green collar phosphoresced around the neck of one, the
forehead of another was cancelled by a line of pink bandaid. None of them
knew where Mr. Brome had disappeared to. At the corner of Passage
Piver, Bob remembered a geomancer of his acquaintance named Bouc Bel-
Air, met at the local grocer's, who practiced his profession on that street.
Shall we go? Wait, went Paul, who had stopped in front of a shoe store. "I
really like those," he said, indicating a pair on display. "I like that kind.
Don't you?"

Bob grimaced at the model in question: its instep was decorated on
either side with a kind of lapel, like a collar, which gave the laces the
appearance of a Texan string tie, knotted, as if around a neck, at the base
of the ankle. They went into the shop. The salesgirl was humble, shy in a
lavender blouse, friendly in a resigned sort of way. Paul plunged his foot
into the shoe, which at first seemed too large, then too small, although
still too large at the same time. Tested, each adjacent size accentuated
one of these defects without entirely managing to eliminate the other. He
tried on, several times, all the half-sizes in both directions, uncertain of
his discomfort, without being able to call on any witnesses other than his

own feet, and the feeling of loneliness engulfed him once more. He raised his eyes toward the footwear specialist: Touch my foot, he begged, just the tip, does it seem all right? Am I comfortable in them? She had neither the will nor the desire to answer. He gave up. They disappeared into Passage Piver.

Bouc Bel-Air was an average man who lived cleanly in small lodgings. He wore the same clothes as anyone else, although his beard and hair were plentiful, almost perpendicular to his skin. All across his cheek, parallel to the arc of the jawbone, this beard showed a long transamazonian gash with several lanes: the tines of a small fork or the claws of a medium-sized lion. No wooden tables or chairs were to be found here, no piece of heavy furniture. The furnishings consisted of rather outdated camping equipment, smacking of salvage: a folding bed, chairs made of tubing over which stretched heavy fabric with faded stripes, in diluted colors, pocked by use. The geomancer greeted his guests around a table of blue plastified hardboard, its circumference streaked with the memory of cigarettes. Then he retreated into what must have been the kitchen, in which they could see a sheet-metal ice box, a butane burner on a cadmium-plated steel stand, and a pantry covered with nylon netting. He returned with a bottle and three dented aluminum measuring cups; they drank. They drank in silence, after which Bouc Bel-Air considered Bob interrogatively.

"It's for him," said Bob, indicating Paul.

Bouc Bel-Air thus turned toward Paul, seemed to study him a moment, then leaned toward a box of sand sitting on the floor near the table, similar in all respects to the commodes that serve for the exoneration of cats. "The principle," he said, "is as follows."

He lifted the heavy box, placed it on the table, and equalized its blond surface with the tips of his fingers. "The principle is as follows," he repeated, removing from his pocket a thick plastic bag from which he poured half a dozen buck-shot pellets into the palm of his hand. He examined them, made them jump in his palm while reiterating that the principle was as follows, seemed to hesitate as to the best way to set forth this principle. Then he apparently renounced his didactic views, for all of a sudden he made his projectiles leap onto the minature private beach.

Instantly, a perfect silence filled the apartment. The external world itself—most immediately represented by Passage Piver—observed same. For several seconds a cluster of children disturbed it; one of them cried distinctly that that's the way it is, Pascal, that's the way it is.

Bouc Bel-Air contemplated the sandy pellets one by one, then the totality of their configuration. Paul and Bob watched him lead his open hand over the arrangement, move it around as though he were taking measurements in the air, and open various compasses with his fingers, on which he then seemed to be counting. After this he leaned back a notch as if to get a better perspective on the matter, all the while carefully massaging the exterior, then the interior, of his nose. Finally he stood and walked into the other room. They heard him run water from the faucet, drink, gargle, and blow his nose between his fingers, which he then rinsed. "The heck's he up to?" whispered Paul.

Bob did not explain how the other had just scattered the pellets, formed the figures, defined the horoscope; how he now had to reflect actively, return, as if to the source of a river, toward the axis of a whole range of partial deductions. He simply muttered, "Shut up, you'll break his concentration."

Bouc Bel-Air reappeared from the kitchen, wiping his hands on a blue dishrag. "It's very clear," he said, reclaiming his place before Paul, who threw Bob a mildly worried glance.

"It's clear," he repeated. "I just have to verify."

"You're not sure?" ventured Paul in the sustained silence.

"I'm sure," said the other, "I'm sure. Just that my confidence does not exclude a certain monitoring."

With a sure hand he groped under his chair for a thick booklet full of minuscule numbers crammed onto poor-quality paper, which must have constituted a kind of astral calendar. He leafed through it jerkily, glancing at the spaces separating the buck-shot, then closed it again; unwilling to part with it entirely, he finally slid the book between his seat and his seat. His body leaned farther forward toward the geomantic tableau.

"It's completely clear. Everything will come in twos, always more or less in twos. This is what will happen: you will meet an energetic man, with greying blond hair, wearing glasses. Glasses, Mars in Aries, don't you see. He should ask you, wait a moment."

Already more detached, Bouc Bel-Air adjusted the joint of his thumb and forefinger over two pellets, then over two others, comparing the spaces by raising his fingers to the level of his half-closed eyes: the lab assistant before his test tube, nodding a professional skull.

"To take part in something," he completed. "Something like an investment. Involving tools, it seems. Machine tools. Naturally, at this degree of precision it can always."

Evasive gesture, like garage mechanics and surgeons. But even so, Venus in the fifth house theoretically meant smooth sailing ahead. As to determining when this meeting would take place, one could not. The heart of the matter, furthermore, did not lie there.

"Where does it lie, Bouc?" Bob wanted to know.

"The heart of the matter lies not in the facts," said the geomancer, "but in their consequences."

"So then," asked Paul, "what should I do?"

"It is my belief that this man . . ." Bouc uttered after reflection, ". . . you should not accept his offer (I'm simply telling you this, you can of course do as you like). It seems to me that it would be better to decline. I could not say why, however."

"Nothing else?"

"Another man," estimated Bouc Bel-Air. "I see him as being closer to you, older than the first, thinner as well (did I tell you the first one's thin?), also tools."

"All right," said Paul, "so I decline."

"No," said Bouc, "this time you go along with it. It's what I recommend, naturally it's up to you to see. Strictly a personal opinion."

He traced in the air a gesture more expeditively rounded than the others, as if he were signing a discharge. "What about love?" said Paul. "Let's hear about love now." Bouc Bel-Air stared at his knees. "Right," Paul said. "Do you take checks?"

TRANSLATED BY MARK POLIZZOTTI

Notes on Contributors

SARAH BARBOUR, Visiting Assistant Professor in French at Wake Forest University, completed her Cornell Ph.D. dissertation on Nathalie Sarraute in 1985. In the summer of 1987 she participated in a Translation Workshop at SUNY-Binghamton.

PHILIP BARNARD teaches in the Literature Department at American University and is currently completing a study of the early-romantic concept of literature in Charles Brockton Brown. Barnard has translated Soller's *Writing and the Experience of Limits*, Severo Sarduy's *For Voice*, and, in collaboration with Cheryl Lester, Lacoue-Labarthe and Nancy's *The Literary Absolute* as well as interviews with Philippe Sollers. Barnard and Lester are currently translating recent writings by Sollers, notably *Théorie des Exceptions* and *Portrait du joueur*.

VICTORIA BRIDGES, Assistant Professor of French Poetry at Wake Forest University, completed her dissertation at Yale on "Le Statut du 'sujet' dans un discours poétique" in 1987.

CATHERINE CUSSET, *Ancienne élève de l'École Normale Supérieure* and *agrégée de lettres classiques*, is now working towards the Ph.D. in French at Yale and writing her dissertation on Sade's *Juliette*.

DEIDRE DAWSON, Ph.D. candidate in French at Yale, received her undergraduate and Master's degrees from L'Université Paul Valéry in Montpellier. She is currently completing her dissertation on epistolary writing as fictional discourse in Voltaire's correspondence.

LAUREN DOYLE-MCCOMBS is a graduate student in French at Yale and is writing a dissertation called "Plotting Novelistic Space: Women in the Novels of Proust and Blanchot."

FRANÇOISE DUBOR is a graduate student in the French Department at Yale and is writing a dissertation on Claudel.

ERIC EIGENMANN is currently working on a doctoral thesis concerning dialogic structures in Pinget, Duras, Sarraute, and Vinaver. He is a lecturer in French Literature at the University of Geneva.

RINDALA EL-KHOURY is a graduate student in French at Yale and is writing a dissertation on Louis-René Des Forêts.

MARIE-ANNE FLEMING is a graduate student in the French Department at Yale.

Pierre Force has taught at the French Institute in Mexico City, Yale University, and the Johns Hopkins University. He recently completed a doctoral dissertation at Paris IV Sorbonne on Blaise Pascal's hermeneutics, and is currently Assistant Professor of French at Columbia University.

Dominique Jullien wrote a doctoral dissertation at Paris III Sorbonne on the Arabian Nights and Saint-Simon in Marcel Proust's *A la recherche du temps perdu,* which will be published in 1989 by Editions José Corti. She is currently Assistant Professor of French at Columbia University.

Joaniko Kohchi, a graduate student in French at Yale, is currently working on the occurrence of male narrators in search of stories from women in Balzac, Barbey D'Aurevilly, and Marguerite Duras.

Leonard R. Koos, a graduate student in French at Yale, is currently completing a dissertation entitled "Decadence: A Literature of Travesty," a study of the phenomenon of decadence in late nineteenth-century French literature.

Marina Kundu is completing her Yale Ph.D. dissertation in the French Department on twentieth-century playwrights Arrabal, Beckett, and Ionesco.

Cheryl Lester, Assistant Professor in English at the University of Kansas, has published articles on Faulkner and, with Philip Barnard, translated and introduced Lacoue-Labarthe and Nancy's *The Literary Absolute* as well as interviews with Philippe Sollers. Lester and Barnard are currently translating recent writings by Sollers, notably *Théorie des Exceptions* and *Portrait du joueur.*

Karen McPherson, Assistant Professor of French at Princeton University, recently completed her Yale Ph.D. dissertation on "The Police and Guilty Women in Four Twentieth-Century Novels," and is continuing to work on "criminal passions" and woman's voice in Beauvoir, Duras, Woolf, and Hébert.

Katrine Pflanze is a graduate student in French at Yale, where she is writing her Ph.D. dissertation on "The Stylistics of Love: Poetic Complicity and the Role of the Reader in Ronsard's *Amours.*"

Mark Polizzotti is Senior Editor at Weidenfeld & Nicolson in New York. His previous translations include works by Maurice Roche, Paul Virilio, Jean Baudrillard, Jean Senac, René Daumal, and the Surrealists. His translation of Echenoz's *Cherokee* was published in 1987 by David R. Godine.

Charles A. Porter is Professor of French at Yale and was recently Special Editor of the *Yale French Studies* on "Men/Women of Letters." He occasionally teaches a course on the Twentieth-Century Novel in France.

Martine Reid, Assistant Professor of French at Yale, has written on Racine, Stendhal, Musset, Nerval, Huysmans, and Proust. She is currently working on a book on Stendhal's autobiography.

Christopher Rivers, a graduate student in French at Yale University, is currently writing a dissertation on Lavater's theories of physiognomy and systems of physiognomical characterization in Marivaux, Gautier, and Zola.

Michael Syrotinski is a graduate student in French at Yale University and is completing a dissertation on the works of Jean Paulhan.

Brigitte Szymanek is currently enrolled in a Ph.D. program at Yale University. She is writing a dissertation on women authors and the French Revolution.

Barbara Vinken is a post-graduate fellow at the School of Literary Criticism, University of Konstanz (West Germany). As a Ph.D. candidate in Comparative Literature at Yale she is working on a dissertation on Richardson, Laclos, and Kierkegaard. She has published articles on Dante and Simon.

The following issues are available through **Yale University Press,** Customer Service Department, 92A Yale Station, New Haven, CT 06520.

63 The Pedagogical Imperative:
   Teaching as a Literary Genre
   (1982) $13.95
64 Montaigne: Essays in Reading
   (1983) $13.95
65 The Language of Difference:
   Writing in QUEBEC(ois)
   (1983) $13.95
66 The Anxiety of Anticipation
   (1984) $13.95
67 Concepts of Closure
   (1984) $13.95

68 Sartre after Sartre
   (1985) $13.95
69 The Lesson of Paul de Man
   (1985) $13.95
70 Images of Power:
   Medieval History/Discourse/
   Literature
   (1986) $13.95
71 Men/Women of Letters:
   Correspondence
   (1986) $13.95

72 Simone de Beauvoir:
   Witness to a Century
   (1987) $13.95
73 Everyday Life
   (1987) $13.95
74 Phantom Proxies
   (1988) $13.95
75 The Politics of Tradition:
   Placing Women in French
   Literature
   (1988) $13.95
Special Issue: After the
   Age of Suspicion: The
   French Novel Today
   $13.95

Special subscription rates are available on a calendar year basis (2 issues per year):

Individual subscriptions $22.00

Institutional subscriptions $25.90

- -

ORDER FORM   Yale University Press, 92A Yale Station, New Haven, CT 06520

Please enter my subscription for the calendar year
☐ **1988** (Nos. 74 and 75)   ☐ **Special Issue**   ☐ **1989** (Nos. 76 and 77)

I would like to purchase the following individual issues:

_____

_____

For individual issues, please add postage and handling:
Single issue, United States $1.50
Each additional issue $.50
Connecticut residents please add sales tax of 7½%.

Single issue, foreign countries $2.00
Each additional issue $1.00

Payment of $ _____ is enclosed (including sales tax if applicable).

Mastercard no. _____

4-digit bank no. _____ Expiration date _____

VISA no. _____ Expiration date _____

Signature _____

SHIP TO: _____

_____

_____

- -

See the next page for ordering issues 1–59 and 61–62. **Yale French Studies** is also available through Xerox University Microfilms, 300 North Zeeb Road, Ann Arbor, MI 48106.

The following issues are still available through the **Yale French Studies** Office, 2504A Yale Station, New Haven, CT 06520.

Single issue
Each additi

- - - - -
YALE F

A check r

Issue no.

PROZAC
fluoxetine hydrochloride

Name _____

Number/Street _____

City _____ State _____ Zip _____

The following issues are now available through Kraus Reprint Company, Route 100, Millwood, N.Y. 10546.

36/37 Stucturalism has been reprinted by Doubleday as an Anchor Book.
55/56 Literature and Psychoanalysis has been reprinted by Johns Hopkins University Press, and can be ordered through Customer Service, Johns Hopkins University Press, Baltimore, MD 21218.